Time Frames

Time Frames

*Japanese Cinema and the
Unfolding of History*

S<small>COTT</small> N<small>YGREN</small>

UNIVERSITY OF MINNESOTA PRESS

MINNEAPOLIS • LONDON

Portions of chapter 2 appeared as "Reconsidering Modernism: Japanese Film and the Postmodern Context," *Wide Angle* 11, no. 3 (1989): 6–15, reprinted with permission from The Johns Hopkins University Press; and as "Doubleness and Idiosyncrasy in Cross-Cultural Analysis," *Quarterly Review of Film and Video* 13, nos. 1–3 (1991): 173–87, reprinted with permission from Taylor and Francis Group. Portions of chapter 3 appeared as "Inscribing the Subject: The Melodramatization of Gender in *An Actor's Revenge,*" in *Melodrama and Asian Cinema* (New York: Cambridge University Press, 1993), reprinted with permission from Cambridge University Press. Portions of chapter 5 appeared as "The Shifting Architectural Codes in Japanese Cinema," *Iris* 12 (1991): 95–110, reprinted with permission from the University of Iowa. Portions of chapter 6 appeared as "The Pacific War: Contradiction, Denial, and Reading," *Wide Angle* 9, no. 2 (1987): 60–71, reprinted with permission from The Johns Hopkins University Press. Portions of chapter 7 appeared as "New Narrative Film in Japan: Stress Fractures in Cross-Cultural Postmodernism," *Post Script* 11, no. 1 (Fall 1991): 48–56, reprinted with permission from Post Script, Inc.; as "Boundary Crossings: Japanese and Western Representations of the Other," *Quarterly Review of Film and Video* 14, no. 3 (1993): 85–93, reprinted with permission from Taylor and Francis Group; and as "Paper Screen: Video Art in a Japanese Context," *Journal of Film and Video* 39, no. 1 (1987): 27–35, reprinted with permission from University of Illinois Press. Images from *Eros Plus Massacre* are reproduced with the permission of Yoshida Kiju and Gendai Eigasha.

Published by the University of Minnesota Press
111 Third Avenue South, Suite 290
Minneapolis, MN 55401-2520
http://www.upress.umn.edu

Library of Congress Cataloging-in-Publication Data

Nygren, Scott.
  Time frames : Japanese cinema and the unfolding of history / Scott Nygren.
    p. cm.
  Filmography: p.
  Includes bibliographical references and index.
  ISBN-13: 978-0-8166-4707-1 (hc : alk. paper)
  ISBN-10: 0-8166-4707-0 (hc : alk. paper)
  ISBN-13: 978-0-8166-4708-8 (pb : alk. paper)
  ISBN-10: 0-8166-4708-9 (pb : alk. paper)
    1. Motion pictures—Japan—History. I. Title.
  PN1993.5.J3N94 2007
  791.430952—dc22
                                              2006033998

Printed in the United States of America on acid-free paper

The University of Minnesota is an equal-opportunity educator and employer.

12 11 10 09 08 07   10 9 8 7 6 5 4 3 2 1

Contents

Preface

The women, who have spent virtually their entire lives inside a geisha house in Gion, climb to the rooftop and look out toward smoke on the horizon. It is 1866, and Choshu troops are on the verge of entering Kyoto, bringing with them the Imperial Restoration and unleashing the modernization of Japan.

The children, who have spent virtually their entire lives inside and nearby an isolated apartment in Nishi-Sugamo abandoned by their mother, travel away from home for the first time to bury the youngest girl, who has fallen and died, at the edge of Haneda international airport. It is 1988, and the four abandoned children are afraid to contact anyone outside for fear they would be separated, and their bond as a family would end.

Consider two films: Tamizo Ishida's *Fallen Blossoms* (*Hana chirinu,* 1938) and Hirokazu Kore-Eda's *Nobody Knows* (*Dare mo shiranai,* 2004). Both films act as parables of interiority at a moment of break, when an outside world remains suspended just before a radical transformation that remains, as yet, both imminent and unimaginable. Both narratives remain inside for the duration of the film, poised at that moment of encountering an unrepresentable exteriority, a horizon. Both films act as allegories of a modern Japan, at the beginning or ending of specific constructions of the nation.

A major premise of this book is that history is not transparent. Historical writing usually proceeds by a kind of integrative accumulation, so that all research and findings are assembled into the appearance of a seamless narrative that nowhere questions its own foundations. The effect is to construct a conception of history as if the past were always already there, simply waiting to be discovered, despite the simultaneous assertion that only the most recent research allows us to see history as it really was.

Historiography is of course more complex than this. New information and methods do more than simply add to existing knowledge; they transform the way we see and know the world. Different discourses compete to account for the events and forces that drive history as a dynamic process, and both the narrative and objects of history change depending on the discursive context through which accounts are produced. The inference that events occurred in the past is accomplished through discourses in the present, in a continual process of oscillation and insight.

At the same time, after Foucault, history is not simply a record of events but also includes how these events were conceived and experienced by the people who lived them. The history of thought and representation is as much a part of history as documented actions, and it plays a determining role in shaping those actions. Information is always incomplete, and recognizing the limits of knowledge in effect at any given moment of the past is as important as recognizing the implicit limits of our own knowledge, which also necessarily remains imperfect. Knowledge always increases, but incremental improvement should not be confused with a total or transparent discourse, which remains structurally impossible.

Japanese film was not simply always available to a world audience, even when it had achieved a substantial scale of national production,[1] and Japanese critics and theorists were similarly delayed in translation and reception outside Japan.[2] Furthermore, these processes were not synchronized, with the result that Japanese films circulated outside Japan long before the work of Japanese theorists.

FIGURE 1. Akira looks out from the rooftop of her geisha house in Gion toward the horizon, where Choshu troops are entering Kyoto. From Ishida's *Fallen Blossoms* (*Hana chirinu,* 1938).

Until *Rashomon* won the grand prize at the Venice Film Festival in 1951, Japanese film was effectively isolated from world distribution and recognition, parallel to the segregation of "race" films in the United States. During the 1950s, Japanese films achieved world recognition, parallel to the reception of Italian neorealist films, but without a contemporary Japanese critical or theoretical context. At this point, classical and modern Japanese literature was increasingly translated, but not criticism or theory. During the 1960s and 1970s, Japanese films received a different kind of world reception, parallel to the French New Wave, while Japanese writing about film began to appear outside Japan. Texts by Nagisa Oshima and Tadao Sato were translated into English, as well as other texts into French and other languages, consistent with the idea of film as artistic style. Throughout these postwar decades, Japanese films made before 1951 appeared in a world context through a sequence of belated rediscoveries and reconstructed narratives of sequential development.[3] During and after the 1980s, reception and translation changed again, so that a new generation of films were both conceived as texts and were accompanied by Japanese theoretical texts.[4] If we think of this moment as postmodern, then it is characterized by a joining of Japanese film and theoretical work as parallel modes of textual construction in a world context.

There are several things that we can learn from this series of events. Film can often precede language as a medium of cultural transmission, and the figural effects of contact through film can then shape subsequent discourse. Film is in no sense a natural medium—its meanings and effects are symbolically constructed as they are in any text. Nonetheless, the ability to view and understand a film can be learned far more easily and quickly than another language. As a result, a specific temporality can affect the transmission of knowledge across cultural contexts, as evidenced by the incremental process through which Japanese film and culture have come to circulate outside Japan.

Since world distribution has meant domination by Western capital, the problem for Japanese film has always been how to achieve world recognition while resisting hegemonic marginalization. This conflict inhabits the Western reception of Japanese films, and its history can allow us to recognize both how knowledge changes and how that knowledge is obscured by a retrospectively constructed nationalist narrative of sequential development.

As Miyoshi has argued, Japanese voices were long absent from English-language studies of Japanese film and culture. We need to recognize the multiple factors involved in restricting and regulating the circulation of Japanese films and texts, from the limits of language and representation to cultural imperialism, racism, and gender discrimination. At the same time, the recent inclusion of Japanese voices can be paralleled by a transformative recognition of how Japanese films as texts have always implied alternative conceptions of the world that were too often ignored as exoticism or style. Films as texts already resist and exceed their nominal status as subordinate objects of study, and potentially challenge and provoke the viewer to change the discourse through which they are conceived.

In retrospect, the production of past historical contexts can be understood in terms of structuring occlusions. The ability of film to circulate in advance of contemporary theoretical work means that film has a radical potential to configure social relations before discursive contact. We cannot eliminate this temporal delay by imagining a circulation of knowledge that did not exist before the 1980s, but we can develop strategies to better understand and learn from the incremental process of how cultural transmission occurs across boundaries.

Accordingly, this book considers how Japanese film histories have been written, in relation to the way that film narratives themselves also imply a sense of history. The histories implicit in films can challenge or complicate official history, as well as the critical reception of the same films. The French word *histoire* means both "story" and "history" when translated into English, and suggests how narrative and history are always bound up together in both films and their histories. The organization of this book, then, embodies a model of how history works, as a continuing process of partial information and inference recognizable as discourses, punctuated by transformative reconfiguration.

A central organizing principle here is that Japanese Film History "begins" after 1945, taking seriously Oshima's argument that the war constitutes a fundamental break in modern Japanese history.[5] The events of Japanese Film History, of course, begin much earlier, but the discourse of Japanese Film History as a disciplinary mode of knowledge in its own right is primarily a postwar invention. Only after this discourse was established were the earlier events revalued as significant, and in this sense were produced by postwar models of knowledge.

The project of the book is in part to deliberately break with such established norms as the conventions of academic writing and the organization of historical narrative in order to open up new possibilities of thought and research. As a result, the text marks a specific intersection of multiple approaches in order to problematize how the field is configured. I hope the book will thereby be able to make a contribution in several areas in return for the benefit it has received from them. Some of these areas include anthropology, history, Japanese literature and culture, art history, architecture, cultural studies, and visual studies, as well as film and media studies and poststructural and postcolonial theory.

The book is also written to be accessible to undergraduates and those new to film and Japanese culture, as well as to graduate students, specialists, and scholars. Narrative elements are designed to facilitate entrance into challenging material while simultaneously working to foreground figural determinants of discursive contexts for those who are interested in the theoretical stakes of this gesture. The project here proceeds from the belief that writing can be both serious and pleasurable, in part to welcome new readers, and its deliberate disjunctions and leaps of thought are motivated in part by the ethical principle that learning should be joyful.

At the same time, some early readers of this book have asked how topics here are discussed in relation to other approaches. These topics include such issues as otherness, language, writing strategies, psychology, domination, and "Western theory." Each of these marks a debate worth pursuing rather than a question of simple clarification.

For example, the question of otherness derives in large part from its very different usage in different contexts. In anthropology and some postcolonial discourses, otherness is often understood to mean abjection and foreclosure, and is rejected as the basis of exclusionary practices. In semiotic and poststructuralist contexts, however, otherness is understood very differently, as the basis of the symbolic capacity that makes us human, and hence as an irretrievable part of all thought and textual representation. In this context, otherness is also understood in ethical terms, beginning with Levinas's injunction to embrace radical alterity. These are complex theoretical and political debates that cannot and should not be oversimplified.

Otherness is bound up with the question of psychoanalysis in Japan, which is neither outside nor identical with psychoanalytic discourses as they derive from Western contexts. The connection argued here hinges on Lacan's use of the term "cogito," which I understand as the moment in Lacan's work that comes closest to Frantz Fanon's project to reconsider the unconscious in relation to historical conditions. By working through the relation of Freud to Descartes, Lacan implicitly suggests that the sense of conscious self conceptualized in psychoanalysis is specific to Western history and discourse, and may not be simply and unproblematically universal. In Japan, the Western model of self has in a sense become universal, insofar as Western history and discourse have become a common legacy throughout the world, but this is not the same as saying that all constructions of self are identical. Again, this is not an issue that can be simply clarified, but invites complex models of incommensurable cultural contexts, at the limits of narrative identity and identification.

The questioning of [Japan] at the beginning of the book may seem convoluted to some readers, who might prefer simply to accept that "Japan exists." However, beginning with Japan as simply existent would return us to precisely the kind of transcendental signified that this book seeks to problematize. As with the discussion of otherness, "Japan" is here being used in two very different contexts. If history is understood as a set of material existents, then questions of language and discourse will appear to be unnecessary and convoluted. However, after poststructuralism, a fundamental distinction can be made between history as event and history as discourse. If history is understood as material events that lie outside discourse, this inference nonetheless becomes possible only by means of the different materiality of discourse itself, and discourse has a different temporality than the events that it makes possible to conceptualize. The distinction between event and discourse is fundamental to the book's project, and hence is discussed directly.

Questions of the West and of theory similarly derive from different contexts. In some postcolonial discourses, nationalist or universalist assumptions combine these concepts into the category of "Western theory" as a critique of cultural imperialism. However, in poststructuralist and other postcolonial contexts, these same concepts are differential and unstable and intersect to critique nationalist and universalist categories. This book recognizes such fundamentally different contexts as multiple discourses, through which figures circulate with unpredictable effects.

This book seeks to reconsider the relations of film and theory, poststructuralism and postcolonialism, and the "non-West" versus "the West." The study of visual media, including art and architecture, together with film, video, and the Internet, makes possible a new kind of comparative project on a world scale that complements the interdisciplinarity and comparative achievements of area studies and comparative literature as models for knowledge. To accomplish this, film needs to be reconceived as neither the passive aesthetic object of applied theory nor as the privileged object of a passive explication. Instead, film can be recognized as an active cultural medium (Gayatri Chakravorty Spivak's phrase),[6] a text bristling with its own propositions and implied discourses parallel to theoretical work in verbal media. From this position, film "speaks" to and transforms "theory" as much as "theory" transforms film. Theoretical work is then placed next to films, conceived as parallel texts rather than as aesthetic objects, and both are situated within historical contexts rather than being imagined as transcendental systems of truth. Past theoretical work is considered as a fundamental part of history, and hence unavoidably mixes insight and blindness in acts of partial knowledge rather than being privileged as true or discarded as obsolete. Figural and discursive differences are thereby mobilized to organize the text rather than national, periodizing, or authorial categories.

What is at stake, then, in historicizing ideas, in order to retell a history of Japanese film? Such historical writers as Ruth Benedict, Takeo Doi, Donald Richie, Tadao Sato, and Roland Barthes may today seem unimportant as sources for Japanese film and culture, since their work has in many ways been superseded by others. However, their work remains important to understanding the history of history as well as the dynamics of knowledge across cultural difference. The point is not the truth or error of their texts as such, but a genealogy of contextual discourses surrounding Japanese film. When did it first become possible to think the thought of Japan in a world context, and then to think specifically of identity, psychoanalysis, representation, and heterogeneity? These questions lead us back to past films and books together, not as sources of truth but as junctures in the possibilities of thought.

Accordingly, this book has a special interest in texts that seem difficult, problematic, conflicted, troubling, and lumpy, the kind of book that many scholars would prefer to dismiss as "discredited" or obsolete. Such books can be symptomatic of thresholds and dislocations between heterogeneous contexts, and the challenge is to understand both their insights and limitations as a model for continuing work at the horizons of knowledge. Like the works of Marx, Nietzsche, Freud, Saussure, and others, who first create the possibility of thinking in modern terms, they mark a genealogical threshold where thought exceeds itself and a new horizon becomes possible. Because such breaks are necessarily produced from within material conditions and established discourses, and can never be simply transcendental in origin, they unavoidably combine old and new in the same rhetorical intervention. Subsequent work then seeks to establish a consistent new discourse uncontaminated by the past, but this "progress" depends on previously uneven texts as its foundation. In this sense, Doi, Benedict, Barthes, and others can be a key to understanding the history of Japanese film in a world context, not a return to discredited ideas. The project is to historicize how these texts mark the beginnings of new fields and possibilities as a part of history itself. Doi is the first to attempt a psychoanalysis specific to Japan, Benedict introduces a critical anthropology, Barthes initiates a semiotic and textual approach to cultural studies, and so on. The politics of anamnesis, or refusal to forget, should include not only the events of history but also should extend to the conceptual transformation and labor that makes such events recognizable.

The structure and strategies of the book are designed to produce specific meanings and effects, at the risk of seeming initially unclear. For example, the book is organized through a montage structure rather than an Aristotelian development, so that the reader is invited to read each chapter in relation to all the others rather than only in sequential continuity. The middle chapter and the Epilogue are designed to be shorter than the other chapters. The middle chapter acts as a pivot at the center of the book, and the Epilogue is a coda. The rest of the book then divides between figural exteriorities most prominent during the relative isolation of prewar cinema and discursive interiorities that characterize a Japan in the world after the war. At the same time, a series of concepts or topics returns in several locations, in a pattern of repetition and difference throughout the text. The purpose of these returns is partly to make it possible to begin reading at any point without undue prior knowledge, but also for points to connect across several contexts. In principle, the montage of the text intersects with a series of relays and displacements, so that the text can simultaneously be read as a network.

Narrative elements in the writing are not simply anecdotal asides but work to foreground figural assumptions inherent in discourse. Material that might seem at first to be disjunctive or extraneous is designed to continually dislocate the text rather than hierarchize ideas according to a traditional specialization and narrowing of topic. If the text works as designed, apparent digressions can make figural determinants recognizable through displacement to an alien context. The reader is also invited to infer connections and implications, without always relying on explicit explanations, consistent with a process of indirect inference and discovery. This strategy is part of an ethics of the text, to position the reader as an active participant in the construction of meaning rather than as a passive follower of the text as authority. The strategy necessarily involves both direct and indirect statement, so that "clarity" alternates with textual agency and figural work.

This is not to say that all or any of the strategies here have been successful, only that new possibilities need to be considered. I hope the gestures here will encourage others to initiate breaks and reconfigurations in thinking about Japanese film, to better conceive of the world we now inhabit.

Acknowledgments

I owe an enormous debt of gratitude to many individuals and institutions that have supported this project through many long years. I would like to express my thanks to Dean Albert Cook of the College of Arts and Sciences and Chair Julian Olf of the Department of Theatre and Film at the University of Toledo, who first sponsored my research travel to Japan; and to Deans Will Harrison and Neil Sullivan of the College of Arts and Sciences, and chairs Pat Craddock, Ira Clark, and John Leavey of the Department of English at the University of Florida, for a summer research grant and for the encouragement that allowed me to continue the writing that led to this text.

I thank the many friends and colleagues in Japan and in Japanese studies who generously helped me in my work, including Akira Shimizu, Donald Richie, Kyoko Hirano, David Desser, Dudley Andrew, Michael Raine, Mitsuyo Wada-Marciano, Abé Mark Nornes, Larry Greenberg, Aaron Gerow, David Bordwell, Naoki Sakai, William Haver, Brett de Bary, Noel Burch, Nagisa Oshima, Noriaki Tsuchimoto, Kohei Oguri, Hiroshi Komatsu, Joseph Murphy, Helen Lee, and Kojin Karatani.

Among my colleagues in film, theory, and academia, past and present, who have responded at conferences and at shared institutions with challenging ideas that made me rethink my own, I would like to offer special appreciation to Michel Marie, Jacques Aumont, Christian Metz, Jean-François Lyotard, Christopher Fynsk, Patty Zimmerman, Michael Walsh, Mark Reid, Sylvie Blum-Reid, Gayle Zachmann, Gordon Bleach, Phil Wegman, Susan Hegeman, Kim Emery, Apollo Amoko, Amitava Kumar, Malini Schueller, Greg Ulmer, Robert Ray, Donald Ault, Nora Alter, Alex Alberro, Craig Freeman, and Barbara Jo Revelle.

All of my work became conceivable thanks to the support and guidance of my teachers and mentors: Hollis Frampton, James Blue, Gerald O'Grady, Paul Sharits, Tony Conrad, Woody Vasulka, and Steina.

I also especially appreciate the undergraduate and graduate students in my Japanese film classes and seminars, who have done so much to question assumptions and provoke further thought on these issues.

To my family, both nuclear and extended, who have supported me through many years, I am deeply grateful: my father, Fred Nygren; my mother Louise Nygren; my brother and sister-in-law, Steve and Alma Nygren; my mother-in-law, Ruthanne Turim; my brother- and sister-in-law, Reuven and Shereen Rahamim; and to many others. I regret that my father and mother-in-law did not live to see this project finished. Above all, I express my love and gratitude to my colleague and wife, Maureen Turim, whose own theoretical work and generosity continually transform our lives together, and to my daughter, Mika, who makes the world come alive.

This text has received the generous support and wisdom of innumerable friends and colleagues, to whom I owe infinite thanks. All of its shortcomings and failures are mine alone.

Introduction

During a time of terrorism, war, and continuing crisis, a book on Japanese film and culture may seem to be superfluous. Yet while directly contesting terror and domination can be crucial, it is not the only event in the world. There is also always the option of introducing a break—an absence in the midst of a conflicted presence—that allows more possibilities to emerge. This book is dedicated to those proliferating alternatives.

Simply stated, this book is about representations of time in Japanese film and culture, the inflections of history that these narratives generate, and the dislocations across cultural difference produced by situating Japan in a world context.

At least this is a plausible description insofar as a book can be said to be "about" something, a problematic phrasing that already implies what is not true: that a book somehow remains a neutral and transparent framework for a separable "content," and that knowledge can be hierarchized into categorical systems and summaries. In this reading, all books are like "high-concept" films; they can be summarized in two sentences or less for a *TV Guide* version of the text.

Books, instead, engage specific sets of determining figures to produce work indirectly by way of a discursive agency and work through the conflicts and misrecognitions consequent in any textual process. In such a reading, this is a book that mobilizes a network of discourses by way of figural dislocation, to track textual intensities across cultural difference, in a heterological General Economy. Unfortunately, the theoretical condensation of this statement, if more accurate, risks becoming unintelligible, since each term depends on counterintuitive arguments that are unavailable at the outset. This can turn an introduction into something like a conclusion, or, at least, a point of return after reading the rest of the book.

Another way of articulating this project is to pragmatically survey its division into sections, chapters, and titles, and at least partly to suggest where each segment may be expected to go. The book is divided into two major sections, composed of chapters 1–3 and 5–7, with chapter 4 ("Kyoto/Venezia") marking a foundational and historical break that inhabits all the others. The Epilogue ("Next") is another break that provisionally

opens on to what comes next. Chapters 1–3 consider the contexts and inversions necessary to theorize history across cultural difference, while chapters 5–7 reconsider what
are normally called "periods" as discourses operating according to different parameters
and principles. Chapter 4 addresses the conflicted moment of break that made it possible to think of Japanese film history as part of a world media economy.

Chapter 1 foregrounds a series of thresholds that are often assumed, or repressed, in
books on Japanese film history. To begin, it suggests the necessity of problematizing the
foundational terms of [Japan], [film], and [history] as volatile and unstable. One point of
departure here is Kojin Karatani's book *The Origins of Modern Japanese Literature,* which
brackets each term of the title as problematic. The chapter then proceeds by considering
the noncategory of the "East" as both metaphysical fantasy and mobile boundary. These
multiple thresholds take the place of a chapter on the earliest Japanese films, which I
consider to be unwritable except by way of these considerations. Writing about the first
Japanese film begs the question of its historical significance, an assumption only determined to be foundational in retrospect. At the moment when films were first produced in
Japan, the discursive context of Japanese film history through which we now evaluate
their significance was not yet in place, leaving broader questions of nation, media, and
temporality still open.

Chapter 2 discusses hybrid cultural contexts by way of the Japanese appropriation
of "humanism" as a way to reconsider the 1920s. The dislocation of appropriated ideas
produces a doubling of texts across cultural difference, and points toward the role of
idiosyncrasy in cultural theory. This chapter too is metahistorical, and, like chapter 1,
argues that Japanese cultural history before 1945 is not directly available as an object of
knowledge without working through foundational problems of placement and context.

Chapter 3 then considers the textual and libidinal incisions of the written body, or
body as text, which acts as a foundational embodiment prior to narrative discourse and
historical agency. The chapter considers "writing" as an intersection of kanji and cinema and moves toward a problematization of psychoanalysis across cultural difference.
What we usually call history is always double, incorporating the intergenerational time
of infancy as it intersects with social history. All knowledge and experience is thereby
embodied, or situated, as specific materialities of media transform economies of infantile sexuality. This chapter addresses the specificity of these configurations in Japan at
the moment of cinema.

Chapter 4 returns to the curious moment when *Rashomon* won the grand prize at the
Venice Film Festival in 1951 and considers the foundational implications of this event for
both Japanese and world cinema. After this moment, Japanese film ceased to be a segregated national tradition, developing in isolation from the West, and became part of a world
cinema history. Earlier periods of Japanese film production were in no sense "pure," since
film itself represents the Japanese appropriation of a Western media practice, but were
foundationally reconfigured after the war as archival materials to be rediscovered. From
this hinge moment, the chapter then proposes a model of history as a process of boundaries and folds, rather than as teleological sequence, in the section "History as Origami."

Chapters 5–7 reconsider the decades of the 1950s, 1960s, and 1980s as different discourses that emerge in specific historical moments and yet exceed those moments in their continuing effects. Chapter 5 problematizes the historical inscription of 1950s Japan as "the golden age of humanist films," both to locate "humanism" as a specific discursive materiality and to trace the unanticipated but ironically productive effects of "humanism" in a Japanese context. Chapter 6 then engages the "Japanese New Wave" in a similar way, to question the implications of categorizing Japanese film through an analogy to the Nouvelle Vague in France. Chapter 7 considers specific effects in Japan contemporary with the emergence of postmodernism in the West that both repeat and invert determining figures that simultaneously circulate elsewhere.

The Epilogue marks an "end" of Japanese film history, as Japan, film, and history begin to dissolve into a world economy, computer media, and heterology. In one sense, nothing "ends," of course, since few media have ever disappeared. What changes are the dominant figures of organization through which we experience and understand the economy of representations that surrounds us.

Interventions and Occlusions

The above survey of topics and trajectories is produced through an assembly of ideas as dynamic and catalytic interventions. Throughout his work, and culminating in his books on cinema, Gilles Deleuze argues that ideas cannot be understood as idealist categories, but only as dynamic machines that do work. As a result, no text is finished, or finishable, because concepts continually radiate outward to additional contexts, only to return to the text, which is transformed by other encounters. The illusion of closed or finished texts is accomplished only at the price of containment within fixed hierarchies—hierarchies that repeat and reinforce the dominant figures of hegemonic transparency. In contrast, an antifoundational historiography recognizes that changes in foundational assumptions are necessary and inevitable, so all texts remain open to perpetual rewriting. Textual ethics then become contingent and figural, neither universally and categorically fixed nor vacuously relativistic, but produced against recognizably disastrous effects that can occur as the result of specific combinations and conditions.

All texts, however, by remaining open to multiple readings, are also most often approached from alternative discursive contexts. These reading formations can easily produce alienated reactions, often in the form of criticisms that a text "fails" to do something else other than what it does. Any single discursive formation unavoidably occludes others, as an effect of incommensurable and often unproblematized foundational assumptions.

Further, given the continuing marginality of cultural theory in a hegemonic media society, the counterintuitive premises of theoretical work are most likely to be initially encountered through misrecognition, parody, and abjection. *Teenage Mutant Ninja Turtles* exemplifies how children first encounter complex ideas, such as genetic recombination, Japanese history, and the Italian Renaissance, through parodic identification with bodily functions and the position of outcasts. The impact of new theory continually places everyone in the position of childhood, relearning foundational assumptions in order to begin again. We are all continually back in the sewer, a site that Georges Bataille mapped with his idea of abjection, at each new foundational break in knowledge. From this nonplace, we attempt to track the pattern of breaks in known discourses and crawl out in pursuit of the asemic figure that just crashed through the landscape. Michel Leiris's term for this effect is *brisées,* a French word from the hunt, describing the subtle pattern of broken branches that indicates the direction of a passing animal.

The effect of these conditions, which are intrinsic to any theoretical work, is that any written text will initially be encountered by way of a commodified reification, and can be easily and appropriately rejected as a mystified set of fetishized signifiers. No work produced and distributed by way of a mass-media consumerist economy can escape these effects. In addition, alphabetic texts incorporate and reproduce their own "resistance to theory," to recall Paul de Man's argument, so that media theory occurs in writing systems that can seem alien and obscure in the environment of visual information that we now take for granted. Any dynamic and radical potential of theoretical work emerges first in a crossfire of reading formations, between the idealist fetishism of hegemonic consumerism and a negative critique that attempts to break through mystification by means of a transgressive alienation.

A theoretical project, however, can only begin when something like Barthes's "third meaning" is recognized, neither an idealist category nor a negative critique, but something else less easily articulated. While all texts remain open to multiple readings, theoretical work asks that readers remain open to the play of allusion and indeterminate readings, to imagine a horizon of possibilities not now self-evident or intuitive. While I do not consider this book to be theoretically innovative, I do begin with the assumption that past innovations can now be taken as a point of departure for further work. The contestation of theoretical arguments is important, but this is not my project here. I am instead interested in reconsidering how history is and can be written as a cumulative effect of multiple innovations across the decentered and conflicted field of cultural theory.

Japanese Names

Japanese name usage in English-language texts approximates in miniature many of the features of indeterminacy and inversion that are discussed throughout the book. Conventional Japanese naming inverts the Western convention of "first name" and "last name" by beginning with the family name and then appending a personal name. Ozu Yasujiro thereby becomes Yasujiro Ozu in English.

Another problem results if we attempt to correct the problem by standardizing Japanese names according to Japanese convention. People with Japanese names living in Western countries commonly invert their names to conform to Western practice, so Sessue Hayakawa is not a translation but a preferred usage.

To further complicate the situation, Japanese usage regularly refers to certain celebrated figures by their personal name alone. Natsume Soseki is commonly known as Soseki, and Ueda Akinari as Akinari. As a result, a name like "Akinari" standing alone in English could mean either a family name according to Western usage or a personal name in the place of a family name, according to Japanese convention.

In effect, one never knows when first encountering a Japanese name in a Western context what name order or usage is being used, and no model of standardized usage will resolve the difficulty. In this book, both Japanese and Western name order will be used, sometimes alternately with the same name according to shifting contexts. The index is alphabetized by family name to minimize confusion, but reversibility is one of the conditions of working across boundaries.

Similarly, Japanese names of films and the substitute titles used in the Western distribution of these films occasionally will invert throughout the book. Again, standardization would imply that one usage has precedence, and inversion operates to unsettle the expectation of a single norm.

Japanese Dates and the Representation of Time

The Japanese dating system has historically differed from the Gregorian calendar of the West, although Western dating has been incorporated into Japanese discourse as a common practice since the 1970s.

Traditional Japanese dating is based on what is called the "reign" name. This is the official name of an emperor to designate an era of rule, in contrast to his personal or family name. For example, the emperor known as Hirohito in the West is known in Japan as the Showa emperor. Dates are then appended to the reign name to indicate in what year of a regime an event occurred, such as Showa 21 (1946). The traditional Japanese system is organized according to lifespan rather than mathematical units like decades and centuries, and it begins with the legendary origin of the emperor rather than the teleological break assumed by the Christian Era.

The traditional Japanese mode of dating is capable of the same precision and accuracy as Western dating, although it is constructed differently. The contrast can help provoke recognition of the foundational assumptions of the Gregorian calendar, at the moment when such assumptions are increasingly obscured by the adoption of the "common era" as a globally acceptable translation of the acronym CE. By recalling this disjunction, I mean to argue that such differences are not trivial, but suggest foundational breaks that continue to inhabit discourse today.

The double dating system through which the modern era rewrites Japanese history can also suggest the double history of infancy and social processes, whereby each generation reconceives its own history in ways that are distinct from its predecessors. Japanese films of the 1950s historicize the 1920s, but because these dates were not yet Westernized inside Japanese discourse, what we now call the 1920s was initially written and conceived as Taisho 8–Showa 5. In other words, a temporal break has been retrospectively recast as a unity by the artificial category of the decade, while erasing the context by which such a recasting has occurred. The period of the so-called Japanese New Wave marks a similar break between Showa and Gregorian temporalities, compounded with its own double history. Following Karatani, this juncture could be represented as a move from the Showa 30s to the 1970s.[1]

1
Thresholds

Why Japan? Film? History?

Books have no beginnings, although we like to imagine that they do.

Once we let go of the illusion that a discourse can be founded in an origin, that effects can be traced to a single cause, and that meaning can be guaranteed by some form of initiating presence no matter how far removed, what then? The topic of this book might once have been thought of as Japanese Film History, but this thought seems already to have reached its limit and passed. Like the writerly books that Roland Barthes loved to read but could no longer write, books on Japan, on Film, and on History are invaluable and even delicious, but no longer possible to believe in as a basis for further work. How did this happen? What do we do next? And how can we rethink these important films and texts that no longer directly represent the world in which we now live?

If beginnings no longer seem logical, an approach can instead be sketched across a series of thresholds that begin to suggest an area of engagement. What is at stake in this process is a questioning of foundational moves that have previously grounded the field and made it possible, and yet no longer seem tenable. And yet, in the same way that Karatani considers Western thought more interesting now that we recognize it as foundationless, so Japan, film, and history become even more significant when unfastened from the ideological and metaphysical preoccupations that once constructed them as knowable categories or a unity.

Japan(s)

One of the questions in approaching Japan, as in any cultural study, is what or whose Japan is being discussed. This problem is not as simple as it once seemed, and not only because a unitary Japan has receded along with universalist models of knowledge. Critiques of nationalist or ethnographic discourses, dividing cultural study between native insiders and scientific outsiders, have also become problematic. In a world where populations increasingly share multiple cultural backgrounds and assume hybrid identities, increasing numbers of people are both insiders and outsiders at once. Inside/outside converge into parameters of cultural knowledge but nonetheless remain multiple in their construction.

An alternative approach could be to pluralize inside/outside configurations according to multiple sites of production. In this model, one can recognize in Japan a specific and now historically based construction of the West, as it has been internalized and become part of a Japanese cultural inheritance. Japan's West in these terms becomes an instructive counterfigure to the West's Japan, and representations of Asia and the East in general, to which Edward Said alerted Westerners in his now long-established *Orientalism*.

The problem today is that these figures and counterfigures now also interact, so Asia recognizes the West's Orientalist version of itself, and Chinese filmmakers seeking an international market can specifically make such films as Zhang Yimou's *Raise the Red Lantern* targeted to meet such expectations. At the same time, U.S. video documentaries like Louis Álvarez and Andrew Kolker's *The Japanese Version* acquaint Western audiences with Japanese appropriations of Western culture for their own purposes. Continuing the figure/counterfigure model in these conditions leads us to a figure of mirrors within mirrors, or mise-en-abîme.

The destabilization of the cultural object is further displaced once we recognize that a rhizomatic networking of multiple mirroring has developed, so that the Japanese community in Brazil produces films such as Tizuka Yamasaki's *Gaijin* that are seen in the United States and Europe, U.S. pop culture is appropriated in different ways from Spain to Indonesia, and so on. It quickly becomes impossible to specify a cultural construction according to any central or binary schema because all such schemas now circulate among multiple sites across the world.

Accordingly, to understand the circulation of tropes throughout a heterogeneous world network of discourses, it can be helpful to isolate a specific border or threshold to study parallel to others. In proposing a discussion of Japan, then, I mean both the Japan available to be read through representations and artifacts historically produced in Japan, and the complex mix of insight and fantasy that characterizes Japan's representations of the world outside Japan. At the same time, the circulation of Japanese cultural history, art, and philosophy outside Japan has its own history, which accelerated in the aftermath of World War II, from Europe to Brazil. As a consequence of the Occupation, for example, U.S. enthusiasm led to both "accurate" and wild versions of Japan, both of which have their own interest, throughout the 1950s and 1960s.

Although the politics of domination clearly governed the historical conditions of the 1950s, when such representations of Japan most flourished in the United States, they did not necessarily govern its representations. In one of the reciprocal inversions that often characterizes the circulation of tropes across cultures, "accurate" historical reports on Japan in books of history and anthropology often assumed Japan's subordination to the West, while fantastic versions from Hollywood to the Beat appropriation of Zen could instead assume a Japanese cultural superiority, regardless of how wildly this was conceived. The complexity and incommensurability of these responses cannot be contained within a unitary category of Western disfiguration, any more than Japanese responses to the United States and the West during the 1950s can be contained in the stock attribution of "derivative."

By the 1980s, increasing numbers of foreigners had been to or lived in Japan, and unprecedented numbers of Japanese increasingly traveled abroad as well. My own research in Japanese archives stems from this period and thus participates in a general cultural movement. My research is not unique, but it is indicative of the increasing hybridity and pluralization of culture that has occurred in recent decades, for which "Japan" operates as a specific case among many, since all hybrid situations exist as single cases, or singularities, and never return to a universalist norm.

The "Japan" of this book, then, is not an insider or expert view of an imaginary "authentic" Japan, nor is it "my" Japan; nor is it simply the West's Japan, nor Japan's response to the West's representations of it, although all of those parameters intersect within this text. Instead, this is a construction of Japan as irretrievably multiple, marked by the heterogeneity of its production within different historical circumstances in Japan and the world from the 1950s through the early twenty-first century. If it is not the "true" Japan, neither is it simply false nor fictional; rather, it configures a specific kind of knowledge marked by a pattern of insights and blind spots like any other.

In the same way, the models of history that inflect film narratives and U.S. scholarly texts in the 1950s, from *Ikiru* to Richie and Anderson's text, are not simply "Western," although they are of course that. They also inflect the making of Japanese films and the

FIGURE 2. Sliding screens turn walls into permeable thresholds that open on to the environment. Katsura Villa in Kyoto became a primary model for modern architecture in the West, where such openings were translated into steel-and-glass walls.

writing of Japanese texts by Japanese filmmakers and scholars for primarily Japanese audiences. They do not thereby become simply the "West's Japan" or "Japan's West" either, although they are of course also that. My argument here is that they mark a join, or fold, across or between cultures at a specific juncture, and cannot be understood within either culture in terms of national enclosure or development.

The circulation of figures of history across cultural boundaries belongs to a generalizeable figure of its own, that of dislocation. By dislocation, I mean the displacement of figures across cultural boundaries so that the asemic determinants of discourse produce new and often unanticipated effects. These effects are in some ways parallel to the process of translation, but specifically characterize the reconfiguration of discourse that occurs when asemic figures rather than semantic signs are at stake. Sudden outbursts of great libidinal intensity, from revolutionary impulses and artistic suicide to mass identifications and catastrophe, are among the primary effects. This book necessarily addresses the figuration of history, because the reconfiguration of time is among the most notable products of figural dislocation.

[Japan]

Why, then, should anyone, Asian or Western, wish to study "Japan" as a specific case?

We could situate this project by rounding up some obvious reasons:

Japan is the second-largest economy in the world and an increasing source of cultural production as well as financial and economic power, especially within Asia. Japan also marks the shift of global wars from Europe to Asia during what the West calls World War II, with the United States subsequently engaged in Korea, Vietnam, and Iraq. Japan has also initiated the growth of Pacific Rim economies and cultural spheres, as a major focus of a world economy.

Another approach would be to note the established proliferation of Japanese corporate products around the world, from SONY, Hitachi, and Panasonic televisions, and Honda cars and motorbikes, to Walkmans, anime, and "Pikachu."

One might also note the important role Japan plays in international scientific discourse, from the International Conference on High-Energy Physics in Osaka, and the High-Energy Accelerator Research Organization in Tsukuba, called the KEK laboratory for its Japanese acronym, to the world's most powerful land-based telescope, built by Japan in 1999 on the summit of Mount Mauna Kea in Hawaii and known by the Japanese name for the constellation Pleiades, or Subaru.

More important, Japan marks the site of an unparalleled body of texts recording an unprecedented process of modernization. In the context of non-Western and postcolonial societies intersecting with a postmodern West, Japan is a pivotal and exemplary case. Japan's rapid modernization, militarization, and closure, and its renewed productivity after military destruction, are not simply an isolated national history. Instead, they represent a transformative process being restaged continuously, with important variations, ever since. Iran's religious revolution and militarized conflict with Iraq and the West do not occur in a vacuum, but are far more meaningful if understood in the context of Japan's nationalist Shinto, invasion of China, and decisive hostility to the West in the 1930s.

But as important as these reasons are, they elide a more fundamental question: What is [Japan]? Do we know if [Japan] constitutes an entity, and, if so, how is it produced? Certainly, a great many people live in an area known to people in the West as "Japan," and anyone who does not live there can travel to a place with that name. But "Japan" as a modern nation begins several times: with the arrival of Commodore Matthew Perry, during the restructuring of governance known in Japan as the Restoration, and after the end of the war in 1945. Each of these Japans dramatically reconfigured its production of social identity and its relation to past events, but most often only the post-1945 "Japan" is recognizable today, together with a specific version of the past that has come to be identified with "history."

The word "Japan" itself is remarkable enough, and has little or nothing to do with the name that "Japanese" use for their nation and society. The English word "Japan" erased the traditional *Nihon* (or "rising sun") in the same way that mercantile imperialism erased local sovereignty in the nineteenth century. Does this mean we could go back to *Nihon?* Of course not, since *Nihon* too was reinvented subsequent to the production of "Japan" as a construction of history and tradition in contrast to the modern nation. Premodern Japan has vanished from any direct representation, just as it has from the region we call "Japan."

Japan today, as Miyoshi and Harootunian argued in 1993, is a *Japan in the World,* and is incomprehensible without the series of contrasts and similarities that constitutes its specific position in a world context. No matter how much ultranationalists and neo-isolationists might wish to imagine a Japan separate from the West, even their most ardent imaginings are themselves a product of Western nationalism and philosophical essentialism.

A postnational Japan has dissolved as a categorical entity not because the institutions and effects of nationalism have disappeared, but because we can no longer locate any such pure or typical site except in the imagination. Bureaucratic formations, however brutal or necessary, are increasingly arbitrary in construction.

What remains of [Japan] is in one sense precisely what Japan has always been: a set of multiply layered and intersecting cultural texts that incorporate the population and terrain of a specific geographical region as part of its discourse. Japan in this sense can and has been reconstituted through the Japanese diaspora outside Japan, from Hawaii and Florida to Peru and Brazil. A postdiasporic Japan is no longer a Japan in which text and terrain can be conflated as inseparable, but becomes, like other cultures, a mobile context that may or may not coincide with the territory known as "Japan."

Then what does it mean to be Japanese? The human genome project has once again demonstrated, if anyone needed to be reminded, that "race" is a cultural construction without biological foundation. Ethnicity is both more complex and multiply hybrid than previously recognized, and impossible to group as unitary and essentialist "races." People who "look" Japanese can be indistinguishable in behavior from Westerners, as many Japanese citizens have discovered over the last fifteen years as diasporic Japanese from

Brazil have returned to Japan for economic advantages. In turn, some Westerners, such as literary scholar Donald Keene or former sumo champion Konishiki from Hawaii, can be more expert in Japanese cultural traditions than most Japanese. Cultural difference between Asia and the West can remain at times profound, but "being" Japanese or Western is a complex and unconscious construction, not a "nature."

The concept of "native" has been displaced and reconceived in a postnational world. Being born and raised in a certain region among a specific people has less to do with being "native" than the process of infancy within a cultural context produced through specific child-raising practices. Infancy is the twin of "history," in its familiar sense of economic and political conditions, so that time is doubly inscribed as a kind of Möbius strip in the unconscious to produce the effect of "native" identity.[1] Conversely, people may feel themselves to be "Western" or "Japanese" without ever having been to the places associated with these names, yet still discover after traveling to such an imaginary home how much of themselves is bound up with the birth context from which they came.

Hybridity has become commonplace but not yet determinative. People now unavoidably inhabit multiple cultural and genetic contexts, yet narrative and cultural conventions still tend to situate us as if we were living lives as ideal categories of ethnic identification. How, then, do we begin to represent a post-Japan that can no longer be identified simply and unproblematically with a territory or a "race," but that continues to be a cultural repository of complex interwoven texts and a generative site of new production? One of the purposes of this book is to displace the concept of [Japan] to slightly offset and resituate the name as inseparable from its many contexts of difference. Japan and the West, for better and worse, are bound up together, and a contemporary project must necessarily study the relation between the two in a condition of irretrievable hybridity. A pure Japan was always a romantic myth, even if it was adopted by Japanese nationalists as much as by Western visitors.

At the same time, the study of Japanese texts and contexts becomes ever more important. Academic programs that have come to be legitimized in terms of traditional Japanology can no longer be taken seriously as privileged authorities on Japanese essence, but, again, once this false foundation is discarded, become much more valuable as translators and guides to the complexity and contradiction of Japanese texts. Japanese study, like Japan itself, is becoming part of the world, not a world apart. The problems that result from this slight displacement are many, and this book will be organized around a number of them. Each "problem," however, becomes a fruitful area of further potential insight and potential research. Nothing, it seems, is more productive in an information economy than a displaced body of texts.

Why Japan?

If the field of Cultural Studies is to be significant, to be what it claims it wants to be, it must address "non-Western" as well as Western texts, materialities, and experiencing subjects. Japan was the first and most determined of so-called non-Western societies to industrialize and modernize, and it provides the longest and most complex and elaborated media record of the modernization process—a process that still governs most cultures on the planet, now under the name of "development." If we are to understand the experience and possibilities of non-Western cultures, there is no better beginning point or orientation reference than Japan. Japan is one of the only major, or large-scale, non-Western countries never to have been colonized by nineteenth-century Western imperialism, and it documents its historical experience extensively through film. Thailand is another Asian culture that was never colonized by the West, but it does not have the same kind of cinematic record. Japan's postwar American Occupation, although profound in its rupture with the past, was brief and came late in its modernizing development. If we are to begin to imagine what sometimes seems impossible, an intercultural set of relationships not governed entirely by the principles of domination and hegemony, there is no better place to start than Japan.

Is it possible to imagine, construct, and participate in a nonauthoritarian network of discourses, one that does not base its operation on an appeal to unconscious or tacit absolutist assumptions, forcibly excluded from question? The problem is complex because all discourses are governed by determining figures outside the domain of symbolic exchange, and neither self-representation nor exterior ethnography is the same as engaging with the unspoken determinants of representation. The possibilities of speaking across cultural difference, if they are to exist at all, emerge from the proliferation of conflicts and paradoxes that mark the boundary between cultures and contexts. Even if such a task seems impossible, the only ethical goal of knowledge work is to move in this direction, since alternatives are untenable. The seductive idea that we can never truly understand, and must therefore leave unthought, any consideration of contexts and agencies other than our own, comes perilously close to reconstructing isolationism in the name of respect for the other.

Any project of representation across difference begins with the dissolution of categories previously thought to be meaningful. Karatani cautions, for example, that "there is no such thing as the non-West," or, in other words, that the non-West is a Borgesian noncategory and cannot represent a substantive or integrated entity. Africa, the Middle East, and Asia in one sense have nothing in common, are entirely distinct as cultural regions, national societies, and ethnic groups, yet they share the condition of impact from combined modernization and Western influence, and struggle in parallel to benefit from the one and resist the other. As a result, the [non-West] both does and does not "exist," having no substantive or foundational value, but nonetheless suggests shared conditions and concerns.

Parallel effects, impasses, and transformations occurring throughout the world recall events in twentieth-century Japan, although as structural revisitations of the same kinds of conflicting issues, not as imitation or following, any more than Japan has simply "followed" the West. Nigerian democracy now struggles for human rights against traditional "feudal" loyalties, as Japan did in the 1920s and again in the 1950s. Iranian "fundamentalism" argues a nationalist appropriation of Islam as origin, as state Shinto did in 1890s Japan. The Palestinian celebration of nationalist martyrdom and suicide parallels the call for direct action and kamikaze attacks in 1930s–40s Japan. The contestations over a

Chilean trial of Augusto Pinochet, initiated by Spain, or of Slobodan Milošević at the
International Court in The Hague, restage the U.S. war crimes tribunal in late 1940s
Japan and return to the same problems of international law: Can legal action gain popular support? Will it have popular legitimacy? None of these developments should seem
unfamiliar to a process of modernization, upheaval, and struggle against Western domination, despite their recurrent appearance in Western media for shock value.

Why Film?

After the advent of hypermedia and the global Internet in the 1990s, film can sometimes
seem like a nostalgic preoccupation of an older generation. Yet film remains an archive
of textual figures and practices that continues to inhabit visual media, and returns everywhere as sets of traces that eloquently articulate cultural and contextual differences. Film
is here conceived as a new kind of writing, or as a type of chemical and mechanical representation characteristic of the modern period, that extends into electronic media and
informs our own moment in history. As a modernist mode of media inscription, film
both constructs a different mode of cultural process and identity in Japan and transcribes
that process into an invaluable series of texts for continued reading, even at the moment
that all such modern representations are displaced into the context of postmodern hypermedia from interactive DVDs to the Internet.

Film is not better (or even ultimately different) than verbal language, but it offers a
different point of access, one in which intelligibility, even if interrupted by unintelligible
elements and passages, arrives more quickly and easily in large-scale texts. Translations
via subtitles or the often lamentable practice of dubbing are possible and do not render
filmic texts unrecognizable (or at least, not always), even though the wide diversity of
translation practices can complicate one's approach to a filmic text. Verbal translation
becomes one issue among many, as well as a moving target since DVDs facilitate multiple translations and hyperlinks to additional contextual references.

Why Japanese Film? Surely this has become an exhausted topic. Surely no book could
add to what is already available, or if it could, it must only be in the direction of more
intensive specialization, language skills, historical research, and cultural sophistication
in Japanology. Or alternatively, it could only be a site for Western appropriation of Japanese "examples" for a preconstituted and ethnocentric "theorization."

But these are, of course, impossible alternatives. There can be no significant encounter
across cultural incommensurabilities without some kind of theoretical framework, conscious or unconscious, to contextualize and thereby render intelligible the representations
and events encountered. There can also be no significant theorization without a deep
and transformative engagement with the specificities and materialities of [history], even
if a poststructuralist rethinking makes it necessary to reconsider what constitutes [history]
and its writing. The question becomes how we go about approaching texts as historically
active constructions so that they interactively inform the present and continually generate
new possibilities.

Japanese Film provides a rich theoretical site for interaction with Cultural Studies that can mutually enrich both cultural theory and understanding of Japanese cultural practices. Such an engagement moves toward a heterological world, reconstructed as an intersection of multiple cultural traditions and identities on the planet. This study proposes Japanese Film History as a site of heterological generativity, available for reading by those who wish to act constructively in a postmodern and postcolonial world. In short, Japanese Film is a resource for working through unconscious habits of hegemonic domination (in the registers of both cultural, molar institutions and of personal, molecular singularities) and moving toward a postimperialist and heterological intercultural agency.

Visual Texts

Media theory and visual culture have intersected productively on many occasions, but they have just as often led to conflicted discourses.

By visual culture, I mean the often-noted emergence of cinema and television in the twentieth century as primary conduits of cultural reproduction, and the apparent shift from verbal to visual means of encoding information. In these terms, breaking from logocentric principles and habits becomes preliminary to any further theorization of new media texts.

Of course, it is not as simple as that. *Fahrenheit 451* stages the fantasy that movies make books obsolete, as if Hitler's book burning were the logical consequence of visual media. If anything, the contrary has proved to be true, with more books being published today than ever before in history. If books seem now secondary to visual media, then perhaps they always were, with cathedral art and public rituals performing the role in the past that cinema and television do today.

More significantly, however, language is itself bound up with the visual and always has been, whether by language we mean the spoken words privileged by alphabetic visualization or the audiovisual complexes figured by hieroglyphs and kanji. Derrida has argued from the beginning that there is no such thing as a society "before" writing, and that the preliterate societies romanticized by Claude Lévi-Strauss in *Tristes Tropiques* themselves depend on surrounding arrays of visual artifacts to record and recall foundational verbal narratives. Supposedly "oral" societies once assumed to be at the origin of literary history turn out to be a phantasm only imaginable from a highly literary context, where verbal codes are assumed as separable and central because of the effects of alphabetic privileging.

Accordingly, the kind of media theory popularized by Marshall McLuhan and Walter J. Ong has ceded to a more complex reading of multisensory inscription. All modes of "writing" are multisensory, even if their effects privilege one mode or another, and writing is always a configuration of sensory registers. The specific characteristics of Western tradition are not understood best as alienated from an "oral" origin or "linear" in organization, but as logocentric, phallocentric, and ocularcentric.

A different, but not unrelated, problem has occurred within film studies in recent decades as film has intersected with other academic disciplines from history to language studies and comparative literature.

After the rapid emergence of poststructural theory in the 1970s, which broke from previous work on film history as pretheoretical, there followed a "return" to history. This "return," however, was rarely explicitly problematized, and research often seemed to assume that historical work could continue where it had left off, as if "history" itself were unproblematic and transcended theorization. As a result, some of the most important interventions in Japanese film history during the 1990s, including work by Hiroshi Komatsu and Kyoko Hirano, have been received as if they simply filled in details within an established narrative rather than implicitly breaking from past models to understand "history" itself differently.

A similar problem has occurred in relation to language studies, which has followed a trajectory like that described by Jean Laplanche, combining a radical break from past ethnocentric models with a recuperative swerve to traditional premises. Laplanche describes a break from narcissistic centering as the unfinished Copernican revolution that Freud discussed, and a recuperative swerve as a Ptolemaic "return" or recentering on established assumptions. At a certain point, Japanese film, like that of other nationalities, reached a pivotal moment when further knowledge seemed to depend on learning the language of its producers. As a result, a new generation of film research appeared that combined language skills with film analysis.

The initial promise of this move was in part to radicalize the field of comparative literature, so that its traditional basis in European literary history could be shifted to include Asian and African languages, among others, and such new media as film. Instead, however, film research can become narrowed to the logocentric assumption that language skills are a prerequisite for any legitimate work on film, effectively reterritorializing international film within language departments. Film on these terms becomes reduced to a subtopic within a national tradition, where the idea of "nation" is preconceived through literature.

In contrast, the visual arts have always tended to be more fundamentally international in character. Artists routinely cross language borders and exhibit work on multiple continents relatively unrestricted by such logocentric regionalization as Anglophone, Francophone, Chinese, and so on. Exhibition politics often regulate choices of artists within language contexts, so that African and Asian modernists, for example, still tend to be unknown in the United States, and even French modernists can be belatedly "discovered" by American audiences, but compared to literary reception the mobility of texts is very different.

When film is considered within the context of the visual arts, it immediately seems international at its foundation and unrecuperable within the frameworks of national traditions. Visual tropes and discourses circulate across language boundaries, even if the majority of American audiences continue to insist on logocentric transparency in viewing. Citations of Yasujiro Ozu appear in films by Jim Jarmusch, while Oshima cites Jean Genet and Roland Barthes, but this circulatory process seems marginal within traditions of "American" or "Japanese" film. Part of the project of this book is to argue that such dislocations and effects are now fundamental to filmic texts, and that national histories themselves need to be problematized and relocated theoretically to account for such moves.

A more productive way of proceeding would be to consider that the visual inscription of filmic texts intersects with logocentric traditions but is not contained by them. The point is not to diminish the contribution of language studies and post-Eurocentric models of comparative literature, but to shift to a visual context where, if anything, the significance of linguistic and historiographic approaches can be better appreciated and understood.

International and national contexts can be reconceived as approaching postnational heterology and local historical agency. The nation does not disappear into a global universalist state where communication becomes transparent, but boundaries are instead transformed into folds, where breaks among incommensurable discourses are marked by abjection and inversion.

In the United States, film studies has become a curious hybrid of "English" departments, where "theory" has most often come to reside, with the visual arts, history, anthropology and innumerable other disciplines. Although cinema programs once seemed ascendant, where these interdisciplinary impulses were resolved within a new coherent area of studies, cinema itself has recently dissolved as a clearly identifiable field, after the emergence of computerized video once again undermined boundaries among text, image, and international contexts. Film studies has become again what it was when it began, a networking of discourses without a disciplinary territory or center.

Speech, foregrounded within a visual context, becomes comprehensible through issues of translation, transposition, and collage, not as a "true" meaning as if singular or guaranteed. "History" becomes any one of a multiplicity of national narratives, whether French, American, German, Russian, Indian, or Japanese, where the figural assumptions located within each narrative become conspicuous features of the text.

Beginning to study films under the circumstance of networked discourses does not require an encyclopedic or Riffaterrean super-reader who already knows all languages and histories implicated in filmic texts. Such an expectation imagines media theory as if it were some kind of Tantric or Masonic esotericism restricted to the very few, in part because such a totality of knowledge would be impossible. Because totality recedes as unknowable, one can equally well begin at any point of contact, as Zen immediacy or situationist frontier. Work becomes possible, productive, and interesting insofar as it is oriented to the collaborative networking of contexts, rather than to an essential "true" meaning founded on a single unitary authority.

A visual text can then be engaged as a series of thresholds, or inscriptions of *différance,* where one discourse hinges on another, and the meaning and effect of images breaks loose from fixed positions to circulate out of bounds. Barthes's *punctum* can be understood as one introduction to such a site within the rhetoric of visual images, as it breaks from recognizable hierarchies of psychoanalysis, ideology, or semiotics to unhinge predictability and containment within a text.

FIGURE 3. Paper screens are knocked down as part of the sexual violence surrounding the Taisho anarchist Osugi, marking a threshold between traditional and modern worlds. From Yoshida's *Eros Plus Massacre* (*Eros purasu gyakusatsu*, 1969).

[History]

The idea of history, as Foucault began to argue, is neither unitary nor universal, yet is constructed through specific tropes of nineteenth-century determinism as if it were.

"History," as the word circulates through both public and academic discourse, is irretrievably bound up with Western metaphysical concerns, from an originary dialectic of Herodotus and Thucydides, through the salvationist teleology implicit in adopting the Christian narrative of time as the "common era" to the categories and principles of nation, origin, and development that were foundational in the nineteenth century. The imagined communities that nationalism constructs, as Benedict Anderson discusses, insofar as they exist in time, are said to be entering "history."

No conscientious historian, of course, would accept such a limitation to historical research, but the term and its limits structure an ability to think through time, in much the same way that all academic disciplines are in part imprisoned by their foundational assumptions. To think "historically" today, one must think past "history" as it has been traditionally conceived and to recognize its construction as itself subject to historicization.

Non-Western societies, that vast noncategory that only appears as a reciprocal figure to the hegemonic position of Western Europe after the age of imperialism, can be multiply reconsidered in terms of how the past has been recorded and transmitted within specific traditions. Asia in particular is notable as having produced an enormous archive of historical transmission, as both written documents and as accumulative narratives of past institutions and occurrences. It is tempting simply to acknowledge this powerful alternative system of knowledge as another "history," but to do so renders invisible the figural determinants that inhabit such a term in a Western context and that are precisely at stake in cultural difference. In this book, I would prefer to restrict the use of the term "history" to that precise construction of temporality that characterizes the nineteenth-century formation of the discipline that goes by that name in the West, leaving alternative temporalities provisionally nameless.

In China and Japan, time has traditionally been inscribed through generational succession as a fundamental unit of measure. In China, a sixty-year cycle organized temporal progression, as the equivalent of a human lifespan, and in Japan the name of the emperor conventionally designated both a reign and an era. From a universalist position, this difference seems trivial, since precise dating of past events can be achieved through this method and a precise correlation of historical records between Mediterranean and Asian civilizations achieved. A postmodern and postcolonial revisiting of time, however, would argue that such differences are foundational rather than insignificant and affect the way that the world is experienced as well as the limits or horizons of thought. This shift is part of a larger move, often discussed in relation to the work of Michel Foucault, to understand the past less as a series of reified empirical events and more as a symbolic and textual process through which events are produced and understood.

Karatani argues that the Showa era came to a foundational end some three decades ago, not when Hirohito, the Showa emperor, died (that came later, in 1989), but when Japanese popular discourse shifted from the Showa 40s (the fourth decade of the Showa era) into the 1970s.[2] About the same time, a parallel shift occurred in reading CE as the name of the Western dating system, from the Christian Era to the Common Era, tacitly acknowledging its increased usage as a shared system outside the Western context from which it derived. As with the widespread use of the Internet, however, the sharing of a system does not render its figural determinants irrelevant or transparent but only less conspicuous in the Western society for which the system continues to seem normal. Everywhere else, the marking of time asserts a double system of historical context and modern chronology, as a sustained disjunctive effect that can never recede into the obvious. Outside the West, that is to say, almost everywhere in the world, the clock and language of the Internet are conspicuously Gregorian and English.

Gregorian English, if we can begin to imagine the Internet in these terms, preconstitutes a set of limits for electronic "communication" that conveniently makes Western metaphysics seem normative and beyond question. Progressive time, as both sequential and directed, anticipates an Aristotelian narrative of beginning and middle, shifting synthetically at the end toward a Kantian transcendence as goal and outcome of history. Francis Fukuyama's argument that the end of history has already occurred and is recognizable as the worldwide triumph of liberal bourgeois democracy seems exactly prefigured by these constructions. The humanist individual moves to center stage as the figure of this understanding of democracy, and the retreat of social process into a narcissistic consumerism seems natural.

"Development," as the word Jean-François Lyotard argues that we now use for what we used to mean by ideology, already assumes the metaphysical apparatus implied by such a common system. One characteristic of the time in which we live is the continued expansion of this particular construction of metaphysical time under the name of "communication" as if it were universal and transparent, while the limits of universalism simultaneously collapse into multiplicity and incommensurability, as Gianni Vattimo argues in *The Transparent Society*. The figure of difference enters into the same, as the "non-West" increasingly takes on the West as both a mechanism of social transformation and as an object of anthropological curiosity and investigation. "Japan" constitutes a site where this complex process of contestation, inversion, appropriation, and investigation can be observed, not as a leader for others to follow but as a model for orientation, departure, and further innovation.

> *It is virtually silent inside Santa Felicità, a small eighteenth-century church in the Oltrarno rebuilt from previous constructions in the 11th and, before that, the 4th century. Just inside the porch, which was built by Vasari in 1564 and retained together with some Gothic columns in the later rebuilding, are two paintings (c1525–28) by Jacopo da Pontormo, representing the Annunciation and the Deposition of Christ. The stone is cold and the air damp, in the middle of winter, a frigid austerity in which to encounter Pontormo's work. These men were citizens of Firenze, or Florence as it is called in English, alluding to Florentia, the name given the town by its Roman founders. Suddenly the door of the church swings open and a group of Japanese tourists appear, walking directly to the Pontormo, where the guide discourses at length about the specific accomplishments of the painter in the context of the Renaissance. Once finished, the group departs as suddenly as it arrived, off to the next site, and the church is as cold and silent as before. In the middle of winter, Firenze is filled with Japanese tourists.*

The foundations of modern European thought, especially as figured through the art and architecture of the Renaissance, have become an appropriate object of curiosity and research by Japanese tourists and theorists alike. It is fitting that Giorgio Vasari's porch leads toward the Pontormo, since Vasari was the writer who first claimed that the chaotic but innovative painting of the previous century was coherent enough to constitute a "Renaissance," and that painters of the cinquecento, the sixteenth century, like Pontormo, now produced their work on that foundation. Vasari can be thought of as the architectural basis of Pontormo's visual discourse, in Karatani's hybrid use of the term "architecture" to suggest both buildings and constructions of thought, despite, or rather, because of the circumstance that Pontormo preceded Vasari in time.

When the Japanese tour Firenze, an encounter takes place that undermines the idea that time flows only in one direction, toward a pinnacle of Western achievement. In a Japanese Florence, Vasari is a metaphysician and founder of that foundationless project we know as Western thought, but which has been appropriated by Japan as a contextual option.

When Jacob Burckhardt wrote *The Civilization of the Renaissance in Italy* in 1860, he ideologically positioned the Italian cinquecento as the origin of the Italian nation, which had been politically constituted during the nineteenth century and which established its provisional capital in Florence that same year. Vasari's *rinascimento* or "Renaissance" is a figural claim for Florentine centrality in the arts that inverts medieval assumptions and aesthetics. His claim becomes folded in turn inside Burckhardt's expansion of "Renaissance" to include the entire civilization of the period, not just painting, an inversion inside an inversion. This double inversion then becomes a model for Western "development," as an engine that drives "history." The Renaissance, initially constituted as a moment of stylistic innovation for political effect, is reconstituted as ideological origin of Western civilization, the mark of its break from a medieval past and its teleological reconfiguration toward an idealized future.

In 1841, Antonio Ramirez di Montalvo reorganized the Galleria Accademia in Florence. He placed all the paintings in chronological sequence to facilitate their study, a strategy that constructs and foregrounds a principle of stylistic development over time. In 1859, the Bargello was converted into a museum and became the repository for sculpture previously housed at the Uffizi. Ancient artifacts were transferred from the Uffizi to a museum of archeology, and the Uffizi was rededicated as a museum of painting alone. Once painting was isolated as a visual medium, the Uffizi too was reorganized in chronological sequence, and stylistic development became the model of art history throughout the West. In contrast, the Pitti Palace, across the Arno, still maintains the classical organization of art as a combination of painting, sculpture, and architecture for cumulative effect. Each room freely mixes artists of uneven quality and from different periods, so that each space is configured to produce variable effects for a visitor moving through the space. The radical break between these two modes of organization and their effects helps clarify how history itself is produced, as an effect of media specialization and chronological sequence.

The model of Japanese Film History that we have received from the 1950s constitutes an extension of the Uffizi to film, to argue its inclusion as one of the arts, and to Japan, as exemplar of the non-West. All the principles are otherwise the same: the isolation of a single medium, the definitive basis of an "origin" in the retrospective search for "first Japanese film," and the consequent arrangement of an otherwise chaotic array of texts as a "development" leading toward later works. This model was produced almost simultaneously in Japan, as *Nihon Eiga Hattatsu-shi (Developments in Japanese Film History)* by Tanaka Junichiro (1957), and, in the West, as *The Japanese Film: Art and Industry* by Joseph Anderson and Donald Richie (1959).[3] Eric Cazdyn argues that Anderson and Richie were probably working from their own abundant sources, despite Noël Burch's suspicion that they simply borrowed from Tanaka. The construction of Japanese Film History, in other words, is neither simply one of alien imposition, even though the model derives from Western foundations, nor of essentialist diffusion, but of a parallel hybrid response: a Western model and a Japanese topic, inscribed by both Japanese and Western writers. This innovation marked a radical move within its contemporary context.

The foundation of this process, however, is not in the books, but in the films that preceded and inspired them. Anderson and Richie, not by accident, dedicate their book to Akira Kurosawa, one of the pivotal figures of what became known as the golden era of Japanese film humanism. In France, Kenji Mizoguchi became the same kind of central figure standing in for all of Japanese film that Kurosawa did in the United States, and one kind of approach would consider how this difference came to be established. More important here is the reinscription of time in the films of both Kurosawa and Mizo-guchi, as working through a figural transformation that opened up a new historical dis-course as a possibility of thought.

In an interrogation of "history," Kurosawa's *Rashomon* reappears as a hinge text, a film that embodies the complexity and contradictions that characterize a moment that Foucault would call an epistemological break. This is ironic, of course, because *Rasho-mon* was the film that first won Western recognition of Japanese film when it won the grand prize at the Venice Film Festival in 1951. The film then became the object of exten-sive critical examination, only later to be set aside as a somewhat minor film once it became clear that major films were produced both before and after it. *Rashomon* came to be seen as a coincidence, the film that the West happened to stumble across out of any number of other, perhaps better, possibilities.

After the decentering of its initial status in the West as a "masterpiece," *Rashomon* becomes unexpectedly significant again because of its pivotal position in founding the possibility of a discourse that cut across boundaries of Asia and the West. Indian film was "discovered" by the West just after this, when Satyajit Ray won recognition for his films at Cannes and Venice in the mid-1950s. *Rashomon* has now become an artifact of a historical juncture, and embodies the conflicted discourses and inversions that mark this foundational moment. *Sansho the Bailiff* in a sense completes what *Rashomon* sets out but fails to do, internalizing a model of history to reconfigure Japanese culture and identity.

Another way of approaching the problem is to consider earlier attempts at writing Japanese Film History in the 1930s and 1940s, as Eric Cazdyn does in *A Flash of Capi-tal*.[4] The two competing models were Marxist or Imperialist, each of which appends a consideration of film to other historiographic projects as a supplement or afterthought. Iwasaki Akira's *Eiga Geijutsu-shi (History of Film Art)* appeared as a companion piece to his *Eiga to Shihon-shugi (Film and Capitalism)* in 1931, and positioned film as a subor-dinate product of capitalist development. Alternatively, *Nihon Eiga-shi (Japanese Film History),* two fifteen-minute films (the third one lost) produced by the Shinko Film Cor-poration and Ministry of Foreign Affairs in 1941, represents film as one of the gifts of Westernization that the emperor had given the people. Not only do both of these earlier histories reject the isolation of film as a privileged object of aesthetic study outside a political context, they also derive its origin in economic or political conditions outside the temporality of "first film."

Even more significant, both histories were written within the confines of a segregated cinema, a mode of Japanese production foreclosed by both popular audiences and serious critics from consideration in the West. Active foreclosure, unlike naïveté or indifference, produces impasses or occlusions even in those who might seem most likely to overcome its effects. Sergei Eisenstein's scathing dismissal of the 1929 Japanese film exhibition in Moscow is only one example of a failed encounter or occlusion. In his afterword to N. Kaufman's 1929 Moscow pamphlet on *Japanese Cinema,* later collected into *Film Form* under the title "The Cinematographic Principle and the Ideogram," Eisenstein claims, the most progressive leaders of the Japanese theater throw their energies into an adaptation of the spongy shapelessness of our own "inner" realism. In its cinema Japan similarly pursues imitations of the most revolting examples of American and European entries in the international commercial film race.[5]

In other words, breaks between the relatively isolated discourses at work within Japan and the West seemed to render even the most significant Japanese films illegible, so that Eisenstein dismissed everything he saw as imitative and superficial. This accusation was typical of Western attitudes toward all of Japanese industrial and cultural production in the modern era, and persisted for most of the twentieth century. One cannot now "correct" the mistakes of the prewar period by simply acknowledging important work across different national histories. One must also acknowledge and theorize the foreclosure that blocked such recognition for so long.

After the 1950s, in contrast to these earlier conditions, Japanese Film History became a foundational discourse that framed all of Japanese film production. Thereafter, it became impossible for many decades to conceive of Japanese film outside the prepositioning of this very particular kind of "history," pivoting on the moment when Japan was re-narrativized as part of a modern and humanist West. Today, as many theorists attempt to undo the foundational break of 1945–51 in order to understand the Showa period as a coherent entity, that same break remains the conceptual foundation on which it has become possible to rethink the pre-1945 period. One instance of this rethinking has been a renewed discussion of the 1942 "Overcoming the Modern" symposium in Tokyo as a problematic precursor of postmodernism.[6] A return to this discussion only became productive after a deconstructive strategy had reframed history, so that it became methodologically possible to distinguish unfinished radical possibilities from the nationalist and militarist rhetoric that simultaneously infected the symposium.

The paradox is that Burch's introduction to Japanese films from the 1930s could only have been written after the 1960s and the countercultural repudiation of both militarism and humanism: "L Before K," as Alan Bass puts it in his introduction to Derrida's *Post Card*. History as unitary sequence can be manufactured only through a series of disjunctive insights and retrospectively reassembled according to chronology, as in Florence, as if the sequence were a unity. The idea that the 1930s precede the 1950s in film was a most difficult arrangement to consider, an idea negated for a generation by the cataclysmic trauma of 1945.

Only after the end of Art History, in the sense argued by Victor Burgin's *The End of Art Theory: Criticism and Post-Modernity,* does it become possible to rethink the aesthetic closure that helped constitute Japanese Film History. Only after postnationalism does it become possible to question the closure of the nation. Only after hypermedia does it become possible to question the closure of film, once the "analog"/"digital" divide collapses into text. History is the materiality of thought and action, produced by an oscillation among multiple discourses all necessarily constructing recognition and misrecognition together. Insights are bound up with blind spots, and code-switching among multiple discourses can make blind spots visible but can never resolve into a totality or universal narrative. Today, in retrospect, Japanese Film History seems to mark a shuttling process, after foundational moves in the 1950s, back and forth from the 1960s to Burch's rediscovery of the 1930s, then from the 1980s to a rediscovery of the 1920s and 1940s. This is how history works, outside the metaphysical demands of genealogical origin and closure.

"History" has become multiple, conflicted, and achronic, nothing like the way it has appeared for so long, and has become unrecognizable to its former self. Not, as Fukuyama imagines, by ending in a teleological triumph of liberal capitalist democracy, but by the collapse of teleology into oscillation and heterology. "History," as a term, so strongly implies the closures of nation and genealogy that a postgenealogical construction of time must necessarily bracket [history] as a thread of contingent and overdetermined narrative within a context of incommensurability and inversion.

Heterology, to borrow the term from Michel de Certeau's *Heterologies: Discourse on the Other,* can be used to describe the condition that we now inhabit, in order to avoid habitual reduction of difference and multiplicity to narcissism and genealogy. In every Copernican move, Laplanche warns us, is the risk of a Ptolemaic recuperation; every attempt to break loose from autocentric blindness can provoke a reciprocal aversion to insight.

In his preface to Deleuze and Guattari's *Anti-Oedipus: Capitalism and Schizophrenia,* Foucault proposes "one might say that *Anti-Oedipus* is an *Introduction to the Non-Fascist Life.*"[7] The question—Is it possible to think in a nonfascist way?—still lingers. Learning to think and imagine differently is one move against the *aporia* of world "development," and the mobility of "history" within heterology is part of that process.

Re/Orientation

"Orient" is a verb, not a noun, which is why it is so hard to pin down as an actual place.

From Protestant England, papal Rome and the Catholic countries seemed corrupted by Oriental despotism and idolatry, and from the United States all of Europe appears as the East. What is at stake in this verb is not a territory, a "race," or a culture, but the metaphysics of the modern positioning itself in opposition to a rejected alternative constructed as an oppressive past.

The "West" imagines itself as the fully self-present modern, the antithesis of medieval autocracy and superstition. The United States, as the West of the West, imagines itself and is imagined by others as the pinnacle of "freedom," "opportunity," and economic success, offering itself to the world as an ideal to be emulated and being baffled by alien hesitation. In World War II, Germany was the East, a domain of barbaric, undisciplined, and savage Huns who had remained outside the civilizing influence of the Roman Empire. More recently, the Soviet Union was certainly the East, in its mystifying secrecy and violent tyranny. And Japan? Like the rest of Asia, Japan was a country that needed to be civilized, even if the civilized values of freedom and democracy had to be brought by force.

Although the West may wish this confusion were superficial and easily corrected by better information, it is instead foundational in Western thought and language. "Asia" was a small province in Anatolia for the Romans, and came to mean everything to the east of what today we would call the Greek peninsula. As a result, English has no term to imagine the vast specificity of the Chinese-Korean-Japanese cultural horizon, despite this region's enormous population, and forces an approach to this world by way of a derivative phrase such as "East Asia" or the "Far East." To begin to unthink this structural conflation, we must ask what seem at first to be absurd questions: Why, for example, do we assume that "Asia" constitutes a unity? The answer that Asia constitutes a continental landmass may seem obvious, but only from a set of assumptions derived from Renaissance mercantile navigation, an approach to the region that mapped a perimeter from the Islamic Ottomans along India to China as a continuous route. Such a unity would have been unthinkable for any of the separate regions before this moment, since overland travel was primary and internal barriers of high mountains and deserts barred conflation of incommensurable terrains and societies.

Not only "Asia" builds historical misrecognitions and conflations into the English language and Western thought. The country now called Japan first became known to Europe as *Chipangu,* a name Marco Polo adopted from the Chinese *Jih-pun,* which in turn was a Chinese translation of the Japanese *Ni-pon* or *Ni-hon,* which means sunrise or "orient." The names "China" and "Japan" were subsequently applied to the Middle Kingdom (the conventional phrase in Chinese to name the region) and the Sunrise land *(Nihon, Nippon)* in order to position those societies as sources of available products for an increasingly hegemonic world market. The name "China," although derived from the Ch'in or Qin emperor as the historical unifier of China, came to denote ceramics produced under the Ming and Qing dynasties. The current European forms of *Japan* (Dutch, German, Danish, Swedish), *Japon* (French, Spanish), *Japao* (Portuguese), or *Giappone* (Italy) derive from the Malay translation of *Japung* or *Japang* in use by sixteenth-century traders at Malacca. Because "Japan" became known to Europe through these relays of travel and trade connections, by 1688 the same name was in use to designate the varnish of exceptional hardness used in lacquerware exported from that country to the West. In other words, "Japan" is the name of both a product and a country, as equated in the Western imaginary. The West's construction of "Japan" is an exemplary case of how distant displacement can erase one meaning and substitute another, the signifieds sliding silently beneath what seem to be authentic sounds. How, then, is it possible for the West even to begin to think of [Asia], [China], and [Japan], when the language itself betrays its speakers and substitutes nonconcepts for dynamic social texts?

The West has for thousands of years oriented itself by turning to the East as an imaginary origin of a metaphysics of light, dawning with the sun at the temples of Luxor and rising among the fire gods of pre-Islamic Persia, while simultaneously expelling the peoples of the lands of this origin as irretrievably barbaric and unable to fully realize the inspiration they initiated. The East for light, the West for law, the Romans used to say. Already a double picture of fascination and foreclosure, of self-defining appropriation and brutal rejection.

Japan, however, is the East of the East, a place where even the Far Eastern societies of China and Korea appear as potential threats from the West. Kublai Khan's threatened invasion was a threat from the West, and Islamic central Asia is in the far West, beyond even the vast expanse of China. From the position of Japan, the Western attempt to dominate Asia through trade has been going on for a long time, stretching back to Islamic trade routes and religious conversions in Southeast Asia long preceding the incursions of Western Europe. Both Islam and Christian Europe represent Mediterranean civilizations seeking to convert Asian populations to universalist religions and incorporate them into imperialist systems of mercantile exploitation. Commodore Perry was simply the latest, and rudest, self-invited guest on the list, despite a politely worded but emphatic "no" that lasted through several centuries of national seclusion.

[Japan], in other words, like the [West], is an idea more than a place, an imaginary and metaphysical construction derived from a complex intersection of accumulated texts and institutions with an environment specifically encoded in relation to those contexts. People in Japan always have the choice as to whether to "be" Japanese, or to be more "Western," as many young people often wish and choose. Of course, as in the West, such choices are made only after the language and institutions of the region already inhabit the people who attempt to choose, making choice always a matter of degree rather than category. Products and styles from the West may circulate freely, but a more radical choice to "be" Western requires as much Nietzschean self-fashioning as any Westerner who seeks to become "Japanese."

Nonetheless, the distinction is crucial: [Japan] is not a people but a discourse network that simultaneously happens to inhabit the people who are native to its terrain, just as the [West] is an idea that inhabits, and is inhabited by, the peoples who are native in its domains. The distinction is crucial because territorial and "racial" identifications of cultural difference have become obsolete, even while embedded traces of "racial" fantasies continue to produce nightmarish effects. Individuals now routinely cross boundaries and learn to love, internalize, and skillfully perform what might once have been "alien" discourses. Fujimoto becomes president of Peru, for better or worse; Yo-Yo Ma becomes one of the world's finest (Western) cellists; Western teens become fans of manga, anime, and Japanese video games; Americans learn to perform Noh music and dedicate themselves to the survival of this ancient artistic form while Japanese teens could not care less. "Race" and territory have ceased to be definitive, as many once imagined they were; while intersecting discourses and texts continue to generate new participants in specific and incommensurable symbolic orders that may never congeal into an international universalist regime.

[Japan], in this text, is multiple: in one sense, a society that has achieved vast international economic success, and is beginning to have a commensurate cultural impact, especially in Asia; in another sense, it is an idea, or set of discourses that are part of the world, and a fundamental part of the process of modernization and the idea of the modern. If we are to understand where we are today, we must understand something about Japan, both because Japan is in the world and because the idea of Japan is fundamental to understanding the modern.

This book will argue that these converging interests are not separable: that Japan and Japanese people belong in the postnational world, and simultaneously that the idea and legacy of [Japan] can no longer be contained within the region called Japan. Japan is in the world in both senses: the world belongs to Japan, and Japan belongs to the world. Reciprocal appropriation has become the hinge and undoing of imperialist appropriation, where isolation and resistance have failed.

To unpack the twist in the Western dance of the Orient, one must return to that curious Western nonconcept known as the "medieval," a figurative construction of history both Mizoguchi and Sato remind us not to forget. Far from being far-fetched, as an appeal to the medieval might first seem to a postmodern viewer, the medieval is fundamental to any reading of Japanese film. Sato argues the foundational difference between Western male gender construction, as it incorporates a principle of ideal love, and the Japanese opposition of *tateyaku* and *nimaime* as incommensurable figures of samurai valor and a weakness for women. Mizoguchi is willing, explicitly in *Sansho* but elsewhere as well, to condemn all of pre-1945 Japanese history as feudal, medieval, a dark ages before the emergence of humanism. His is a view in accordance with the most absolute version of the Western metaphysics of light, casting aside everything outside the Enlightenment into the realm of superstition, brutality, tyranny, and evil. Junichiro Tanazaki, however, praises darkness as a zone of fertile and intimate regeneration. This more "traditional" Japanese view of darkness marks Mizoguchi's films as much as the Western metaphysics of light: evil in *Sansho* tends to occur in broad daylight.

The "medieval" functions as a lacuna in Western post-Enlightenment thought, to block out historicization of how East and West were refigured in Europe as preliminary to any possible Western self-definition after the Renaissance. "Medieval" Christianity was not unitary, but radically disjunctive through Ostrogothic, Byzantine, Carolingian, Norman, and twelfth-century modes, a complexity masked and repressed by the need of "modern" Europe to imagine itself as single cohesive entity. The twelfth-century Bulgarian heresy of Albigensianism was officially repressed, but it infected dominant orthodoxy nonetheless with its grandiose polarization of two Gods locked in eternal struggle. "Darkness," as a figure of evil, was born in this context, a late "medieval" moment of contestation against the Moors, their expulsion from Spain as partial recompense for the Ottoman conquest of Constantinople, and the displacement of that internal Iberian violence against the Jews, the strange native groups who were "discovered" to inhabit the Americas, and eventually the Africans in the slave trade. Although "whiteness" as we know it in the United States today would not be constituted until the late nineteenth century, "darkness" was produced as a determining figure in the late medieval conflation of metaphysics and "race" that emerged through the conflict with the Moors.

One irony of the Enlightenment is its secularized adoption of the late medieval metaphysics of light as foundational for rational thought. As a consequence, thought would be locked into a system of repetition through the continuing realignment of misogyny, racism, and intolerance with "humanism," despite the best jabs of Voltaire and the alternative

figures of Leibniz and Spinoza to offset this. The reign of the cogito, that sovereign subject, had begun, extending its dominion of darkness, as well as of light, across the earth.

This is the kind of Enlightenment that Douglas MacArthur brings to Japan in the
year zero of 1945, a self-defining benevolence and democracy compatible with autocracy
and condescension toward the Japanese. Out of this idiosyncratic mix, the Occupation
marvel of forced democracy would be born, positioning Japan in a paradoxical situation
of opportunity and foreclosure against which filmmakers began to act. Japanese films
in the 1950s proposed radical shifts in narrative construction to refashion agency out
of conflicted circumstances. "Japan" was reinvented as a positive darkness inscribed
against a metaphysics of light, a "style" that produced effects as strong as the "action" of
the narrative and that tacitly posited a textual agency alongside that of official humanist characters. The hybrid texts so produced oscillate between "Japanese" and "Western"
constructions of visual discourse, in a way that has yet to be fully read. Neither celebration nor condemnation of these films' "humanism" allows us to consider how these texts
are irretrievably double, and how the instability, paradox, and conflict implicit in this
doubleness is what gives these films their intensity.

Difference and Foreclosure

Edward Said's work on Orientalism remains a pivotal introduction to the figures of Western ethnocentricity that inhabit Western representations of the "East," from Eastern
Europe and the Middle East to Asia. Said's text initially appeared at the same moment
as Louis Althusser's critique of ideological representation and Foucault's discursive
models of power, and can be best understood as part of a shared project. In this context,
Said's intervention works to call attention to tacit figures of power and fantasy that circulate through both popular and academic representations of Asia. To achieve this, Said
inverts the Western assumption of a unitary "East" in opposition to a complex and multiple Western tradition, and instead argues a unitary West opposed to a complex series
of different societies that cannot be contained in a single term like "East."

Said's text, however, like all texts, is open to multiple readings, and one version of Said
reifies his strategic inversion of unity and multiplicity as if it guaranteed a truth of the
West. Insofar as this counterpremise facilitated the breakup of Western colonialism by
national liberation movements, it again became strategically productive. Insofar as the
premise becomes foundational rather than strategic, it risks reconstituting the essentialist
hierarchies of Western metaphysics that it seeks to oppose, from a grand binarism to a categorical foreclosure of the other. Said, in this version, is sometimes combined with Frantz
Fanon's critique of the Western foreclosure of the colonial subject as an abject Other, in
order to appropriate foreclosure and turn it against the West. This move unfortunately
forgets that Fanon was arguing a theory of madness in order to liberate those who suf-
fer, and instead romanticizes suffering as if it were a solution rather than a symptom.

It can be helpful to remember that Fanon's work was contemporary with Lacan's,
during the period when Lacan initiated a critique of orthodox psychoanalysis as the
appropriation of Freud as support for a conformist identity in Ego Psychology. Lacan

argued that Western thought derives from a foreclosure of the otherness necessary to produce a self as individualized subject, and that the cogito represents the source of alienation and neurosis, not its cure. He then linked foreclosure and the cogito as foundational constructions of the Western subject, structurally indistinguishable from psychosis. In so doing, he shifts from otherness to the Other, to distinguish the relation of self and other from the Symbolic order of language that constitutes this relation. The problem for Lacan lies in the repression of sexual difference as accession to intersubjectivity and the Symbolic order of language, and the alternative collapse of the subject into the Imaginary imprisonment of mirror identification and foreclosure.

Homi K. Bhabha's innovation in postcolonial theory was then in part to connect Fanon's theory of the Other as abjection and foreclosure with Lacan's Other as an opening of the cogito to the reconfigurative agency of the Symbolic order. One effect of this move is to oscillate between sexual difference and cultural difference, as an interiority and exteriority of a historically situated Symbolic. After Bhabha, the Other becomes a pivotal concept that unhinges ethnocentric closure and universalist grand narratives, and instead operates as a method to navigate among incommensurable discourses by way of the determining figures so often repressed within speech and experienced phenomena. Bhabha's innovation does not reject opposition, as a politics of resistance to domination, but relocates it as a figural ethics. Opposition becomes a contingent figure, crucial in some contexts but counterproductive in others, rather than a universal narrative. Said and Bhabha both mark junctures in the theorization of cultural difference, and they continue to be more often contested and misrecognized than worked through.

Asemia

All language is open to negational critique and deconstruction, but this does not mean that all language thereby becomes devalued and impossible to engage. Terms like Japan, film, history, West, culture, exchange, and construction are all problematic and contested. As a result, a certain play with language is unavoidable, to both speak and unspeak at the same time. A productive *aporia,* as a limit or horizon of thought and discourse, can be the result.

A conceptual paralysis or aphasia can be another effect, however, where it seems impossible to produce or read any text because all terms are unstable. Derrida's phrase "nothing outside the text" argues that no essentialist self-guaranteeing meaning is available to ground language in unconsidered foundations, and no transcendental signifieds escape the symbolic process through which meanings and effects are produced. As a result, the only possible way to proceed is through language that we know is inadequate and can never simply and directly say what it means, but must always work through the indirect processes of contextual relays and indeterminacy.

Theoretical work necessarily transforms the idea of language from stable categories to provisional and dynamic projects, parallel to Deleuze's idea of cinema. All terms are potentially open to reconsideration, but only a few terms can and will be selected and worked through at specific points, to change their available set of connotations and effects.

Terrain

What field of study or terrain is implied by, or invited by, the intersecting ideas of Japan, Film, and History?

Film history, as it was initiated in the 1950s, extended the model of art history to film, as an international arena of visual practices, combined with the literary idea of an auteur, or director, conceived as primary artist in the studio production of cinema. Japanese film history was then a subset of these models, transforming the sociological and mass-media analyses of the 1930s and 1940s. By the 1960s, cinema became institutionalized in U.S. universities, primarily, but by no means exclusively, in departments of art and English. Art departments recontextualized film and video as practices of new media parallel to painting and sculpture, and hence restored to the borrowed model of art history a new set of practices. English departments, under the name of Film Studies, resituated the understanding of film parallel to such literary models as nationality, period, author, and genre. Since English departments then curiously became the primary site for U.S. reception of French poststructural theory, film theory became radicalized very early in the institutional emergence of the field.

By the 1970s and 1980s, a "return" to history marked a reconsideration of historical materials after the intervention of new theoretical methods and concerns. A deepening concern with historical specificity coincided and partially overlapped with a shift to a comparative literature model to combine national film histories with language specificity. Japanology, institutionalized in part as Japanese language and literature departments, then played a double role to both open up the Eurocentric field of comparative literature to non-Western traditions and to reconsider film in relation to Japanese language and cultural history. Anthropology departments, which had already engaged with film and video within a discourse of Visual Anthropology, positioned a field of Japanese ethnographic film as a potential contribution to Japanese film studies, leading to such innovative contributions as *The Japanese Version* by Louis Álvarez and Andrew Kolker (1991). By the 1990s, a degree of recuperation had set in, and film, rather than combining productively with multiple disciplines from art and literature to history and comparative languages, began to recede to institutional appropriations of film within predefined parameters of diciplinary knowledge. The situation of film studies then began to be called "in crisis," by theorists as divergent as Mitsuhiro Yoshimoto and Robert Ray. The one area to emerge that promised to recontextualize and reinvigorate cinema was Cultural Studies, but this often devolved in practice to an analysis of whatever popular culture materials were most immediately available, and foreclosed both Japan and history as considerations.

This book proceeds from an as-yet-imaginary field of Media and Cultural Studies, not so much from institutional context and precedent as from multiple trajectories both inside and outside the field. Film, in my view, logically invites a theorization of historical materialities and effects in multiple media, in the direction where poststructuralism, postmodernism, postcolonialism, and postnationalism begin to converge and intersect. The vectors of multiple post-'s invite inflection by theories of libidinal intensities from feminism and queer theory to Bataille, to propose a merger of Cultural Studies and General Economy. Such a project seems to me to engage most effectively the contemporary problems and issues of what has come to be known, for better or worse, as an information economy.

As a result, this book is written neither as a specialist approach nor as a universal overview, but instead operates as a generalist strategy organized around the principle of an ellipsis. As Derrida argues in *Points de suspension,* translated as *Points . . . ,* an ellipsis is a trope of political agency, always open to otherness, both as the enormous range of valuable texts already available in the area of Japanese film history and as future replies, contestations, and new information. No mastery or truth is possible in these terms, but rather a dynamic model of continual learning as reconfigurative process, without permanent foundational assumptions. Accordingly, this book argues for a catalytic approach to film and media materialities situated in the gap between disciplines, languages, and cultures, irretrievably lacking mastery in any single discourse. My hope is that this strategy may generate new approaches to film and cultural studies, as well as offering a new introduction to Japanese film in an information context.

2

Dislocations

The fecundity of a Picasso or a Matisse made them cruel models for a generation of artists who were still, as a group, grappling with their attempt to understand the Western tradition, and just at the time when contemporary European artists were in full rebellion against it.
—J. Thomas Rimer, *Paris in Japan*

This inversion, which transforms our mode of perception, does not take place either inside of us or outside of us, but is an inversion of a semiotic configuration.
—Karatani Kojin, *Origins of Modern Japanese Literature*

Plural Time: Modern, Modernization, Modernism

Modernism and postmodernism form problematic contexts for the consideration of cultural issues in Asia. Clear categories and a unilateral concept of progress tend to dissolve into a multilateral dynamics of meanings and effects across cultural difference. For example, to what extent has the Western tradition of humanism paradoxically operated as a modernist force throughout this century in Asia, despite its classical and antimodernist role in the West? Cinematic realism and Western-style individualism seem to be continually reconstituted throughout Asia as progressive modes of representation from 1930s Japan to contemporary Vietnam, regardless of the prevailing official ideology. In contrast, to what extent have Western modernist practices drawn on Asian models to deconstruct those same ideologies of realism and individualism in the West?

Part of the problem has to do with the polyvalence of the word "modern." Modern, in one sense, refers to Europe since the Renaissance, as in "the history of modern Europe." This usage identifies "modern" with Neoclassicism, the Reformation, and the Enlightenment. Modernization, in contrast, suggests nineteenth-century industrialization, romantic and revolutionary values, and the transformation of society into a global political economy. Modernism, yet again, suggests the revolution in artistic modes of representation that characterized the era of twentieth-century media. Each of these modes of modernity conflicts with the others, yet these conflicts are often masked by the unitary term of "modern."

In Japan, modernity arrived suddenly and simultaneously, collapsing together the incommensurable discourses of the modern that had developed incrementally in Europe. In this regard, Japan is like all other countries outside Europe for whom modernity was sudden and external to social development, rather than gradual and internal. As a result, European ideas of development and progress became transposed into new social modalities where past events no longer followed the same trajectory toward the present. Instead of "development," Japan experienced the modern as a series of inversions, or what Karatani calls *tento*. The teleological narrative that the West had come to identify with time itself was unhinged as an effect of historical conditions outside the West, and time became open to reconfiguration.

Double Coding

Charles Jencks in his book *What Is Post-Modernism?* defines postmodernism as a mode of "double coding" that combines modernist and traditional techniques outside any progressivist hierarchy that would valorize one at the expense of the other.[1] Jencks primarily addresses formal aesthetics in terms of architecture and painting, and engages neither the issues of history and ideology that Jameson foregrounds nor the concerns with legitimation and language games expressed by Lyotard.[2] Nonetheless, this characterization makes it possible to rethink certain aspects of Japanese cultural history previously marginalized as trivial, derivative, or unintelligible in relation to the dominant progressivist model derived from humanist ideology and retained by Western modernism.[3] Films such as Osanai and Murata's *Souls on the Road* (*Rojo no reikon*, 1921) or Ozu's *I Failed, But . . .* (*Rakudai wa shita keredo*, 1930), previously discounted insofar as they seemed clearly imitative of D. W. Griffith or Buster Keaton, can be reconsidered in terms of postmodernism's concern with pastiche as a legitimate form of aesthetic organization. The conflict of humanist individualism and an antihumanist traditionalism in Mizoguchi's *Osaka Elegy* (*Naniwa eregy*, 1936) or Kurosawa's *Ikiru* (1952) seem less clearly progressive and more problematic in terms of postmodernism's interplay of humanist realism and antihumanist modernism.

If postmodernism is conceived in the West as a nonhierarchical free play of traditionalist and modernist signification without teleological determinism, is it possible to discuss a postmodernist reconfiguration of Japanese culture where Western values of humanism and antihumanism seem reversed in their relation to tradition and the modern? Can Asian societies in general be theorized in terms of an alternative access to a postmodern situation?

These questions open the possibility of rereading the dynamics of cultural difference between Japan and the West, outside the cultural evolutionary models that have informed the writing of most art and cinema histories in both Japan and the West. A discontinuous and reversible model of history now seems more productive in conceptualizing cultural difference, as is partially suggested by 1980s exhibitions in both Paris and New York of Japanese modernist painting that previously was trivialized and ignored in the West as merely derivative. It now seems unnecessary to categorize all non-Western artistic developments as gradual progress through fixed stages toward the latest Western innovation. As a result, it becomes possible to rediscover Japanese modernism on its own terms.[4]

Japanese Modernism

To discuss postmodernism in a Japanese context, one must first reconsider the role and function of modernism in Japan. Part of what is at stake here is the comparative role of cinematic realism in the United States and in Japan, both during the peak decades of modernism from the 1920s to the 1950s, and in the periods of late modernism (as Jencks positions the art of the 1960s) and postmodernism since. This text will argue that classical Hollywood conventions often valorized (although misleadingly) under the name "realism" served to reinforce dominant cultural ideology in the West, while functioning to deconstruct dominant values in Japan. The roots of this inversion across cultural difference can be found in the transitional period of the late nineteenth and early twentieth centuries in Europe and Japan in the artistic movements that swept through painting, literature, and theater, and later affected cinema. Although the influence of Japanese traditional culture on the formation of Western modernism is well known, in many respects the situation in Japan was the reverse: it was Western tradition, not Western modernism, that played a key role in the formation of what we might call "Japanese modernism." The Meiji era in Japan corresponds to the historical moment when Japanese influence was greatest in Western art, and was characterized by a great Japanese enthusiasm for all things Western. Yet during the Meiji period, the "modern" came to signify the influence of Western traditional values, specifically the ideology of humanism and the formation of an individualist subjectivity, as the metaphysical counterpart of industrial development. Traditional Western metaphysics, discussed so extensively by Derrida through his analysis of Western philosophy and art, are inverted through cultural difference in Japan to function as a modernizing influence.

Modernism as a term has been used to describe Western artistic developments beginning as early as the 1830s, but especially the decisive move away from realism usually dated to correspond with the intervention of Cubism at the beginning of the twentieth century. Impressionism and Postimpressionism are transitional movements in the development of Western modernism, and they coincided with the Meiji era in Japan when social and artistic change first decisively engaged Western modernization. In the West, the academic tradition maintained values with their roots in Renaissance humanism: realist bourgeois portraiture, landscapes of a categorically uncivilized nature, and illusionistic perspective with its stress on the single individual's point-of-view. These values were reconfigured during the Classical and Romantic eras, as Michel Foucault argues in *The Order of Things,* to become the dominant ideology of humanism for which the West is now known. Although discontinuous in its development even in the West, humanism is mythologized as universal, unitary, and progressive. History was rewritten during the nineteenth century to imagine all social formations as marking fixed evolutionary stages leading toward the West as center and outcome. Anthropology and psychology become the key discursive formations to position humanism as central, and representational principles specific to this ideology are mythologized and valorized as "realism." Realism, as the concrete embodiment of what Derrida calls the metaphysics of presence, directly affected the invention and design of photographic and cinematographic cameras, and later the development of classical Hollywood style. It is through being against the humanist ideology inherent in realism that Western modernism defines itself.

Japonisme

Western modernism turned to traditional Asian aesthetics as an alternative to the French academic tradition dominant in the late nineteenth century. Claude Debussy, for example, turned to Javanese Gamelan music as a model for compositional strategies in *La Mer*. Non-Western traditions were thereby counterposed to the established rules of Western tradition as a means of generating new aesthetic models. Although the Asian influences of Chinoiserie and Japonisme date back to the seventeenth and eighteenth centuries in Europe, this deliberate juxtaposition of two radically different cultural traditions was fundamental in forming what came to be known as "modernism" in the West. As an example of nineteenth-century Japonisme, as Colta Feller Ives has documented in *The Great Wave: The Influence of Japanese Woodcuts on French Prints,* Japanese traditional aesthetics played a crucial role in the development of Western Impressionist and Post-Impressionist painting. As early as 1856, the French etcher Félix Bracquemond discovered Hokusai's *Manga (Sketches)* in Paris, just three years after Commodore Perry had successfully forced his official reception by the Japanese Shogunate. In the four decades from 1860 to 1900, Western painters influenced by ukiyo-e, or Japanese woodcuts, included James Abbot McNeill Whistler, Jean-François Millet, Edouard Manet, Claude Monet, Vincent van Gogh, Paul Gaugin, Mary Cassatt, Henri Toulouse-Lautrec, and Pierre Bonnard. Ironically, one of the best collections of ukiyo-e in the world now open to the public is Monet's collection housed at Giverny. This irony is reversed in Japan, since traditional woodcuts had already begun their stylistic decline by the time of their discovery in Europe.[5]

The intervention of the Japanese model during the formative period of Western modernism allowed artists to challenge Western assumptions about perspectival depth and illusionistic figuration, which in turn had served to naturalize the ideology of nineteenth-century empiricism and humanist individualism. In contrast, artists restructured visual representation with a new attention to surface, color, and linear inscription borrowed from the Japanese brocade print, a process that transformed illusionism into a more self-conscious representational practice closer to what we now theorize as textual construction. Although Western modernism retained many aspects of humanist ideology, such as progressivism, the artist as individualist hero, and an expressive concern with myth, its attack on realism undermined that ideology in its most naturalized form. In retrospect,

Japonisme could be said to have allowed Western modernism to initiate a sustained, if partial, deconstructive role toward the dominant ideology of humanism in the West. The term "deconstruction" is used advisedly here, since in its specific sense it refers to an analytic technique and not an artistic practice. Nonetheless, the modernist intervention at the level of image construction precisely addresses the unconscious subordination of imagery within alphabetic writing that Derrida attributes to the West. Derrida himself has written of such literary texts as those of James Joyce or Maurice Blanchot as being preferable to the texts of classic philosophy insofar as they tend to foreground their own compositional tropes. In this sense, we may consider modernism as a deconstructive practice (as opposed to deconstructive theory) insofar as it problematizes and reconstructs the naturalized sign of realism.

Western modernism, in its deconstructive role toward humanism, could not and did not have the same impact in Japan. Rather, it was the metaphysics of humanism itself that came to play something like a deconstructive role against the so-called feudal values of the Meiji era. Feudalism was conceptualized during the modern era in Japan as a means to categorically discard the established social order. "Feudalism" itself as a term mythologizes Japanese historic traditions in much the same way that humanism does for the West. "Feudalism" implicitly positions all of Japanese history as analogous to the medieval stage of Western development, and imagines that history again as unitary, without internal contradictions. As such, the term becomes an extension of humanist ideology open to deconstruction. As used in this book, feudalism refers to the adaptive continuation of multiple traditions in Japan in their mythologized unitary form. Humanism, as an alien and external tradition for Japan, both unified the past and introduced a means for decisive change.[6]

The complex set of inversions that marks the sudden transformation of Japan into the modern era is not reducible to a simple opposition, but instead is part of a complex and heterogeneous specificity. Nonetheless, the recognition of inversions within the dialectical model of Western thought produced the illusion of a totalized opposition between East and West. Any understanding of Japan must now account for both its specificity and the Western hallucination of opposition.

Madness and Authenticity

In contrast to the bohemian excess associated with antirealist avant-garde movements in the West, such excess in Japan was associated with living through the premises of Western subjectivity. Two examples are the painter Yuzo Saeki and the Japanese literary movement known as the "I-novel," or *watakushi-shosetsu*. Saeki conceived of his move to France in 1924 as liberating, as J. Thomas Rimer describes in *Paris in Japan: The Japanese Encounter with European Painting*. His Western teacher, Maurice de Vlaminck, "looking at the young Japanese painter's work, told him that in order to develop his own talents, he must abandon all the [Western] academic styles that he had been taught [in Japan] in order to find his own unique voice." After an extended residence in Paris in search of the subjective authenticity that his mentor demanded, Saeki finally committed suicide in 1928. "To locate the self and to cast it up on the canvas without any cultural supports proved an effort that eventually consumed him."[7] Hisaki Yamanouchi, in *The Search for Authenticity in Modern Japanese Literature,* records that the *watakushi*-novel movement at the turn of the century was similarly plagued with madness and suicide. This movement was a Japanese response to Western naturalism that foregrounded what must have seemed the greatest novelty of that style to Japanese writers: the "romantic aspiration toward the fulfillment of the ego."[8] Yet displaced to a Japanese context, the ego proved unstable. The "search for authenticity," which derives from the ideology of an inner subjective truth unique to the West, had no basis in the psychoanalytic formation of Japanese identity. Any attempt to live through those premises, as Yamanouchi describes, risked the self-contradiction of an imitated authenticity:

> How could Western culture and their native tradition be reconciled to one another when often it persuaded them to hate whatever of their own culture and themselves they had been reared to respect? They felt compelled to imitate and *thus* be authentic, a contradiction that obviously gnawed at their consciousness. Consequently they came to suffer from insecurity and identity crises. These circumstances are partly responsible for the many instances of mental breakdown and suicide among modern Japanese writers.[9]

Ironically, Western encounters during the same period with an unconscious outside the boundaries of the individualist ego risked similar collapse. The madness of Nietzsche and Van Gogh, regardless of cause, became emblematic of the juncture called modernism. The discovery of an unconscious theorized in the West through psychoanalytic models of collective structure coincide with the limits of individualism felt in many domains: the closing of the American frontier, the rise of evolution as a model of human origins, the Marxist critique of capitalist ownership of the collective means of industrial production, the Nietzschean critique of humanism, the invention of cinema and radio as new mass media, and so on. These encounters, both Japanese and Western, engage the double process of history by which the psychoanalytic formation of the self coexists and interacts with the diachronic transformations of social relationships, each in its own time scale and means of signification.

Topic as Relational Self

Takeo Doi is one of the first theorists to raise the question of a culturally specific psychoanalysis. Perhaps precisely because of this, he remains a vexed figure whose works can be problematic. In some respects, Doi seems to be a humanist who studies the characteristics of traditional Japanese identity as a pathology that inhibits the formation of an individualized subject. Conversely, he can also be read as a reactionary nationalist who privileges specificity as the foundation of Japanese uniqueness.[10] Neither of these readings, however, can fully account for his project. Doi began his work in the 1950s, as a contemporary of Lacan and Fanon. Although preceded by Kaison Otsuki, who in 1912 was the first Japanese psychologist to refer to Freud, and in many ways superseded by later theorists like Takatsugu Sasaki, Doi remains historically important as a pivotal figure.[11] In his books *The Anatomy of Dependence* and *The Anatomy of Self,* he contributed significantly to a psychoanalytic model of Japanese subject formation during the postwar era. His work initially helped articulate the specificity of Japanese conditions for psychoanalysis in a field that has also come to be known as transcultural psychiatry.[12]

Doi argues that Japanese identity is different from the West's in its promotion of dependent relationships, which he terms *amae.* Since his theses of maternal dependency correlate with Japanese child-raising practices, where physical contact with the mother tends to be sustained far longer than in the West, Doi's theories can be read as based in material conditions and not some mysterious Japanese essence. The significance of this shift cannot be underestimated, and it suggests the radical potential of psychoanalysis in postwar Japan. The conceptual framework of psychoanalysis transforms "mentalities," previously imagined as ethnically or biologically determined, into social practices. As such, the self is then open to political reinvention.

Doi's formulation of dependency, however, can be misleading because it defines the Japanese self as a lack of Western individual autonomy. Since Doi himself identifies *amae* with the ideological premises of Japanese culture, to position Japanese identity formation in terms of a lack presumes from the outset a Western centrality. This implicit humanism in Doi's argument invites deconstruction unless we understand his use of the term "dependence" to lack the pejorative characteristics associated with it in the West. Doi's *amae* can function as the psychoanalytic basis of a self unlike the classical Western subject characterized by interiority, unity, and categorical separation from the other. In contrast, traditional Japanese identity appears as multiple, decentered, and relational. The *amae* self is dispersed among relationships with numerous others, and the other is always bound up in any possible subject position. The *amae* personality might be better described as a relational subject, or *topic,* to borrow a term from Japanese linguistics, which functions to form emotional interdependency as the basis of Japan as a consensus society. In these terms, the *amae* model of identity formation parallels the Lacanian model of a split subject, which cannot be conceived separate from otherness. Again, a traditional Japanese formation is linked with a modernist practice in the West. That link here involves both transcultural psychoanalytic theory and the interiorities of history.

Yet the relational self in traditional Japanese society is bound up with patriarchal authority, so consensus is always formed from the top down. The hierarchical authority in each social group, whether corporation, family, or psychoanalytic practice, initiates the terms of the consensus to be reached. As a result, the introduction of Western subjectivity not only breaks apart the relational self but also breaks the hierarchy, making it possible to reconceive social responsibility within a democratic and socialist context. This is the preoccupying theme of many films of the immediate postwar and post-Occupation period, such as Kurosawa's *Ikiru* and Kinoshita's *Twenty-four Eyes* (*Nijushi no hitomi,* 1954).

Ikiru, for example, represents a cultural *méconnaissance* or misrecognition of Western individualism, which can only be conceived as a reversal or otherness of the *amae* of an established consensus society. In the film, the central character, Watanabe, learns he has cancer and embarks on a search to discover what purpose or meaning his existence might have in postwar Japanese society. In his search, individualism is first conceived as personal selfishness, as represented by Western-inspired or modified establishments dedicated to personal indulgence, from cheap bars to dance halls and strip joints. Only later, after a series of intervening stages, does Watanabe reconceive of individual rights as the process of becoming a person who can make independent choices and initiate action. It is important, when considering this narrative, not to allow the humanist ideology which clearly makes Watanabe the center and ideal of post-Occupation Japan to erase the doubleness implicit in the film: the Japanese critique of Western selfishness as coexistent and co-valid with the American critique of Japanese consensus society as authoritarian, paralyzed, and incapable of individual action. Occupation Japan remains interesting as a boundary area between what were then called "feudal" and humanist constructs, and it can be read both ways, backward and forward in historical sequence, as a continuing critique of each by the other.

Modernism in *Ikiru* is a volatile, unstable force. Splitting the category, to distinguish a "Japanese modernism" from a Western modernism, plays on the word to indicate some parameters of its indeterminacy. Looking back at a circulation of tropes across the cultural difference between Japan and the West during the earlier part of this century, history appears as something like a Möbius strip: Japan's past seemed like the West's future, and vice versa. The purpose of this model is to help explain narrative incidents or tropes that remain puzzling in the context of other methodologies. Noël Burch, for example, notes two such enigmas at the margins of his argument in *To the Distant Observer:* Kinugasa's failure to take his film *A Page of Madness* on his trip to Europe in 1929, and the contradictions in Japanese war propaganda as viewed by the West.[13] Kinugasa's *A Page of Madness* (*Kurutta ippeiji,* 1926) has by now often been celebrated by Western critics as a radical text in some ways more innovative than the most avant-garde work accomplished during the same period in the West,[14] but Kinugasa inexplicably failed to exhibit the film to Western audiences when he had the opportunity to do so. Such Japanese war films as Takasa's *Five Scouts* (*Gonin no sekkohei,* 1938) seem oddly pacifist to Western audiences, lacking racist caricatures of the enemy and foregrounding personal suffering and solidarity among the soldiers, but there seems no doubt that these films functioned as effective propaganda.

Paradoxical Modernism

To proceed from here, one needs to move to a different level of complexity. Although the exchange of humanist and antihumanist traditions might be said to have played reciprocal roles in the formation of Japanese and Western modernisms, the question still remains of the relation between these two modernisms. Once the plural dimension of modernism enters into a circulation across cultural difference, discourse tends to become marked by paradox and the unthought of each culture, as it approaches *aporia,* or the collapse of meaning.

The most familiar example of paradoxical modernism in Japanese film is Yasujiro Ozu. As Mitsuhiro Yoshimoto has argued, Ozu's films are simultaneously considered to

be traditionalist in a Japanese context but are treasured as modernist in the West by critics as diverse as Burch, on one hand, and David Bordwell and Kristen Thompson, on
the other. Ozu's characteristic style, as Burch first argued, functions like Western modernism to deconstruct the assumptions of humanist ideology, but was formed during the
militarist period of Japanese isolationism. The isolationism of the period invited both an
emphasis on traditional values and innovation in cinematic form outside the conventions of Hollywood classical practice. Ozu's development of traditional Japanese aesthetics within cinematic form consequently parallels the adaptation of Japanese tradition by
Western modernism, although Ozu's follows from entirely different circumstances. The
characteristic features of Ozu's style, such as 180-degree reverse shots, "incorrect" eye-
line matches, and intercut environmental scenes out of continuity sequence (what Burch
calls "pillow shots"), function to decenter and de-dramatize the Western emphasis on
character and action.[15] As Bordwell and Thompson have observed, centrality of character and action is embedded in classical Hollywood conventions.[16] These conventions in
turn function to embed humanist values in the dominant stylistic system through which
Western cinematic narrative emerges. Accordingly, Ozu's style functions to deconstruct
the assumptions of Western humanism.

FIGURE 4. The abstract modernism of Japanese tradition, as represented in Ishida's *Fallen Blossoms*.
According to Donald Richie, the modernist sets of Hiroshi Shimizu's *Dark Pearl* (1929) may not
derive from those of Marcel L'Herbier's *L'Argent* (1928), since the minimalism of modern Japanese
coffee shops paralleled traditional Japanese architecture.

Mizoguchi, however, is no less paradoxical a figure in this respect than Ozu. Both his early and late films concerning women, ranging from *Poppies* (*Gubijinso,* 1935) and *Sisters of the Gion* (*Gion no shimai,* 1936) to *My Love Has Been Burning* (*Waga koi wa moenu*, 1949) and *Street of Shame* (*Akasen chitai*, 1956), are at best ambivalently feminist. As David Desser has pointed out in his book *Eros Plus Massacre,* the Japanese critic Tadao Sato considers Mizoguchi's "worship of women" as a "special Japanese form of feminism."[17] However, the role of suffering woman as an object to be admired with great outpourings of sympathy is a well-established traditional trope familiar from Noh and Kabuki. In a sense, the "Japanese feminist" sensibility, or *feminisuto,* is precisely antifeminist in that it functions to reinforce the oppression necessary to idealized suffering. The structure of the society that creates suffering is never itself significantly problematized. Yet it is precisely this trope of suffering women that Joan Mellen, in her book *The Waves at Genji's Door,* seems to celebrate as more powerfully feminist than images of women in Western films. Again we have a link between Japanese tradition and Western modernism, which here paradoxically joins reactionary values in Japan with social change in the West.

Progressive feminism seems inextricably connected with patriarchal domination as the same cinematic trope shuttles back and forth from Japan to the West. One must be careful here not to confuse issues of aesthetics and ideology in a manner that recalls the *dialogue des sourdes* of formalism and Marxism. Nonetheless, it is important to register the reversal of values within the trope of suffering women depending on whether it is read in a Japanese or Western context. One could go further and consider that Mizoguchi's quote of *feminisuto* sensibility in a modern cinematic context precisely creates the ambivalent trope of *feminisuto* as feminist. In Mizoguchi, the question remains open: Does *feminisuto* representation in a modern context provoke feminist change, or does it recuperate feminism to a traditional role of normative oppression? Either way, the paradox is genuine.

Avant-Garde Occlusion

Although the revaluation of early Ozu and Mizoguchi by Western modernism can seem paradoxical, the influence of Western modernism in Japan itself approaches *aporia*. Several factors contributed to a situation where primarily conservative or humanist aspects of Western modernity were influential in Japan. In part, only conservative instructors were available for visiting Japanese students because the "progressive painters whom the Japanese came to admire—Dégas, Monet, Van Gogh—seldom if ever took students." Yet if the study of conservative technique may have been forced on them by circumstances, Japanese artists also made specific choices of their own. Rimer speculates that "the question of national sensibility may also help to explain why certain trends in European art—Cubism, Surrealism, Futurism, Dadaism, among others—seem to have been less attractive to the Japanese than Impressionism and Post-Impressionism."[18] It should not be necessary to resort to an overly broad concept of "national sensibility," as Rimer does, to account for the preference in techniques and movements evidenced by Japanese artists. Their choices derive from the deconstructive effect of the Western humanist tradition in a Japanese context and the consequent collapse of meaning inherent in deconstructing humanism itself. The presence of humanism in Japan functioned not only to introduce new ideas but also to unify the past as a mythological "feudalism." Any deconstructive moves against humanism itself thereby undermined not only the modern, but the history of Japan as the Meiji period had come to conceive it, erasing any position from which to proceed.

As a result, the most radical movements in Japan from the point of view of the West, from Dada and Surrealism to anarchism and sexual liberation, remained far more circumscribed than might be initially imagined. Since these Western modernisms depend on a Kantian humanism to work against, that itself remained opaque to a majority of Japanese in the 1920s and 1930s, the most radical and avant-garde of Japanese projects could easily become occluded as fundamentally illegible. In addition, the Japanese avant-garde was severely suppressed by the militarists in the 1930s in a systematic effort to exterminate all radical thought. This in itself is no different than parallel suppressions of the avant-garde in Germany and Russia during the same period, but, unlike those countries, the Japanese avant-garde did not achieve recognition in the West before the war. Consequently, Japanese avant-garde movements were not recognized and preserved in Western museums and histories as Expressionism and Constructivism were until belatedly embraced by the nations from which they came. The achievements of the Japanese avant-garde, for the most part, vanished into an abyss of unrepresentability in both Japan and the West until their rediscovery in the very different context of the 1960s. Understanding this process of contextual legibility, occlusion, and delay is important to a theorization of how history works, as well as what it represents.

Japanese artists who arrived in France after World War I seemed to have been mystified by the attack on the academic conventions that the Japanese were still working to interiorize. Contemporary European artists were in full rebellion against the Western representational tradition at precisely the historic moment when Japanese artists were struggling to understand it. The confusion of the Japanese situation should not be dismissed as an inability to keep up with progressive values in the West, but rather as a critique that illuminates a paradox of Western modernism. Despite the deconstruction of humanist ideology inherent in Western modernism, the artists who most strongly articulated these positions, such as Pablo Picasso, Henri Matisse, Jean Cocteau, or Sergei Eisenstein, were publicized or marketed as extreme individualists. An earlier generation of Japanese artists had deliberately worked to bring back to Japan a codified system of techniques based on the French academic tradition and that represented Western standards to the Japanese. Insofar as later Japanese students were able to respond initially to new styles in painting that rejected this same academic tradition, it was by seeking out individual artists as mentors, as individuals, and responding to their style as a new set of rules or operations to be performed on alternative subjects.[19] The limits of their ability to recognize avant-garde work in the West corresponds to the limit to which these developments could be recuperated within the model of extreme individualism.

Most often these styles were linked with Western subject matter, such as portraits of Europeans or landscapes and cityscapes around Paris, but when turned to the Japanese context they could prove too destabilizing for successful performance. Japanese artists who studied in the West "found on their return a need to adjust their skills, expectations, even the strategies used to develop their maturing talents, to the realities of Japan, in terms of society, environment and reward. Many, especially those who returned to Japan from Europe with advanced stylistic commitments, found this period of adjustment an awkward, painful and a sometimes surprisingly protracted one."[20] In Japan, the collective relationships of a hierarchical consensus society were dominant and predetermined. The deconstructive aspects of Western modernism against the dominant ideology of humanism in the West paralleled or drew on collective structures of culture and subjectivity theorized by psychoanalysis, Marxism, formalism, and linguistics. Insofar as Japanese artists modeled themselves after an individualism that sought to represent such collective determinations, they became isolated and powerless on their return to Japan. Japanese artists influenced by Western modernism were placed in the odd position of imitating a Western authenticity that in turn imitated Japanese tradition to oppose Western humanism. Far from being rebellious in Japan, this alternative modernism in many ways mirrored or was recuperable by the dominant conservative and antimodernist Japanese tradition. "Homecoming exhibitions" of Japanese artists returning from Europe were welcomed but were seen as novelties, posing no coherent threat to the established

FIGURE 5. Appropriation of U.S. pop culture preceded the invention of an alternative cinematic style congruent with traditional Japanese aesthetics. From Ozu's *I Failed, But . . . (Rakudai wa shita keredo,* 1930).

regime. Insofar as Japanese artists sought in Western modernism's borrowing of Japanese tradition a modernism to position against Japanese tradition, they became caught in mirrors within mirrors, an *aporia,* or collapse of meaning. Impressionism and Postimpressionism in retrospect seem like a brief interlude when Western and Japanese modernisms, borrowing from each other but moving in opposite directions, appeared to recognize common values but were instead deceived by mirrors.

Antihumanism and Recuperation

A reconsideration of modernism across the cultural difference of Japan and the West, then, leads to principles of inversion, paradox, and *aporia*. Humanism and antihumanism play inverse roles in the conflict of tradition and modernism in Japan and the West: each culture turns to the other for traditional values that function to deconstruct its own dominant ideology. Japan borrows humanism from the West as a component of Japanese modernism, just as the West borrows antihumanist elements from Japanese tradition to produce Western modernism. At points where discourses of the modern intersect between Japan and the West, traditional and modernist values are likely to seem paradoxically intertwined. Attempts to directly identify or exchange modernist developments between the two cultures are likely to approach *aporia*. These considerations may now help illuminate the methodological enigmas cited above.

   To return to Kinugasa, cross-cultural exchange between Japan and the West has sometimes seemed to be a history of unfortunate coincidences and missed opportunities. Noël Burch, in a footnote, expresses his disappointment that Kinugasa toured Europe but failed to show his most powerful film, *Page of Madness:* "Kinugasa's decision not to take *Page of Madness* with him on his tour of Europe in 1929, to take only *Crossways,* a far more academic 'Western-style' film, might indicate that he was not, indeed, aware that his masterpiece would most likely have been hailed as such by critics and an elite audience who accepted and admired *Caligari, La Roue* and *Potemkin,* all of which had gone much 'further' than *Crossways*."[21] If modernism functioned inversely in Japan and the West, Kinugasa might well have felt that the "academic 'Western-style'" of humanist filmmaking evidenced by *Crossways* was not just more likely to be positively received by a West seen as predominantly humanist, but was more significantly modern. *Page of Madness* might have seemed like a minor novelty in comparison, and less effective at challenging traditionalist values.

   A symptom of the tendency toward paradox and *aporia* can be found in the problem of power in the cross-cultural theorization of social change. It can be helpful here to reconsider Burch's theoretical revaluation of 1930s films as suggesting an alternative modernism in Japan, ironically associated with Japanese chauvinism and ultimately militarism. The link is ironic because this alternative Japanese modernism approximates Western modernism, which Burch wishes to link with leftist ideology. Western modernism was capable of political alliances on both left and right (for example, André Breton and Constructivism on the left, Ezra Pound and Futurism on the right). Nonetheless, according to the progressivist conventions by which the history of modernism has often been written, one might imagine that a move closer to Western practice would be associated with social change. Again, in Japan, the reverse was true. To the degree alternative Japanese modernism approached Western modernist practice, it was marked not by clear progressivism but by traditionalism. Only by the 1960s did it become possible to disentangle a Western or "universal" modernism from the risk of transparent recuperation by ultranationalists.

Burch values Japanese films of the 1930s precisely insofar as they challenge the humanist assumptions of the dominant economic class in the West. Yet this class analysis leads to self-contradiction, as Burch himself notes in discussing the wartime films: it is, he acknowledges, "instructive to observe the extent to which the mode perfected during the previous period of political and ideological reinforcement of the traditional values, was directly compatible with the requirements of propaganda in a wartime situation. This is another aspect of a complex dialectical process, involving more than one uncomfortable contradiction."[22] In other words, antihumanist ideology in a Japanese context, far from extending democratic principles past the ownership of a privileged class, is compatible with totalitarianism. The antihumanist values that Burch persuasively argues as a critique of Western hegemony are never clearly distinguished in Japan from the authoritarianism that dominated the consensus society of the militarist 1930s and the Stalinist practice of social revolution during the same era.

The question of radical potential and militarist recuperation returns in a postmodern context through the debates that have come to surround the 1942 symposium "Overcoming the Modern." In this wartime discussion, a radical critique of Western hegemony is seamlessly merged with a nationalist rhetoric of Japanese imperialism, inviting a deconstructive rereading of this unstable conflation. Burch's project, however, is preliminary to such a move, and argues for the possibility of a radical potential in even the most unlikely of contexts which remains unread, unfinished, and yet still available as a resource for further agency.

Deconstructive Humanism

The question of deconstruction in Japan, however, can be as vexed a topic as that of postmodernity. Karatani once mischievously remarked that Japan has no need for deconstruction, because Japan was never constructed. To engage Karatani's suggestive and multivalent intervention, it helps to consider what he means by "construction." In *Architecture as Metaphor,* Karatani proposes architecture as a figure through which to consider Western thought from a position exterior to that tradition, partly to call attention to "construction" as a central and foundational principle within the West. In this sense, Japan's different tradition outside the West can only be deconstructed, paradoxically, by the introduction of construction.

In his most recent work, Karatani then argues for the Kant in Marx, or the continuing foundational assumptions of Kant that survive and inhabit a Marxist discourse. A consistent pattern or figure can be recognized here as the representation from the outside of a unity that appears impossible from the inside. Kantian idealism, like that of

Hegel, appears in the West as precisely what Marx opposes in his call for a materialist history. Yet from outside the West, Kantian assumptions appear to coincide with, rather than oppose, Marxism. Asia never constructed an opposition between idealism and materialism, never imagined that the world could be divided and categorized in this way, so any call for a materialism necessarily and paradoxically implies the idealist counterposition that it opposes. Aristotle and Plato alike are alien producers of unexpected effects in Asia and remain inextricably bound up together as Western.

The external position of Japan makes it possible to historicize what the West conceives as a universal history, and to consider how the Kantian subject is reciprocal with a Marxist empirical project and is co-defined by it. To Marx, Japan was simply a feudal society, a nineteenth-century exemplar of institutions and practices continuous with medieval Europe. Ironically, all these ideas come together in Japanese film through modernist representations of Marxism in terms of a humanist individualism in a feudal context.

In the 1920s, *mobos* and *mogas,* alternatively translated as "Marx boys and girls" or "modern boys and girls," represented a counterculture of Japanese youth. The films that Bantsuma made during this period displace the figure of the *ronin,* or masterless samurai, from Tokugawa Japan to become a provocative figure of intervention for social justice against the ruling class. The inversion of the *ronin* from social marginality to retrospective *mobo* is a key move in these films.

Choshu's Question

The possibility of a deconstructive humanism allows us to rethink the several positionings of Japan, including those by Marx, as simply "behind" the West. Faced with the challenge of an expansionist European imperialism, through both the arrival of Commodore Perry in 1853 and in the battle of the Shimonoseki straits in 1863–64, Japan produced an innovative and unexpected response that continues to resonate today. *Shishi* activists, or anti-Western samurai, in the province of Choshu began firing on Western ships passing through the Shimonoseki straits in 1863. Their action triggered a counterattack by American, British, Dutch, and French ships in 1864, whose sailors went ashore and dismantled the Choshu gun emplacements. After this encounter with overwhelming force, Choshu abandoned its anti-Western absolutism and began Westernizing its military, including peasantry in ranks previously restricted to the samurai class. This action then led to the Restoration in 1868, in which Choshu played a key role, and proliferating effects from political and sexual anarchism to reactionary militarism. The intersection of radical potential and militarist atrocity, often represented in the same moment, people, and events, becomes a major concern in Oshima's later work, from *In the Realm of the Senses* and *Empire of Passion* to *Taboo.*

Choshu, initially among the most vehement rejectionists in continuing to mount military resistance to Western incursion, reversed its strategy to become the strongest advocate of institutional change within Japan. Having determined that military resistance was futile and self-destructive, Choshu seized on modernization as an inevitable and fundamental change. However, its reversal inverts Western assumptions of superiority by transforming the threat of imperialist domination into a question: Is it necessary to Westernize in order to modernize? Once this question is raised, regardless of the variety of answers subsequently proposed in response, the seamless identification of modernization and the West was already broken. In effect, the actions of Choshu deconstruct the ideological basis of Western colonialism at the moment of its mid-nineteenth-century insistence, and anticipate the multiple alternatives to it that followed.

Choshu marks a movement of reverse appropriation, whereby from the Western move to appropriate Asia into its own narrative and political economy, Japan seizes modernization as a trope that can be turned against the West. This move is then repeated throughout African and Asian liberation movements, continually reinvented without direct repetition, as Western principles of nationalism, self-government, and revolution are appropriated and refigured as the means of producing an anti-imperialist break.

The Choshu inversion is not, of course, a deconstruction in any direct sense, but rather embodies a symptomatic response that prefigures and becomes retrospectively legible through the parallel of deconstruction in a postmodern context. Choshu represents a response to the West that not only resists domination but also reconfigures the terms in which it is thought. Rather than a subordinate position behind the West, Choshu produces the parallelism of an alternative practice of the modern, nowhere intended but irretrievably inscribed.

FIGURE 6. Post-Taisho *mobos:* three modern young men in *I Failed, But . . .* (*Rakudai wa shita keredo,* 1930).

Occlusion and Rediscovery

By the 1920s, Japan and the West had come to occupy incommensurable discourses of the modern, each blind to the figuration of the other. While the West continued to pursue a teleological narrative of Western superiority and exclusion, Japan was inventing a radical alterity, not in terms of its traditional culture, but within the modern. While the West saw Japan as an exotic past, reminiscent of a medieval West, Japan recast its past as an origin of national modernity that positioned the West as an equal. The ideology of race, as an overdetermined figure of cultural evolutionism, condensed many of the dissonances and misrecognitions of this period into a single trope. In 1924, the United States passed a racial exclusion law, excluding the Japanese in a general prohibition of Oriental immigration, that fundamentally worked against any rapprochement between a modernizing Japan and an insistently imperialist West. One of the unresolved problems of history today is to assess how much U.S. exclusion contributed to the derailing of Japanese progressive politics in the 1920s and Japan's subsequent decline into the "dark valley" of 1930s militarism.

Since 1945, the discourse of the modern from the Japanese 1920s has become occluded in both Japan and the West and open to multiple narratives of partial recovery. Immediately after the war, Japanese films from *Ikiru* to *Twenty-four Eyes* refigured the 1920s as an interrupted continuity, so that Taisho and early Showa discourses of the modern were positioned as an origin of 1950s humanism. By the 1960s, a counterculture refigured the 1900–1930 era as a period of radical potential never achieved in Japan, and rediscovered an avant-garde through *Page of Madness* and a radical politics through Yoshida's *Eros Plus Massacre*. By the 1980s, the same period had been refigured again, through an archeology of early cinema practices, from the *benshi* to paracinema, that now seemed hybrid and postmodern. None of these versions of recovery is simply true in the sense of rendering others false; instead they open onto the proliferation of multiple discourses and effects from pivotal junctures in time. The specific formation I have sought to articulate here is the humanist inversion that seems less recognized than other effects.

It becomes possible to reconsider the different function and effects of modernism in Japan and the West because of a postmodern context that problematizes any unitary model of modernist progressivism. If we are to consider postmodernism as a concept relevant to Japan, we might consider it as characterizing a period in which this different positioning of traditional and modernist values continues, but develops a degree of self-reflexivity analogous to but not identical with the nonteleological interplay of traditional and modernist values in Western postmodernism. A postmodernist conceptualization of Japan invites a reconsideration of the relation between force and signification. Signifiers and systems have become increasingly shared within cross-cultural exchange, with business suits in a capitalist Japan and sushi served to Western executives studying consensus models of management, yet the vectors of force driving these signifiers through systems of meaning remain different between Japan and the West. In postwar films from Ozu's *Early Summer* (*Bakushu,* 1951) to King Vidor's *Japanese War Bride* (1952), the polarization

Figure 7. Japanese poster for George Stevens's *Giant* (United States, 1956).

of Japanese and Western appearances still predominates. Such categorical separation of traditions across the Pacific has virtually vanished. Nonetheless, suits and sushi still function differently even if they look the same.

Doubleness and Idiosyncrasy

Parallel to the dislocations produced in Japan by the impact of the modern are dislocations in "Western" cultural theory produced by the encounter with Japan. Derrida argues a similar idea in *Dissemination* when he writes that "the rule according to which every concept necessarily receives two similar marks—a repetition without identity—one mark inside and the other outside the deconstructed system, should give rise to a double reading and a double writing." Like the postmodern, "Western" critical theory has a problematic relationship to Japan, as it does to any cultural region outside Europe. On the one hand, many theoretical methodologies that historically have developed in the West, from psychoanalysis and Marxism to structuralism and poststructuralism, fundamentally break with biologizing or racist ideas of cultural difference that dominated Western thought before 1945. As such, these methodologies are an invaluable resource for decolonizing narratives of national identity and history. On the other hand, with the exception of Marxism, these same methodologies have tended in practice to consider primarily Western cultural representations. As a result, they can ironically appear outside Europe to be an extension of past cultural imperialism, despite the foundational break with Eurocentric domination that constitutes their project. A resistance to "Western theory" has accordingly developed, often through Marxist, nationalist, and/or humanist discourses that are themselves, in a double irony, equally Western. "Theory" itself is a misleading term for the multiple activities usually grouped under the name "poststructuralism," since it implies a unity where there are only heterogeneous approaches. "Theory" also implies an opposition to practice, as if all postwar developments could be dismissed as a retreat to idealism rather than an engagement with the materialities of thought. As a result, in yet another irony, several so-called theorists are unwilling to accept the term to describe their work.

The process by which these ironies of reciprocal misrecognition and exclusion have begun to break down is now itself a part of history. Many of the pivotal debates that mark this encounter in film theory surround the publication of three texts: Noël Burch's *To the Distant Observer* (1979), Roland Barthes's *L'Empire des signes* (1970, translated into English as *Empire of Signs* in 1982), and Edward Said's *Orientalism* (also 1979). Burch's work extends some of the principles and strategies of Barthes's *Empire of Signs,* which is itself bound up with questions surrounding a shift from verbal to visual modes of inscription, and hence from literary models to film. Said critiques figural assumptions within Western discourse of the East, parallel to Derrida's and Lyotard's work on tropes and to Althusser's and Foucault's work on ideology and discourse. H. D. Harootunian's introduction to the recent electronic republication of Burch's text helps testify that the significance of these debates has not diminished and remains an entry point for any serious discussion about Japan in the world.

Through this circuitry of interventions, theoretical methodology enabled a critical reading of an alternative cultural context, while cultural difference conversely functioned to help read the limits and character of critical methodology itself. My interest here is in a specific case of non-Western cultural production where cross-reading becomes an issue, and neither a cultural tradition in its own terms nor critical methodology per se suffices as a controlling discourse. Discussion surrounding these texts, like parallel work in Japan at the same moment, was moving toward a double writing, in which exteriority and interiority were mobilized next to each other as parallel formations.

Since the time of these debates, most discussion of national cinemas has tended to move away from these central methodological problems, back toward more basic, traditional issues of industry analysis, historical accuracy, and auteurist stylization. In part, this is an understandable and even welcome development, given the important recent work in national cinemas from China and Southeast Asia to India and Africa. Yet this new access to materials should not obscure or petrify the theoretical argumentation on which comprehension of these new materials must be based.

To engage current problems in cultural heterogeneity, one might accordingly begin by reconsidering this cluster of key interventions that generated productive work in the field. By juxtaposing developments in several different areas of activity that either partially overlap or are usually considered separately, it becomes possible to avoid centralization in a single text and problematize assumptions implicit within different discursive formations. As part of its break with past approaches, this process of circulation exceeds dialectical models and instead produces supplementary connotations of discrepancy, misrecognition, and destabilization.

In this fashion, one could somewhat arbitrarily identify two or three relatively stable areas of activity that function to orient (to use and displace a loaded term) work from that period. First, extending the techniques of literary and textual analysis to the domain of cultural studies is now long established, but remarkable in the example of Barthes's *Empire of Signs*. Second, the reorientation of political and ideological analysis toward the domain of cultural forms remains productive, as in Scott Malcomson's critique of Barthes and Burch in *Screen* (1985) based on Said's *Orientalism*. Last, in a slightly later development, the necessary empirical detail of a specific cultural practice is transformed by a younger generation of historians. Original materials once available only in native languages begin to be translated or studied by a new generation of historians who are frequently bilingual (native to Japan and writing in English), such as Hiroshi Komatsu, Kyoko Hirano, Keiko MacDonald, and others.[23]

The problems that these developments suggest can be posed by imagining an intertextual dialogue of multiple voices. Voices can be imagined as being generated by the positions from which individual texts are written without restricting the discourse to these texts alone. The pursuit, application, and cross-referencing of these positions by other writers become part of the voices as well. This approach as a technique of contemporary criticism has been pursued elsewhere by such writers as Jane Gallop in *The Daughter's Seduction,* and is part of a critical era produced by such operations as the split writing of Derrida's *Glas* and the multiple voices or equivocity of Joyce's *Finnegans Wake*.

Empires and Signs

A first voicing, or intersection, of this material might be Scott Malcomson's critique of Barthes (1985) in relation to Tony Rayns's introduction to the new generation of Japanese filmmakers that emerged in the 1980s (1986).[24] Malcomson argues Said's position, that the West inevitably perceives the Orient as a projection of its own Other, thereby inevitably casting it in the form of exotic opposition. Since Said's publication of *Orientalism* in 1979, the study of Orientalism has become a field in itself, with an increasingly nuanced analysis of complexity and multivalence at stake.

Orientalism, as an enthusiasm in the West, developed in the seventeenth and eighteenth centuries through the collecting of objects, such as ceramics and furniture, that was made possible by developing trade routes to the East. In its original context, the Orient seems to have included everything east of Vienna, so that Egypt, Arabia, India, and the Far East were all equally and interchangeably intriguing. Moorish disguises in opera (for example, Mozart's Turkish Ambassadors in *Cosi Fan Tutti*), mock Egyptian furniture styles that followed Napoleon's conquest of Egypt, and ceramic collections from China coexist with fake Oriental landscapes done in oils such as can be found in the queen's chamber at Fountainebleau.

Malcomson, without recalling the historical details, argues that this position is still maintained by Barthes's presentation of Japan in terms of an absolute difference from the West. Rayns then advocates an alternative position: that Japan, now completely industrialized and a major participant in an international information economy, has more in common with the West than it does in contrast. He goes on to clarify that this does not mean he wishes to deny all cultural specificity to Japan, but rather that any such specificity must be rethought in the context of an international economy where the same outweighs and recontextualizes such difference.

Barthes, of course, has already anticipated such a critique in his original formulation of *Empire of Signs,* when he argues that he is articulating an imaginary place that he will call Japan and that has no necessary connection with any real place of the same name. To Malcomson and Rayns, this must seem like an inadequate effort to be clever, and it does not undo the damage: romantic implications emerge precisely from positioning Japan in the place of the Imaginary. Malcomson is not alone in criticizing Barthes's late work as if it retreated to an aestheticized idealism in contrast to his earlier, more "political" concerns. It is in this context that Victor Burgin rereads *Camera Lucida* and complicates the idea that Barthes's later writings seem to betray the positions taken in his earlier texts.[25] But there is more to be said.

The commonality of the West with modern Japan is, of course, also a romantic vision, but one that implies a return to universal humanism. Rayns's allowance for cultural specificity repeats the humanist subordination of difference to the status of local color or national character, which simply reinforces hegemonic normativism that foundational difference can work to resist. Although Malcomson, and implicitly Rayns, accuses Barthes of a romantic fascination with tradition and a corresponding blindness to modern Japan, both remain blind themselves to the suggestions of a political unconscious implicit in

Barthes's conjunction of imagination and history. The radical potential of *Empire of Signs* remains to be read: a relocation of history from Western teleology to determining figures embedded within a culturally specific terrain. The problem is not whether tradition or the modern prevails, but how the relation of tradition to the modern is figured. But this is not simply what Barthes says, so Malcomson's and Rayns's critiques also remain pivotal.

The critique of late Barthes carries the conflicted intensity of a partial insight. On the one hand, a negative critique can call attention to the narrow and self-indulgent aestheticism that seems at times to infect Barthes's writing, undermining and unnecessarily limiting his best contributions. For example, Barthes seems to treat the impassivity of Japanese facial expression while playing *pachinko* exclusively in aesthetic terms, without noting the control of *pachinko* by *yakuza,* or Japanese mafia, and the relation of impassivity to power. Such moments can make Barthes's comments seem superficial and insensitive. On the other hand, dismissing Barthes altogether trivializes and forecloses his many contributions to the theorization of the text, desire, and the unexpected. Barthes, like other figures that mark a break, necessarily combines productive and counterproductive moves in the same texts.

Isolating *Empire of Signs* from Barthes's other later works makes it easy to misread his project as if it were simply a recuperative idealism, claiming to be a truth of Japan. But to dismiss these later texts as simply inconsistent with his earlier work misreads the break within his writing and can enthusiastically miss the point of what work these later texts perform. If *Empire of Signs* can legitimately trigger alarm bells of ethical responsibility, casting doubt on the privileged role of an outsider's aestheticism, it is also part of a larger project that opens many doors for further interventions. In the context of such other late work as *Camera Lucida, Barthes by Barthes,* and *The Pleasure of the Text, Empire of Signs* helps initiate a textual reading of visual images in the context of memory, indeterminacy, and desire.

For most of his career, Barthes was convinced that the analog character of camera images, as a mechanical index of events, set them outside the methodologies of textual analysis. Only late in his life was he able to think through the textuality of camera images, and his difficulty suggests the significance of this divide in thinking. Anticipating digital images as encoded texts, Barthes's textual images relocated what had been assumed as photography's seamless bond to the real as an arbitrary process of signification and inscription. After this juncture, camera images and Japanese writing seem equivalent as visual modes of inscription, but without any appeal to an imaginary pictographic realism that once motivated such a comparison.

Once situated as parallel writing systems, photography and Japanese writing intersect and combine with other modes of visual representation to produce a decentered textuality that precedes the experience and thought produced through it. All participants are produced by, inhabit, and reproduce visual texts as the symbolic environment that characterizes human life. To engage this symbolic text, Barthes adopts a series of antinominalist strategies that relocate visual images in a network of connotations without denotative center and open onto an unconscious of the text. He then reclaims desire and pleasure as productive textual strategies, refusing to cede pleasure to the fetishized objectifications of hegemonic consumerism. This move necessarily follows after an ascetic resistance to pleasure in his earlier works, a principled resistance productively continued in Laura Mulvey's theorization of the male gaze and Hal Foster's *Anti-Aesthetic*. Yet Mulvey, too, next asked why she enjoyed films, despite the seemingly omnipresent objectification of the gaze, a question she took up in her subsequent but less famous work.

After Barthes and Mulvey reclaim pleasure as a strategy of radical reinscription, two other projects logically follow and retrospectively transform the reading of Barthes's work. The first is a rereading of aesthetic discourse, to deconstruct the narcissistic conflation of pleasure and irresponsibility implicit in isolating aesthetics from social history, taken up in such works on postmodern ethics as Lyotard's *The Differend*. This direction leads Lyotard toward a figural ethics, working through how a foundationless play of the text is incompatible with social irresponsibility, a project argued by refusing the malicious falsification of Holocaust deniers. The second, dependent in part on the ethical intervention of the first, reads outward from Barthes's play of the text to imagine a ludic indeterminacy of allusion and asemic inference that can act as a generative precondition for experiment and innovation. Barthes's texts remain double, operating at an unresolved juncture of privatized aestheticism and textual play.

Speakers and Limits

Barthes's position in *Empire of Signs* might be located as parallel to that of Jean-Luc Godard and Anne-Marie Miéville's film *Içi et ailleurs* (France, 1974), where another kind of doubleness operates. On the one hand, Godard and Miéville's images of Palestine are motivated by rhetorical tropes of political commitment and social conscience, and yet precisely because of this commitment those images are driven within the film to a point of self-imposed limitation. The filmmakers argue the impossibility of any adequate image of Palestine being produced by a non-Palestinian, that is, by a European, a Westerner, parallel to Louis Althusser's critique of "who's speaking?" in any hegemonic representation of difference.

Sol Worth pursued similar conclusions in his collaboration with Ted Adair to give cameras to the Navaho from 1966 to 1972, at approximately the same historical moment as Althusser's critique. Their goal was to facilitate film documentation of a non-Western society that might be less biased by Western cultural assumptions than films by outside anthropologists.[26] Worth and Adair's project, of course, overlooked both the ideological assumptions built into the camera as apparatus and the many decades of extensive Western cultural collaboration developing cinematic codes to articulate such documents. As a result, the Navaho films were often as much preoccupied with the camera as cultural artifact as they were engaged with a means of representation. But not all Navaho were naive about cinema. John Ford had shot *The Searchers* in Monument Valley and employed a number of Navaho to play Apache in the film. Commercial assumptions were likely to prevail even in films produced by outsiders, as an available vernacular through which to narrativize events. What differences Worth and Adair were able to discern in Navaho filmmaking were far more subtle than initially anticipated.

A similar situation marks the aftermath of the 1970s feminist critique of male domination in Classical Hollywood Cinema, when a few women began to be able to direct but were far more likely to succeed if they reproduced dominant conventions. Although the democratization of new media remains crucial on grounds of social justice and equal access, new users are no guarantee of a different visual discourse. Instead, new film- and video makers are far more likely to produce a document of the camera as a material exteriority or a fiction that derives from dominant commercial films than an innovative break with past practices. Expectations that those previously disenfranchised from dominant media can simply and directly take up tools of authentic self-representation are perhaps more naive than the approaches of new filmmakers themselves. Peoples and discourses are not biologically identical but only historically linked, and this discrepancy or sliding of participants under discourses often becomes visible in films by new producers.

Içi et ailleurs argues that Western support for non-Western causes all too easily slides into an Oedipalized identification with subordination and a rage against power, so that a double figure of identification and foreclosure infantilizes the other and perpetuates powerlessness in the name of opposing it. Ironically, a "hard" resistance to Orientalism can simply reconstitute Orientalist fantasy on different grounds. As African Americans and feminists have observed in other contexts, abjection and idealization are both objectifying stereotypes. Neither the primitive beast nor the noble savage, and neither the irrational feminine nor the idealized woman, is an image that allows the other to speak. Deleuze and Guattari argue instead against Oedipalization as the mechanism by which the cogito reproduces itself as a foundation of Western ideology.

As an initial response to this problem, Miéville and Godard redirect our attention to the location of the Imaginary in the West, as mass-produced and consumed within the totalized information economy represented by television. In their next film, *Numéro Deux* (France, 1975), the Western Imaginary has become figured as an incestuous anality, an aggressive compound of narcissism and abjection as a colonizing foreclosure of otherness. In *Içi et ailleurs,* we cut back and forth continuously between images of the Palestinian conflict and images of a French working-class family watching television. The doubleness or dilemma might be formulated something like this: Westerners cannot *not* think of the struggles of non-Western societies; to simply not think would be fundamentally irresponsible. However, any such thinking unavoidably engages the operations of the Western Imaginary and must be addressed directly as such. Barthes's text does this, or perhaps implies this, by its playful thinking through of Japan in terms of desire and the Imaginary. However, if we are to recognize and build on this problematic, we must do more than simply allow the differential construction of Japan in *Empire of Signs* to remain a closed text, which would indeed open its formulations to a romanticized recuperation. We must instead, like Oshima, continually rewrite *Empire of Signs* as a text open at every point to further intervention and make explicit in this work of writing the dilemma or doubleness implicit within Barthes.

Theorizing History

A second voicing of the material, as an intertextual configuration of contemporary cross-cultural methodologies, might be the historian's critique of Noël Burch's *To the Distant Observer.* Burch, more than anyone, has taken seriously the differential conceptualization of Japanese formal signification and inherent ideology that Barthes proposed. Briefly, Burch first argues that the formal elements of traditional Japanese aesthetics, as reinterpreted by Barthes in terms of decentered space and textuality, were adapted to film during the 1930s, long before the popularity of Japanese film in the West during the 1950s after *Rashomon* won at Venice. More significantly, he then argues that the resulting formal practices articulate the ideological values of a nonhumanist consensus society that Burch associates with Althusser's rereading of Marx.

In one sense, this sliding over of Japanese traditional aesthetics such as *wabi, sabi,* and negative space into the deconstructive domain of decentering, and of the consensus society of Japanese patriarchy into Althusserian Marxism, is open to the same critique as that of Barthes by Malcomson. (Malcomson includes Burch with Barthes in his critique, although without elaborating his position to this degree.) It sees the East in terms of the West and imagines somehow that the East is always already there before us where our latest theoretical methodologies allow us to arrive. This tendency of Western argumentation is complicit with certain contemporary arguments in Japan, for example, that Japan has always already been postmodern and feminist, positions that represent too complex

FIGURE 8. A working-class sushi automat in the Asakusa district of Tokyo, a hybrid of tradition and mechanization.

a misrecognition to go into fully here, but which function to support a neoreactionary closure of Japan to Western influence and ideological change.

One symptom of this sliding-over process, the unconscious transference from East to West and vice versa, is the problem of totalitarian politics, which Burch himself acknowledges is unresolved within his text,[27] namely, the militarist dictatorship that contextually surrounded and supported the development of a Japanese national style and that corresponds with disturbing precision to the unresolved issue of Stalinism in Althusser's own texts. This occurs despite Burch's lack of naïveté about his project, which he carefully situates at the outset, not like Barthes in terms of the Imaginary, but by quoting Maurice Merleau-Ponty's assessment of the interest of reexamining non-Western societies:

> The point is not to seek truth or salvation in the pre-scientific or the philosophically preconscious, nor to transfer whole segments of mythology into philosophy; in dealing with these variants of mankind who are so different from us, our aim should be to gain further insight into the theoretical and practical problems which confront our own institutions, to gain new awareness of the plane of existence in which they originated and which the long record of their achievements has made us forget. The "puerility" of the East has something to teach us, if only the narrowness of our adult ideas.[28]

Ironically, a book that otherwise seems to have little in common with Burch (in other words, does not share Burch's postessentialist and rigorous textual analysis), that is, Joan Mellen's *The Waves at Genji's Door,* shares this feature with *To the Distant Observer:* that it seeks in the East a cultural correlative to Western ideological developments, in Mellen's case, feminism. Mellen sees in Japanese film, such as Mizoguchi's *Life of Oharu,* far more powerful treatments of the situation of contemporary women than she finds in commercial films in the West.

In this second, historicist voicing of the material, however, I am thinking of a different kind of critique, namely, that Burch gets his facts wrong. Like Barthes himself, Burch is not a specialist in Japanese studies. Barthes and Burch both visited Japan briefly (according to this critique) and based sweeping interpretations of cultural dynamics largely on the novelty value of first impressions. As a result, Burch is sometimes quite mistaken as he describes films in terms of what he imagines the plot to be. For example, his description of *Souls on the Road* completely misconceives its story.[29] This kind of problem—that of inadequate understanding of Japanese films by Western observers—will continue to be corrected by the new generation of historians, and by the reinvention of Japanese film history through careful serious examination of the original materials by native speakers.

Nonetheless, Orientalist and historicist critiques of Burch's text do not exhaust its arguments. Despite the problems with Burch's work, it remains the only book in English to seriously raise theoretical questions that derive from poststructuralist issues. Again, as with *Empire of Signs,* an active rewriting is necessary that treats *To the Distant Observer* as a text open at all points to further work, as a text that raises many serious questions without mobilizing all the resources necessary to answer fully, thereby generating unresolved intertextual momentum.

If historians can critique Burch, the opposite is also true: Burch's text stands as an implicit open critique to all those historians who would pursue historical artifacts as self-defining objects already positioned within the hierarchical organization of linear time and centralized space dictated by humanist ideology. This hierarchy centers the West as ultimate frame of reference and value in order to organize the material, and it is this hierarchization that so frequently goes in the West by the name "history." Linear organization of the material can function as a logocentric projection of time based on the alphabet's prioritization of diachronic grammar over the synchronic display of visual representation, a division masked by the repression of the polychronic configurations potential in writing. Space becomes centralized insofar as Western Europe and the humanist values of Western civilization are represented as the center to which all history and all other cultures, including Japanese, can be claimed to aspire by predefinition. Nothing of course could be less true, and the rewriting of history toward a more complex and adequate intertextual simulacrum of multiple cultural dynamics will require the contemporary methodological issues and questions raised by Barthes and Burch as well as the ideological and empirical methods of Said, Mellen, and the new historians.

The Politics of Historiography

Herein lies the third voicing of this array of intertextual forces: an ideological critique of the writing of history. Textual/ideological questions are unavoidable because these problems are inherent in the language through which one writes. An already ideologized dialectic is embedded in the terms East/West (implicit in the categories of Orient or Far East), as if these already formed a magical polarity rather than a juxtaposition of different social and cultural constructs. Not only East/West, but other ideological polarities, such as man/wife and representation/object, saturate the English language. In writing, one might continue to use such terms, knowing they're incorrect, to produce a problematic intelligibility without constant neologisms. Similarly, terms such as "Gothic," "Cubist," and "Structural Film" continue to be current in art and film history, despite their known misrepresentations. In such writing, one expects acquaintanceship with the critique of these terms integral to their continued usage, much as one continues in English to say "the sun rises." (The derivation of "Orient" is from the Latin *oriens,* rising, rising sun, east, from *oriri,* to rise.) One knows differently, but the history of a knowledge system is preserved as a trace in the circulation of an established and familiar discursive figure.

Accordingly, doubleness emerges as both a product of, and a strategy to negotiate, cultural difference. It is not enough to simply open a discourse among these different texts, since discursive analysis already too easily implies the dialectical processes of the Western imagination. In placing different critical projects next to one another, such as Third World ideological critiques of the Western Orientalist imaginary, and Western poststructural readings of Asian cultural dynamics, one cannot simply assume a potential new whole made of oppositional components. Necessary schisms remain an integral part of the process of analysis that can never be recuperated into a single, unproblematic and unified whole. The point here is that there is not and cannot ever be a transcendent or idealist solution to the juxtaposition of separate cultural languages, knowledge systems, or representations. Any attempt at ultimate synthesis would be yet another imaginary position. If the West can only conceive of the Orient by speaking or writing through the Other of Western ideology, then it is also true that the West appears to the East in terms of its own Other. Any adequate representation of heterogeneous cultural dynamics will necessarily involve a split writing (to use Derrida's term for the formalization of this practice) among a Western and Eastern doubling of ideology and of Otherness.

Kurosawa's *Ikiru* remains a classic text that demonstrates this operation. As noted earlier, the film is structured around a double system of values: the Japanese critique of Western selfishness and the American critique of Japanese consensus society as authoritarian. Despite earlier discussion of Watanabe in the context of Doi's psychology, a return to the film after Barthes, Burch, and Said makes it possible to reconsider the self as being folded into a social field.

In *Ikiru*, after Watanabe learns he has cancer, he goes through an extended crisis that ultimately results in his taking individual action against the bureaucracy to build a city park. The operative node of this conflict rests between *giri*, or the traditional Japanese concept of obligations, and "rights," a concept that in the West implies individual initiative,

Figure 9. An oil-storage tank as traditional still life. Traces of the proletarian Tendency film in Ozu's *An Inn in Tokyo* (*Tokyo no yado,* 1935) produce an effect like Fernand Léger's cubist industrial landscapes.

action, and accomplishment. Within the framework of *giri,* obligations to larger social groups "naturally" precede those of smaller social units. As a result, obligation to the emperor was paramount because the emperor represented in his body or person the entirety of Japanese society and culture. After the emperor, any position of social authority follows along the same principle, so that feudal lord and corporate *(zaibatsu)* director become interchangeable, and the patriarch within the family is owed duty as the person responsible for that social group.[30] Personal "rights," while not forbidden (as are personal pleasures in the traditional Western ethical mapping of the body), are simply last in priority. In other words, pleasure, including sexual pleasure (presumably restricted by patriarchy to exclusively male control), is forbidden not in itself but only if it conflicts with a higher obligation. The entire feudal system operates through the body; corporations in some sense are similarly linked in English through the cognate of corporate and corporeal. The feudal structure finds its organization through a bodily representative: the physical body of the Father through the phallus is transferred to the physical body of the emperor as phallus of the nation,[31] and sexual pleasure is also determined by the imaginary "possession" of the phallus.

In *Ikiru,* Watanabe personifies a misrecognition of human rights followed by a Nietzschean transvaluation. Individualist human rights can at first only be conceived as a reversal or otherness, an opposition to the established system of priorities. If human rights are now paramount, rather than obligation to the emperor, then personal selfishness must be the rule. As a result, Watanabe begins his search for meaning through Western-inspired institutions of personal indulgence, narrativized as a series of cheap bars, dance halls, and strip joints. After this period of self-indulgence, Watanabe becomes fascinated with the younger generation, which, however, only conceives of autonomy as survival and self-interest in a new world based on the violation of social norms. Watanabe's final stage of development is the transference of the concept of autonomy from its imaginary site in the younger generation to his own cancerous body. The body of tradition, terminally ill and no longer able to sustain power over the cultural domain of representations, is transformed or rewritten into the body or person of individual rights, the person who can make choices and initiate action. As is well known, the second half of the film is then a complex series of flashbacks intercutting between Watanabe's actions and their effects, consequences and decipherment among his personal group of co-workers and immediate family.

The reinvention of self documented in the film is not so much the passive adoption of a Western identity as a new mode of self actively and provisionally fashioned at the intersection of incommensurable norms. The border zone between so-called feudal and humanist contexts opens the possibility of a series of transfigurations, as fluid recombinations of death, self, and agency. The decentered social initiative that Watanabe eventually embodies is never guaranteed; he is haunted everywhere by counterfigures of disease, addiction, hallucination, and suicide. The doubleness of the situation generates multiple possibilities, from reciprocal critique to madness and social agency.

If we maintain this doubleness and extend out from the film, this reading can function as a valuable critique of recent developments in U.S. society. The desire for a body or personal representative of collective social processes has been signified by the election of political figures from FDR to Reagan, who are best known through their media images, and by a resanctification during the 1980s of the corporation as the ideal organization of the economy. The persons of corporate directors (Ross Perot, Lee Iacocca, et al.) are then cast into heroic form by the media (a process inevitably dismissed as a "production device"). Similarly, sexual pleasure has been newly included as an acceptable "right" within the system of consumer society, primarily allocated through the phallocentric domain of male-oriented pornography, from the Internet to major hotel chains, and pornographically influenced fashion and narrative design. The hierarchization of sexual power articulated through most pornography coincides with the so-called renewal of family values in the sense that the latter aspires to reestablish traditional patriarchy through the defeat of the Equal Rights Amendment and other militantly antifeminist measures. All of these developments bypass what function as traditional values in the West: the humanist principles of democratic/rationalist argumentation, individual enterprise (what used to be known by the term "industry" with a lowercase *i*), and romantic sexuality in the sense of individual choice. In short, the United States, it appears, is trying to recast itself in terms of an empire, a process Umberto Eco refers to in *Travels in HyperReality* as neofeudalism. As Eco points out, since we no longer live under feudal conditions, any such attempt to recast contemporary society as a feudal domain exists solely in the domain of the imaginary, in the tacit analog of corporate centralism to a land-based warrior aristocracy (hence the frequent pop fantasy motif of juxtaposed swords and computers). In the West, this imaginary construct has become dominant through its appearance in mass media. In Japan, a similar phenomenon began in the 1960s, as television narratives of feudal samurai began to function as stand-ins for loyal salarymen in a corporate economy. One of the unresolved questions of comparative cultural analysis is why either society should so wish to recast itself.

If "doubleness" is a useful term, then it refers not only to the unavoidability of the process by which each society observes difference by means of its own Other, but also to the simultaneity of a double process. If this is a dialectic, then it is at least a double one, of two societies coexisting in their attempt to conceive of each other. Japan's view of the West through its Other is as valid, as problematic, and as unavoidable as the West's conception of Japan through its own Other. This approach does not reject a dialectical analysis where it indeed operates, frequently within rather than between cultures, and most often and clearly in Western culture, but acknowledges an alternative and simultaneous operation of dislocation across cultural difference. Doubleness here articulates a parallelism of multiples that cannot be resolved into a dialectical opposition of same or other. Several consequences follow. First, of course, this situation demands an increasing sophistication in the utilization of the term "otherness" as a means by which to inscribe difference. (A related example here will be to consider King Vidor's 1952 film *Japanese War Bride* to sketch the limits of this approach.) At the same time, the juxtaposition of a double process of otherness and unconscious ideology demands recognition as such in terms of a split writing. This strategy becomes an essential component of any attempt to formulate difference without resorting to an imaginary unifying discourse.

FIGURE 10. Prewar Miki Masu on a sign for a bar in the Gion district of Kyoto.

In this context, it is sometimes the most familiar things that most reward rereading. For example, it is perhaps the contemporary neofeudal impulses of the West that make Kurosawa's earlier film, *No Regrets for Our Youth,* continuously interesting in a Western context. In this film a humanist resistance to feudal power is the ideological means of telling the story of the 1930s, of pre-Occupation Japan. Rather than seeing the Japanese misrecognition of Western "rights," we see here instead the alienation, significant gestures and limits of Japanese humanism under the unrestricted hegemony of militarist imperialism. The continuing appeal of this film in the West undoubtedly draws on a reading of the female lead character insofar as she suggests the position of women on the left in the United States after the defeat of the ERA under the Reagan administration. Here a split reading and writing intersects through the juxtaposition of Western reading formations with the discursive formations of feudalism and humanism within the film.

Figuring the Border

Because doubleness as an approach foregrounds the necessary distorting process of the Imaginary or Other as a means by which difference can be conceived, what Lacan calls *méconnaissance,* or misrecognition, becomes significant as a symptomatic text of where real difference lies. ("Lies" is precisely the right word here, with its double meaning in English of "falsifies" and "is situated," the condition of articulating difference through misrecognition.) In some senses, what could be dismissed as individual and ephemeral idiosyncrasy is sometimes the site where the most interesting and suggestive articulations of difference can be observed. I am thinking now of those incidents or narratives, frequently anecdotal in form, that are too often dismissed as entertaining interludes in an analysis, but that might better be taken somewhat more seriously. For example, Jack Seward writes of a mysterious sign in Occupation Japan that reads "Dirty Water Punishment Place," which he realized only later was an attempt at a literal translation of the Japanese for "Sewage Treatment Plant." If this anecdote seems amusing, the effect cannot be reduced to a superior attitude toward bad English. Laughter is in part a comic symptom of the incompatibility of languages and the inability to translate directly from one to the other, and the inevitable shift or *différance* that emerges at these boundary sites.

Another, more telling example can be found in John Christopher Morley's *Pictures from the Water Trade*. Morley's is both a trivial and an interesting book, for many of the same reasons as Joan Mellen's novel about Japan, an often-unread parallel to her text on feminism and Japanese film.[32] In both Morley's and Mellen's books, which cannot in any sense be taken seriously as academic research or comparative cultural analysis, we read the same story: that of a Westerner frustrated by a cross-cultural love relationship in Japan. These books are simultaneously naive and oddly touching precisely because they report on a lived-through *méconnaissance,* the attempt to sincerely enact in its fullest and most complete form (that is, in its plenitude) the positioning of cultural difference through its psychoanalytic dimension, through the figuration of the symbolic Other as a sexual other. That cultural difference can somehow be engaged or resolved by a romance is based on unquestioned humanist assumptions about an imaginary universal emotional response. What is especially interesting about each of these texts is not just the failure of these romantic attempts, but the traumatic and disruptive effects of this failure on the protagonist. One is reminded of the psychiatric clinics in Japan designed to treat Westerners who are supposedly suffering neurotic consequences from an attempt to remain in Japan and live as a Japanese.[33] Not only do the romances fail through the unacknowledged confusion of otherness and difference, but the failure functions in such a way as to destabilize the protagonist's attempt to maintain authority and centrality in his or her text. The unconscious of the text is unintentionally evoked, and that unconscious is in a sense represented through madness. The text itself opens into the domain of the symbolic Other, not the sexual otherness of romance reminiscent of the mirror stage. These intimate, even embarrassingly personal texts, should not be dismissed simply as what in fact they also are: idiosyncratic and narrow travelogues, isolated within their own specificity. A symptomatic and deconstructive reading much more strongly highlights the (unavoidable) processes of *méconnaissance* involved with dislocation across cultural contexts, much more viscerally and effectively through the body than its cognitive formulations through academic analysis alone. This situation recalls Derrida's concept of literature, relatively aware of its own tropes, in contrast to logocentric philosophy, which struggles to repress its determining metaphors. It is not literature here, but paratexts, documents surrounding the "serious" work of cultural theory and adjacent to it, that come into question.

Similarly, to pursue a doubleness for the moment, a symptomatic reading of Kurosawa's *Something Like an Autobiography* functions in much the same way: although by no means embarrassing or naive, unlike the cited Western texts, and in some ways self-conscious about its own procedures, Kurosawa's text unavoidably evokes the same kinds of discrepancies between intentional language and the unconscious of the text. In *Something*

Like an Autobiography, we read a text not entirely dissimilar, however unintentionally, to *Roland Barthes by Roland Barthes:* the representation of a single life by someone who does not exactly believe that a single life exists separable from the Other. We are reading an equivocal work of authorship by someone who does not believe in the authority of an author. Interestingly, we can see the same process at work in Jacques Aumont's description of Eisenstein's autobiography in *Montage Eisenstein,*[34] namely, that all of what the Western reader's expectations would anticipate as important details are left out: no information on childhood traumas, interiorized memories, or subjectifying moments that draw us into character depth and recast the role of the individual in history as a dramatic subject in Aristotelian terms. Instead, in Kurosawa (as in Eisenstein and Barthes), we read a sustained contemplation of shifting rhetorical tropes configured in relation to shifting historical circumstances and group process.

Idiosyncrasy is not a value for its own sake, but is foregrounded insofar as it functions as the *punctum,* to use Barthes's term from *Camera Lucida,* within the conflicted picture of cultural heterogeneity: the illuminating or captivating detail where desire comes into play, where psychoanalytic configurations inform the text, and the unconscious of the text emerges. Culture ceases to appear as a one-dimensional system of binary oppositions and approaches instead a libidinal economy, as Lyotard calls it, a project of dislocation informed by doubleness and idiosyncrasy that articulates cultural dynamics in a decentered, multiple, and indeterminate fashion. The result of such a project may risk conflict among the tropes of postcolonial, postmodern, and poststructural analyses, but we should be wary of any moves in cultural theory, especially those projecting themselves as "new," that do not go so far even as this. The risk instead would be a lapse back to empiricist, logocentric, or humanist assumptions already irretrievably problematized by contemporary conditions and critical methodology.

To summarize, any project across cultural contexts must be compound and reversible: no universal system or grand narrative (*grand récit,* to use Lyotard's term)[35] exists that transcends cultural difference, but no cultural specificity thereby escapes critical evaluation. Reading across cultural boundaries is always at least double, and doing so articulates both cultural situations, that of the reader and that of the read, unavoidably and simultaneously. No absolute truth-value can ever inhere in any reading or metareading, but cultural difference can at times be most evident at idiosyncratic junctures that undermine and multiply the imaginary transcendence of unitary approaches.

As a last example, Sogo Ishii's black comedy, *The Crazy Family,* idiosyncratically provokes an articulation of cross-cultural conflict and the figuration of *différance* by parodying the Japanese integration of Western values. Ishii's film reconstructs an Ozu-like family intimacy within a new American-style suburban house (called a "2x4"). This combination of figures generates a Nietzschean explosion of incompatible trajectories. Open warfare breaks out among the three generations, the house is destroyed, and the family relocates to an empty space under a thruway overpass. Such idiosyncratic texts can be more suggestive of positional *différance* within a libidinal economy than a systematic accounting of cultural differences, insofar as a destabilization of meaning thereby enters into the account being given.

3
Incisions

The term *aufschreibesysteme*, as God revealed it to the paranoid cognition of Senate President Schreber, can also designate the network of technologies and institutions that allow a given culture to select, store, and process relevent data.

—Friedrich A. Kittler, *Aufschreibesysteme 1800 / 1900*

Hybrid Writing: Configurative, Categorical, Dynamic

A bouquet appears, perhaps toxic like a cognitive *Fleurs du Mal,* as a cluster of questions: What does it mean to write history? What does it mean to write? What is writing? What is the body of writing that we read? What body is being written, marked, figured by and through writing? How is the body written before it can engage in the act of writing?

What story is being written in history, and what history is written in the production of stories? The French *histoire,* combining the English "story" and "history" in a single word, prefigures the theoretical attempt to read the relation of narrative to history, and the way narrative inhabits even the most rigorously scientific of historical projects. Every film produces a narrative that embodies historical assumptions, and that implies potential historiography. Film narratives exist next to historical narratives, just as Deleuze conceives of cinema next to philosophy, proposing parallel constructions of time but in a different discourse and in a different writing system.

Aufschreibesysteme, a word that Dr. Schreber invents, is cited in the title of Kittler's 1985 text *Aufschreibesysteme 1800/1900.* Kittler's translators render this term into English as "discourse networks," to evoke Foucault's work on the exteriority of discourses produced as artifacts of any given historical moment and Kittler's engagement with linked discourses through the exteriorities of media, technologies, and institutions. A more precise translation of *aufschreibesysteme* would be "system of writing down," or "notation system," with the added inflections of potential madness and/or embodied effects. The production of any knowledge or narrative through a discourse is "a function of instructional practices and technologies," resulting from "a specifically trained coordination of children's eyes, ears, and vocal organs. It is a discipline of the body."[1]

Lacan argues that the learning of "language," a term that in his usage normally includes writing, inhabits the sexual body through which the infant accedes to the Symbolic. Sexual and perceptual organs alike are organized and regulated through the incorporation of language and/as writing, as well as the symbolic productions of movement, hand,

and voice. One such production is the interior voice of Kantian and Romantic metaphysics, which Kittler argues is produced as a male mind or spirit dependent on the body
of the Mother, but this is only one of many possible configurations of the body and subsequent discursive effects. Takeo Doi's psychoanalytic theorization of *amae* may seem
similar as a Japanese principle of longing for dependency, but it is produced very differently. Kittler's usage of *aufschreibesysteme* not only implies the incorporative regulation
of the infantile body, but opens onto comparative identities and effects across contextual
or cultural difference.

After Derrida, the concept of writing has expanded to include all exterior processes
of recording, processing, and retrieving of information, from alphabets and hieroglyphs
to labanotation, phonography, cinema, computer programs, and even speech itself. Derrida's project of *Grammatology,* or the study of *grammae,* recorded marks, intersects with
Kittler's *aufschreibesysteme* to compound consideration of what is at stake in the contemporary study of "writing." The inscription of signifying marks, from petroglyphs to
tattoos, operate as the framework through which the human body is configured to inhabit
different symbolic productions of the world. The study of writing systems as a network
of technologies and institutions locates the material conditions through which discourses
are produced, thought takes place, and agency has effects.

History is always double, divided between a personal history of infancy and a social history of adult institutions, as Giorgio Agamben suggests in *Infancy and History*. Infancy
marks the singular moment of accession to the Symbolic, by which each person enters into
social history at a different point. The intergenerational transmission of knowledge that
characterizes the human situation means that social history always intersects with infancy
and is continually reconfigured through it. Agamben's use of the term "infancy" addresses
the same configurative forces that Freud addresses in psychoanalysis, but avoids the
assumption that a Western individualized and interior psychology is universal. "Infancy"
allows us to historicize the idea of the unconscious, as de Certeau has also done in *The Writing of History,* and to leave open the question of how psychoanalysis relates to such other
societies as Japan, where the cogito was not a historical foundation of the modern self.

To work through the materiality of writing and the body, we need to consider the
intersecting discourses of writing, psychoanalysis, and cultural difference. These intersections never add up to a synthesis, but instead generate the figure of a network. Networked
discourses operate semi-autonomously, yet in combination produce unanticipated effects
not predictable from any single context.

Graphic Writing

Much of the debate about Chinese writing is generated by conflicting definitions of writing, as effects of metaphysical or ideological assumptions. Derrida shifted the foundations
of the debate in *Of Grammatology* when he argued for a necessary and extensive redefi-
nition of "writing" to include all recording systems that store, process, and retrieve information. As a consequence, new media from cinema and computers to phonography and
radio can be reconsidered as writing systems, consistent with the semiotic break that

reconsiders media production as specifically coded rather than only shapeless analog copying. Cinematic imagery has since been theorized as simultaneously active in indexical, iconic, and symbolic registers, parallel to the relegitimation of allegory by Angus Fletcher and of postmodern appropriation of pastiche. Deleuze continues the relocation of the graphic image in *Cinema 1* and *2* as a cultural reconfiguration of knowledge. He places cinema "next to" philosophy and thereby implies that both are capable of propositional logic as well as figural assumptions, but in different media contexts.[2] Film and media theory now routinely address a broad range of textual effects in different media, from foundational assumptions of narrative discourse and production of viewer position to libidinal investments and political hierarchization.

Linguistics, however, functions as a discipline from the traditional definition of writing as the graphic transcription of speech. Derrida asks that linguistics reconceive itself both to theorize speech as a kind of writing and to recognize the privileging of speech and subordination of writing as logocentric effects. The most difficult task he proposes is to see the alphabet as a graphic machine that produces logocentric disciplines from philosophy to linguistics. Most linguists, however, find it difficult or impossible to imagine the extent of foundational inversion that Derrida's work implies. Linguistic study has for so long been based on the centrality of verbal communication that its displacement can seem absurd, even as visual media saturate society.

The difficulty of moving from one set of assumptions to the other should not be underestimated. Roland Barthes spent much of his career convinced that the camera image was a purely analog phenomenon that remained outside analysis, and only at the end of his life did he begin to engage with the visual image as text. In retrospect, the assumption of camera imagery as analog now seems linked to some of the twentieth century's most powerful myths, from nationalist and ideological propaganda to advertising and commodity fetishism. The unconscious habit of equating camera imagery with the Real, and seeing digital image processing as a lie or threat, functions as a modern form of magical thinking. Images are assumed to be things, and constructed representations are imagined as guarantees of truth.

Film and media scholars argue that the effective response to this condition is to reread media representations as multiply coded texts, rather than lament their predominance as a decline. Dominant media, however, continue to reinforce logocentric assumptions that verbal language is central to social communication, that it can be located inside the visual image of a human body, and that visual information in excess of these assumptions can be understood as background. Corporate television so insistently mass-produces these assumptions through its program conventions that it can become difficult for most people to imagine any alternative. The modern era is structured as an oscillation between disciplines that encounter textual effects at the limits of knowledge and a public media sphere governed through classical metaphysical assumptions. These conditions complicate the interdisciplinary work necessary in media and cultural studies, since individual disciplines often encounter others by way of their mass-media stereotypes and hegemonic context.

The problem here is not simply a matter of theoretical work but of overcoming the aversion of iconophobia. Iconophobia recurs throughout Mediterranean civilization, from

Protestant northern Europe and the Jewish diaspora to the Islamic Middle East, from Byzantine iconoclasm to the modern censorship of new media, as a reaction against the fixed iconography of Catholic and Orthodox traditions and the supposed moral decay of the abject body. Foucault addressed the genealogy of the specifically Western abjection of the body in his work on the history of sexuality, tracing its genealogy to late Roman discourses.

Such concerns contribute to the idea that the study of the Chinese written character is heavily invested with ideological modes of language and abjection, in conflict with grammatological reconsideration. This debate in miniature suggests the incommensurability of discourses and contestation of cultural assumptions around the world. Abjection and violence flare when the incommensurable representations of another discourse seem to interfere with the ability to think, act, and exist in one's own. A politics of the text, or *pouvoir/écrire,* is at stake in the acts of "reading" and "writing." Grammatology acts not to hierarchize some modes of writing over others, but to recognize the graphic materiality and figural foundations of discourse as their limits and boundaries, in order to negotiate *différance* and the heterological intersection of multiple contexts.

The Eisenstein/Pound Thesis

A common misperception in the West is that Chinese characters are pictographic, parallel to myths of Egyptian hieroglyphs before Jean-François Champollion's decipherment. Many of the problems surrounding this misconception in the context of cinema and literature hinge on the extensively debated work of Sergei Eisenstein and Ezra Pound.

Eisenstein recognizes that only 10 percent of Chinese characters visually resemble their meaning but shifts to comparison of combinatory characters and montage. Nonetheless, his cinematic comparison leaves camera shots in a position analogous to characters, undermining his attempt to differentiate characters from pictographs.

Pound similarly concentrates on combinatory characters, in the context of poetic images rather than camera shots, and compares such combinations to poetic figuration grounded in concrete referents. As with Eisenstein, the assumption of transcendental signifieds undermines his work on combinatory figures.

John DeFrancis, in *The Chinese Language: Fact and Fantasy,* reviews more recent theories of Chinese writing that make Eisenstein and Pound untenable to modern linguists. Although there is common agreement that the earliest characters were pictographic, later characters became more stylized and less easily recognizable as resembling their signifieds. Some linguists argue that characters today are no more likely to be recognized as visual images than the letter A is likely to be seen in the West as its originary pictograph of an ox head. Characters can be divided into three groups: those that continue to maintain a visual resemblance make up about 10 percent, while those that are primarily phonological are another 10 percent. All other characters, contrary to what Eisenstein and Pound seemed to imagine, combine a semantic element, or "radical," with a phonetic element that indicates how the combinatory character is to be pronounced.

Despite this general agreement, there are nonetheless competing theories without consensus about several basic issues, and perhaps even a resistance within linguistics itself to the study of writing. DeFrancis exemplifies the phonological position, and continues to advocate the marginalization of characters through the increasing use of Pinyin as an alphabetic system. Others, strongly attacked by DeFrancis, continue to use or propose such terms as "ideograph" or "logograph" to describe the character as linking a single graphic mark with a monosyllabic meaning. Curiously, this debate seems entirely circumscribed by Western metaphysics, devolving to equally ideological assumptions of phonological logocentrism or transcendental signified. What seems most difficult is to engage the operation of the Chinese character as simultaneously based in a graphic figure and a phonic sound. Each character thereby operates as part of a visual-phonic double network, resembling other characters with the same radical while linking homophonically with other characters that have the same pronunciation.

The irony of the Western attempt to separate visual and sound elements of Chinese writing can perhaps be suggested by the groundbreaking work of Bernhard Karlgren, whom DeFrancis celebrates as foundational for his phonocentric argument. Karlgren first demonstrated that it was possible to reconstruct the pronunciation of medieval Chinese by a close textual analysis of Xu Shen's *Shuo-wen chieh-tzu,* completed in 121 CE but revised and edited during the T'ang and Sung dynasties. The irony is that the *Shuo-wen chieh-tzu* is the first systematic and comprehensive Chinese dictionary, and it introduced the convention of grouping characters by their radicals, a nonalphabetic system of organization followed ever since in Chinese and Japanese dictionaries.[3] Traditional Chinese scholarship always conceived of characters in visual terms, as demonstrated by the radical system, despite DeFrancis's appropriation of Karlgren's *Shuo-wen chieh-tzu* for phonological argument.

In Japan, the writing system becomes even more complex, layered, and networked. Each *kanji,* as the Chinese character is called in Japanese, is given both an *On* and a *Kun* pronunciation, combining the ancient pronunciation of Chinese at the time when kanji were introduced into Japan with a Japanese word of equivalent meaning. Words and compounds derived from the *On,* or Chinese, readings, now circulate through the Japanese language together with words of Japanese derivation, like the use of Latinate and Greek words with Anglo-Saxon in English. Since Chinese grammar differs from Japanese, a specific practice developed of writing classical Chinese with annotation allowing rearrangement of word order according to Japanese grammar. Accordingly, Classical Chinese scholarship is called *Kanbungaku* in Japan, named for the study of texts written in *kanbun,* or annotated Chinese. Further, Japanese contains words for which there are no equivalents in Chinese, so two syllabic scripts were invented to intersperse with kanji in order to add the missing words. These scripts are called *kana* and mark particles, affixes, and other non-Chinese words in the text. Kana are of two types: *hiragana* for words considered to be of Japanese origin even if imported long ago (like "tobacco"), and *katakana* for loan-words still seen as foreign in derivation (like "konpyutaa"). Japanese writing practices today combine the *on* and *kun* readings of kanji with two types of kana, mingled with arabic numbers and some *romaji,* or roman letters, to produce the most heterogeneous writing system in the world.

FIGURE 11. Kanji and *romaji* inhabit the same sign at a train station in Tokyo.

Figural Writing

Chinese writing also means what has been written in characters.

Eisenstein and Pound both blur the distinction between legendary origins and poetic figures, on the one hand, and structural elements of writing, on the other. As artists and critics, they are not so much vague as intuitive, combining incommensurable discourses for figural effects. After their dismissal by linguists, Eisenstein and Pound were then reconsidered by Derrida as proto-grammatologists, initiating a necessarily unfinished move toward an unthought theory of the text.

Derrida argues that the arts produce a grammatological research into the determining tropes of writing, and throughout his work he alternates between studies of literature and of philosophy, sometimes directly juxtaposed as in *Glas*. What is conventionally called "literature" foregrounds the determining tropes that remain repressed in philosophy, and poetic figures inhabit discourse as preconditions and limits of thought.

Part of the problem is that modernization of Chinese and Japanese writing systems depend on a repudiation of traditional and classical models of the text that nonetheless remain determinative from within, just as they do in the West. After 1945, both China and Japan simplified the appearance of characters and reduced the number of characters in use, in order to promote universal literacy. In Japan, the approximate reduction was from 17,000 to 1,850 kanji. Even before this, Japan had shifted toward a vernacular usage of characters more closely matched with everyday pronunciation, and hence phonological in effect. Maejima Hisoka first proposed the abolition of Chinese characters in 1866, initiating what came to be called the *genbun itchi* movement to unify spoken *(gen)* and written *(bun)* languages. He was promoting mass education, and had been convinced by an American missionary he met at the shogun's school for Western learning in Nagasaki that kanji were abstruse and confusing. In 1884, the Kana Society *(Kana no Kai)* was established to promote writing in the Japanese syllabary, and in 1886 the Romaji Society *(Romaji no Kai)* was established to encourage use of the Roman alphabet.[4] Although Chinese characters were eventually reduced and simplified rather than replaced, the effect of these efforts was to indirectly shift kanji toward vernacular and phonocentric usage, as later popularized through the new field of "Japanese literature." In an unrelated but parallel development, a new writing style called *kogo* gradually emerged after 1868 to replace the classical writing style or *bungo*. *Kogo* was adopted in primary-school textbooks in 1903 and became the dominant prose style, paralleling the emergence of naturalism.

As a combined result of these different events, the classical tradition of Chinese scholarship was marginalized in both China and Japan, parallel to the decline of classical Latin and Greek in Western education. *Kanbungaku,* however, returns us to the determining figures of Japanese culture, from T'ang poetics to Tokugawa discourses, that continue within the phonocentric modern. Derrida, in *La Carte Postale,* argues that Plato inhabits Freud, whether acknowledged or not, and parallel textual effects inhabit Asian representational practices. H. D. Harootunian's *Toward Restoration: The Growth of Political Consciousness in Tokugawa Japan* and H. Richard Okada's *Figures of Resistance: Language, Poetry, and Narrating in "The Tale of Genji" and Other Mid-Heian Texts* are two recent examples of rereading historical texts for both historical insight and effects on the modern. The purpose is not nostalgia, but a displacement of texts as resources for theoretical work.

François Cheng's *Chinese Poetic Writing, With an Anthology of T'ang Poetry* is one such book that helps reconsider the operation of the Chinese written character. Cheng, writing in 1977, produces a complex and detailed approach to Chinese writing practices that complicates both pictographic and phonological assumptions. A discourse of Jacobsonian semiotics enables him to depart from the translation convention of figural transparency and instead concentrate on effects specific to the materiality of the Chinese text.

Perhaps no one, however, has contributed more to this rethinking of Chinese writing than Thomas Lamarre, in his *Uncovering the Heian: An Archeology of Sensation and Inscription* (2000). Lamarre necessarily engages a double project. On the one hand, he has extended Deleuzian concepts to complicate modern understanding of early Japanese writing. He argues that translations of Heian literature into modern Japanese conform to ideological norms of phonocentrism and repress complex visual effects simultaneously active in the Heian texts. On the other hand, he also traces the reciprocal relationship in the nineteenth century of phonocentric reforms with nationalism, so that an ethnolinguistic unity becomes both imaginable and foundational for formation of the modern state. One implication of his work is that the privileging of spoken language is bound up with nationalist ideologies of romantic identification, ethnic homogeneity, and discursive closure. Cinema as a visual medium does not simply escape these hegemonic operations, since the ideological reduction of camera images to classical transparency reproduces the same effects. However, the radical potential of writing systems from kanji to cinema, by way of the visual materiality of the text, opens onto the world of heterogeneity and *différance*.

Kanji Intertext

What is the relationship of the Chinese written character to the production of cinematic imagery by nonalphabetic cultures such as Japan? This question, perhaps unanswerable, remains fascinating because of the series of imaginary propositions by Eisenstein, Pound, and others concerning the Chinese written character.[5] These propositions, once they are known to be based on false premises, can be reread to illuminate Western metaphysical assumptions at work during the historical juncture when cinema emerged as a dominant medium of representation. These representational assumptions, in turn, can clarify the impact of cinema on non-Western cultures and lead us back to questions of intertextual and grammatological relationships among such different graphic codes or modes of writing as characters, syllabic script, the alphabet, painting, printmaking, and cinema.

The Myth of a Natural Language

On this basis, let us return to the Eisenstein/Pound thesis and the erroneous view that Japanese writing is imagistic, and that combinations of characters form strings of readily identifiable images. In this reading, one imagines characters as if cinematic montage or a natural poetry were formed directly from everyday experience. Linguists have long since argued that the Chinese character, or kanji in Japanese, is no more imagistic than the Roman alphabet to its contemporary users, and that written characters have become just as abstract and nonrepresentational. Nonetheless, Eisenstein appears to have had no doubts about the concrete and immediate representational quality of kanji when he wrote his essay "The Cinematographic Principle and the Ideogram." He begins by arguing a privileged historical origin for naturalistic imagery:

> [T]he principle of montage can be identified as the basic element of Japanese representational culture.
>
> Writing—for their writing is primarily representational.
> The hieroglyph.
>
> The naturalistic image of an object, as portrayed by the skillful Chinese hand of Ts'ang Chieh 2650 years before our era, becomes slightly formalized and, with its 539 fellows, forms the first "contingent" of hieroglyphs. Scratched out with a stylus on a slip of bamboo, the portrait of an object maintained a resemblance to its original in every respect.[6]

Eisenstein then derives a "second category" of abstract combinations based on primary pictographic "objects":

> The real interest begins with the second category of hieroglyphs—the *huei-i,* i.e., "copulative."
>
> The point is that the copulation (perhaps we had better say, the combination) of two hieroglyphs of the simplest series is to be regarded not as their sum, but as their product, i.e., as a value of another dimension, another degree; each, separately, corresponds to an *object,* to a fact, but their combination corresponds to a *concept.* From separate hieroglyphs has been fused—the ideogram. By the combination of two "depictables" is achieved the representation of something that is graphically undepictable.
>
> For example: the picture for water and the picture of an eye signifies "to weep"; the picture of an ear near the drawing of a door = "to listen."

He then acknowledges the comparison to cinematic montage that has motivated his study of kanji, but inverts the sequence of argument, presenting cinema as if it derived from a naturalistic writing that preceded it:

> But this is—montage!
>
> Yes. It is exactly what we do in the cinema, combining shots that are *depictive,* single in meaning, neutral in content—into *intellectual* contexts and series.

Reading the same argument in reverse order, we can restore the sequence of a speculative quest for origins: beginning with montage, Eisenstein seeks its equivalents in different historical contexts. By so doing, it becomes clear that part of what is missing from this argument is the difference between photographic imagery and the abstract and symbolic figuration of kanji.

Pound makes virtually the same argument as Eisenstein about the Chinese character, but with no overt reference to cinema. Pound's assumptions about kanji are integral to all of his work, but his most noted text on the subject is his 1918 editing of *The Chinese Written Character as a Medium for Poetry,* a study of Japanese aesthetics written by Ernest Fenollosa before the latter's death in 1908. The Pound/Fenollosa text argues a "natural connection" between signified and signifier in Chinese writing:

> Chinese notation is much more than arbitrary symbols. It is based upon a vivid shorthand picture of the operations of nature. In the algebraic figure and in the spoken word there is no natural connection between thing and sign: all depends upon sheer convention. But the Chinese method follows natural suggestion. . . . The thought-picture is not only called up by these signs as well as by words, but far more vividly and concretely.[7]

Despite the absence of a direct reference to cinema in Pound's work, the Pound/Fenollosa text goes on to connect kanji with movement:

> It might be thought that a picture is naturally the picture of a *thing,* and that therefore the root ideas of Chinese are what grammar calls nouns. But examination shows that a large number of the primitive Chinese characters, even the so-called radicals, are shorthand pictures of actions or processes. . . .
>
> A true noun, an isolated thing, does not exist in nature. Things are only the terminal points, or rather the meeting points, of actions, cross-sections cut through actions, snapshots. Neither can a pure verb, an abstract motion, be possible in nature. The eye sees noun and verb as one: things in motion, motion in things, and so the Chinese conception tends to represent them.

Pound and Fenollosa imply a comparison to cinema by comparing verbal nouns or moving things with snapshots. At the same time, this linguistic connection of representation and motion recalls Benjamin Lee Whorf's assertion, formulated as early as 1936, that the "Hopi actually have a language better equipped to deal with . . . vibratile phenomena than is our latest scientific terminology."[8] The common intertextual element operating in all these arguments is the Western interest in non-Western modes of representation as models for theorizing Western technological and theoretical developments during the modern era, ranging from cinema to relativity. The taxonomic dimensions of this period's attempt to connect representation and motion has been explored by Gilles Deleuze in *Cinema 1: The Movement-Image,* a text that through its reconsideration of Henri Bergson suggests the psychological and philosophic implications at stake.

Yet Eisenstein and Pound stop short of the more radical thesis of Whorf and Edward Sapir that there is "a relation of habitual thought and behavior to language," a thesis that rejects any fixed and universal signifieds from which to derive representation.[9] Eisenstein and Pound's underlying assumption instead seems to be that a material world conceived in terms of motion is best represented by imagery "naturally" connected with a referent conceived as preexisting. By so doing, they perpetuate a myth of the natural sign, a central premise of all logocentric discourse, and one that cuts across otherwise vast ideological differences between the two artists. Before Charles Sanders Peirce's distinction of symbolic, iconic, and indexical signs helped clarify the problem,[10] Eisenstein and Pound collapsed all three types of signification into a single concept of the Chinese character as identical with photographic representation.

If we characterize this period as one constituting an epistemological break between the premodernist and modernist eras, we may reread work that marks and produces such a juncture as plural, in that such work unavoidably combines elements of both periods. Eisenstein and Pound make imaginary use of kanji to deconstruct the idealist categories of Western metaphysics, yet they remain complicit with Western metaphysical assumptions by appealing to the myth of the natural sign. In *The ABC of Reading,* Pound argues an implicit empiricism by equating "the ideogrammic method" with "the method of science." In *Guide to Kulchur,* he restates the same premise by arguing that the first principle of Kung (or Confucius) was "to call people and things by their names, that is by the correct denominations, to see that the terminology was exact."[11] The natural sign prescribes a hierarchy of values that positions signification as secondary to a primary presence of the thing represented, a hierarchy implicit in the term "re-presentation." Derrida, throughout his work, deconstructs this notion as a characteristic feature of the logocentric discourse associated with alphabetic (sound-based) writing. He discusses hieroglyphs as a nonalphabetic mode of inscription and questions the Western impulse to construct a myth of cultural origins by imagining alternative systems of writing as closer to a presence of meaning.[12] Such a myth, Derrida argues, inevitably represses the process of writing and embeds Western ideological assumptions in a metaphysics of preexisting objects fully present to a logocentric construction of meaning. Cinematographic representation, once assumed to be natural, carries with it the hierarchical values of Western discourse that form the basis of all Orientalism. Orientalism, to use Said's term, here signifies the appropriation of non-Western societies into Western discourses through the imaginary positioning of the other as childlike and/or primitive, congruent with the positions of master and slave that have evolved through phases of military, economic, and cultural imperialism.

Today, it can be useful to read Eisenstein and Pound against the grain, together with a generation of early filmmakers from Viking Eggeling to Charlie Chaplin, who believed in cinema as a universal language. Today, they appear as makers of a myth of cinema that characterizes not written characters but the Western imaginary. A reconsideration of the Eisenstein/Pound equation of kanji and cinematographic object might help illuminate these ideological assumptions, present not only in the films and theoretical writing of this period but in the cinematic apparatus itself as perceived by non-Western societies.

Too often, the relationship between writing and film has been studied as an issue of adaptation alone, or, at best, of translation, without ever questioning the parallel construction of meaning within the apparatus of the alphabet and that of the cinema. In turn, studies of film, even in an international and cross-cultural context, too often assume that the *dispositif* of cinematic representation exists independently of the cultural and historical values embedded in the cinematic apparatus.

The camera image, rather than being recognized and studied as a specifically Western mass production of perspectival space and individualist point of view, is too often treated as if its mechanical and indexical mode of signification guarantees a presence of meaning that transcends cultural barriers. The isolation and interiorization of subjectivity that develops with the transcription of sound through the alphabet finds its complement in the projection of perspectival illusionism into representational space. The unified hierarchization of space posits a visually distanced object as the reciprocal of the individualized subject's point of view. The social and psychological practice of this panoptical cone of vision, as delineated by Foucault and Lacan, embeds a categorical and hierarchical opposition of subject and object into both language and perception.[13] These Western ideological practices conflict with the relational and process-oriented practices associated with kanji, yet they persist both in the formulation of kanji as equivalent to camera imagery and in the introduction of cinema to non-Western societies as a natural and universal language.

Suggestive Practices

The search for a universal language so prevalent among early filmmakers and theorists originated in the eighteenth century. Jacques Derrida has traced a history of grammatology to this period, a history most easily summarized here by reference to Gregory Ulmer's discussion of Derrida's work in *Applied Grammatology*. Ulmer argues that the eighteenth century was marked by "a theological prejudice—the myth of an original, primitive language given to man by God" together with a "'hallucinatory' misunderstanding of hieroglyphics," by which "the hieroglyph was excessively admired as a form of sublime, mystical writing."[14] As summarized and quoted by Ulmer,

> Derrida credits the work of Frerèt and Warburton (one working with Chinese and the other with Egyptian writing) with creating an "epistemological break" that overcame these obstacles, thus "liberating a theoretical field in which the scientific techniques of deciphering were perfected by the Abbé Barthélemy and then by Champollion. Then a systematic reflection upon the correspondence between writing and speech could be born. The greatest difficulty was already to conceive, in a manner at once historical and systematic, the organized cohabitation, within the same graphic code, of figurative, symbolic, abstract, and phonetic elements."[15]

In one sense, Eisenstein and Pound reverse the "epistemological break" instituted by Nicolas Frerèt and William Warburton to imagine kanji as naturally connected with the

thing represented. Yet Derrida also credits the work of Pound and Fenollosa as show-
ing "the limits of the logico-grammatical structure of the Western model, offering instead
a writing that balanced the ideographic with the phonetic elements of writing,"[16] thus
constituting the next historic step after Frerèt and Warburton in the development of
grammatology as a field. Ulmer, in turn, concludes his own work on contemporary grammatology by extending Marie-Claire Ropars-Wuilleumer's discussion of Eisenstein in
Le texte divisé as a basis for theorizing the textuality of cinema. The paradox of Eisenstein and Pound's work on kanji is that a move backward theoretically is combined with
a move ahead in cinematic and graphological practice.

If an imaginary reading of kanji produced cinematic and graphological innovation
as a basis for the development of grammatology in the West, then what was the effect of
introducing cinema to a nonalphabetic society such as Japan? In this context, another
noteworthy component of Eisenstein's cinematic argument on the ideogram is the complete repression of Japanese cinema. Since Eisenstein introduces his essay by arguing that
"cinematography is, first and foremost, montage," he then is able to dismiss all of Japanese film as the work of "a country that has no *cinematography*. . . . The Japanese cinema
is excellently equipped with corporations, actors, and stories. But the Japanese cinema is
completely unaware of montage."[17]

On this basis, Eisenstein argues that Japan is genuinely "cinematic" only in its traditional, non-Western culture. He thereby extends to film the influence of Japanese tradition on Western modernism, well documented elsewhere as *Japonisme* in such studies as
Ives's *The Great Wave: The Influence of Japanese Woodcuts on French Prints*. Yet by 1929,
the year Eisenstein wrote "The Cinematographic Principle and the Ideogram," the Japanese had already produced a decade of important work in film. For example, Osanai
and Murata's *Souls on the Road* (*Rojo no Reikon*, 1921), Kinugasa's *A Page of Madness*
(*Kurutta Ippeiji*, 1926) and *Crossways* (*Jujiro*, 1928), and forty-four films by Mizoguchi
(now lost) had all appeared by this time. Especially ironic in this regard is Kinugasa's
European tour of 1929 with *Crossways*, a tour that in retrospect seems a landmark of
missed cross-cultural opportunities between Japan and the West. If, as Noël Burch suggests, Kinugasa chose *Crossways* rather than *A Page of Madness* to show to the West because
he may have believed it to be more Western in style,[18] then he could only have fulfilled
Eisenstein's doubts. If Eisenstein could have seen *A Page of Madness,* he could not have
doubted that montage was a powerful part of cinematic form in Japan, yet Kinugasa's
choice of *Crossways* suggests that Japanese filmmakers saw the West in terms of its own
premodernist traditions as much as Eisenstein privileged tradition in Japan. Both Kinugasa and Eisenstein chose to mirror an alien culture's traditions back to itself in hopes of
gaining an acceptance that was denied precisely because modernist issues were avoided.

As it was, Eisenstein's dismissal of Japanese film remained part of a larger underesti-
mation and misunderstanding of Japanese modernism throughout the West that continues today. Western appreciation of Japanese *jidai-geki,* or period films such as Kurosawa's
Roshomon (1950), long preceded acceptance of *gendai-geki,* or films about contemporary
life such as *Ikiru* (1952), even though both styles of film were consistently produced in
Japan. Similarly, traditional Japanese woodcuts have been collected in the West since the

time of the Impressionists, but the avant-garde work being produced in Japan while the West collected woodcuts was ignored by the West until the retrospective exhibitions of 1910–70 at the Musée national d'art moderne in Paris in 1986, and of 1890–1930 at the Japan Society in New York the following year.[19]

Western inability to comprehend the significance of Japanese modernism seems rooted in the same hierarchical values that generate Orientalism. Western modernism super-imposed a unidirectional cultural evolutionism on the cross-cultural process of history, with the end point of the evolutionist model being the contemporary West. This dominant teleology has apparently blinded the West to the possibility that traditional Occidental values might play the same ambiguous and partially deconstructive role in Japanese cul-ture as Japanese tradition did for Eisenstein and Pound. Only with the postmodernist appreciation of multiple directionality, cultural difference, and grammatological practice has it become possible to consider the Japanese route through modernism to the present historical moment.

Grammatological Questions

By this circuitous route, is it now possible to conceive of a plausible interrogation of kanji and cinema that does not lapse into magical attributions at some point? If we con-tinue to assume that the relation between the written character and cinema is significant, then that relation must be reconceived as indirect in its operation, and not direct and unproblematic as in the Eisenstein/Pound formulation. The quest for concrete imagery and a transparent identification of signifier and referent in written characters can now be set aside as an illusion. Instead, one might more productively consider multidirec-tionality and multiple figuration in the inscription of kanji, and its parallel to the so-called traditionalist organization of actors and space in the films of Mikio Naruse and Yasujiro Ozu. While kanji do not lack sequentiality, they are far more spatially complex and multidirectional than alphabetic graphemes, both internally (a single character may incorporate as many as seventeen different brush strokes) and in the reversibility of read-ing required for intelligibility. In contrast, the alphabet minimizes spatial articulation by a radical reduction in the number of graphic units and develops complexity through sequence.

It can be tempting to look at classical Japanese film texts in these spatialized terms. Ozu's films, for example, lack the psychological interiority and climactic action of West-ern drama from Aristotle to Ridley Scott's *Black Hawk Down* (2001). Ozu's *Early Summer* (*Bakushu,* 1950), for example, like many Japanese novels, instead foregrounds relation-ships among characters and slight shifts in attitude that suggest significant consequences left unrepresented in the film itself. Derrida posits interiorized subjectivity and central-ized action as derived from logocentrism, which is in turn a cultural effect of alphabetic writing. Conversely, one might relate Ozu's relational subjectivity and decentered action to the relatively spatialized structure of Chinese writing and the mental processes or metaphysical assumptions this mode of writing might produce.

This approach easily generates a conceptual model for analyzing the relationship between certain novels and films in Japan. Ichikawa's *Odd Obsession* (*Kagi,* 1959), for example, is a film version of Tanizaki's novel *The Key* (*Kagi,* 1956). The film ends with an action-centered climax not unlike *Hamlet,* with virtually every character on screen dead. In Tanazaki's novel, no such action occurs, but only a slight shift of attitude by a central character that suggests that calculated murder might be a possibility. Similarly, in Naruse's 1954 film version of Kawabata's *The Sound of the Mountain* (*Yama no Oto,* 1949), the father and daughter-in-law leave the house for a dramatic separation scene in

FIGURE 12. A Kenwood portable audio advertisement with a catalog of beetles.

a public garden, while in the novel these characters remain in the house and their future separation is suggested through a shift in emotional positions among them. Can we account for these changes by the separate cultural traditions associated with Japanese literature and the imported Western medium of film, and hence by a metaphysics derived from ideographic inscription as opposed to logocentrism as a model for cinematic action?

To some extent, this reading seems valid. Yet in Tanazaki's *The Key,* the shift of attitude that suggests the possibility of murder occurs in a private diary, a form of private written confession linked not only with the diary tradition of Japanese literature but also with the I-novel, or *watakushi-shosetsu,* a Japanese novelistic form modeled after the centralized authority of the subject in Western literature. In other words, the influences and counterinfluences of Japanese tradition and Western logocentrism occur within both novels and films and cannot be reductively identified on a one-to-one basis.

One can recognize a limited homology between the internal organization of ideographic and alphabetic writing and the dominant modes of social and spatiotemporal organization of the cultures that practiced them. The spatialized construction of kanji seems congruent with the relational and synchronic aspects of traditional Japanese culture as invoked by Barthes's *Empire of Signs,* as the Chinese character is with the spatialized symbolization of traditional China theorized by Marcel Mauss. The sequential alphabet, in turn, parallels the dominant progressive or diachronic organization of history according to Western metaphysics. A conception of history as sequential and progressive emerged in the West from the sixteenth to the nineteenth centuries, contemporaneously with the expansion of printed alphabetic text as the dominant mass medium of communication. A possible thesis relating modes of thought to modes of writing depends here on the conception of historical periods as the equivalent of social laboratories, an analysis made plausible only by moments of cultural closure that isolate the effects of one writing system from another. It is more difficult, however, to theorize the precise regulatory interplay of a system of writing with its cultural context to derive specific effects. Neither writing system has ever existed in a pure isolated state but always functions in relation to other forces. Only by deconstructing an ideology of direct unitary causation and all idealized binarisms that categorically oppose one system to another can one perhaps begin to theorize a circulation of signifying practices in relation to modes of writing.

Chinese characters are not internally sequential as the alphabet in their operation, but neither can they be idealized as a purely synchronic function. Unlike the petroglyphs found in Michigan's Upper Peninsula or in central California, where geometric pictographs appear in spatialized groups, the spatial complexities of Chinese characters are linked in sequences to construct sentences. The temporality of ideographic textual dynamics are, then, more complex than a binary opposition to the alphabet might imply. An analysis of time and motion within ideographic reading might better be developed analogous to Lyotard's analysis of time and color within the abstract paintings of Albert Ayme.

Further, in contrast to the Chinese use of characters exclusively, multiple modes of writing have coexisted in Japan for centuries among kanji (the Chinese characters) and kana, two different syllabic scripts. The two kana are hiragana and katakana. Hiragana is a syllabic system designed to clarify the mismatched relationship between the polysyllabic

Japanese language and "monosyllabic" Chinese characters. Katakana is a second syllabic system, identical in grouped phonetic units to hiragana but used exclusively for foreign words. This traditional complexity has apparently facilitated the contemporary inclusion of *romaji* (the Roman alphabet) as a parallel but noncentral system within a plural interplay of writings. If the goal of applied grammatology is, as Ulmer argues, the development of multiple writing practices that combine features of both hieroglyphic and alphabetic systems, then the Japanese have inadvertently arrived at such a communications environment through cross-cultural conflict and exchange.

This sustained multiplicity of writings parallels the simultaneous continuation of both traditionalist and Western figuration in the arts, visible in the Japanese route toward modernism earlier in the century, and it may illuminate the theme of juxtaposed modernism and tradition that pervades Japanese cinema throughout its history. A corresponding juxtaposition in the West of the classical fine arts tradition and modernism during the first half of the twentieth century might be related to the simultaneous currency of printed alphabetic text and the "new hieroglyphics" that Vachel Lindsay saw in film. The disjunctive modes of alphabetic and cinematic writing could be considered as generating a double tradition of representation in the West, even while cinema derives from logocentric metaphysics in its construction and provides the most direct influence of logocentric values on non-Western cultures.

Any theory of the cinema in its relation to kanji would today need to be grammatologically based in this plurality of writings and figuration. As a result, directly predictable effects now seem impossible, having been displaced by a play of differing modes of inscription within the same textual space, where tensions and intensities can perhaps in part be interpreted in relation to historical circumstances that isolated the effects of one system or another, a condition no longer present.

Cross-Writing

Christian Metz has addressed several issues related to cinema and writing in the context of his *Language and Cinema*. He argues first that if a parallel between written language and cinema is based on both being recording techniques, then different sensory orders and different kinds of recording are involved. The alphabet's recording is restrictive, in that it transcribes only the phonemic elements of sound identifiable as elements of language. That transcription is never exact, since written forms of language diverge from actual pronunciation and alternative dialects. Alphabetic writing is also modified by punctuation, a nonphonemic script that partially represents rhythm and intonation. Nonetheless, the alphabet's restrictive recording differs from cinema's indexical and metonymic processes that visually transcribe reflected light unrestricted by any preestablished units of coded signification.

Yet Metz's usually precise description lapses into mystification when he comes to ideographic writing. Ideographic script, according to Metz, records "discrete elements of social experience" or "purely mental, non-perceptible" elements. These contradictory phrases seem to suggest that ideographic writing directly records Ferdinand de Saussure's referent or signified, or somehow both at once. But in terms of sensory order and mode of recording, so-called ideograms are both visual and restrictive: insofar as they are identifiable as iconically representational, they record only those morphic elements of social experience identifiable as part of the written code. The term "ideogram," still unavoidably in use to name this mode of writing, is itself based on an inaccurate identification of inscription with a signified. Despite this, Chinese characters are signifiers, not referents or signifieds, and circulate in Japan within a field of other signifiers through multiple codes and modes of writing.

Derrida's appreciation of Frerèt and Warburton is based on their recognition of "figurative, symbolic, abstract and phonetic elements" within the same graphic code. Yet too often, kanji (again now referring to the Japanese term for Chinese characters as a component of their multiple writing system) are discussed only in their figurative aspect. Even with as careful a theorist as Metz, this figurative aspect is immediately reduced to a signified or a referent, and we are returned to the myth of a natural language. However, kanji in themselves are plural in their mode of signification in a way that the alphabet is not. A single character, for example, the one for "water," combines a morphic figure 水 iconically linked with a brook and two swirls of water. At the same time, that morphic figure is abstracted into a system of limited brushstrokes that makes iconic identification unnecessary or unlikely in practice. The link of each kanji with spoken words is never unitary: each kanji always has at least a Chinese name (in this case, *sui*) and one or more Japanese words as parallels or adaptations (*mizu* or *mina-*). Kanji thereby incorporate plural sound signs and the arbitrary and symbolic characteristics of verbal language.

It is important not to imagine kanji as simply reversing the signifier/signified relationship Saussure proposes for verbal language, itself modeled on an alphabetic or logocentric conception. The signified that Saussure proposes in his model of the verbal sign is an image or concept, but one that is necessarily unrestrictive. No code exists that prescribes how each speaker will visualize or conceive of the signified for each word spoken. In contrast, kanji prescribe specifically and restrictively the verbal signifiers attached to each abstract visual figure, even though those verbal signifiers derive from at least two separate language systems, Chinese and Japanese. In other words, alphabetic and ideographic writing are in no sense opposites or reversals of sound/image relationships but instead function on completely separate principles. Kanji position an array of restrictive signifiers, usually plural in both figurative and verbal aspects, while alphabetic words link a sequence of abstract letters to one or more unrestricted images or concepts.

The logocentric effects of alphabetic inscription have already been theorized. Phonocentrism positions a subjective interiority, while an unrestricted signified conversely positions the other as a silent nature, where language and writing is repressed. The desire to appropriate and control a nature conceived as uncoded is embedded in the unrestrictive recording apparatus of cinema. Cinema simultaneously industrializes or mass-produces the perspectival space of bourgeois individualism while dynamizing its single point of view through the illusion of motion. In short, the cinematic apparatus mechanically reproduces the logocentric metaphysics of an interiorized subject through its perspectival point of view, subordinates an unrestrictive or uncoded formation of nature to the centrality of the viewing subject, and moves that relation through time according to the diachronic prioritization of logocentrism. In a non-Western society, cinema functions to introduce such logocentric values, unanticipated by those expecting a neutral recording device, while bypassing the alphabetic writing that shaped cinema's origin.

Pouvoir/Écrire

Close analysis is necessary to articulate the tensions and complexity intrinsic to the coexistence of kanji, kana, and cinema in modern Japan, together with the marginal use of *romaji,* most often for visual design. Extended analysis of the materiality of writing is sometimes confused with formalism, yet it becomes postformalist when theoretical work engages a materiality of language and thought in relation to social and political contexts. Beginning with *Discipline and Punish,* Foucault moves in his later works toward a conception of *pouvoir/savoir* (power/knowledge). In this model, power is considered as formative, while discursive formations that derive from power also function to distribute and regulate the flow of power among the participants of each given discourse. Derrida responds to this theory by the suggestive subtitle *"pouvoir/écrire,"* or power/writing, which he appends to "Scribble," his introduction to a reissue of Warburton's *Essay on Egyptian Hieroglyphics*. What does power/writing suggest for a study of multiple writing practices that include kanji, kana, and cinema?

One route to this analysis might be by way of a conception of voice. The formation and distribution of power in any situation can in part be determined by who is allowed to speak and who is not, who speaks for whom and who is spoken for. The position of voice is also embedded in the circulation of desire, in the politics of the family, where language is first learned and power first distributed. Takeo Doi, in his *Anatomy of the Self,* argues that the Japanese self is split like the Western subject, but along different lines.[20] Doi's conception of the traditional Japanese self is regulated by the dominant characteristic of *amae,* or dependency, which functions as the psychoanalytic foundation of a relational subject, as we see represented, for example, in Ozu's films. Doi argues that this relational subject is split in its formation between *omote,* a public self organized by social obligations, and *ura,* an intimate self associated with *uchi,* the in-group of any familiar or domestic arrangement. For our purposes here, it is interesting that Doi associates *omote* with writing and *ura* with its interpretation. *Ura* is not precisely language but rather is the unspoken element in communication, implied but never contained in the coded and restrictive figural and verbal elements of traditional writing practices. *Ura* is what the Japanese context implies when communication is said to be "wet" with emotion. In contrast, language and imagery from the Western expressive and realist traditions seem "dry" in Japan, since meaning tends to be either direct and on the surface or absent.

Derrida argues that writing precedes language in his analysis of logocentrism. Analogously, we might consider that the writing of *omote* precedes the interpretation of *ura* and constructs a position outside the *différance* of kanji and kana, where an unrestricted flow of feeling occurs. In Japan, according to Doi, nature is not an other or object, as in the West, but a space where the split between *omote* and *ura* dissolves.

In this model, it becomes possible to conceive of the redistribution of power at stake in the Japanese use of cinema. Ozu's *Early Summer* (*Bakushu,* 1951) indeed functions according to traditional aesthetics to invoke *ura* as a strong suggested response to apparently banal verbal exchanges. Yet as in so many of his films, the daughter, Noriko, breaks with the arranged-marriage choice of her parents to voice her own desire. Her independent subjectivity is central to Ozu's representation of a shift of attitude, yet it is ironic because Noriko makes a traditionalist choice in a man who reminds her of her dead brother killed in the war. It is in this multidirectional and ironic play of memory and desire, authority and autonomy, direct and indirect statement, and tradition and modernization, that one can begin to trace the *pouvoir/écrire* of multiple writing practices.

Ozu is only one of many sites to observe the indirect operation of *pouvoir/écrire*. A specific but significant subset of Japanese film involves direct intertextual links between literature and film. An extensive overview of this specific intertextual relationship has been attempted by Max Tessier in his catalog for the 1986 exhibition at the Centre Georges Pompidou in Paris, *Cinéma et littérature de l'ere Meiji à nos jours au Japon*. *Pouvoir/écrire* provides a model for tracing the effects of multiple writing practices in and among these texts insofar as it functions to distribute power and desire within social formations. Yet writing practices also produce effects within films without literary connections. Further, they undergo a significant shift in their activity by their recontextualization in video. Video, with its digital image mapping, is equally capable of both figurative and abstract construction, of mixing imagery with ideographic and phonocentric writing with equal facility. In this, video differs from film, which despite the practice of titling (titles, subtitles, intertitles) and use of verbal text within the mise-en-scène, conventionally functions to subordinate or repress writing in favor of image dominance. In contrast, video foregrounds the full range of multiple writing practices across its raster surface, thereby becoming a site where *pouvoir/écrire* seems unavoidable for analytic access to textual practice.

Pouvoir/écrire can also help correct for the tendency still implicit in Doi to assume that being Japanese is necessarily identical to a specific kind of self. Doi's theorization of Japanese specificity can be enormously helpful to the degree that a film is working with or against traditional aesthetics and values. However, any suggestion that these conditions and effects characterize all Japanese people today unavoidably devolves into restrictive stereotypes. People who live in Japan, and those acquainted with modern Japan, know that there is no natural Japanese self, but only different modes of traditional or modern identity that can be practiced according to context. In this sense, identity is performed in Japan just as Judith Butler argues it is in the West, although the available choices and contexts may be different. *Pouvoir/écrire* can make it possible to conceptualize an exteriority to psychoanalysis in the context of cultural difference, parallel to Derrida and Foucault's critique of psychoanalysis as a discourse, and theorize traditional or modern identities as the effects of multiple conditions and material practices in the same context.

The nihilistic comedy characteristic of Japanese new narrative filmmakers of the 1980s, such as Ishii, Morita, Sai, Itami, and others, is a site where we can see this kind of *pouvoir/écrire* at work. Compare the logic of inscription in Sogo Ishii's *Crazy Family* (*Gyakufunsha Kazoku,* 1984) to that of Ozu. Most commentary on contemporary Japanese film emphasizes the reappearance of an Ozu-like family in an advanced state of disintegration. But in *Crazy Family,* the landscape as well becomes an integral surface for this refiguration of intimate relationships. As in many Japanese films of the 1980s, the family is represented by three generations: grandparents obsessed by memories of the militarist era, children narcissistically entranced by personalized electronic devices, and parents suspended between as destabilized protagonists. The initiating action in *Crazy Family* is the parents' move with their extended family to a newly built "2x4," or American-style suburban house, so named because of its standard building material. The move, and the consequent chaos it triggers, is framed in the film by two sequences more typical of avant-garde filmmaking than conventional narrative practice. At the beginning, suburban housing tracts are represented through traveling shots from a car reconstructed by single-frame stop motion. As a result, houses fly by as if in a flicker film, in a repetition of architectural form that suggests a hallucinatory state of mass production. At the end of the narrative, in a style similar to Terayama's experimental theater-based films, the family demolishes its 2x4 piece by piece and relocates in a vacant field under a thruway overpass. In this new space, the family reconstitutes itself in terms of multiple narcissisms, with each individual isolated within separate stacks of consumer possessions. The 2x4's transformation of the family into the space of American individualism, as represented in the film, leads to a collapse of communication and serial autism. In terms of the space of this final inscription, one should note the emptiness of the space as a radical force, marked by the linear trajectory of the overpass as track of the machine. Read as *pouvoir/écrire,* this emptiness and trajectory suggest the effects of logocentric values on Japanese relationships. The environment, previously a coded component of Japanese architectural space in the form of a garden, is erased and becomes a tabula rasa. The West's conception of nature as neutral object is reinscribed as a powerful void, and as a means to erase established or naturalized relationships deriving from Japanese tradition. The automobile's overarching trajectory positions teleological direction as the sole and dominant relation now possible in this context, a directionality that eliminates *ura* for the sake of parallel motion.

Topics and Subjects

Lacan rarely mentions Japan in his work, but when he does the result is both curious and suggestive. In his first seminar, *Les écrits techniques de Freud,* he compares the technique of psychoanalytic therapy to Zen: "The master interrupts the silence arbitrarily, with a sarcasm, a stamp of the foot. So proceeds the research of meaning by a Buddhist master, according to zen technique. . . . The thought of Freud is the most perpetually open to revision."[21] In his preface to the Japanese translation of *Écrits,* he positions Japan outside psychoanalytic practice: "This demonstrates that wit in Japan is the same as the most common discourse, and is why no one who inhabits this language needs psychoanalysis, except to regulate relations with sub-machines—especially with the most simply mechanical of clients."

As Jean-Luc Nancy and Philippe Lacoue-Labarthe argue in *The Title of the Letter: A Reading of Lacan,* Lacan's essay "The Agency of the Letter in the Unconscious or Reason Since Freud" circulates around the principle that the letter is bound up with the structure of language, the subject and reason as *ratio* or *logos*.[22] The letter in question is the phonemic particle that inflects the double articulation of language, as a splitting between phonemic and semantic components, as well as its approximation by the elemental unit of the alphabet. In "The Seminar on the 'Purloined Letter,'" written two years earlier, in 1955, and included as the initiating essay in the French publication of *Écrits,* Lacan clarifies that the letter is not a transcendent or metaphysical phenomenon, but a materiality in plain sight made invisible by habit. Derrida's response to Lacan's "'Purloined Letter,'" in *The Post Card, from Socrates to Freud and Beyond,* further extends the figure of the letter to the postal system as social network of circulating texts.

Ellie Ragland-Sullivan observes that Lacan's "letters" often represent the effects of language, especially as the impact of otherness on the body through the differentiation of erotogenic zones.[23] Letters are bound up with organs as abstract signifiers prior to an Oedipalized entry into the Symbolic, and the consequent incorporation of an ideal self into the subject of language. Nancy and Lacoue-Labarthe comment that agency could also be understood in W. V. O. Quine's sense of "propositions which could be substituted by a *letter* used as a symbol in the calculus (of symbolic logic)."[24] In other words, the letter in its materiality represents a calculus of the body, through which biology is transfigured into discourse.

Two kinds of questions then follow. If the materiality of the letter is bound up with specific effects in Western discourse, which Derrida summarizes as a logocentric metaphysics and Karatani calls "architecture," then what effects are produced by nonalphabetic writing systems such as the Chinese written character or cinema? Is it possible to think past the limits of thought imposed by the foundational writing system that makes discourse possible?

No one today is able to sustain an unproblematic identification with the effects of classical writing systems, whether alphabetic or not, because of the intervention of modern media. The normative situation now is to inhabit multiple writing systems, and the disjunctions among them open onto the thought of an exteriority previously unthought and unthinkable. Agency has become reconfigured into an other-than, or postidentity, where classical identity and identification are situated alongside an unconscious or alienation as point of departure. No one today is simply "Buddhist" or "Islamic" or "Christian," but must either be insistently so, as a neofoundationalism, or participate in a "secular" discourse inhabited by surviving figures from past narratives.

The Operation of the Kanji in the Unconscious

The problem of developing theoretical models for the construction of agency and self in non-Western cinemas can be approached through the site of Japanese film. Although Japan constitutes a highly specific case, it is only through such specificity that conceptual strategies can be effectively generated that might be more widely applicable to Asia,

Africa, and other cultures negotiating the conflict between tradition and modernization. To begin, Ichikawa's *An Actor's Revenge* can be considered as a kind of tutor-text to unravel how sexuality and gender roles are figured by cinematic technique.

While psychoanalysis has been an effective tool for addressing subject formation in Western cinema, problems unavoidably arise in any attempt to extend this model to Japan. Japanese film instead operates at the juncture of Western psychoanalytic methodology and cultural difference. As before with critical methodology in general, psychoanalysis enables a critical reading of an alternative cultural situation, while cultural difference conversely functions to help read the limits and character of psychoanalysis itself. It becomes necessary to problematize non-Western cultural production as a site of intersecting discourses, so that cultural specificity and psychoanalytic methodology can potentially interrogate, destabilize, and transfigure each other.

Questions that then need to be addressed range from psychoanalytic theory and the unconscious of the text to issues of *écriture* and representation. How does psychoanalysis function in Japan without the tradition of a Western cogito on which the methodology is based? While the fundamental insights of psychoanalysis cannot simply be discarded, neither can the subject construction of Western interiority be assumed. What does it mean for Lacanian theory to posit a *je* and a *moi* in a language such as Japanese where pronouns are dropped? Or to posit a "letter in the unconscious" in a nonalphabetic culture? These questions not only invite consideration through Takeo Doi's analyses of the

FIGURE 13. A restaurant in Shinkuju in the 1980s. To read the sign as "bad English" would miss the point: libidinal intensities easily emerge at sites of syntactic dislocation.

amae (dependency) and *uchi* (in-group) character of a Japanese psychology but also necessarily situate Doi's work historically in the era of postwar humanism. Equally important are questions specifically addressed to Lacanian methodology raised by Takatsugu
Sasaki, Hiroyuki Akama, and other members of the Groupe Franco-Japonais du Champ
Freudien.

The question of the subject in its relation to writing can be pursued through issues
that arise in the Japanese reading of Lacan, as in Takatsugu Sasaki's essay "Mettre la
psychanalyse en japonais," and the attempt to imagine the operation of the kanji in the
unconscious. The role of cinema is pivotal here, as a nonalphabetic writing that circulates
simultaneously with kanji in positioning a multiple and shifting agency as postidentity
in postmodern Japan. Yet studies of film, even in an international and metacultural context, too often assume that the *dispositif* of cinematic representation exists independently
of the cinematic apparatus. The camera image, rather than being recognized and studied
as a specifically Western mass production of perspectival space and individualist point
of view, is too often treated as if its mechanical and indexical mode of signification guaranteed a presence of meaning that transcended cultural barriers.

The Melodramatization of Gender

Ichikawa's film *An Actor's Revenge* (*Yukinojo henge,* 1963) has long been acknowledged
as an eccentric tour de force. Donald Richie, in *Japanese Cinema,* remarks that "In *The
Revenge of Yukinojo,* [Ichikawa] triumphed over his material so completely that the result
is something of a masterpiece—though just what kind is difficult to say."[25] I would like
to consider the film as the site of contestatory discourses of power and gender identification, through a play of apparently contradictory theatrical and cinematic styles. Specifically, the film foregrounds melodrama as a style that uneasily pivots between traditional
Kabuki theater and Western cinematic realism. As such, it invites a reconsideration of
the role of Shimpa, the Japanese popular theater often described as melodramatic, in its
relation to cinema and Japanese culture.

Shimpa derived from a form of political theater designed to promote liberal political
thought before the establishment in 1890 of the first Japanese constitution, and it embodied emerging middle-class values parallel to the role melodrama played in France after
the Revolution.[26] All but forgotten after the triumph of Shingeki, or Western-style realist
theater, and Shingeki-influenced cinema, Shimpa marks a boundary between what later
would become clearly delineated Western and Japanese traditions in both political organization and narrative representation. By the 1950s, these different traditions came to be
known as "feudalism" and "humanism," yet both terms are sweeping generalizations that
erase the complexity and contradictions within each tradition. As such, they mythologize
cultural difference as a polarization of unitary transhistorical forms.

An Actor's Revenge sets Kabuki and Western melodrama against each other, as two
forms of excess, in order to destabilize the assumptions inherent in each. "Feudal" and
"humanist" distributions of power are both undermined through an ironic intertextual
bracketing of modes of representation associated with each. These modes can be seen to

regulate the distribution of power and the relative positioning of women within discursive formations.

At the same time, gender destabilization in the film provides a means of discussing the difficult question of psychoanalysis in a Japanese context. Gender identification is undermined by the deliberate casting of Kazuo Hasegawa (Yukinojo) as an *onnagatta,* the type of male Kabuki actor who specializes in playing female roles, and the actress Ayako Wakao in romantic love scenes. This juxtaposition recalls the historical moment in Japanese film when women first replaced *onnagatta* in female roles during the 1920s, and undermines any simple sense of what constitutes gender identification.

Textual Features

According to Donald Richie, Ichikawa was assigned to remake *An Actor's Revenge* as punishment, "almost a calculated insult," by the Daiei studio after its dissatisfaction with his productions of *Conflagration (Enjo,* 1958), *Bonchi (Bonchi,* 1960), and *The Outcast (Hakai,* 1962). This "old tearjerker," or "tired melodrama," was seen by the director and his wife, Natto Wada (who adapted the scenario), as "so bad as to be good."[27] In short, the scenario is conceived as a melodrama at the historical moment when negative attitudes toward the form begin to reverse into a positive appreciation. Appropriated shortly after its release into the Western concepts of "camp" and pop art, Ichikawa's reinscription of melodrama can perhaps now be reexamined on its own terms.

The story centers on Yukinojo, a celebrated Kabuki actor during the Tokugawa period who, as an *onnagatta* or *oyama,* specializes in female roles. During a performance at the Ichimura Theater in Edo (Tokyo), he recognizes Lord Dobe and the merchant Kawaguchiya, who were responsible for the ruin and suicide of his parents. He seeks vengeance through subterfuge, most significantly through the manipulation of Lord Dobe's daughter Namiji, who has fallen in love with him. Economic depression has produced a rash of burglars, who by turns interfere with or assist Yukinojo's schemes. Eventually, Yukinojo traps his enemies by a charade in which he pretends to be the ghost of his dead father, and, overcome by exposure and guilt, they kill themselves.

The story is filled with instances of social corruption and class power. Lord Dobe and Kawaguchiya exemplify the alliance of samurai and merchant classes that dominates Tokugawa Japan. Kawaguchiya's speculation in the rice market is characterized as greed responsible for the famine and uprising that devastates the city. Lord Dobe claims that the Shogun is in his power because of Namiji, linking his corruption directly to the nominal ruler. When the story of Yukinojo's father Matsuuraya is told at the end of the film, Lord Dobe is revealed as the former magistrate of Nagasaki, the sole Japanese city where even limited trade with the West was permitted during the rigid isolation of the country enforced by the Tokugawa shogunate. Lord Dobe had been bribed by Hiroyama, whose "rare clock" had been smuggled from abroad, and then conspired with Hiroyama and Matsuuraya's clerk Kawaguchiya to blame Yukinojo's father for the crime. Matsuuraya, driven mad by the false accusations, committed suicide.

At the same time, numerous roles are mirrored by parallel relationships or names.

Ohatsu, a woman boss of a band of burglars, is infatuated with Yukinojo, mirroring across class lines Yukinojo's aristocratic affair with Namiji. Yukinojo's "real" name in the film is Yukitaro (Yukinojo is his stage name, which partially explains why his enemies do not recognize him), a name mirrored in Yukitaro's rival Yamitaro, a burglar and Ohatsu's principal cohort. In a tour-de-force performance not untypical of Kabuki, the same actor plays the roles of both Yukitaro and Yamitaro. This doubling is then noted within the film when Yamitaro claims he feels as if Yukitaro were his brother, and again when Ohatsu remarks that their profiles are similar. Yamitaro is in turn rivaled by another burglar, Hirutaro (*Yami* means dark and *Hiru* means light), Yukitaro is rivaled by yet another burglar, Heima Kadokura (a former fellow student of the sword instructor Issoshai at the Tenshin School, where the school "secrets" are recorded on a piece of paper that turns out to be blank), and so on.

Part of the doubling cuts across the difference between stage performance in Kabuki and offstage "life," that is, the film's representation of the characters' social context. Ichikawa's film has often been noted as an antirealist experiment with all the artificial and theatrical devices available to a filmmaker at the Daiei studio in Kyoto. Yukinojo maintains his *onnagatta* costume and performance both onstage and off, creating several layers of sexual ambiguity during love scenes, especially with Namiji. The wide screen becomes an arena for graphic display: a horizontal fan fills the screen against a red background, a fight is filmed as slashing swords isolated by light against total darkness, a rope stretches completely across the screen (again isolated against darkness) with the characters pulling the rope offscreen. In addition, any sense of historical realism seems willfully and even frivolously violated. Authentic Kabuki music alternates with a muted jazz trumpet or violins and vibraphone, and outdoor scenes can seem conspicuously painted as if to recall Western landscapes. Traditional Kabuki and Western-style cinema reflect each other as equally artificial constructs.

The effect of all these proliferating plot turns, conspiratorial revelations, character doublings, and formal devices is to create a narrative maze in which rational comprehension of all detail becomes difficult or perhaps impossible on first viewing. Narrative clarity tends to dissolve into an illusion of infinite recession, as in a hall of mirrors. In this, the story is not unlike the Byzantine workings of many Kabuki plays (or eighteenth-century opera in the West), but the film does not stop there.

Plural Intertextuality

If *An Actor's Revenge* seems like a labyrinthine text in itself, another part of its fascination comes from a layering of intertextual references so complex that the effect of infinitely receding mirrors extends well into the social fabric of Japanese film history and cross-cultural influences between Japan and the West. First, Ichikawa's film is a remake of Teinosuke Kinugasa's *The Revenge of Yukinojo* (*Yukinojo henge,* 1935), a film made during the militarist period of closure against the West as strict as that of the Tokugawa regime in which the story is set. As in the Ichikawa film, the Yukinojo character in the original film also maintained his *onnagatta* role both on and offstage, and the same actor again performed the roles of both Yukinojo and the burglar (and in the first film, of Yukinojo's mother as well). Further, as is well known, Ichikawa specifically chose the same actor who had starred in the 1935 film to re-create his role in the 1963 version, and Ichikawa's scenarist, Natto Wada, adapted the original scenario by Daisuke Ito and Kinugasa, which had been based on a novel by Otokichi Mikami.

Interestingly, the actor involved had changed his name between films, reversing the film character's adoption of a stage name after he left Nagasaki. When the actor had moved from Shochiku to Toho, he had been forced to leave his stage name of Chojiro Hayashi behind and revert to his birth name of Kazuo Hasegawa. In a famous incident, a Korean gangster hired in part by the Shochiku labor-gang boss slashed Hasegawa in the face with a razor; only afterward did the public sympathize with the change and accept his new name.[28] Hayashi/Hasegawa's face was then reconstructed through extensive plastic surgery, making his "real" face as much an artificial construction as that of his *onnagatta*'s role's makeup. Shortly after Ichikawa's film, Kobo Abe's novel *The Face of Another* would make the trope of plastic surgery and new identity a metaphor for the Japanese experience of cultural change; by 1966, Hiroshi Teshigahara had made Abe's novel into a film.

In 1963, Ichikawa's choice of Hasegawa for the role of Yukinojo already suggested the violence of identity change between the militarist period and the post-Occupation cinema of "modern" Japan. This disjunction specifically resonates with the difference between Kabuki tradition and Western realism: the enforced mythologies of militarism that attributed divine origin to the emperor had been displaced by the humanist realism of the American Occupation as a vehicle of an equally imposed ideology. For those Japanese who had lived through the militant enforcement of such contradictory ideologies, a cynical distance tended to undermine absolute belief in any single system of meaning, as can be seen in the films of the Japanese New Wave contemporaneous with Ichikawa's film.

But many more ironies surround the names of personnel associated with *An Actor's Revenge*. Kinugasa, the director and co-scenarist of the first version, is best known in the West both for his 1920s experimental films, *A Crazy Page* (*Kurutta ippeiji,* 1926) and *Crossways* (*Jujiro,* 1928), and for his later *Gate of Hell* (*Jigokumon,* 1953). However, Kinugasa was himself originally an *onnagatta* at the Nikkatsu film studio and played the heroine in such films as Eizo Tanaka's *The Living Corpse* (*Ikeru shikabane,* 1917). Kinugasa led the 1922 *onnagatta*'s strike against Nikkatsu to protest the introduction of women to play female roles in films, before making a career change and becoming a director. Although Kinugasa had between these two periods reversed himself to also lead the fight to modernize Japanese filmmaking, his 1935 production of a film narrative centering on an *onnagatta*'s revenge unavoidably recalls the conflict between traditional Kabuki stylization and Western cinematic realism earlier in Japanese film history.

Unfortunately, few complete films from this period survive, even at the Film Center of the National Museum of Modern Art in Tokyo or in the Matsuda collection, and *The Living Corpse* is so far extant only through written descriptions.[29] This was the period when *onnagatta* and *benshi* dominated Japanese film production, together with the exaggerated Shimpa techniques for which Tanaka was primarily known. Tanaka, however, idolized Ibsen and attempted to introduce "new-style" films beginning with *The Living Corpse,* substituting such devices of Western realism as location shooting for the theatricality of Shimpa. According to Anderson and Richie, Kinugasa's female appearance in the film was contradicted only by heavy workmen's boots that he wore due to the heavy mud encountered during November shooting. No one objected, however, because "the audience had not yet been trained to expect the illusion of complete reality."[30]

The Living Corpse, then, apparently participated in a remarkably mixed style of film in some ways unique to Japan, but also indicative of the intersection of traditional non-Western aesthetics with cinematic representation. The omniscient style of camera narration characteristic of Western realism is framed by the *benshi* as interpretive narrator, location realism combines with contradictory costume elements, and photographic realism combines with *onnagatta*. This mixed text is conceived as a move against the theatricality of Shimpa, and marks what is perhaps Kinugasa's most important role as an actor in early cinema. Although Kinugasa's relationship to Western modernism has been debated, concerning his avant-garde films like *A Crazy Page,*[31] the effect of his disjunctive stylistic background on his interest in antirealist filmmaking has yet to be discussed. Ichikawa, in remaking *An Actor's Revenge,* is in some ways more faithful to Kinugasa's film experience than Kinugasa's original version could be. Through his deliberate undermining of cinematic realism by studio theatricality, Ichikawa reconsiders precisely those early conditions of production that helped shape Kinugasa's wildly diverse career, and incorporates those into his remake as a critique of the text.

Daisuke Ito, who co-wrote the original *Actor's Revenge* scenario with Kinugasa, was himself a major director of silent films. Ito originated the *chambara* or swordfight film, which re-created the fight scenes of previously filmed Kabuki and Shimpa plays with greater cinematic realism. Curiously, *chambara* films are linked with ideas of left-wing social activism that circulated in Japan during the 1920s, and often feature an outlaw hero fighting against a corrupt and oppressive social order. The most famous actor portraying such outlaw heroes was Tsumasaburo Bando, but Hayashi/Hasegawa was almost as popular.

Although, again, few films survive, it is possible to draw some guarded conclusions from Ito's only extant silent film *Jirokichi the Ratkid* (*Oatsurae Jirokichi goshi,* 1931), together with Buntaro Futagawa's *The Outlaw* (*Orochi,* 1925) and Tsuruhiko Tanaka's *The Red Bat* (*Beni Komori,* 1931).[32] These are all films that can be considered as part of the Ito school, through their increased physicality of performance combined with dynamic camerawork and editing during combat sequences. Most interestingly, a comparison of *The Outlaw* and *Jirokichi* suggests the kind of innovations Ito introduced. *The Outlaw,* in today's postmodern terms, is a far more experimental film. The climactic fight scene at the end of the narrative is represented through a series of stylized combat tableaus directly transposed from Kabuki: the central character is tied in by police ropes drawn across the screen like a spider's web, and a close-up presents his face in cross-eyed anguish as if in a Sharaku ukiyo-e (Edo-era woodblock print) portrait of a Kabuki actor. Intercut with this, the film rapidly jumps across static compositions of the surrounding police in a machine-gun rhythm of staccato Soviet-style montage. Accordingly, *The Outlaw* follows a paradoxical pattern of inversions where Western modernism and Japanese traditional aesthetics seem to coincide. In contrast, Ito's own film *Jirokichi* radically eliminates both such theatrical effects and disjunctive montage, substituting a dynamic style of physical performance and cutting on action to center attention on character within narrative continuity. Yet even in *Jirokichi,* as Burch has noted of Ito's style as perpetuated in *The Red Bat,* visual stylization exceeds Western continuity norms. Rapid swish pans (for example, between two men at a tense moment) interrupt Western conventions of narrative action, but in Ito seem designed to intensify viewer involvement with screen action.

It is perhaps impossible to reconstruct with any historical certainty how the *benshi* (or *katsuben,* as *benshi* for cinema were called) interacted with specific films. However, Shunsui Matsuda's *benshi* performances on the soundtracks that now accompany both *The Outlaw* and *Jirokichi* suggest that *benshi* performances were stylized both independently of the narrative and in relation to shifts of visual style. In Matsuda's *The Outlaw,* the *benshi*'s voice frequently interrupts the action, as, for example, to introduce each new character as they appear on screen. This unavoidably produces a Brechtian effect of distancing the viewer from total identification with the action. In contrast, in Matsuda's *Jirokichi,* the *benshi* narration conforms far more precisely to the outlines of the action visualized on screen, inviting a more direct identification with the central character within narrative continuity. The difference demonstrates possible innovations within the mixed textual construction of *katsuben* performance.

FIGURE 14. Chojiro Hayashi as Yukinojo, the *onnagatta* role in Kinugasa's *The Revenge of Yukinojo* (*Yukinojo henge,* 1935). This actor (but under his birth name of Kazuo Hasegawa) plays the same role in Ichikawa's baroque remake, *An Actor's Revenge* (*Yukinojo henge,* 1963).

Accordingly, such tropes as national xenophobic isolation, a name change masking violence, the transposition of the *onnagatta* role within cinematic realism, and swordfights against social oppression, all extend past Ichikawa's film text into its social and historical context. Ichikawa's easy mixture of realist and antirealist devices recalls and transforms the discordant styles within a text that characterized early Japanese cinema. Of course, one could object that any Japanese film could be traced to its origins in early cinema, but such an objection would miss the point. Ichikawa's *An Actor's Revenge,* through its concatenation of specific and highly charged intertextual citations, invites consideration of the cultural and cross-cultural contexts in which narratives are produced. These contexts are situated at the intersection of Japanese traditional theater and Western cinematic realism and are addressed in *An Actor's Revenge* by a rereading of melodrama.

Melodrama as Avant-Garde

In the histories of Japanese cinema available in English, melodrama is usually treated briefly. The predominant view is that melodrama can be equated with Shimpa, or "New School Theater," the form of Japanese theater characteristic of the Meiji era. Shimpa originated in the 1890s and maintained a dominant popularity from about 1900 to the mid-1920s, and was the primary source both of cinematic style and of film actors and directors during the early period. Shingeki, or "Modern Theater," thereafter displaced Shimpa as a primary cultural influence, beginning with experiments in theater in 1909 and becoming dominant in cinema by the 1930s.

Opinion has then often diverged in ways that leave Shimpa equally marginalized. Most often, Shimpa has been dismissed by both Japanese and American writers as a transitional, "half-modern" movement, not yet sufficiently realist to sustain audience attention as a fully adequate representation of the modern age. Tadao Sato, for example, argues that its character types were drawn from Kabuki, and dismisses its "antiquated forms" once Shingeki appears. Donald Richie refers to Shimpa as "almost instantly fossilized," and again contrasts it to a Shingeki-influenced cinema that seems obviously superior because "Shingeki at least concerned itself with a kind of reality." Faubion Bowers, in his classic postwar text on Japanese theater, dismissed early Shimpa as silly and insignificant melodrama and again reserves praise for the "serious" theater that followed with realism. Alternatively, Noël Burch praises Shimpa, but as a form of resistance to Western models of narrative form that preserved elements of traditional Japanese theater. Burch argues that the originators and practitioners of Shimpa knew little or nothing about the Western models they were supposedly emulating, and as a result unavoidably recapitulated the traditions they sought to abandon.[33] The difficulty with either of these positions is that neither examines Shimpa on its own terms. Both instead immediately slide past Shimpa to another form privileged as "serious" in its influence on cinema, regardless of whether realism or an antirealist reading of Kabuki is so privileged.

Yet Shimpa, even when it is described by its detractors, is clearly an energized intersection of conflicting forms, an unstable and multiple movement that functioned as a pivot between traditional Japan and the modernized West. Shimpa directly derives from the "Political Dramas" *(soshi geki)* originated by the Liberal Group in 1888 to promote the policies and platforms at stake once the Meiji constitution would be put into effect in 1890. Yet Shimpa is also clearly related to efforts made to reform Kabuki, to imports of Western plays, and to contradictions between Western and Kabuki norms of representation. In Kabuki, Danjuro IX's nationalistic "Plays of Living History" (beginning in 1878) and Kikugoro V's "Cropped Hair Plays" (beginning in 1879) both radically broke with the prescriptive stylization of Kabuki that characterized the late Tokugawa period. Danjuro sought to eliminate the inconsistencies of traditional Kabuki texts and rewrite them as unified nationalistic propaganda based on historical research. Kikugoro first adapted a Western play into Japanese and staged performances in contemporary dress; cropped hair indicated the recent abolition of feudal social distinctions and the hairstyles that had signified them. Both Danjuro and Kikugoro adapted Western models of narrative construction (history, theater) to promote the social and political agendas of modernization, yet they pursued these representational goals within the framework of Kabuki.[34] As a consequence, both produced performances that mixed styles as freely as Shimpa.

Shimpa as a term first refers to the work of Kawakami Otojiro, beginning in 1891 with his elimination of overt political material from the "Political Dramas" he had been writing. Enough legends surround this "sensational charlatan," who is acknowledged as the "father of modern drama in Japan," that he seems like a Meiji version of O-Kuni, the woman whose dance in the bed of the Kamo River supposedly created Kabuki. One narrative claims that an audience member once murdered one of Otojiro's fictional villains because he was supposedly unable to distinguish between art and life even in the initial stages of realist aesthetics.[35] (Godard restages a similar story in *Les carabiniers* about the confusion of art and life for viewers of early cinema.) Another narrative claims that Otojiro, after touring Europe and America with Shimpa, returned to Japan in 1902 to stage a version of *Hamlet* in which the central character entered on a bicycle.[36] This particular story (also appreciated by Burch) joins Shakespeare with a signifier of the European avant-garde, since the bicycle was in the late nineteenth century the principal emblem of the modern among bohemians.[37] European tradition appears avant-garde in Japan, in a mirror reversal of the paradoxical link of Japanese tradition and Western modernism noted in *The Outlaw*. In *Origins of Modern Japanese Literature,* Kojin Karatani argues that the onset of the modern period in Japan is characterized by a series of such inversions, or *tento*.[38]

Shimpa after 1895 was capable of mixing forms of representation in a way that can perhaps only be appreciated in the West after the postmodern transvaluation of pastiche and contradictory styles within the same work. Both men and women appeared on stage at the same time in female roles,[39] a circumstance often criticized as partially regressive or progressive but not appreciated as a meaningful contradiction in itself that usefully problematizes representation. Shimpa also first combined film with live performance in "chain-drama" *(rensa-geki),* as early as 1904 and as late as 1922, with significant popularity beginning in 1908.[40] In this mode of representation, exterior scenes were shot on film and alternated on stage with live performances for interiors. In its capacity for such innovative mixed forms, what is called melodrama or Shimpa in Japan ironically seems to share certain features with what in Europe is called avant-garde: a passion for the politics of representation, a distanciation from total identification with any single system of meaning, and a disruption of the ontology and epistemology of the image.

Shimpa, it could be argued, was a volatile generator of tropes that first marked the collision of Japan and the West. As such, this marginalized form functioned to help produce the determining tropes that served to orient Japan's entry into the modern period, and that are later repressed in dominant forms of representation from the 1930s on. Ichikawa's *An Actor's Revenge* redirects our attention to what is called Japanese melodrama through a text informed by a complex intertextual understanding of melodrama's multiple determinants. The determining tropes of Shimpa then begin to self-destruct through representational contradictions made apparent by their recontextualization in an era of dominant cinematic realism. The film reinstates the representational indeterminacy of the period when Shimpa was dominant, and signification had not yet become comfortably polarized into the mythologized terms of tradition and realism.

In *An Actor's Revenge,* melodrama appears as a boundary site between Kabuki and cinematic realism. Through an inversion, by which melodrama is reprioritized long after it had been conceived as superseded by realism, the style is made to comment on the logocentric assumption that realism is central. In part, the film recalls the historical origins of realism for Japan in a mode of excess, undermining realism's pretensions to an origin in an objective, mute nature. *An Actor's Revenge* retells a melodramatic story of love and vengeance by freely mixing realist and antirealist devices, and by so doing suggests that a totalized illusion of realism depends on a denial of sexual difference and of class violence. Through a strategy of excess, realism is seen as grounded in a desire for power over the other, both ideologically and sexually.

Ichikawa's reinscription of melodrama, however, also relocates Kabuki as a necessarily complementary mode of excess. By 1912, Nikkatsu had divided its production into Shimpa ("New School"), which signified the production of dramas in contemporary settings at its Tokyo studio, in contrast to Kyuha ("Old School"), the period dramas produced at Kyoto.[41] From the historical break that marked the emergence of Japanese melodrama, Shimpa and Kabuki reinvented each other in a way that mixed traditional/modern and Japanese/Western values. As a result, neither Kabuki nor Shimpa is the Tokugawa theater or European melodrama it may at first appear to be. At Nikkatsu, Shimpa worked to redefine the parameters of period drama not as a tableau transposition of Kabuki but as a domain in which a middle-class Meiji personality type confronted tradition. At the same time, Shimpa preserved the character stereotypes of Kabuki, producing a specifically Japanese version of melodrama. As described by Sato, these types are the *tateyaku* ("standing role"), the *nimaeme* ("second"), and the *onnagatta*. The *tateyaku* is the male lead of the Kabuki troupe, who represents the idealized Bushido samurai who never places romantic love or family interests above his loyalty to the feudal lord. The *nimaeme,* in contrast, were weak men who fell in love with geisha or prostitutes and preferred to commit suicide with them rather than subordinate emotional intimacy to Bushido. The *onnagatta* played all female roles, but especially the idealized woman whose virtue is demonstrated by the degree of sacrifice she endures. Sato argues that these values contrast sharply with feudal ideology in the West, in which warrior virtue is identified with romantic idealism. In Shimpa, excess functions to reinforce polarized values of good and evil, as in Western melodrama, but the ideological terms so valorized are quite different.

Kabuki was itself often a form of social protest against a corrupt Tokugawa regime. Sato relates the Kabuki male character split to the difference between samurai tradition and the emerging merchant class during the Tokugawa period, with their respectively different attitudes about the role of women. Ito's active translation of such protest elements into left-wing *chambara* films reinscribed Shimpa melodrama as a critique of emerging Japanese capitalism, constructing a parallel style from different sources to the Western melodrama that had emerged in the West during the capitalist development of industrialization. In Ito's reweaving of the multiple determinants that characterize a specifically Japanese mode of melodrama, the *tateyaku* becomes the vehicle for an Old Left trope of heroic socialism. The ironies of this formation become especially obvious once feminism emerges as a component of social critique.

Kinugasa's mid-1930s *chambara* is more ambiguous: although his narrative's representation of a corrupt elite might suggest an extension of Ito's critique to the militarists by then in power, Yukinojo's dedication to his vengeance also suggests an ethical purity valorized by Japanese fascism. Given the intensifying repression of dissent during the 1930s, Kinugasa's text hides behind a double reading: the corrupt elite could just as easily be read as the dominant Westernized class that revolutionary fascism considered itself to be fighting against. Ichikawa's satirical quotation of the trope of a corrupt dominant class after the Occupation recalls both Ito's and Kinugasa's prior usages. Early *chambara*'s anticapitalist protest is recalled in the context of renewed post-Occupation capitalist development, but so are the ambiguous consequences of such protest during the militarist period and the Occupation.

By satirical displacement, Ichikawa does not so much negate the social critique of *chambara* as turn our attention elsewhere. The film problematizes an identification of social activism with an unconsidered conjuncture of *tateyaku* and a realist aesthetic. As such, a principal target of the film's critique becomes the samurai humanism of postwar period films by Kurosawa and others, including such "masterpieces" celebrated in the West as *Seven Samurai* (*Shichinin no samurai,* 1954). Although Anderson and Richie have argued that Mifune is "definitely a post-war type," Sato argues that Kurosawa's casting of Toshiro Mifune is a classic example of the *tateyaku* role.[42] Yet Mifune's role in *Seven Samurai,* as has often been noted, is to defend the peasants rather than exploit them. Kurosawa's samurai tend to revive early *chambara*'s reinscription of *tateyaku* as socialist protest, but Kurosawa shifts the politics by developing the character of individual samurai. The *tateyaku* role is reinscribed once again to suggest humanist individualism, but still within the value system of Japanese melodrama, the traces of which remain in Japanese cinema long after the surface style of exaggerated action has disappeared. In *Seven Samurai,* the enemy has also been recast from an oppressive dominant class to the chaos of uncontrolled criminals, a shift that ironically returns the samurai to a position of legitimate, if temporary, authority over the peasants who mistrust them. Ichikawa's Yukinojo in part satirizes this recuperation of democratic activism (whether socialist or humanist) by the unavoidably rigid hierarchies of feudal heroics condensed within the figure of the *tateyaku*. Equally important, his film undermines the embedding of this contradictory figure within the naturalizing form of a totalized realism.

In Ichikawa's *An Actor's Revenge,* the "truth" of both social oppression (Yukinojo's reenactment of his father's ghost to confront his enemies) and of sexual difference (Yukinojo's theatrical construction of sexual identity juxtaposed with Namiji as voyeuristic object) is represented as a confrontation of the theatrical against a dominant realism. The most significant danger is the violence of representations embedded in ideological rigidity, and the effective response is not vengeance but *jouissance,* a play of forms. If the characteristic activity of *chambara* from Ito through Mifune is to valorize a negational rage against social oppression, then the figure of Yukinojo works to undermine the categorical absolutism enforced by negation. Through its parody of the Hasegawa type of social protest *tateyaku,* Ichikawa's melodrama works to reverse the tendency toward representational identification with totalitarian control that has characterized both the Left under Stalinism and the humanism of corporate hierarchization. In contrast to the similar concerns of Oshima's *Night and Fog in Japan* (*Nihon no yoru to kiri,* 1960), Ichikawa further plays with the problem of how to reinscribe violence into a positive project of textual pleasure that unlocks the anxious isolation of the subject.

Gender Indeterminacy

The parodic figure of Yukinojo functions as a playful critique of what Lacan would call the paranoid construction of the cogito and its dependence on a categorically objectified other to defend itself against anxiety. Nowhere is this parody more fully developed in *An Actor's Revenge* than in the treatment of gender. The juxtaposition of *onnagatta* and actress in a love scene generates contradictory tensions that cannot be resolved within any expectation of a unified text. This juxtaposition recalls the same mix of performers of female roles in Shimpa, at the "origins" of "modern cinema," but here recedes into an indeterminacy that cannot be contained by an imaginary progress toward one representation or the other.

This destabilization rests on the simple device of sustaining the images of both *onnagatta* and actress within the conventions of a love scene characteristic of realist continuity, inviting the same emotional transference and identification with character that classic cinema constructs. As a result, the viewing subject is placed in an untenable position. It is not just that identification is undermined by transgressive sexual implications, but that those implications become undecidable. If the images of what appear to be two women together suggest a lesbian relationship, then an eroticized image of an *onnagatta* as a male offstage also shifts the appearance of female costume toward transvestism. Is the woman a voyeuristic object of male desire mirrored back by the man's cross-dressing? Or the man an image of the woman's narcissistic desire for a weak *namaeme,* literalized in the form of emasculation? The effect of receding mirrors earlier observed both textually and intertextually is here reinscribed at the position of emotional identification to trouble the formation of the subject.

One might object that such tensions are a mirage created by seeing the film out of context, that *onnagatta* are completely conventional in Japanese tradition and that only Westerners would imagine sexual complexity by misreading an *onnagatta* as if he were a transvestite. Yet this objection overlooks the 1958 passage of the antiprostitution law in Japan, a law designed to bring Japanese sexual practices into conformity with the appearances demanded by the West. It also overlooks Ichikawa's many previous films, such as *Conflagration* (1958), *Odd Obsession* (*Kagi,* 1959), *Bonchi* (1960), and *The Outcast* (1962), which specifically represent a neurotic or perverse psychology in a Japanese context, some adapted from novels by Tanazaki and Mishima, which themselves are psychoanalytically informed. Since the Meiji period, numerous translations of Western texts (both books and films) have circulated in Japan, often the same texts through which Westerners develop their own unconscious assumptions or reading formations through which they interpret the world. Unavoidably, many Japanese have become well aware of how Westerners are likely to view certain things, and have often incorporated Western discursive formations into their own work. Tanazaki and Mishima are but two examples. Wim Wenders's nostalgia in *Tokyo-ga* for an imaginary Ozu-style Japan to the contrary, no pure Japan has ever existed. This fantasy is of recent invention, and is inextricably linked in Japan with a xenophobic and authoritarian right wing seeking justification for an imaginary cultural superiority over Japan's Asian neighbors and the West. In the United States, a fantasy of an innate Japanese difference is linked with a similar narcissism, one that imagines that only ignorance of Western formations of knowledge and power would explain any limit to American cultural totalization.

Cultural difference remains, but not through ignorance of the West. Multiple determinants always affect the complex intertextual formations we call culture, never any single source. Accordingly, as *An Actor's Revenge* seems to demonstrate so well, texts can be constructed that invite multiple and even contradictory readings. The process of cross-cultural translation is unavoidable, and the film functioned from the outset in both Japanese and Western readings, a doubling that contributes to its effect of receding mirrors.

For Lacan, of course, mirror identifications are a mark of the mirror stage and its unavoidable component of undifferentiated aggressivity.[43] Lacan argues that during the period when a child first identifies the image in the mirror as a signifier of the self, that image is still relatively undifferentiated and remains transferable among other children. This phenomenon, which he terms a transitive relationship, means that children at this stage are unable to distinguish conceptually between others and themselves. Transitivism leads to both the spontaneous identification of children with one another, and simultaneously to intense unresolvable disputes whenever desires come into conflict, since the child has no conceptual apparatus to clearly distinguish intersubjective difference. For Lacan, this apparatus requires the locating of the self in language, a project accomplished through gender differentiation. Accordingly, Lacan warns against appeals to emotional identification, often produced in the name of "humanism," as a means of resolving conflict.

In these terms, the undecidability of gender relationship in the *onnagatta*/actress love scenes becomes a mark of its cinematic "language" and its displacement of fetishized love object toward a representation of *jouissance*. Located at the site of narrative and visual mirroring, *onnagatta* and actress become interchangeable or transitive. The classic realist camera image that constitutes woman as the object of the gaze is equated with the theatrical construction of the idealized female object by the male. In other words, the realist image that embeds woman in a naturalized objectification is itself seen as a mask, and the "truth" of the realist image is recast as a mask of power.

The formation of the body in representation becomes a contested terrain through the sexually ambiguous figure of Yukinojo, so that mastery of the other by reduction to a unitary object becomes impossible. Reciprocally, the plural representation of gender raises the questions of authorship and authority in textual construction. Ichikawa has never been identified with the single set of concerns classically used to identify the body of work belonging to an auteur. Instead, his work has been remarkably diverse and open to a play of contradictory forms similarly impossible to master by reduction to a unitary object.

In Yukinojo, the body becomes a scene of teaching, in the sense in which Gregory Ulmer refers to Lacan's seminars as a combination of the psychoanalytic scene and pedagogy. However, here the disciplinary boundaries that frame the possibility of the subject are themselves called into question.

Psychoanalysis/Melodrama/Other

Who is watching, or is expected to watch, a Japanese film? How does a Japanese film assume and imply an imaginary viewer as ideal position from which to experience the diegesis? The issue at stake in these questions is how to develop theoretical models for the construction of subject positions in non-Western cinemas, a problem that can be approached through the specific site of Japanese film. Accordingly, I would like to consider the metapsychological construction of a subject prior to the possibility of a voice, and the shifting or reinscription of subjectivity in a modernizing culture, by setting Naruse's *Sound of the Mountain* (1954) next to Ichikawa's *An Actor's Revenge* (1963).

The interest in writing about Japanese subject formation is that the stakes are very high. There is no legitimate way to extract questions of subjectivity from related discourses of history or national identity and their reciprocal implications in language, writing, and representation. At the current historical moment, postmodernism and postcolonialism intersect to problematize all past discourses that depend on the universalisms of a grand narrative. As a post-Lacanian project, the consideration of cross-cultural subjectivity can trace one genealogical derivation from Alexander Kojève's lectures on Hegel in the 1930s as a key break in the dominant dialectical discourse of Western thought.[44] Echoes of this break can be found in Lacan's "Agency of the Letter in the Unconscious or Reason Since Freud" (1957),[45] in which psychoanalysis can be discussed only in relation to writing and philosophy, and in Derrida's *Post Card* (1980), in which Freud is situated within the dialectical tradition between Plato and Hegel.

Alleged Impossibility

The alleged impossibility of psychoanalysis in Japan has most often been argued according to a cultural difference between Western and Japanese constructions of subjectivity.

In these terms, psychoanalysis has been argued to be relevant only to the Western construction of an interiorized subject, or cogito. Takatsugu Sasaki of the Groupe Franco-Japonais du Champ Freudien cites Kojève in this regard:

> Il l'a écrite au retour de son voyage au Japon, en 1959: "Tous les Japonais sans exception sont actuellement en état de vivre en fonction de valeurs totalement formalisées, c'est-à-dire complètement vidées de tout contenu 'humain' au sens d'"historique.' Ainsi, à la limite, tout Japonais est en principe capable de procéder, par snobisme, à un suicide parfaitement 'gratuit.'"

> He wrote on return from his voyage to Japan, in 1959: "All Japanese without exception are presently in a state of living by function of totally formalised values, that is to say completely empty of all 'human' content in the 'historical' sense. Hence, at the limit, all Japanese are in principle capable of proceeding, by snobbism, to a perfectly 'gratuitous' suicide."[46]

Sasaki notes the connotation of Hegel in Kojève's use of the term "historical" in this quotation and the anticipation of Mishima's suicide a decade later. Interestingly, Sasaki not only concurs but then argues (in 1988) that the situation remains unchanged in Japan. Roland Barthes, in *Empire of Signs,* presumably derives his articulation of Japanese culture as empty from Kojève's earlier comments. Barthes's and Noël Burch's still-later interest in Japanese culture as the absence of Western historical humanism can rightly be criticized as a sophisticated form of Orientalism. Sasaki's interest, however, seems to be in the break between Japanese formalization and a humanist subject.

Sasaki credits Takeo Doi as the sole exception to a general absence of psychoanalytic research in Japan before the Groupe Franco-Japonais du Champ Freudien. Doi theorized oppositions between *ura* (reverse side, like the lining of a coat; related in Doi's use to *kokoro,* mind-heart) and *omote* (face), and between *uchi* (in-group) and *soto* (outside). He argued that *amae* characterized relationships within any in-group or *uchi,* such that subjectivity operated as a shifting relational process within a group, rather than by the Western expectation of an interiority separate from a social other. *Uchi* can be variable and can range from the family to one's coworkers to the nation as a whole, but in each case *uchi* is opposed to those outside the group with whom one is not intimate. Intersecting with the *uchi*/*soto* distinction, but not identical to it, is the *ura*/*omote* division. *Omote,* or face, is the formalized public appearance that the Japanese subject constructs in a social context. *Ura,* variously translated as the reverse, wrong, back, or other side (as in the palm of the hand, the tail of a coin, or the flip side of a record), represents one's deepest feelings apart from one's public face, and is often in conflict with *omote*. *Ura* might be spoken within an *uchi,* but it would never be expressed in public. Doi argued that these distinctions function quite differently from the inner/outer and mind/body oppositions familiar to Western metaphysics, whereby the inner/outer distinction is mapped onto cogito/other (individual self/group) rather than *uchi*/*soto* (in-group/outside). These theoretical distinctions help account for psychological differences between individuals raised according to the different child-rearing practices between Japan and the United States. Traces of these distinctions can be found throughout Japanese cinema, both in representations of the individual and family, and throughout Japanese culture, specifically in the construction of space. Later, I will discuss the importance of spatial representation in Naruse's film *The Sound of the Mountain* (*Yama no oto*, 1954) to articulate the conflict of tradition and modernization in Japan.

The Sound of the Mountain represents as well several difficulties with Doi's theoretical distinctions. First, Japanese culture is now (has always already been) irretrievably hybrid. The traditional subject position articulated in Doi's *amae/uchi* is shattered by Kikuko's break from her family to an enforced individualized independence. Furthermore, that break is already inscribed by its representation in novel or film, both artistic modes of representation borrowed from the West. Second, as noted earlier, Doi's representation of a subject constituted through a relational group process is unavoidably pejorative. Doi's *amae*, or dependency, is a concept figured from the outset as inferior to Western independence and the humanist values dominant at the time of Doi's writing.

Ironically, Doi's assertion of a distinctive Japanese psyche is both imaginary in its assumed categorical isolation from the West and imagined to be inferior to the West it imagines as separate. National difference is simultaneously asserted and subordinated to the West, parallel to the emergence of a "New" Japan in the 1950s–1960s within the Cold War alliance led by the United States. Herein lies the third problem with Doi: its structural inability to historicize the language through which it constitutes its psychological difference.

The post-Lacanian Groupe Franco-Japonais du Champ Freudien both marks the limits of Doi's approach and relocates research at precisely those boundaries of psyche, language, and history that Doi's psychology is structurally unable to address. Hiroyuki Akama, Shin'ya Ogasawara, Kunifumi Suzuki, and others all examine characteristics of Japanese language in relation to the question of psychoanalysis in Japan. Takatsugu Sasaki specifically reconsiders the problem of a relational subject through M. Arimasa Mori's investigation of Japanese shifters, thereby avoiding the problem of *amae*'s imaginary inferiority to humanism.[47] Sasaki also describes Mori as having taught Japanese for more than twenty years in Paris to French students, thereby also repeating his own repositioning of theory from an imaginary cultural purity to a site of cross-cultural hybridity.

M. Mori, according to Sasaki, argues that Japanese shifters function as second-person address, making it almost impossible to speak in the first person in reference to a third. Mori calls this characteristic of the Japanese language a "binary rapport" (*rapport binaire*) and describes the function of the Japanese *je* (*watashi*) as a "*tu pour toi*," an intimate you for the other you with whom one speaks. According to Sasaki, the Lacanian concepts of the other and, even more problematically, the Other (*le grand Autre*) are thereby virtually inexpressible in Japanese. Elsewhere, Tooru Takahashi has similarly argued that psychoanalytic therapy is impossible in Japan, because the analysand's *je* is inextricably implicated in the analyst's discourse, making the isolation of an interior string of verbal associations impossible.[48] Sasaki and Takahashi seem to agree that psychoanalysis in Japan can work only as a theoretical project apart from therapeutic practice.

However, at this point the Groupe Franco-Japonais du Champ Freudien may perhaps reach its own limit, being unable to address problems of writing within the language-centered discourse of what now circulates under the name of Lacanian methodology. In *The Sound of the Mountain,* the psychological isolation of an individualized *je* is not absent from Japanese culture, but has perhaps been inscribed as much through the visual representation of film as it has through verbal language. Kikuko achieves the ambiguous perils of independence in a garden constructed for the deep space of visual perspective, in short, in a "landscape," as Kojin Karatani uses the term to suggest the Western prepositioning of space prior to the centering of an individual subject within it.[49] The camera space of film and television may have functioned throughout the twentieth century to problematize the traditional Japanese subject by dislocating the viewer into an alien construction of space, as an extension of and parallel to the *watakashi-shosetsu* (or "I-novel") literary movement that Karatani ironically deconstructs in his *Origin of Modern Japanese Literature.* This ideological construction of the cinematic and televisual apparatus pre-exists its adaptation for traditional Japanese aesthetics and concerns, thereby hybridizing even "the most Japanese" of filmmakers, such as Ozu or Naruse, as part of their textual project.

A Textual Unconscious

Lacan's emphasis on the agency of the letter within the discourse of the unconscious calls attention to writing in its constitution of a subject, also theorized as inextricably bound up with an other. At this point, Derrida intersects with Lacan in such texts as *The Post Card, The Purloined Poe,* and *Taking Chances* and provides a means to rethink the assumed basis of psychoanalytic theory in individualized therapeutic practice.[50] Instead, the problematics of the text emerge as preceding the constitution of subject and other already assumed in clinical therapy (itself embedded in medical discourse). The question is not that therapy becomes impossible or irrelevant here, but that it can be approached only by means of the text. What then characterizes the intersection of psychoanalysis and text in Japan? In these terms, melodrama is a performative text that can be conceived as in some sense "preceding" psychoanalysis, by configuring the metaphysical relationships of the family in a public space prior to the formation of subjectivity.

As is well known from Peter Brooks, melodramatic formulas and stereotypes function as an allegory of psychoanalytic forces within the family rather than as a "realist" representation of an interiorized psychology within individual characters. Although deriving historically from theatrical innovations linked to the secularization of ethical values after the French Revolution, melodrama became mass-produced as a model for cinema at the same historical moment that Freud first theorized the unconscious. Melodrama preceded cinema as a Western import to Japan, where it also became a model for narrative film, but it became mixed in Japanese culture with the theatrical traditions of Kabuki deriving from popular culture during the Tokugawa regime. As discussed above, the play of melodrama and visual realism in Ichikawa's *An Actor's Revenge* functions to problematize social class and gender positioning. In this film, satirical metadiscourses of social class power and gender positioning destabilize any single subjective identification and introduces instead a paradoxical shifting subjectivity that is alternately centered and decentered. The representational playfulness that so strongly characterizes this film functions in part to foreground the space, or "landscape," within which subjectivity is figured. At the same time, a shifting subjectivity is constituted across multiple spaces that work to foreground the process of inscription prior to the possibility of a subject.

The question of the subject in its relation to writing leads through issues that arise in the Japanese reading of Lacan, as in Takatsugu Sasaki's essay "Mettre la psychanalyse en japonais," and the attempt to imagine the operation of the kanji (Chinese characters) in the unconscious. The role of cinema is pivotal here, as a nonalphabetic writing that circulates simultaneously with kanji in positioning a multiple and shifting subjectivity in postmodern Japan.

In this context, the reputed impossibility of psychoanalysis in Japan can be linked with Peter Brooks's argued parallelism between melodrama and psychoanalysis, to consider melodrama in Japanese film as a metapsychology mapping the possibility of a Westernized subject since the time of the Meiji modernization. Brooks argues that melodrama can be considered as an allegory of psychoanalytic forces, yet theorists from Lacan to Tooru Takahashi have questioned whether a subject of psychoanalysis is possible in Japan without the logocentric traditions that construct the Western cogito. By reading melodrama in terms of conflicting formations of subjectivity in Japan, cinema can be understood in parallel with Karatani's postmodernist critique of the Meiji era *watakushi-shosetsu* (or "I-novel" experiments with first-person narrative).

4
Kyoto/Venezia

I see a ruined gate, where the rain continues to fall. The site has been abandoned for some time now, either for newer areas of development or as an unpleasant reminder of past injustices and devastation. Yet the gate still shimmers with ghosts, phantasms, specters.

Samurai Humanism

Rashomon was released in Tokyo in August 1950 and went on to win the Grand Prize at the Venice Festival in 1951, and then the Academy Award for Best Foreign Film in 1952. The film marks a juncture between film history conceived as an exclusive development of Western Europe and the United States and a world cinema including "non-Western" societies. Japanese Film History, in a sense, "begins" here: not because the West "discovered" Japan, or because Japan first achieved international acclaim, but because previously isolated lines of development from Asia and the West first intersected at this point.

This juncture then transformed all earlier Japanese film into a progression leading here, and all that followed into future departures. The discourses of Japanese Film History that pivot on *Rashomon* are still with us today, not only in Japan but throughout the world, as determining configurations that inhabit knowledge and power and mark its limits and possibilities. Any discussion of Japanese Film History today inevitably turns on a fundamental break in cultural history that begins to become accessible through a reconsideration of *Rashomon* as a text.

The public policy goal of Japan since the Meiji Restoration in 1868 had been to achieve world recognition parallel to that of Western nations, a goal achieved in one way for the first time at Venice. Since 1951, many other non-Western cinemas have joined Japan in world distribution and recognition, beginning with India in 1955, when Satyajit Ray's *Pather Panchali* premiered at the Museum of Modern Art in New York and then won recognition at Cannes. In subsequent decades, films from Latin America, China, Africa, Southeast Asia, and other parts of the world, as well as such minority cinemas as African

American film from within the United States, have gained access to world circulation and audiences, so that a world cinema today seems very different from the Euro-American context that controlled world markets through the end of the 1940s. *Rashomon* is a hinge not just between Japanese isolation and world recognition, but between dominant Western assumptions and the possibility of a genuine world cinema.

Rashomon, as a pivotal text that allows an initial approach to this cultural break, is not here conceived as a "masterpiece" or a work of "genius," despite its many celebrations in these terms. The auteurist rhetoric that greeted the film's initial appearance in the 1950s had the instrumental purpose of drawing attention to a film not previously known, but has since become part of a historical discourse as well. *Rashomon* together with its multiple critical receptions now form a set of artifacts from which we can address the problem of cultural change on the model of break and reconfiguration. To distinguish this complex of artifacts from an isolated reading of the film as pure object, we might consider *Rashomon* and its surrounding critical texts as the function R. Rather than seeing *Rashomon* as an important moment in film history, as if history itself were already known, we might better consider R as a break in thought, knowledge, and representation that reconstructs the assumptions on which historical narratives themselves are based.

Pivot

I understand "Japanese Film History" here as a mode of postwar discourse, parallel to the way Karatani writes of *The Origins of Modern Japanese Literature,* where the title is intended ironically and each word is meant to be conceived in brackets. The quest for an origin is inevitably a retrospective project to legitimize a current discourse, seeking to reconfigure the past as a mirror of the present. The question of origin is most strongly associated with the emergence of nationalism in the nineteenth century and its struggle for legitimation, and is bound up with the ideas of "Japan" and of "the modern" to produce a model for organizing time into a narrative of "history." After the interventions of poststructuralism, postmodernism, postcolonialism, and postnationalism, all these assumptions begin to seem arbitrary, begging the questions of how to write history and where to begin.

In order to reconsider an approach to the materials and organization of "history," I would like to reposition *Rashomon* and its multiple contexts as a pivotal site from which to "begin" to rethink time in relation to culture, and the specific constructions of "history" as interior to modes of discourse. As a pivotal site, *Rashomon* marks several junctures or intersections, each of which repositions the film at a gap between contexts rather than within a recognizable category. The film lies between the Occupation era and Japan's regaining of independence as a "modern nation." It also circulates between the "West" of the United States and Europe and the "East" of Asian culture, problematizing what either of these might mean. In addition, it marks a transition between Japanese film as a locally specific practice, partly as a result of deliberate isolationism and partly as an exclusion parallel to that of "race" films in the United States during the 1930s, and participation in a world cinema economy. At a later moment, *Rashomon* marks a juncture of contestation between Donald Richie's and Tadao Sato's conception of 1950s Japanese film as a "Golden Age," and Burch's argument for an alternative "golden age" in the 1930s that casts the 1950s as a decadence. None of these moves constitutes a simple "progress" or "decline" but instead opens on to a complex process of reconfiguration in which cinema reciprocally engages and is engaged by the dynamics of culture.

"Culture," of course, is as nonobvious a term as "history," but let me leave that aside for the moment, except to say that in this text both are considered as partial representations of what Georges Bataille calls a General Economy. The possibility of bringing all discourse to a halt by legitimately stopping to interrogate every term is only one of many potential occlusions that make it difficult to reconsider *Rashomon*.

Occlusions

Films from the 1950s now seem the most difficult for audiences to watch. They appear dated, old, forgettable. Films made today are so much "better," or mobilize political or theoretical arguments far more effectively. Why bother? Films like *Rashomon,* after all, have been abandoned for a reason. There are no computerized special effects, no ideological sophistication—only a name, which like "Los Angeles," "hysteria," or "Kleenex" has become a cliché, even while its etymological source has been forgotten.

A first problem that develops when *Rashomon* appears on screen is a tendency toward occlusion by one of two currently competing discourses. On the one hand, techno-corporate triumphalists may dismiss the film as "primitive" or, conversely, appropriate it as a kind of camp or nostalgia. Cultural critics, on the other hand, can equally dismiss the film as a sellout to American ideology and domination, negating the cultural identity of Japan that needs to be rediscovered as counterpoint to Western hegemony. Both of these initial responses, however, share the characteristic of rereading the past in terms of the present and claiming an "accuracy" of interpretation for developments outside the parameters of the film in its own context. Such a reading is not simply "wrong," especially if it proceeds by deliberate misreading for innovative effect, but can be deeply misleading if it obscures the context and available resources through which a filmic text was initially configured. A first problem, then, requires learning how to set aside current discourses and return to a textual zero from which to imaginatively reconstitute the film on its own terms. If such a zero is ultimately impossible, it is also necessary as at least a theoretical position from which to begin.

Another kind of occlusion comes from disorientation and a sense of semiotic weightlessness, which occurs once the imaginary ground of one's own current discourse is suspended. Like a cosmonaut trying to read English in the Roman alphabet (*romaji* in Japanese) on the International Space Station, basic textual communication can suddenly seem illegible. If a film cannot be simply appropriated to a current discourse or knowledge system, then where does one begin? Surely one knows too little to say anything, and the text remains closed to those outside the language, the culture, the period. Those who are most committed to the ethics of cultural difference are ironically those who become most disempowered by this kind of *aporia*. As a result, responsible viewers can become isolated from fundamentally different texts, imagining that ethical refusal constitutes the only possible reading. Yet this is precisely where textual analysis begins and why it is important as a strategy.

If one cannot know the intentions of the filmmaker or share the context of the film's production, the film becomes a Deleuzian machine at first approach. Representations are already suspended from the kind of artificial groundings in "interpretation" that Deleuze and Guattari warn us against in *Kafka,*[1] and we are left with a set of figures and discourses that multiply intersect and form configurations on their own terms. Initially, as with attempting to decipher an untranslated language, the viewer looks for repeating patterns across contexts, to accumulate links and connections to specific images. Unlike verbal language, the sound and visual text of film opens relatively quickly to this kind of reading, which is why the medium is important in a multicultural world. Film represents perhaps the easiest access available to being inside an alternative cultural context, and it may be fundamental to developing the heterological skills necessary to navigate and negotiate in today's information economy.

Even though this effect may be strongest for a viewer outside Japan, it occurs inside as well. The younger generation in Japan tends to consider Japanese film as something from the past, and relatively unimportant in an electronic era of high-definition television, computers, and video games. Japan never considered *Rashomon* that important, and industry representatives were supposedly amazed when Giuliana Stramigioli, head of Italiafilm, recommended that it be sent to Venice for the 1951 festival competition. According to Donald Richie, Japanese critics had not liked the film, and everyone in the industry was shocked when it won the grand prize. The question might well be raised, then, Whose film is it? A Japanese viewer might well seek insider knowledge from a Western viewer, asking why the West responded so strongly to such an unlikely film.

When I was in Tokyo, a representative of the film industry once told me an anecdote that might illuminate this dilemma precisely by its opacity. Japanese film executives, according to this anecdote, were so mystified that the West liked *Rashomon* that they puzzled endlessly over the possible cause. Eventually, they decided it must be because Westerners like gates (*Rasho mon* means "the Rasho Gate" in Japanese), and rushed into production such other "gate" films as *Gate of Hell,* and so on. In the United States, this story often provokes anxieties that some kind of racist trivialization of Japanese intelligence is implied, a reaction that ironically only adds to its narrative significance. In Japan, self-deprecatory remarks and jokes are a conventional part of social courtesy and seem at times inversely proportional to the degree of status or power actually held by the speaker. This difference in social courtesies often makes an important Japanese speaker seem absurdly modest to an American, and an American who cites his or her accomplishments seem rude and boastful to a Japanese. The mutual misrecognition involved in such an exchange mirrors what I take to be the narrative of the joke itself, which is that communication across cultural contexts is not obvious even to extremely intelligent and capable people.

Insofar as Western and Japanese viewers look to each other for explanations of *Rashomon,* the film's reception devolves to a hermeneutic wish that someone else somewhere knows the secret code that explains its significance and effects. Precisely because insider knowledge is no necessary help in this unlikely case, the film becomes an excellent place to begin. *Rashomon,* in short, approaches a theoretical limit of zero all around, with all potential viewers as equally outsiders.

Necessarily beginning, then, with what Deleuze and Guattari call an "experimental" reading, an outsider can decode the text from within through an engagement with repeating configurations of images, links, and connections. Once launched on this process, the text is not sealed from outside contexts but inverts the usual status of critical materials surrounding a film. Rather than assuming that a film is an illustration for an established interpretation, the film instead becomes the primary visual text and all other critical materials become secondary to it. Beginning with the image text on its own terms, all relevant contexts can become reconfigured by the film, rather than the other way around. In other words, rather than fitting *Rashomon* into "history" as preconceived, *Rashomon* can itself be read as a narrative of history, a propositional argument addressing how narratives of history can and must be constructed.

A last occlusion I will discuss here that interferes with an initial reading of *Rashomon* is the assumption that images are secondary or supplementary to writing. Even for enthusiasts of Derrida, the idea that "writing" needs to be reconceived to include more than a literary text seems difficult in the United States, where the reception of Derrida's work has been shaped by his initial repurposing for literary criticism. If film is conceived as a "writing" of its own, and not just an illustration of a script, then its specificity might be located in an unanticipated capacity for combining thought and feeling, outside the assumptions of Western metaphysics that prepositions mind and body as opposites. As a Deleuzian machine, cinematic writing can be conceived as operating without originary legitimation through an artist's intentions and instead generates effects as an autonomous text, parallel to such other verbal texts as *Kafka*. Through what Deleuze describes as the "movement-image," cinema writes in terms of dynamic figures parallel to concepts.[2] In these terms, cinematic sequences are not only emotionally engaging, but simultaneously function as propositional arguments. One of the primary accomplishments of Deleuze's works on cinema is the argument that cinema operates "alongside" or next to philosophy, rather than being an illustration of or a supplement to it.[3] In the same way, I read *Rashomon* and all other films as propositional arguments addressing the demands of history "next to" more traditional texts on history in kanji or *romaji*.

Rewriting Japanese Film History

Alan Bass explains in "L Before K" that "one of the major concerns of [Derrida's] *The Post Card* is the possible subversion of what is usually taken as a fixed sequence—e.g. Socrates before Plato, the passing of an inheritance from a prior generation to a succeeding one, the death of the old before the young. What if the usual and seemingly fixed sequence were reversible? What if each term of the sequence contained within itself the principle that subverts the usual progression? What could there be between each term and itself that would operate this subversion?"

I would like to argue, and not simply for the sake of being theoretically perverse (although sometimes this can be an interesting option), that Japanese Film History begins in 1951, the year that Kurosawa's *Rashomon* won first prize in Venice. I am not suggesting, of course, that Japanese film appeared *ad nihilo* at this moment, that no Japanese films were ever produced before the American Occupation, or that film had never before been conceived in historical terms by Japanese writers. Nor am I suggesting that only the West can legitimize films and the writing of history, nor even less that the publication of a history in English establishes any particular significance.

By perverse, I mean the risk of seeming to raise the specter of Western ethnocentrism in a project to provide an exteriorization and critique of it. Precisely because it has become so difficult to accept the naturalized ideologies of 1950s films and critical histories, it becomes challenging to imagine an era in which such assumptions were not only possible but were invisible and unconscious. In order to reach this point, I would like to suggest that *Rashomon* can be considered not just as a narrative in history, but a foundational narrative of modern history.

In this approach, 1951 marks the convergence of several different trajectories that, once met, transformed the writing of Japanese Film History both retrospectively and successively, such that it is difficult even today to think past the limits of the historical model that achieved hegemonic transparency at this moment. The multiple threads that formed this convergence include not only the prize at Venice, but the eventual publication of *The Japanese Film: Art and Industry* by Anderson and Richie in 1959, and the regulatory dislocation of the Japanese film industry exercised by the American Occupation forces between 1945 and 1952. In other words, 1951 represents an epistemological break in the relationships among Japan, cinema, and history in both Japan and the West that allows us to rethink Japanese Film History in genealogical terms.

Books and essays on Japanese Film History written today continue to appeal to such classical categories as nation, period, genre, and auteur, as if these classifications could negotiate the problems of postmodern and postcolonial hybridity, intersecting diasporas and nomadic thought. The textual heritage that continues to generate these categories pivots in the field of Japanese Film History on *Rashomon*/1951. A genealogy of this mode of writing history leads to a deconstruction of the trajectories and forces that intersect at this site.

A genealogical approach, as Foucault argues beginning in *Madness and Civilization,* demands that we reconsider history as it is conceived from within the process of historical change, by means of discursive and institutional formations of power susceptible to collapse and reconfiguration. In part, this asks us to recognize the point within discourse at which it first becomes possible to think historically in specific terms that are later reimagined as if universal. This point of break or rupture is never simply identifiable with a single date, person, or event, but can be indirectly observed through conflicted representations across a series of incidents and artifacts that symptomatically embody a radical dislocation of figures and discourses. The year "1951" marks one such break, one that is worked through by the time of Anderson and Richie's text and is anticipated by postwar transformation, but does not simply progress or develop from the one to the other. The prize

at Venice instead marks the point at which postwar change can be reconceived as a progress toward *Rashomon* as international event, and imply a later explicatory development
of this newly possible circumstance.

If international acclaim seems to recontextualize Japanese film within the postwar
humanism of the West, international recontextualization is in turn appropriated by Japan
as the medium of a new postwar cultural identity. In other words, Japan tacitly and
remarkably turns Western appropriation on its head by redeploying the figural determinants of Western discourse for its own ends. In response to the Reverse Course of American Occupation policy from 1948 to 1952, Japan invents a Reverse Appropriation to
translate and reconfigure Western tropes for different effects, as a foundational move
that makes a postwar modern Japan possible, unexpected, and innovative. By the 1970s,
the Western system of dating is incorporated into conversational Japanese, as Karatani
attests, shifting a normative sense of time from imperial reigns to the humanist teleology
implied by a "common era." This shift of temporality is prefigured by narrative production during the 1950s, especially in film, where humanist conventions of narrative construction become the vehicle for a reconfigured cultural text. In retrospect, *Rashomon* acts
as a hinge between modalities of time and cultural context at stake in a moment of radical break. To recover the multiple possibilities of a text occluded by ideological positioning, one can begin by rereading *Rashomon* as the initiating text of Japanese Film History.[4]

Godzilla Meets the Uffizi

Rashomon is the explicit point of departure for writing *The Japanese Film: Art and Industry,* as Anderson and Richie explain in their Authors' Foreword:

> Ten years ago this book would never have been written; there was a need for it but no
> audience. That there is more of a need now not only reflects the increased excellence of
> Japanese films during the past decade but also the world-wide interest which this excel-
> lence has aroused. One of the last film industries to create a national style, the Japanese is
> now one of the last to retain it.
>
> A major point this book will attempt to make is that, long before *Rashomon,* the Japanese
> cinema had attained a level which deserved but did not receive international recognition.

In other words, *Rashomon*'s success is pivotal in the constitution of Japanese film as a
national cinema within international discourse, and it creates the possibility of a retrospective historicization to account for its emergence.

At the same time, a genealogical approach also demands that we reconsider what we
imagine to be unities, and recognize fractures and dislocations where we assume there
are only additions and corrections to an established model. *Rashomon*'s prize at Venice
means several different things in different contexts, some of which are deeply in conflict.
To the West, it suggested that Japanese film had matured to the point where international
recognition was deserved, even though in retrospect later theorists beginning with Noël

Burch question whether the stylistic shifts that characterize Japanese films of the 1950s might not as easily be considered a decline. To Japan, it meant that Western recognition, in one sense the overriding goal of national policy since the Meiji era, had at last been achieved. Long-standing bitterness associated with Western assumptions of superiority, from Commodore Perry's incursion in 1853 and the Triple Intervention of 1895, to Eisenstein's dismissal of Japanese filmmaking as uninteresting, finally had a resolution in a narrative of success.

Rashomon marks a moment when the contestations of Western and Japanese imperialisms had apparently been resolved after extensive and intensive violence, and Japan had finally found a place in the world economy. That this place is now once again necessarily contested only further demands that we reconsider how that place was first established, as a point of departure for all that has happened since. The obstacles to rethinking history in this way are so numerous as to defy consideration here, but often they derive from an internalized violence that marks the construction of a world framework at this moment. It is easier by far to rely on the supposed neutrality of a chronological list of events, as if this constituted history, beginning from a nominally arbitrary "origin" such as the invention of cinema and proceeding in sequence through to the present. However, this constitutes its own violence against history and forecloses the kind of project I would like to join here, namely, to consider not just what has happened but how history works.

It is important to remember that the organization of history as a chronological sequence beginning from an origin is itself a relatively recent strategy for understanding culture through time, and it is linked both to the nineteenth century as a specific context and to the hierarchical categorization of knowledge into specializations. As discussed earlier, it was not until the mid-nineteenth century that the Uffizi Gallery in Florence was reorganized so that the collected materials were redistributed to specific institutions according to categorical types. Painting was gathered at the Uffizi, sculpture went to the Bargello, and artifacts were relocated to the newly created Museo Archeologico. The materials were then arranged in chronological sequence to emphasize their "development." Foucault destabilizes this arrangement by declining to accept the idea of Western civilization as an unbroken developmental unity from the Renaissance to the twentieth century. He argues instead that many conflicting discourses and epistemes characterize the West, and that the idea of developmental unity is one such specific discourse, itself identifiable with the nineteenth century, which might in turn be linked to the mass culture of industrialization and the formation of national identities.

The Pitti Palace across the Arno River in Florence, which retains the mode of organization in practice prior to this reorganization, exhibits a mixture of different types and periods of art arranged for effect. After Lyotard, we might consider the Pitti's mode of display as a rhetoric of visual images rather than the logical discourse of the Uffizi and its companion institutions. As such, the Pitti's rhetoric of images inhabits the discourse of art history in the same way that Derrida argues that the tropes of literature inhabit philosophical discourse. Art history, in turn, is the model for writing histories of cinema, regulated by the assumption that cinema is a new but still categorically separable mode of art comparable to the difference in media between painting and sculpture.

The postmodern questioning of such assumptions derives from the very different argument that multiple media and the various arts are all implicated in one another as modes of textuality, and that texts are always deeply embedded in the specific cultural and historical contexts from which they emerge. The implications of these questions for film history, although substantially begun by such books as Deleuze's *Cinema* and the collaborative text on the French cinema of the 1930s, *Générique des années 30,* by Michèle Lagny, Marie-Claire Ropars-Wuilleumier, Pierre Sorlin, and Genière Nesterenko, is far from concluded, and is still only beginning to be thought in relation to questions of cultural difference outside the West.

Rashomon as Hinge Text

Rashomon/1951 provides a site in and of textual history through which we can consider a number of interesting possibilities that make possible a rethinking of history, film, and Japan, in part parallel to the historiography of Kittler. In Kittler's work, as described by David Welbury, the dates 1800 and 1900 denote "discourse networks—the linkages of power, technologies, signifying marks and bodies—that have orchestrated European culture for the past two hundred years." Here "1951" also functions like such dates as 1947, 1874, 1933, 1730, and 1227 that punctuate Deleuze and Guattari's *Thousand Plateaus,* and map the intersections of conflicting cultural configurations with specific moments in history. Such junctural moments open onto an array of discourses, beginnings, and effects. Foucault, Kittler, and Deleuze and Guattari suggest a number of such strategies and models to reopen history as a question, rather than prefigure it as a closure, a finished product, an already-known.

As one beginning, the title *Rashomon* itself has become a trope in the English language, spoken in the public media (sometimes even used as a verb) as a term suggesting cultural or ethical relativity, and in more recent usage as an undecidable situation of multiple conflicting stories. As such, the word has come to function within popular culture to name a phenomenon similar to what Derrida would call "undecidability," or what Lyotard would describe as a "differend." *Rashomon* has also been written about rapaciously, and has become one of the most noted and interpreted films of the entire century among both journalists and scholars. At the same time, the film itself has virtually vanished from view and is rarely exhibited or seen today despite its availability on videotape and DVD. In other words, *Rashomon* has become a cultural marker that everyone takes for granted and no one consciously considers, as with most figures of speech. This is the figure, I would argue, that inhabits all of Japanese film history and makes it possible.

As another beginning, the story of *Rashomon* is, if not well known, at least readily recoverable. At the end of the Heian era, a crime occurs, and four different conflicting versions are reported in a police court. These conflicting reports are retold under the ruined gate of Kyoto in the rain, after which one of the story re-tellers adopts a baby found near the gate as his own, and a priest says his faith in man has been restored.

The story of the story is also readily available. Its basis can be found in two stories by Ryunosuke Akutagawa called "Rashomon," from which little was taken except the image of the gate and its period in time, and "In a Grove," which consists of seven separate and conflicting testimonies before a police court without other explanation or conclusion. These stories were adapted by Kurosawa with the addition of a framing narrative to introduce and resolve the material. The film's popular reception in the West seems to have been related to both its novelty as a relativistic narrative and to its exotic locale, historically set in "medieval" Japan. If placed in history as a developmental sequence, the film seems to allegorize the Japanese experience of World War II as a period of uncertainty and violence, followed by hope for a new future.

After that, the film becomes more complicated, and the text seems to break down. The film's reception seems irretrievably split between modernist and classicist discourses, which read very different implications from the film, while the film itself is divided between the Akutagawa narratives and Kurosawa's additions in a way that eludes easy, or any, resolution. Despite its figural unity as a term in everyday speech, *Rashomon* as text quickly collapses into a series of incommensurable projects, only one of which is the relativistic narrative commonly acknowledged.

The prospect of *Rashomon* as multiple incommensurabilities, or narrative mise-en-abîme, marks its different position as constituting history as such, or an idea of history that makes its narrativization in relation to certain ideas of "film" and "Japan" possible. This positioning of *Rashomon* considers it as a hinge text, between two epistemes or cultural configurations, that constitutes the possibility of a recognizable national cinema in a world context. As such, it makes new modes of narrative possible within the determining figures of a new episteme, but, simultaneously, it remains filled with unresolved traces of the break between epistemes. The new episteme instituted by *Rashomon,* which has often been called the "golden era" of Japanese humanist films, then departs from the figural determinants of its initiating text while repressing its instabilities and uncertainties. Eventually, this means repressing the film itself, which begins to appear "dated" or even unwatchable because it does not operate according to the figural determinants that it institutes.

The conflicting modernist and classicist discourses that regulated *Rashomon*'s reception now make the film appear to be proto-postmodern, a film that is doubly encoded, to use Charles Jencks's phrase, in both classical and modernist modes. To historicize the film, however, which here means to recognize *Rashomon*'s role as metahistorical, requires us to remember that the possibility of reading classical and modernist codes at once would remain unthinkable for several decades. One basis of *Rashomon*'s status as conflicted text is the assumption before postmodernism that classical and modernist approaches mutually exclude each other.

By classicist discourse, I mean the reading of the film in terms of Classical Hollywood Cinema, a reading that seeks to ground the film by means of humanist identification, logical unity, and narrative closure. In these terms, the film becomes a hermeneutic puzzle, challenging the audience to solve the film as problem and determine the single true story as if obscured by multiple conflicting reports. Richie proposes such a model, although he discards it, and one part of the critical response to the film depended on this approach.

By modernist discourse, I mean an engagement with narrative fragmentation, stylistic innovation, and moral relativism. The alternative critical response to *Rashomon* was that it precisely denies any single "correct" reading and insists that all truth is relative and "subjective." Because of its containment of narrative indeterminacy within the ideological construction of subjectivity, this discourse also celebrates *Rashomon* as foundationally based in the creativity of Kurosawa as individual artist.

Modernism by the 1950s was safely established within the domain of the museum world, specifically as painting within the gallery circuit of New York City, as regulated by the influence of the Museum of Modern Art and the critical discourse of Clement Greenberg. Film, however, was dominated by the commercial Hollywood industry in a way unprecedented before the war. For Japanese film to cross over from a local, isolated Japanese audience to a world audience dominated by the U.S. economy required a shift from a modernist appreciation of Japanese aesthetics to a popular identification with humanist characters and narratives.

One of the ironies of *Rashomon* is that it seems to have taken a modernist critical discourse to initially celebrate its narrative innovations, but its popular reception opened the possibility of Japanese film distribution on the world market in an era of humanist films. Conflicting cultural configurations are afterward hierarchically resolved by subordinating "Japanese" materials such as mise-en-scène to a humanist narrative structure and trajectory, as in *Throne of Blood, Ugetsu, Sansho the Bailiff, Life of Oharu,* and the many other historical narratives that dominated foreign distribution of Japanese films in the 1950s. This "aesthetic" or stylistic arrangement mimes the power relations between U.S. ideological humanism and Japanese subordination to it, but power is disguised under the name of "style" in order to conform to the prevailing ideological norms.

Folds in Time

If humanist films become possible through the success of *Rashomon,* then we can also read backward to consider what came before this determining break. The "before," in this case, is not locatable in the immediately preceding years of the postwar era but is constituted by a leap to the 1920s. The choice of Akutagawa as source of literary material for adaptation to the screen is neither an accident nor a neutral choice from across an evenly distributed array of possible Japanese literary sources. The significance of this source specifically derives from the period of liberal politics and cultural experiments that immediately preceded the militarist period.

That this leap is not arbitrary can be recognized by a parallel formation in several other important films from the postwar period, most notably *No Regrets for Our Youth* and *Twenty-four Eyes.* Both of these films invest considerable narrative energy in the proposition that the 1920s was an era of liberal values and opportunities equivalent to the 1950s, while the militarist period was a dark shadow that intervened and brutally delayed the fulfillment of a liberal society. The project of these films is to establish the humanist ideology of the 1950s as based in Japanese developments, not simply as imposed by the American Occupation. As such, the project cuts several ways: on one hand, it naturalizes American ideology as if purely Japanese, parallel to the official pretense that the Constitution dictated by Douglas MacArthur was actually written by the Japanese. On the other hand, it also retrieves crucial concerns of identity and agency that reestablish Japanese initiative, parallel to the artistic and industrial development that followed. In other words, the link to the 1920s was a complex innovative move, or fold, of history back on itself, that has multiple and sometimes unanticipated effects.

The argument here is that history does not simply "progress" or continue from one era to another in any additive way, but is transformed at moments of radical breaks between one set or configuration of determining assumptions and another. Further, the break of "1951" paradoxically locates an initiation of history conceived as an unbroken continuity, and ironically depends on a binary opposition of discarding what is old and "feudal" to embrace what is new and "humanistic." Kojin Karatani characterizes this period of the break as being marked by a series of inversions, or *tento,* after which the inversions that constitute the break are forgotten or repressed. Commenting on an unpublished paper by William Haver, Brett de Bary explicates this pattern:

> William Haver has lucidly analyzed the reasons for this paradoxical quality of Karatani's historicism by elaborating on Karatani's notion of an inversion, or *tento,* as the origin of Japanese modernity. Karatani's inversion, Haver notes, presents us with a model of knowing, or "discovery," which is doubled, constituted in equal parts of "blindness and insight." As Haver writes, "'origin,' or *kigen* in Karatani's deployments, refers both to the originary 'event' of a dialectical *tento,* and at the same time to the *forgetting* and repression of that event . . . origin as the originary forgetting of one's historicity."[5]

The fold, as a term introduced by Deleuze, allows us to recognize a complex reconfiguration of time that marks the "origin" of humanist developmental history as instituted in the 1950s in Japan. The humanist resolution of *Rashomon* (incompatible with the operation and effect of Akutagawa's stories) marks a radical break with all that has come before, parallel to similar abrupt disjunctions in other important films such as *Sansho the Bailiff* or *The Life of Oharu.* The logical organizing premise here is that all history before the end of the war could henceforth be sweepingly unified under the single category of "feudalism," in opposition to the "humanism" that follows. This binary system depends on an identification of the militarist era with the samurai class of premodern Japan, an identification the militarists themselves conceived and encouraged through the appropriation of Bushido as a model for industrial militarization. This identification, however tenuous, is then folded onto a Western model of history through the category of the "feudal." History thereby becomes a system of equivalences within a universal model of cultural development based on the West as norm, so that the period of Japanese history dominated by the samurai class is proposed as a direct parallel to medieval Europe. Such parallel features as an agricultural economy dominated by a military class come to the foreground in this model, while anomalies of cultural difference are subsumed as inconsequential.

History is then doubly folded back on itself, in a maneuver reminiscent of origami, by the inversion of the 1920s as linked to the 1950s. The later humanist-era assumption of Japanese progress toward a Western-style democracy is founded on a complex play of same and difference in the field of time unprecedented in narratives of Japanese history before the Occupation. History changes shape, by a process of folding and refolding, so that moments previously disregarded as insignificant and unrelated suddenly come to the foreground and seem linked and determining. Alternative folds of the previous militarist regime, such as the identification of national industrial development with Bushido or the linking of a modern central authority with an essentialist origin in the Yamato lineage, are then either inverted or set aside as irrelevant. Recognition of *Rashomon*/1951 as a site of such refolding allows us to reconsider how history is and can be written.

History as Origami

Let us now, after these considerations, roll back the film and begin again.

> *I see a ruined gate, where the rain continues to fall. The ghosts move forward, asking to be questioned.*

One of the distinguishing features of any text that marks a fundamental break in the construction of history is a refolding of time. By a "fold," I mean to build on Deleuze's concept *("le pli")* in *The Fold,* but to argue that a fold in time is anterior to any historical narrative that imagines itself as universal. The classical model of time in the West is dependent on the Renaissance fold of the fifteenth century onto the earlier classical periods of Greece and Rome, rendering all time in between as "medieval," a "middle ages." Normative history in the West has followed this interruptive model ever since, no matter how inapplicable it may be to societies outside Europe.

Rashomon is set at the end of the Heian period, the classical period of Japanese history when the emperor supposedly reigned directly (even though the Fujiwara family actually directed the government), before the shogunate emerged as the actual seat of authority, rendering the Imperial throne merely nominal in power. It takes little imagination to see this historical site as an allegory for the end of the Restoration Emperor, from Meiji and Taisho to Showa. The ruined gate we see at the beginning of the film marks the decline and disintegration of the Heian period, as well as the devastation of the bombing at the end of the Pacific War. *Rashomon* begins, then, with a fold of the militarist Japan of 1931–45 onto the Heian period long ago, not unlike how the militarists themselves might have wished to conceive of history. However, this is all past, and the present is another problem.

1920s:1950s

Many commentators have noted Kurosawa's derivation of *Rashomon* from two stories by Akutagawa Ryunosuke, who, as is often added, committed suicide in 1927. Several of the critical pieces that surround *Rashomon* detail how Kurosawa borrowed elements from two different stories and combined them in the film version, together with a few additions of his own. What tends to be overlooked is the specific fold of the 1950s onto the 1920s, a move that marginalizes the militarist period of 1931–45 as an aberration, an unaccountable nightmare. Akutagawa was a modernist, and much of the Western controversy surrounding the supposed "moral relativism" of the film in fact derives from Akutagawa's story, "In a Grove." Although the suggestion of the 1920s may seem incidental here, as if it were of no more importance than Kurosawa's choice of other texts from Shakespeare to Dostoevsky, there is more at stake than that, and the figure of the 1920s:1950s fold circulates through several key films from this period.

No Regrets for Our Youth (1946), Kurosawa's first major success in the postwar period, was explicitly based on the conjunction of the 1920s and the postwar era. The film derives from the Takikawa Incident of 1933, when Yukitoki Takikawa was forced to resign his post as a Kyoto University professor due to his supposed "Communistic thoughts."[6] In *No Regrets,* this incident acts as a dividing line between the Marxist and modern era of the 1920s, when it was still possible to imagine that an egalitarian society might emerge from the Meiji Constitution, and the "dark valley" *(kurai tanima)* of 1931–45 when militarism took over.[7] Grounding a postwar narrative in the 1920s is an innovative response to the American Occupation, as noted earlier, since such a move claims democracy as already Japanese, and not simply imposed from outside. This narrative gesture salvages Japanese autonomy from within the imposed rules of the Occupation, rather than simply acting as a denial of U.S. control. As a later consequence, this move helps sustain Japanese commitment to liberal/labor idealism from the 1920s even when the United States reverses its policy in 1948 and turns away from radical change.

Kinoshita's *Twenty-four Eyes (Nijushi no Hitomi,* 1954) retells the same explicit narrative from the position of a schoolteacher, repeating a modern commitment to education as a foundational resource against tyranny. In this case, the teacher is also a woman, who again experienced the 1920s as a time of learning and growth, the militarist period as a nightmarish regression, and the postwar period as a renewal of 1920s liberalism.

Double History

Recognizing the fold of 1920s:1950s suggests as well that history is always at least double. The social and economic context that one inhabits as an adult is always offset from childhood by perhaps twenty years. Historicizing childhood makes it possible to recognize the foundational assumptions of each generation, introjected as if natural at the moment of each person's insertion into history. Giorgio Agamben approaches this model in *Infancy and History.* In the figuration of time, infancy always acts as an outside, an unpredictable exteriority as part of the generational process of regenerating history through the body. More important, a double history represents not just childhood memories but moments of intensity, formative instances of identity and social reality that are thereafter offset and relived.

In the 1920s, Kurosawa (born 1910) and Kinoshita (born 1912) were both teenagers emerging into adult identities, while by the 1950s both were playing leading roles in the renewal of the film industry. Oshima (born 1932) was sixteen when the United States reversed course in 1948 and substituted right-wing anticommunism for its previous left democratization policies, an experience his generation experienced as a profound betrayal like that of the militarists. Within a few years, the generation that was to become the Japanese New Wave saw imperialist history overthrown as lies, then democratization rhetoric equally renounced as false. As a result, Oshima's radicalization as a student activist at Kyoto University was founded on an angry cynicism, and his attack on the emperor was meant as a blow against foundational denial and falsification in postwar Japan. What this generation felt as the double betrayal of militarism and AMPO (the Japan–U.S. Mutual Security Pact) then became the basis of their work in the 1960s. Similarly, Kohei Oguri (born 1945) remakes his postwar childhood of 1956 Osaka into *Muddy River* (*Doro no kawa,* 1981) as a postmodern filmmaker, incorporating not just the events of the period but also its neorealist mode of representation.

Directly or indirectly, as autobiography or as social activism, childhood intersects with history not as expression but as countertext, generating dislocations and intensities by continually refolding time.

Tento

Karatani's idea of an inversion, or *tento,* as Haver explains, is founded on the repression of an originary event—"the originary forgetting of one's historicity." *Rashomon* marks such an originary moment for what we now call Japanese Film History, in that it simultaneously initiates international awareness and appreciation of Japanese film, yet is organized according to a set of procedures that are immediately abandoned and forgotten, never to appear in another film again. Not even the attempted remakes of *Rashomon* have done more than to cite one of several incommensurable discursive aspects of the film, and the proliferation of critical analyses that surround *Rashomon* attest as well to the difficulty of working through what may be fundamentally unresolvable conflicts that characterize the text.

As a material artifact embodying a moment of historical break, *Rashomon* has several recognizable features that offer parallels with other break-point texts. One is a redistribution of audience, both uniting and dividing previously unresponsive groups in unexpected ways. Western audiences seem to agree only that the film is important, to the surprise of Japanese at the time of its production, who considered it a minor work. Past that, Western reception divides between those who seek to appropriate the text to the status of popular action film as a murder mystery, and those who instead cast it as a modernist and existentialist art film confronting the relativity of knowledge. Among contemporary Hollywood films, perhaps only *The Matrix* similarly attempts to combine popular-culture suspense action with metaphysical impasse, and it is this cutting across the imaginary boundary between fine art and popular culture that helps establish *Rashomon* as important. After erasing these boundaries to create a Western audience, however, subsequent films, distributors, and audiences promptly reestablish them, so within a few years Japanese films in the West can easily be divided between the samurai action films that come to be identified with the name "Kurosawa" and so-called art films that curiously combine traditionalist works like those of Ozu with ambiguous modernist films like *Woman in the Dunes*.

Another recognizable feature of the break is the conflict of trajectories within the film that mark a suspended project, a narrative half told and abandoned, rather than resolved, as unrepresentable. In other words, the film is doubled as originary event and its forgetting at once. Horror films have been analyzed as the displacement of history into an aesthetics of anxiety that represses or forgets originary events. *The Cabinet of Dr. Caligari* can be discussed as a narrative suspended between the atrocities of World War I and the aestheticized horror of *Nosferatu* and the *Frankenstein* films that follow.

The multiple inversions embedded in *Rashomon* mark it as a site of a refolding of narrative possibilities, and the limits of what can be thought or represented within a narrative discourse. Since narrative unavoidably inhabits all representation of history, often as an unacknowledged figure, we benefit by taking seriously the reworking of narrative figuration in *Rashomon*. Film narrative inevitably produces a telling of history as well as being produced out of historical conditions, and this narrative formation engages audiences as a figural framework through which the events of the current moment can be thought and shared.

Audience intensity, through mass response or a small but dedicated base, can mark the reciprocal internalization and deployment of specific figures available through film, thereby affecting the next cycle of production. Insofar as this is true, figures of film narrative participate in the production of history as the working through of the possibilities of available discourse. This is neither a magical nor a robotic process, but a production of textual materiality that mobilizes libidinal and economic forces in relation to viewers. The discursive formations through which viewers engage films thereby become potential sites for a reconfiguration of insight and agency.

Moments of historical break are marked by multiple inversions of the kind that Karatani calls *tento*. Films like *Rashomon* can be understood as representing such moments as a kind of origami. By origami, I do not mean to suggest a casual metaphor but rather a recognizable process, for a multiple refolding of discursive fields according to a design or figure that is not visible until the work of folding is completed and forgotten. In the 1950s, the figure that became visible came to be called "humanism," as in "the golden age of humanist cinema," yet exactly what constitutes the "human" is not obvious. In "Japanese humanism," the "human" is constructed through a specific combination of features appropriated from "the West," but as a combination that would have been recognizable nowhere in the West.

5
Reconsidering Humanism

The 1950s

What we now understand as Japanese Film History begins in the 1950s, as an effect of
the break marked by such films as *Rashomon*.

This should not be a surprising assertion, except that it seems to go against the grain
of virtually all discourse surrounding the topic of Japanese Film History. Established
discourse assumes that we already know when Japanese Film History began, and that
beginning can be located with reasonable certainty close to 1900, with Shibata Tsunekichi's *Maple Viewing* (*Momiji-gari,* 1898), a strong candidate for the first surviving film
produced in Japan by a Japanese filmmaker. An earlier film may yet be discovered, but,
no matter, the principle is the same: the assumed beginning of Japanese Film History is
the first film produced in Japan by someone Japanese.

The problem is that no one in the first decades of the twentieth century CE would have
thought of film in these terms, and this is true of the West as much as of Japan. Film
began as an innovation without a history, a modern novelty popularly known to all and
hence unnecessary to consider in terms of a specific history. History begins only when a
combination of circumstances develops that requires a rethinking of events previously
taken for granted as merely novel. The passage of time is only one such circumstance,
so that the 1940s marks the moment when a new generation appears that has no longer
already seen all the films that have been made, and retrospection becomes an issue. Henri
Langlois is justly famous in France for anticipating the imminent historicization of film
by collecting materials in the 1930s, and the Museum of Modern Art in New York City
is equally famous for its inclusion of cinema as one of the arts in the 1930s. Film, however, only began to be understood historically in the late 1940s, when the Cinémathèque
Française opened its doors to future New Wave filmmakers, and MoMA began distributing its collection of historical films to audiences who had never seen them.

Certainly there were attempts in the 1930s to write about film historically, and these
efforts are invaluable as prototypes for the histories initiated in the 1950s. However, in

the 1930s, film history invariably was initiated as an offshoot of another topic, as an industrial or economic history that happens to cover cinema, or of modernization that includes
the arts. To think historically about film required an extension of thought from some
other topic, such as the "traditional" (that is, precinematic) arts. In Japan, as Eric Cazdyn
discusses, two of the earliest attempts to historicize film positioned film as an extension
of capitalism or nationalist modernization. Iwasaki Akira's *Eiga Geijutsu-shi* (*History of
Film Art*, 1931) was written as a companion piece to *Eiga to Shihon-shugi* (*Film and Capitalism*), and *Nihon Eiga-shi* (*Japanese Film History*, 1941), two fifteen-minute films (a
third is lost) were produced by the Shinko Film Corporation and the Ministry of Foreign Affairs as part of imperial development and the war effort.[1] In other words, "Film
History" did not yet exist as an autonomous and presumptive discourse.

History, as it emerges in relation to cinema as well as all other arenas, is a discourse
before it can become a narrative. Before the search for the "first use of the close-up" or
some other technique, or for the "first feature-length film," the domain of "cinema" as
constituting an object of study must first be established. What makes it reasonable or
even possible to distinguish "cinema" as an independent area of study rather than subordinating it, as all early nomenclature does, to a previous field, through such terms as
"motion picture" or "photoplay"? Even if we acknowledge cinema as a domain, why do
we need to assume that an understanding of the field can be best produced through an
overriding chronological sequence rather than through studio, genre, star performer,
director, or some other mode of organization?

Determining figures of "cinema" and "chronology" needed to be established before
"history" could construct its narrative. Once these figures were in place, the search for
"earliest use of a technique" or "first film" became logical effects, but not before. The
debate over whether there could be such a thing as a first use in a fundamentally collaborative and decentered medium only marks the limits of this discourse, but does not
yet unhinge it.

The twist in thinking through this process in Japan is that this "history" appears to be
imposed from the "West," as if an alien and ethnocentric Western discourse appropriates
Japanese culture for its own ends. Despite the general appropriateness of skepticism toward the West as a dominant figure of cultural imperialism, a reading here limited to
imperialist appropriation can overlook a number of incisive innovations in the development of a postcolonial culture.

Japan, according to John Dower, uniquely distinguished itself in the aftermath of
World War II by "embracing defeat."[2] This can be a helpful if misleading suggestion
toward rethinking the resistances of Japanese essentialism to questions of "history," but
it does not go far enough. Who was defeated, and who embraced the consequences of
the war as a defeat? If we understand "Japan" as the continuity of political figures that
once staffed militarist imperialism, and were rehabilitated by the U.S. Occupation to become the postwar Liberal Democratic Party (LDP), then, yes, these figures "embraced
defeat." But Japanese filmmakers were not unequivocally supporters of either militarism
or the LDP, and much of the most significant cinema embraced the end of the war as the
"defeat" of militarist imperialism and the liberation of democratic and socialist idealism

buried since the 1920s. For these Japanese, the postwar was a liberation, not a defeat, and the embrace of "history" from those who had helped defeat the monstrosity of militarist ultranationalism was a benefit. "History" for the Japanese Left and for many filmmakers was a means to rethink the institutionalized atrocities that modernized Japan had become, and open the possibility of another Japan only dreamed of in the past.

These filmmakers refigured the discursive assumptions of Japanese films to produce what misleadingly became known as "Japanese humanism." The West welcomed the opportunity to imagine that Japan was adopting the normative view of "history" that the West took for granted, but something very different was at stake in Japan. After postmodernism, we can begin to understand that a specific hybridity was constructed in Japanese "humanist" films of the 1950s, which can be understood neither as a self-effacing acceptance of Western universalism nor as a betrayal of a previous golden age of Japanese cultural difference, as Noël Burch has argued. The specific hybridity of the 1950s was constructed along the fault line of a utopian "humanism" far in excess of what post-1948 U.S. policy wished, together with a tacit but visceral residue of imperialist identification and trauma working out its effects.

The key postcolonial figure here is not the adoption of Western ideas as if universal, but the appropriation of specific Western discourses by the non-West to produce its own ends. That this remains important as a postcolonial move can be seen today from Wole Soyinka's call for "rights" as a Nigerian weapon against its military heritage, to the embrace of Xianity by former Tiananmen activists as a means of refiguring Chinese identity against bureaucratic submission. There is nothing passive or subordinate about such moves, nor do they represent any more a "triumph" of the "West" than the influence of Manichaeanism in medieval Europe represented a domination by the East. The essentialist imaginary that hopes to resist modernization's brutalities by seeking a pure national identity uncontaminated by foreign influences is not only xenophobic and dangerous, but it misses the point. The most effective, and perhaps only, resistance to the threat of cultural domination is not the (impossible) expulsion of the alien, but a renegotiation of the other on different terms. *Black Athena,* regardless of its arguments for or against African roots of Western culture, is noteworthy as a narrative appropriation of the West within an African discourse. That this could be a liberating move should not be overlooked. What appeared in the 1960s to be overwhelming cultural imperialism has inverted to an increasing appropriation of Western cultural elements by non-Western cultures, a pivotal shift that has come to characterize the world after postmodernism and postcoloniality converged.

In other words, things are often not what they seem. The moment of apparent "triumph" for Western universalism, as Gianni Vattimo argues, has inverted into a heterology of cultural hybridities.[3] Singularities of non-Western appropriation of Western effects have produced a proliferation of hybrid cultures, each living simultaneously in a "Western" and "non-Western" world of its own making, regardless of and in excess of Western attempts at monopoly and domination. Chakrabarty's name for this phenomenon is "provincializing Europe."[4] Only the West, in this postcolonial world, seems backward, still bound up in a narcissistic mirror of imaginary auto-universalism, unable as yet to come to grips with the incommensurability of multiple cultural differences that have come to inhabit the world after colonialism. Only the West continues to imagine multiplicity as devolution away from the universalism of imperial transparency, and to mistake the proliferation of regenerative hybridities for decay.

In Japan, as previously noted, the Showa 1930s gave way to the 1970s, as Japanese public discourse adopted the convention of "Western" temporality that was still radical in the 1950s. By this time, however, a slight displacement had already made it clear that the ideological transparency of universalism had vanished. The substitution of CE or "common era" for AD or "anno Domini" seems obvious as a convention outside the West, while seeming arbitrary only to those for whom a Christian narrative teleology remains unthought and unquestioned. "CE" is a small but typical example of the appropriation of the West into non-Western hybridities, and another site of inversion and postcoloniality.

Japan is a tutelary site for understanding the processes of inversion, displacement, and appropriation that mark the end of Western imaginary universalism and the opening of a postcolonial possibility. Although Western capital flows now circumnavigate the world in nanoseconds, and financial institutions have replaced the ancien régime of direct colonization, the possibility of a world apart from a system of domination simultaneously begins to be imaginable. That wish, that desire, that utopian dream had one of its entries into the world in 1950s Japan, and we benefit today from rereading how this occurred, to better understand how the proliferating restaging of this event characterizes the continuing possibility of a world simultaneously postmodern and postcolonial.

Ikiru

Ikiru, "to live." A word fraught with epistemological resonances of Being and Becoming. The title was left untranslated in U.S. distribution, perhaps with the intention of exoticizing the text, but the word can also suggest the untranslatability of Japanese postwar experience. The film defies the humanist ideology of authenticity and transparency by narrativizing the difficulty and obscurity of becoming a humanist individual.

Several conspicuous features mark this film: First, the film never received the popular acclaim in the West that greeted historically set narratives, or *jidai-geki,* such as *Rashomon, Seven Samurai,* or *Sansho the Bailiff. Ikiru* marks a blind spot of Western audiences to Japanese modernity, a symptom of how an evolutionist history continues to operate as a popular reflex, so that the West remains fascinated by the other as if identical with a feudal past.

Second, *Ikiru,* as much as any film, is a prototype for the Nouvelle Vague, the New Wave of filmmakers in France who, informed by a self-created film history and critical self-training, invented new visual and sound strategies of representation in the late 1950s and 1960s. *Ikiru* either anticipates or directly incites the French critic-historian generation. *Ikiru* initiates a direct use of filmic materiality as a strategy of representation, which, although fundamental among avant-garde filmmakers around the world, remained revelatory within a narrative film. Materiality intervened as a radical alternative to nineteenth-century theatrical and novelistic models for narrative representation in film, with mass-produced premises from actors, sets, and costumes to character development and facial expression as signs of interior psychology.

Three moments in the film stand out: the image of an X-ray that begins the film, the voice-over narrator's direct address to the audience, and Watanabe's departure from the doctor's office after learning that he has cancer. The full-screen X-ray immediately breaks with the realist convention of an establishing shot to relocate identity in the nonocular-centric domain of radiation and alternative imaging. The direct-address voice-over (a device that Godard later makes famous) rejects transparency to ground film narrative in a dialogic relation between filmmaker and viewer. Watanabe's reaction to learning of his imminent death is represented through silence on the soundtrack, which switches abruptly to the noisy sound of traffic within an uncut shot as he realizes he is in the middle of the street. In all three cases, the materiality of image and sound displaces classical conventions of dialogue, transcendent realism, or expressive acting.

Third, the film produces what we now in postcolonial terms call a hybrid identity, although the film anticipates the theorization of this effect by several decades. In 1945, Ruth Benedict wrote *The Chrysanthemum and the Sword* as a guide for U.S. forces to understand the people of Japan, and her book then became a best-seller when it was published the following year. As an anthropologist, she articulated a series of complex differences between Japanese and Western traditional identities as the effect of very different historical conditions and discourses.[5] Part of her work contrasts Western principles of human rights to the feudal system of obligations, or *on*, in Japan.

In a postcolonial context, Benedict's work is often discussed as if it were simply discredited and obsolete, but the situation is more complex than that. The problem with Benedict's text is that she exaggerates both the isolation and the robotic control of tradition, as if culture produced homogeneous and deterministic effects that approach biology. Benedict argued, for example, that the traditional Japanese language had no word for "rights," although *minken* has been in use for this concept since the Meiji era. Politically, her work seems consistent with the idea that Japan could not become democratic without U.S. guidance, while critics pointed to the progressive politics of the Taisho era as a legacy on which a nonfascist modern Japan could be built.

However, Benedict's discussion of the traditional Japanese system of obligations remains unparalleled in English, without which films from *Ikiru* to Oshima's *Ceremonies* (*Gishiki*, 1971) would make little sense. She also helps us understand how humanist individualism is constructed through such personal celebrations as birthdays, and how such events would seem self-centered and rude within Japanese social traditions. Benedict's book can now be reread as a snapshot, documenting a specific moment of felt contrast between conflicting identities and discourses. As such, both its insights and its exaggerations are instructive.

Ikiru reinscribes the same historical conditions that inform Benedict's work, but the film rejects the book's mechanistic antinomies and proposes instead a hybrid and reconfigurative process. The narrator tells us that Watanabe "has been dead for the past twenty-five years," again bracketing the time between the 1920s and 1952 as meaningless. However, this living death is identified with a fascist bureaucracy paralyzed by endless deference to authority, suggesting that feudal hierarchies were destructively imposed on the modern era by the militarists, rather than being either traditional or innate. Watanabe's imminent death from cancer viscerally inscribes the end of any fixed identity and propels him into uncertainty and nomadic desire. He systematically works through a series of possible postwar identities, borrowing from both Japanese tradition and Western humanism, before he performatively refashions himself.

Initially he returns to his family, then seems to begin an affair with a younger woman, both of which would be familiar and predictable actions for a traditional older man in crisis. Both of these appear as irretrievably lost or useless in a modern era, but his memories of his now-dead wife and his son's childhood significantly revolve around a baseball game. Before militarist neofeudalism, in other words, Japan was already a hybrid society. Baseball may have come from the West, like tempura, but now is as deeply Japanese as the family. At the same time, what is at stake in family history is not biology but an exteriority of the unconscious. Childhood formations of self are neither intentional nor genetic but are constructed through embodied symbolic processes known to us through psychoanalysis. Changing the foundational construction of the self within social discourse is tantamount to death, as a symbolic embodiment of total loss.

Within the alternative discourse of "democracy" is the promise of a different kind of self, founded on the "freedom" of the individualized subject. What the Occupation proposes as "freedom," however, appears in the film as irresponsible self-indulgence. Watanabe's experiment with alcohol, strip clubs, and dissolution positions Western "humanism" as narcissistic excess, and quickly appears as another dead end. Many Asian critics continue to feel that American "freedom" promotes selfishness and greed without respect for others. Today, this critique of the West is voiced with greatest intensity in the Arabic and Islamic world. In *Ikiru,* individual "freedom" appears as a season in hell, an inferno of isolation and loss within mechanized desire. This hell is nonetheless productive, and an artist like Dante's Virgil acts as Watanabe's guide through the underworld.

Eventually, Watanabe becomes determined to build a park to benefit a neighborhood, fusing individual initiative with social responsibility. He forges a new role for himself out of the ruins of tradition and humanism, both of which seem exhausted and fatally flawed. If Asian cultural traditions respect the dynamic group process of social interactions, this seeming openness is rigidly controlled and undermined by patriarchal authority. However, if democratic humanism seems to offer freedom from authority and domination, this opportunity is equally compromised by a regressive egocentrism and social irresponsibility. Watanabe's refashioning of self combines Western agency with Asian respect for group process, while rejecting both Western self-indulgence and feudal deference to authority. Far from being natural, as Rousseau imagined, Watanabe's socially responsible agency is a complex construction, produced only through a visceral passage of death, hell, and rebirth.

At the moment of his renewed sense of purpose, Watanabe climbs the stairs in a restaurant next to a young person's birthday party that he does not attend, a significant coincidence and displacement that suggests his hybrid reconfiguration. A younger generation will be born into a humanist individualism, as constructed through such nontraditional personal celebrations as birthdays, but a productive refashioning of self lies between discourses of tradition and modernization, in excess of either in absolute terms.

Fourth, an origami-like structure of time organizes the film. *Ikiru* begins with a relatively Aristotelian trajectory of narrative beginning, middle, and end, as exposition, trials, and outcome, then appears to reach a narrative conclusion midway through the film. The narrative then unexpectedly continues with a complex array of flashbacks after Watanabe's death that reconstruct, through the discourse of others at his funeral, his motivation and agency in the last months of his life. The nonchronological array of flashbacks, organized within a model of social discourse, is set against the Aristotelian development of part one, like modernist and classical narratives parallel to what Charles Jencks would later call double coding as a foundational characteristic of postmodernity. What Deleuze calls image-time and image-motion are here deployed as parallel strategies, within the same film, where neither takes precedence.

Ikiru stands as a pivot-text between *Rashomon* as a conflicted and destabilized narrative and the Japanese humanist films of the 1950s, such as *Ugetsu* or *Sansho*, that fully adopt a Western classical model as dominant mode of narrative organization. The folding of time in part two necessarily complicates and displaces the humanist transfiguration of part one into a transgenerational process that requires others to decipher and reconstruct what Watanabe became. The transmission of Watanabe's agency to others transforms the individualist claim of self-sufficiency and Being into a paradox. Being and interiority, experienced in humanist terms as an authenticity and guarantee of meaning, are only possible as an effect of discourse, as an intergenerational formation prior to the possibility of becoming an individual. As in Deleuze's *Foucault*, interiority is argued as an effect of discourse, so that both the Western individual and Japanese *uchi* are produced as a consequence, not a cause, of social context.

Ugetsu

Ugetsu acts as a sign of completed transition, a text fully produced from within Western classical conventions of unity, closure, and Aristotelian hierarchies (a single overarching trajectory of Beginning-Middle-End and the elevation of a central plot over secondary subplots). If we compare *Ugetsu* as book and as film, the translation into Western conventions becomes apparent. *Ugetsu monogatari* originates as a series of nine tales by Ueda Akinari, published in 1776. The nine tales produce an interlocking network of repeating ideas and events that embody the fabric of life during the Tokugawa regime. Capital and neurosis, represented as mercantile practices and the supernatural, are two of its central concerns.

In Mizoguchi's 1953 version of the text, one tale is prioritized as central, its characters made primary, and a second tale is relocated as a subplot. "The House amid the Thickets" ("Asaji ga yado") is selected as the main story because of its setting in the sixteenty-century Japanese civil wars, the same time setting as *Rashomon,* as a historical parallel to the immediate postwar trauma of the 1950s. "The Lust of the White Serpent" ("Jasei no in") then becomes a secondary narrative to complicate and parallel the action, according to Western usage of secondary characters. The other seven tales, characters, and thematic concerns are omitted completely. More important, the network model of narrative organization is replaced by Western unity, closure, and hierarchy to produce a narrative system of subject positioning within sequential development. Although this narrative strategy was often defended during the 1950s in the United States as necessary to adapt literary complexity to the constraints of the screen, this is an ideological fantasy that characterizes the period rather than a truth. Other films from Kurosawa's *Dreams* to Jarmusch's *Mystery Train* demonstrate that such an assumption derives from an ideological failure of imagination and that networked multiple narratives are easily possible in film.

The diachronic subject of Western conventions reproduces the Kantian metaphysics of interior expression and exterior empiricism that marks the foundational assumptions of Classical Hollywood Cinema. Displaced to Japan, the humanist metaphysics produced by these narrative conventions are proposed as a model of postwar experience within a new sense of history, which prefigures the popular adoption of the "common era" of historical chronology by the 1970s. Narrative is again bound up with history, an effect suggested by the French word *histoire,* which means, as discussed earlier, both "story" or narrative and "history."

Western appreciation of Japanese "style" then subordinates cultural difference to the status of national character, local color, or personal directorial flourish. However, we can alternatively consider such effects as a tacit countertext that inhabits the visual discourse of Western narrative conventions and remains available to be read.

Japanese humanist films do not simply adopt or adapt to Western conventions as a transparent normativism, but engage in what could be called a reverse appropriation as strategy of generative survival. In an international economy that only recognizes narratives in humanist terms, Japan appropriates this set of conventions in reply to the Western appropriation of Japan as exotic object and feudal past. Far from transparently accommodating humanist metaphysics as universal and natural, Japanese films continually inscribe textual resistances that both inhabit and sit next to a dominant humanist discourse. The transparency of humanist narrative and the opacity of Western conventions are situated in the same place, much like a modernist poem that oscillates between semantic effect and the materiality of the letter.

Once again, the Japanese text is not simply a source for or naive precedent of Western modernism but instead is a different kind of modernism within the same historical moment.

Totalization/Teleology

Fredric Jameson, in *The Cultural Turn,* dismisses the critique of totalization and teleology in order to pursue his project of restoring a Marxist discourse in a postmodern context. This is unfortunate because the postmodern critique of totalization and teleology is crucial to distinguish political agency from totalitarian discourses. It is also unnecessary because postmodern premises do not imply a rejection of totalization and teleology as such, but instead paradoxically resituate them as contingent tropes that can be radical and progressive in some contexts and totalitarian and reactionary in others.

Japan anticipates and lives through this seeming paradox as a heterological set of intersecting discourses in the 1950s. In one context, Western humanism and socialism are represented as a unity, based both on the *mobo/moga* tradition of the 1920s and the New Deal administration of the early period of the Occupation from 1945 to 1948. Japanese Marxists, emerging from wartime imprisonment and still working from the 1920s ideas of Marxism prevalent before militarists blocked international communication, initially welcomed the U.S. troops as liberators who ended the Japanese militarist regime. Occupation policy at this moment promoted democracy, unionization, and women's rights, and a brief period of U.S. military presence expected to end in 1948. Only after the Reverse Course of 1948–52 were all these policies replaced by a restoration of leaders from the militarist period, corporate domination, and patriarchal norms during an extended Occupation designed to reposition Japan as a military ally against a Stalinist USSR. The Left represented this moment as a betrayal, and the Japanese Communist Party (JCP) simultaneously revised its own agenda to correspond to the Stalinist correct line during the Cold War. As a consequence, an entire generation grew up during the 1950s between two competing propaganda systems, both of which claimed universality and the future as legitimizing principles.

This is the generation that became the "Japanese New Wave," and Oshima's early films at Shochiku radically critique both the betrayal of a radical left by the JCP and corporate brutality as it had come to dominate Japan. *Cruel Tales of Youth* (1960) embodies despair and violence as the primary experience of a younger generation in corporate Japan, and *Night and Fog in Japan* (1960) critiqued the betrayal of student radicals by an authoritarian JCP. Oshima had been a leader of the student movement in demonstrations against the emperor at Kyoto University in 1951, and his film production derives from his own lived history, represented as the crushing of student radicalism between Japan's 1950s corporate nationalism and the JCP.[6] Oshima's citation of Alain Resnais's *Night and Fog* in the title of his 1960 film claimed a parallelism with the situation in France, where films also narrativized a repudiation of fascist atrocity followed by the competing totalitarian propaganda systems of the United States and the USSR. The later alliance of student and labor activists that characterized the 1968 uprising in France became possible only after working through the conflicts between these different trajectories in the 1950s, and events in Japan both prefigured and contributed to later activist developments in the West.

Japan in the 1950s, then, is suspended between two incommensurable discourses, each of which is further split into competing factions. An official discourse, which dominates public media and Japan's international image, identifies democracy and freedom with the corporate nationalist policies of the emerging neoconservative LDP, locked in Manichaean combat against the "Communism" of the JCP and the USSR. The emblem of this state discourse became Japan's commitment to a military alliance with the United States in the treaty known as AMPO. In contrast, a complex and dynamic subculture opposed this treaty and dominant discourse, ranging from the ultranationalist movement claimed by Yukio Mishima to student radicals. These conflicting counter-discourses grad-ually reconfigured a new Japanese identity in terms of protest, which only today is begin-ning to be unpacked and problematized.[7] The protest movement achieved international recognition by the 1960s, but its formative period during the 1950s remained under-ground and was strongly affected by the emerging antinuclear movement. This Japa-nese subculture invites comparison with the Beat movement in the United States and Existentialism in France, but it operates independently according to forces and motiva-tions within Japan.

The films produced during the 1950s are conventionally called "humanist," but they embody a conflicting set of incommensurable discourses and competing factions. Appar-ently dominated by Classical Hollywood Cinema norms of unity, closure, and Aristo-telian hierarchies, the films also embody a countertext to dominant discourse that is positioned within a "humanist" context as "Japanese style" or "national character." Re-read as a countertext, the multiple figures of "Japanese style" operate as an alternative writing system set next to logocentric transparency and produces a double discourse within a hybrid text. In the context of Cold War conformity, one of the prerequisites of producing a countertext was that it remain tacit or invisible within a "humanist" reading yet simultaneously produce alternative reading formations. Many of the most interesting films of the 1950s dissolve into fractured and multiple discourses, nowhere resolved or resolvable through the trope of a universalist "humanism," until the determining trope of "humanism" itself is called into question in the 1960s. During and after the 1960s, "humanism" becomes identified with the propaganda image of corporate nationalism as an object of critique, but before that moment the memory of an alternative radical human-ism from 1945 to 1948 remains resonant. Japanese "humanist" films are often governed by an uncomfortable oscillation between these very different possibilities of what "human-ism" can produce.

Kant in the East, *Mu* in the West

How is history written in cinema? If we understand cinema as "next to" philosophy, as Deleuze proposes, rather than as an aesthetic object of philosophic discourse, then cin-ema is also "next to" historiography, rather than simply being an illustration, whether true or false, of a history imagined as already known. Mizoguchi's *Sansho the Bailiff* (1954) is not simply an artistic work or an illustration of history but also can be considered as a remarkably interesting project of historiography. *Sansho* is not only a narrative set in the Heian period, but actively intervenes in historical discourse to disrupt and transform the way that history can be thought and written. At the same historical moment that made *Sansho* possible in Japan, underground and countercultural movements in the United States were similarly reconfiguring the way that history can be thought and lived.

In one sense, *Sansho* works to popularize postwar conceptions of history as marked by a grand caesura that imagines all prewar Japanese culture as "feudalism" and all post-war events as "democracy." Since the American Occupation ended before *Sansho* was produced, and this binary narrative of history circulates through numerous films, the "feudalism"/"democracy" figure cannot be understood simply as an external imposition but needs to be addressed in terms of its appropriation and redeployment within Japan.

Sansho sets its tale in Heian Japan, the era traditionally conceived as the golden era of Japanese cultural history prior to the emergence of samurai domination. As such, the film refuses to condemn only the samurai class as precursors of 1930s militarism, but instead identifies the initial emergence of the feudal manorial system during the pre-samurai Heian. *Sansho* ambitiously contructs a grand, epic narrative in order to indict all Japanese history as founded on brutality and slave labor, beginning with the classical era. As a result, the critique of "feudalism" as antidemocratic coincides with a class analysis of the control of production and the mobilization of forced labor, so that the "people" of the narrative doubly figures in terms of "human rights" and as social class.

None of this, however, addresses the more fundamental problem of how history is written in cinema, but considers only the narrative effect.

Part of the difficulty in approaching cinema as a historiographic practice derives from the hybridity of writing systems and reciprocal reading formations implicated in cinematic representation. Since the twentieth century, multiple writing systems intersect in every society and at every point of inscription. The emergence of cinema, video, and other modern modes of inscription did not render the alphabet or Chinese written characters obsolete, except in fantasies like *Fahrenheit 451*, but instead have generated hybrid writing practices among multiple systems in use. In the West, the roman alphabet, arabic numbers, and cinema intersect in television and computer contexts. In Japan, kanji and kana similarly intersect with arabic numbers and cinema to configure a different hybridity of writing practices that inflect the formation of verbal and visual discourses. A consideration of how history is written in cinema comes up against these hybrid writing practices as a complex figural horizon that inflects the possibilities and limits of narrative discourse through which history can be thought and represented.

Further difficulties complicate the analysis of writing systems. These are perhaps exemplified by the technocentric fantasy that a writing system can be equated with a single, especially immediate or current, set of effects, as if writing constituted a physical cause rather than a figural limit. Any legitimate consideration of writing as a figural horizon for film must begin with the recognition that social practices are only indirectly related to writing, and hybridity is one of several means to decipher such compound indirect effects.

The use of kanji in modern Japan, for example, has been transformed by the encounter with the West, both in the radical nineteenth-century *genbun itchi* ("unifying spoken *[gen]* and written *[bun]* languages") movement, which redefined Japanese writing as phonocentric, and in the postwar reduction of recommended kanji to about two thousand characters from the traditional use of some seventeen thousand. Once the Japanese writing system is reconceived as phonocentric, the use of hiragana to record Japanese spoken language by such women as Sei Shonagon and in the Heian period (tenth–eleventh centuries) is retrospectively refigured as a precursor of modern literature—once, as Karatani observes, phonocentric discourse makes literature itself conceivable as a category.

The full effects of these changes emerge sometime after their introduction, as a new generation internalizes the shift in grammatological conditions as an assumed and unconscious norm, so that the decade of the 1950s proceeds from prewar conditions of writing interacting with a new postwar system. New writing practices are thereby inevitably marked first by circumstances no longer relevant to later production. Accordingly, we need to distinguish among several configurations and practices of the same writing system over time.

The reconfiguration of writing in the unconscious is what makes Friedrich Kittler's use of *aufschreibesysteme* or "system of writing down" (Dr. Daniel Paul Schreber's term) helpful, insofar as it suggests the parallel of internalized writing to a psychotic embodiment. Kittler's term in part implies Lacan's argument that the construction of the cogito as Western identity is structurally indistinguishable from psychotic foreclosure, insofar as it is based on the categorical exclusion of the other from the self. For Lacan, the cogito is grounded in misrecognitions negotiated in relation to language, irretrievably bound up with writing, as he suggests in the title of his essay "The Agency of the Letter in the Unconscious." Yet non-Western cultural identity can also be theorized in terms of internalized writing systems, and foreclosure of alternative configurations is inevitable, even if that foreclosure does not necessarily categorize the other. What is foreclosed is not thought or discourse as such but the scale of ease or difficulty in producing specific effects, so that some representations, by way of an unconscious practice of Occam's razor, begin to be experienced as spontaneous or natural, while others seem abstract or labored.

Another problem comes from the hybrid indirection of camera images, so that cinematic practices are generated parallel to different writing systems, even when a specific system is not directly in use. What came to be known as the Japanese national style in the 1950s was generated in relation to the reciprocal effects of kanji and landscape painting, modes of inscription that are not kept categorically separate in Japanese cultural tradition. Yet this "style" alternates with camera conventions introduced from the West, which in turn developed in relation to roman writing, logocentric metaphysics, and the construction of camera conventions as an ocularcentric "realism." As a result, Japanese films incorporate a hybrid practice of representation, distinct from the hybrid writing systems that are in use in Japan. Representational practices shift from a Japanese to a Western metaphysical context, in each case generated through the practice of specific but different combinations of writing systems.

Japanese films from the 1950s can be significantly reread outside the historically situated discourse of "national style," if we instead consider cinema as "next to" philosophy as a parallel conceptual process. In these terms, the shift from Japanese to Western "style" in *Sansho* can be reread as a cinematic text embodying propositions about cultural difference as it is being worked through in 1954 Japan.

One such proposition emerges from the Kannon figure in *Sansho* that the father gives to his son Zushio at the moment of his dismissal from government service for defending local farmers from abusive edicts, with the injunction that all men are equally deserving of compassion.

Men are created equal. Without mercy a man is like a beast. Be sympathetic to others.

Kannon, the Buddhist figure of compassion, is constructed here as if it were a signifier of human rights, through the restatement of Buddhist principles in phrases reminiscent of Japan's postwar constitution. In the English subtitles, Kannon is described as the "goddess of mercy," a reference recognizable enough in a Buddhist context as Kannon, the bodhisattva of compassion. Why is Buddhism presented as if it were a form of Western humanism? Rather than dismiss this narrative figure as an ahistorical device justified by poetic license, one might better consider the historiographic possibilities and effects of such a move.

Kannon here evokes a series of contexts that intersect with and complicate the narrative. Buddhism was introduced to Japan at the beginning of its historical development (536 or 552 CE), together with the Chinese written characters that first made written historical records possible. Sutras and images were brought together from Korea, relayed from China, where they had been translated and copied from Indian sources. Cultural transmission to China became possible across the Silk Road in the first and second centuries CE, connecting Han China to the Kushan empire in central Asia. The Kushan and Gandhara empires were pivotal in the sculptural development of the Buddha image, whose classical appearance was once attributed to Hellenistic influence in the wake of Alexander's conquest of western India and later revised to Roman influence during the first and second centuries CE. Chinese sculptural images were copied from Buddha figures developed in relation to Western classical idealism, so that the Occidental metaphysics of ocularcentric representation accompanied Buddhism to Japan.

Sutras in turn were translated into Chinese characters from Indian alphabetic texts, inverting the traditional Western assumption that the alphabet is the inevitable end product of grammatological development. The phonocentric character of alphabetic writing, together with the ocularcentric image of classical idealism, combines sound and image as a figure of cinema, a mode of textual production, like *Sansho*'s Kannon, carried around in a small box. Kannon is also the etymological basis for the manufacturing trade name of Canon, the multinational corporation known best for its photographic and video cameras.

In multiple ways, the Kannon figure suggests that the West has always been present in the East, coinciding with the beginning of Japan's historical era. The Shoso-in, an eighth-century repository storehouse at Todaiji temple in Nara, the first permanent capital of Japan, confirms this idea, including artifacts from the late Roman Empire that arrived over the silk route through the T'ang China capital of Ch'ang-an, at the end of the classical period, when this earlier contact between West and East was still possible.

Rabindranath Tagore, during the late nineteenth- and early twentieth-century independence struggle in India, responded to the thesis of classical Western influence by counter-arguing that the Buddha image could just as well have developed from Asian sources independent of the West. This contestation over cultural heritage participates in a postcolonial discourse that is equally relevant in *Sansho*. What matters here is not so much whether art history can be decided in favor of Western or Asian determinants as the dispute itself as a figure of historical contestation and appropriation. What seems from the West may in fact be Asian after all, so that the Kannon marks a pivotal position of potential cultural inversion. The human-rights discourse conjoined in *Sansho* with the Kannon inverts also, so that what appears at first to be Western influence is instead claimed as having always been already Japanese.

The figure of cultural inversion that inhabits the Kannon image in *Sansho* is further compounded by Ernest Fenollosa's discovery of the early seventh-century wooden Yumedono Kwannon at Horyuji temple in 1884. Fenollosa was curator of Oriental Art at the Museum of Fine Arts in Boston, and was one of the few to appreciate and rescue premodern Japanese images and texts during the Meiji era of radical industrial modernization. His discovery of a Kannon inside the earliest of Asuka-era Buddhist temples still standing in Japan marks a moment of cultural inversion during the Meiji period, when Western interest in ancient Japanese arts paradoxically plays a role in the reinvention of Japanese tradition by a modernizing Japan.

This incident of Buddhist history would not seem so significant if Buddhism itself had not been so caught up in the late Meiji contestation over tradition and modernization. In the 1890s, the Meiji 20s, a neotraditionalism began to emerge in reaction to extensive Westernization. Nativists began to define Japanese cultural traditions against "foreign" influences from the West, first attacking Japanese Christians and "disrespectful" historians, then Westerners and Chinese, and then Buddhism as an alien tradition. To re-imagine Japan as a modern nation, tradition was radically reconfigured as a nativist essentialism, so that Shintoism and Buddhism were transformed into an imaginary opposition, even though the two had been intertwined and mutually influential since the earliest moment of Japanese recorded history. The separation of Shinto and Buddhism, the subsequent withdrawal of state support from Buddhism, and the popular sentiment for rejecting the religion culminated in an iconoclastic smashing of Buddhist statues, which was expressed most violently at the eighth-century Nara temple of Kofukuji, where tossing Buddhist images into bonfires became a daily routine.

Mizoguchi's calculated retrieval of a Buddhist image to represent Western ideas of human rights inverts the prewar militarist abjection of Buddhism into a figure of resistance within Japan. "Mercy," or compassion for the mass of people suffering under feudal enslavement for the benefit of the few, conjoins militarist domination with the Heian manorial system as a doubled object of resistance, folding history back on itself to imagine all of prewar Japan as uniformly tyrannical and oppressive. The "dark ages, before human beings had emerged," in the words of the film's opening intertitles, extends in this narrative of Japanese history at least through 1945.

At the same time, the conceptual limit of this fold recedes into paradox, since it simultaneously depends on universalist models of history that assume Western centrality and the very different idea that what appears Western has always been inside Japan. The category of "dark ages" and the narrative premise of "feudalism" in *Sansho* depends on an implicit universalization of Western history, and the acceptance of an evolutionist model of cultural progress, willing to assume an inevitable worldwide development through the stage of "medieval" or "feudal" society preliminary to modern humanism and democracy. In contrast, the inversion of the West into Kannon, a figure bound up with the introduction of Chinese writing and the possibility of Japanese history itself, emerges as foundational of a resistance to domination within Japan and a different idea of history.

Kannon derived from the Chinese Kuan-yin, and in turn from the Indian bodhisattva Avalokiteshvara, undergoing a gender change as he/she crossed the mountains. Avalokiteshvara was a male incarnation of Buddha who emerged as a significant figure in Mahayana Buddhism contemporary with Christ as an incarnation of the Hebrew idea of God, while the female Kuan-yin is figured parallel to the receptive side of Yin-Yang philosophy as it permeates classical Chinese thought. Kannon, as a "goddess of mercy," figures in *Sansho* parallel to what Vattimo calls "weak thought," a conceptual practice that engages with the other while refusing any imaginary position of mastery. By way of a transsexual bodhisattva, *Sansho* unhinges universalist historical categories that it initially seems to assume, and places gender and race in play with democracy and social class as figures at stake in a game of domination.

Gender is configured as a component of the Japanese national imaginary after the success of the *genbun itchi* movement and the new writing style called *kogo,* which replaced classical writing as a result. The new style treated writing as phonocentric, parallel to the Japanese understanding of alphabetic writing, and redefined its purpose as a recording of everyday vernacular language use. This made literature possible in the modern sense, as Karatani argues, and simultaneously reconfigures past Japanese writing practices as a history of literature. Women writers of the Heian, whose writing in the Japanese vernacular was once assumed as secondary to the male writers who wrote in Chinese, are instead seen as the first authentic examples of a Japanese national literature. Sei Shonagon, Murasaki Shikibu, and others can be located within a discourse of nation and literature as an origin of gendered authenticity.

Sansho's Kannon, through its appeal to human rights and the strong representation of female suffering under "feudalism," in part seems to argue for the liberation of women, as do many other Mizoguchi films. The *"feminisuto"* paradox of Mizoguchi, however, is that female suffering is also a classical trope within Japanese traditional narratives to idealize endurance despite unchanging conditions. The suffering of women as such wobbles unstably between these two poles of reading, as a call for freedom or a repressive celebration of noble sacrifice. The women in *Sansho* figure in additional ways to rewrite positions in history.

Anju, as is often noted in discussions of the film, sacrifices herself to make her brother Zushio's escape from slavery possible. The representation of her suicide can be cited as an example of what has been seen as Japanese national style. Tamaki, Zushio and Anju's mother, is similarly represented in crisis at the end of her appearance within the film, but is figured very differently. These two sequences speak to each other as eloquently as the two sisters in *Sisters of the Gion,* with similar effect.

Anju's death is represented indirectly through compositions of her body, facing away from the camera, within a natural environment. She walks into a lake, appears further away, then in a third and final shot has disappeared beneath the surface of the water, leaving only a concentric ripple. Her action is distanced and expressionless, while the composition reframes the environment so that she is surrounded by foliage in the first shot, standing between a live tree and a barren one in the second, and then disappears next to a single barren bush in the third. The indirect representation of intense feeling by means of elements in the landscape is consistent with Japanese painting. Within the discourse of traditional Asian aesthetics, this is not to be understood as a pathetic fallacy, as it would appear in Western melodrama, but as the participation of humans and the environment in the same cyclic processes of life and death. In contrast to classical Western assumptions of foreground subject and background object, Asian tradition constructs humanity as part of the environment and not outside it.

As a mode of textual inscription, the play of multiple elements within a complex visual figure could be said to parallel the operation of what Derrida names as the "hieroglyph," a figural complex of sound and image elements in contrast to the phonocentric transparency of the alphabet. This, of course, is similar to Sergei Eisenstein's and Ezra Pound's idea of the Chinese character as a complex figure, although neither could have accepted the idea that such an effect could be produced within a cinematic mise-en-scène. Japanese "national style," as exemplified by Mizoguchi, produces such complex figures by distributing equally significant elements throughout the frame that can only be meaningfully understood as a reciprocal play of signifiers inclusive of presence and absence. As a propositional text, this sequence inscribes female suicide through a sequence inflected by the figural logic of kanji, without the close-ups of facial expression that classical Western cinema uses to imply the subject of an inner voice.

FIGURE 15. Sign of national tradition or class oppression: *Byodo-in*, near Kyoto, is one of the rare surviving examples of Heian architecture.

When Zushio discovers his mother, Tamaki, at the end of the film, the sequence instead concludes with a crane shot, moving away from the directly expressed grief of Zushio and Tamaki into a panoramic long shot of the distant beach and sky. If this is meant to imply a Buddhist emptiness, the crane shot more powerfully suggests a transcendence of material concerns; if we are meant to imagine an attitude of *mono no aware,* an acceptance of things as they are, we are also presented with a grand vista like the one at the conclusion of Mikio Naruse's *Sound of the Mountain*. The vista here, as there, positions the viewer as a master of space, a transcendental omniscience beyond the objective concerns of the world, a metaphysical site first constructed by Kant. What seems in one sense to be a Zen landscape folds into a Kantian transcendental subject.

The omniscient subject of the crane shot derives from the operation of logocentric metaphysics, imagining a vast interior space as an oppositional category to an exterior empiricist history. That this position should coincide with an emptiness of composition reminiscent of Zen works to undermine any easy positioning of the narrative within the categories of nation or style. As a propositional text, the sequence positions the blindness of Tamika next to the powerless sight of Zushio, while only the viewer can master events. If the sequence of Anju's suicide doubles Western feminist liberation and Japanese traditional idealized female sacrifice within a figural inscription, the ending sequence sets Tamika's blindness against Zushio's eyes within a panoramic vista that mirrors the Kantian subject. We are left with a scene that suggests Lacan's essay "Kant and Sade," so that atrocity underlies the possibility of historical change, and we are left uncertain whether the atrocity is past or yet to come.

If *Sansho* reconfigures the possibilities of Western historiography through a process of cultural dislocation, inversion, and transformation, then activities in the United States during the same period are implicated in a reciprocal intertextual process bound up with Japan.

The same Fenollosa who discovered the Yumedono Kannon at Horyuji in 1884 produced draft translations of Japanese poetry that were later revisited by Ezra Pound. Pound's work on the Chinese "ideogram" became the basis for his theories of Imagist poetry and part of Western literary modernism.

By the 1950s, intersections with Japanese and Asian culture began to produce different unanticipated effects in the United States. Jack Kerouac and Allen Ginsberg became interested in Buddhism in New York and, when they moved to California, discovered that Gary Snyder and Kenneth Rexroth shared their involvement. The Beat movement became identified with Buddhism through such texts as Kerouac's *Dharma Bums* and Ginsberg's "Sunflower Sutra" (1955), which, like other Beat appropriations of Buddhism, dislocated figures from Asian culture into a Western context of an Anglophone literary tradition, popular culture, jazz, and alienation. William Blake and Charlie Parker were mixed with Zen in a countercultural project to break with the dominant militarist, corporate, and consumerist mass culture that emerged during and after the Korean War. In 1950, John Cage began producing music based on chance operations generated from the *I Ching* (the Chinese *Book of Changes*) and by 1952 had composed *4'33"* as a duration of silence.

Cage's position in this array of activities helps clarify the effect of interjecting Asian textual figures during the period. During the same decade when a dominant mass culture produced and circulated such neo-Orientalist narratives as Daniel Mann's *Teahouse of the August Moon* (1956) and John Huston's *Barbarian and the Geisha* (1958), another America was engaging with Asia according to a very different cultural logic. While dominant studio narratives are interesting insofar as they articulate the limits, contradictions, and occasional subversions of Western stereotypical constructions of Asia, avant-garde and countercultural interventions reverse the process to reconfigure Western discourse in relation to Asian figural elements. Neither area of Western cultural production engages with Asia on its own terms, but both generate hybrid texts that rewrite the limits and possibilities of historical knowledge.

The position of Zen in 1950s America can be understood in part through the figure of D. T. Suzuki, who popularized Zen in the United States by reinventing it outside its Japanese context in terms of the phenomenological "experience" that William James constructs as a secular model for comparative religious practices. By the 1990s, Suzuki became a figure of considerable contestation, as scholars debated the degree to which he was implicated in the support of 1930s militarism by schools of Zen in Japan. This problem, as important as it became later, was occluded during the 1950s by the immediacy of Japan's defeat and the interest in reconceiving possible relationships across cultures. Suzuki's interpretation of Zen emptiness, or *mu,* as a psychology of experience was generally welcomed as a productive rethinking of tradition in a modern universalist context, as 1950s humanism imagined itself to be.

Several occlusions, then, inflect the 1950s introduction of Zen into U.S. culture. American artists and audiences were generally unaware of the authoritarian and hierarchical institutional contexts in which Zen was conventionally practiced throughout Japanese tradition, and Suzuki conveniently overlooked any issue of his own complicity with militarism and its atrocities in his public self-representations. One aspect of the period invites reconsideration of these considerable omissions and a reading through the gaps to uncover hidden conflicts and incommensurable discourses.

Another approach, equally important, is to consider how the figural elements that emerged from these conditions worked to produce their effects. In a decade when theoretical models for cultural study available in the United States were primarily existentialist and phenomenological, the dislocation of *mu* into Western discourse approximated what Derrida would later theorize as absence. The Beat deployment of Zen emptiness worked to reconceive Western metaphysics as foundationless, without the presence of Being that drove both existential anxiety and consumerist fetishism. As with Eisenstein and Pound's creative misunderstanding of Chinese characters as "ideograms" that generated proto-grammatological projects of innovative textual practices, so *mu* in the 1950s worked to prefigure an absence at the basis of representation that was nowhere else possible within available discourses.

The silence of Cage's *4'33"* and the emptiness of Beat Zen reconfigures Western identity in response to the televisual enclosure that first emerged in the aftermath of World War II as a refusal of the mass subject constructed by utopian advertising in relation to its seductive objects. As a figural gesture, *mu* in the West acts both politically to render propaganda foundationless and simultaneously to reread the electronic screen as a facade of empty representations. Alternative modes of representation and agency begin to proliferate during the 1950s, from rock music and underground film to protest activism, and the foundationless site of *mu* operated as a hinge to allow circulation among seemingly incommensurable new discourses.

Stan Brakhage's 1958 move in *Anticipation of the Night* to a post–Jackson Pollock filmmaking strategy based on continually shifting movement, focus, and light, like Andy Warhol's reduction of cinema to a machine in films like *Kiss* and *Sleep* (both 1963), radically reconceives visual textuality outside the claims of presence. Both cinemas implicitly introduce a structuring absence into cinematic agency: through the imaginary goal of a fully "subjective" camera, Brakhage produces a cinema without a defining object, and through the equally imaginary position of a fully mechanical camera Warhol proposes a cinema without a subject. The interventions of the late 1950s avant-garde initiate an irretrievable break in cinema with expressive realisms and open on to modes of inscription within the materiality of the visual text. Much of the innovative film and video of the 1960s will develop this break into a heterogeneous array of visual rhetorics, and the force of this break can be recognized in the figure of *mu* as it appears in the U.S. counterculture of the 1950s.

History is refigured in the process, as the progressivist trajectory of Western civilization toward the transformation of Asia into a universalist humanism begins to appear as foundationless as the consumer utopianism of television. The radical rejection of an Aristotelian narrative trajectory in post–Brakhage/Warhol avant-garde film for cinemas of duration and temporal multiplicity marks a break in how time is narrativized as a model for historiography. In the United States, cinematic historiography remains divided between a dominant mass cultural practice that has itself changed in significant ways but nonetheless remains within recognizably classical parameters, and multiple autonomous media practices that continue to assume an irretrievable break with classical metaphysics. Cultural difference in the United States after the 1950s begins to be figured through sound and image media as a sustained oscillation between a mass cultural interiority and alternative media exteriorities. This oscillation not only characterizes the United States but inflects the possibilities of reading films from other cultural contexts and moments in history that are not always so polarized.

Reconsidering *Sansho* as a propositional text, rather than in terms of national character and personal style, makes it possible to address foundational figures of cultural difference within the film as a complex horizon of thought and possibility at a specific moment in history. Far from being a formalist reduction or over-reading of details, a foundationalist reading situates the question of political agency in history. Postwar Japan emerges in the midst of the transition from an industrial to an information economy, and political agency shifts from the "direct action" of 1930s assassinations and militarist aggression to the mediated action of symbolic protest. The foundational parameters of

FIGURE 16. The working-class amusement park in Asakusa, narrativized as part of the immediate postwar period in Chiba's *Downtown* (*Shitamachi*, 1957).

1950s representations are a site through which it becomes possible to map how this transformation occurred as a means to understand its achievements and limitations. When the 1960s begins with a cynical break with the "failure" of 1950s protest, a new discourse begins with the foundational assumption that agency is always constituted as a symbolic intervention in the social text, so that contextual performance becomes the central means through which to reinscribe history. The production of this new foundational insight is in many ways the work of 1950s cinema.

Shifting Architectural Codes

At the end of Mikio Naruse's *Sound of the Mountain* (*Yama no oto,* 1954), the father, Ogata Shingo, bids a reluctant and poignant farewell to his daughter-in-law, Kikuko, in a large public garden in Tokyo.

> SHINGO. A wide place . . .
> KIKUKO. A well-designed vista makes it look wider.
> SHINGO. What's a vista?
> KIKUKO. A perspective line.

The empty vista dwarfs the characters and reinforces their isolation from one another. To a Western viewer, the setting reinforces the representation of a young woman expelled from a family home into the outside world. Still, Shingo and Kikuko's parting remarks directly commenting on the perspective construction of a garden vista seem remarkably disjunctive. Other, more complex and less obvious significations are being suggested in the domain of constructed space.

Architecture in cinema cannot be identified directly with either the specialized design function separate from the actual building suggested by the Western word "architecture" or the craft of house construction embodied in the Japanese word *zoka*.[8] The concept of architectural codes in film addresses a different issue: the visual representation of architecture or *zoka* in the camera frame, or the problem of signification through spatial codes. Space is always constructed on film in relation to the camera, whether these constructs engage architectural design or traditional craft, set or location, conscious innovation or intertextual convention, or a combination of all of the above. In the example from Naruse, a shift in the organization of space from interior intimacy to exterior depth articulates both changing social relationships and a repositioning of the experiencing subject. This shift cuts across the architectural codes of buildings and gardens to imply the architectural organization of the camera space through which we see the film, a camera space introduced through historical contact with the West and tied to the sustained conflict of modernization and Westernization, which functions as a central concern of so many Japanese films.

Such problems and issues related to space and architectural codes circulate widely among Japanese film texts. These can be discussed by a series of digressions and returns, away from and back to the Naruse film as a reference point, to amplify components of a signifying process. *Sound of the Mountain* is not seen here as a master text that explains all others but as specific figuration to weave together and coordinate multiple threads of meaning unraveled intertextually.

Naruse's film is adapted from Kawabata's novel of the same name, but with a different sense of emphasis. As Peter Grilli has noted, Naruse omits Kawabata's fascination with such eccentricities as Shingo's claim to have heard the mountain, which gives the novel and film their shared title, and instead concentrates on painstakingly reconstructing the Kawabata home in Kamakura as the setting for the narrative.[9] This emphasis on architectural space suggests the means by which Naruse visually translates the themes of Kawabata's text. The ending of the film also differs from the novel: in Kawabata's original, Shingo and Kikuko remain at home as at the beginning, with shifting attitudes implied within an unchanging situation. In the film, Naruse continues his concern with space by inventing the separation scene set in a vast garden.

In both film and novel, the narrative represents postwar stress on the traditional family system through a father/daughter-in-law relationship, not unlike the repeating father/daughter trope in Ozu. Shingo, as patriarch, is deeply concerned with his son's wife, Kikuko, who was raised before the war and continues to represent the traditional female ideal of selfless service to her husband and her parents-in-law. In contrast, Shuichi, the son, is indifferent to Kikuko and becomes involved with a mistress, Kinu. In the story, both women become pregnant at the same time, but Kikuko, in the traditional relationship, has an abortion, while Kinu, representing a break with tradition, determines

to have the child. It is this image of the barrenness of tradition and the fertility of modernity that Naruse represents by the parting in the garden.

To a certain extent, the representation of architecture in film appears to refer simply
and directly to a historical context, with the style of a specific period chosen to reinforce
the impression of realism within a *jidai-geki*, or period film. As a result, it can be helpful for a Western viewer to be able to distinguish differences in style from the Heian
through the Tokugawa. Knowing the difference between such locales as a Shingon Buddhist temple and a Fujiwara mansion, or an Edoite's private residence and a Yoshiwara
geisha house, can sometimes help clarify the narrative situation. However, this kind of
distinction will not take us very far because film is a medium of visual representation,
not a transparent reconstruction of history. In Shinoda's *Himiko* (1974), for example, the
story of female shamanism during the semihistoric Yayoi epoch is set in deliberately
stagelike artificial buildings, to emphasize that we have no complete or infallible knowledge of the period. In other words, even within the visual style of realism, it is necessary
to interpret the film's understanding of history, and not simply identify its period through
architecture as if signification could be direct and unproblematic. In Naruse's film, the
appearance of a vast garden space, like that of Kenrokuen of the Maeda family in Kana-
zawa or of Shugakuin Villa in Kyoto, is unusual compared to the small-scale intimacy
expected of the traditional tea-garden aesthetic, as at Joju-in, Katsura Villa, Nanzenji,
and Ryoanji in Kyoto, or many others elsewhere. Why does Naruse choose this kind of
garden to represent change within the tradition?

In a *gendai-geki*, a film set in the period contemporary with its production, it becomes
necessary to interpret not only the film's representation of a historic moment but also the
traces of past architecture reinscribed in the present. For example, seventeenth-century
teahouse architecture and gardens have had a lasting effect on Japanese domestic architecture. Many teahouse elements persist to give contemporary housing its recognizably
Japanese character: tatami mats, which define both the size and the surface of the floor,
shoji (paper screens) to separate rooms, a minimalist aesthetic that leaves rooms primarily empty and unadorned, with functional items concealed in closets unless actually in
use, a tokonoma or alcove built into the main room designed to display a single art object,
such as a hanging scroll, and so on. When a television appears in the tokonoma in a
Japanese film, we are seeing a profound shift and doubling of Japanese styles in a single
architectural figure, which would be invisible without knowing this context.

At the same time, the revolutionary impact of the Meiji era, with its importation of
Western building styles, continues to affect the definition of public space in film. The
concept and construction of public space was introduced to Japan during the Meiji era.
Because Japan had no architectural tradition to draw on for such construction, the first
public buildings were direct replicas of famous Western edifices, or more functional ware-
houses and offices as in the nineteenth-century merchant quarter of Yokohama. By the
1920s, it had become fashionable for houses to have a "Western room," with heavy furniture that fixes the individual at a single point in space, in contrast to the fluid open space
of Japanese tradition. Such a room plays a very important role, for example, in Kurosawa's
No Regrets for Our Youth (*Waga seishun ni kui nashi,* 1946) as a setting for Westernized

Japanese liberals to advocate individualist principles in education, and for the heroine to play Western music on a piano. In Kurosawa's *The Bad Sleep Well* (*Warui yatsu hodo yoko nemuru,* 1960), in contrast, a luxurious Western home is the setting for ruthless capitalist individualism, and the impersonal public space of an office building is the site of murder. The Western-style architecture of public space and furnished homes is frequently represented in Japanese films in such ambivalent terms, as the site of contradictory responses to the impact of Western individualism.

In contrast to the Western tradition of central space and fixed furnishings, it has often been noted that pre-Meiji Japan had no tradition of *agora* or central public space in the construction of towns and villages. As Masao Yamaguchi writes, "For Japanese of the pre-modern period, it seems that it was the boundary between the village and outside areas that was crucial, rather than a concept of central space. The boundary of the village was that ambiguous space where "in" merged with "out." It was for this reason that bridges built on the river that marked the boundary were considered to be malevolent as well as beneficial."[10]

In Japan, social areas are traditionally decentered and intimate, constructing proximate relational interactions, in opposition to a boundary marked by ambivalence and the unknown. This structure is repeated throughout Japanese culture. To cite only one historic example, the origins of Kabuki theater are to be found in O-Kuni's public performances in the dry bed of the Kamo River, which divides Kyoto. This river marks a

FIGURE 17. A repeating spherical design at irregular scale undermines the depth of perspective, flattening the visual field to produce a proximate relational space at Joju-in, the garden of the Kiyomizu temple in Kyoto.

boundary space both inside and outside the city for performances that triggered strongly ambivalent responses among early audiences and were marginal in every sense of the word.[11] In film, Imamura's *Why Not? (Eijanaika,* 1981), represents public disturbances at the end of the Tokugawa era as occurring around and across a bridge.

Because of this characteristic feature of Japanese culture, the contemporary Western concept of decentering, as used by Derrida and others, has found many parallels in Western studies of Japan. Roland Barthes has discussed the role of the center in Japanese tradition in his *Empire of Signs,* and Noël Burch has raised the problem of decentering in film through such means as this discussion of Ozu's editing in *To the Distant Observer:*

> The pillow-shot may also be regarded as an expression of a fundamentally Japanese trait. Like Ozu's mismatching, it is not simply a signature, an individual stylistic trait, but a culturally and complexly determined sign of dissent from the world-view implicit in the Western mode. This mode, of course, is profoundly *anthropocentric,* as demonstrated by the rules of centering applicable both to composition within the frame and to the whole camera/diagesis relationship. Prolonged or "unmotivated" absence of human beings from the screen in a fiction feature film functions as a departure from the codes. . . . Ozu's pillow-shots have a similar de-centering effect when the camera focuses for a moment, often a long one, on some inanimate aspect of Man's environment.[12]

Burch argues, as does Barthes, that spatial decentering is not simply a formal arrangement, but a structure grounded in a specific ideology of relational subject positions.

Space is also organized in the way described by Yamaguchi inside the traditional Japanese home, with empty rooms separated by shoji forming multiple decentered spaces within which intimate relational exchanges occur and marked by the outside door as boundary. In Naruse's film, the traditional system of polite exchanges within the domestic environment is violated by Shuichi's indifference, and this abandonment ultimately leads Kikuko to the boundary of the home as the site of fearful change. At this boundary, she arrives at a public space so vast as to be unusual in traditional gardens, which were in any case closed to the public in the premodern era.

As familiarity with the Japanese intertextual context develops, a disjunction between appearance and textual analysis begins to emerge. Once the realist assumptions of constructed space as background for dominant action begin to recede, the metonymic and indexical functioning of architecture as historic referent or trace begins to appear as one among many operations in the domain of the symbolic. A well-known monument or type of building can function not only to identify period but also frequently works to establish geographic location, just as the film appearance of the Golden Gate Bridge or the Empire State Building iconically represents specific cities as narrative contexts for American viewers. Many of Ozu's so-called pillow shots, creatively misrepresented by Burch as narratively empty in order to develop an analogy to the pillow word in Japanese verse, actually function in this way. Burch is not precisely wrong, since the formal analogy of Ozu's visual technique to rhythmically repeating formulas in poetry is helpful, but he omits the referential element present in both Ozu's films and in the poetic technique. In general, abstraction and representation coexist in the Japanese arts, rather than moving categorically toward materialist realism or "pure" form. For example, the repeating image of gigantic oil-storage tanks in Ozu's *An Inn in Tokyo* (*Tokyo no yado,* 1935) immediately locates the narrative in the industrial section of Tokyo. The appearance of an Akita dog near the beginning of *Early Summer* (*Bakushu,* 1951), foreshadowing the young woman's ultimate decision to marry a man from Akita, has a similar function by nonarchitectural means. This function is not limited to the films of Ozu: Oshima, for example, incorporates Osaka castle within the wide-screen frame of *The Sun's Burial* (*Taiyo no hakaba,* 1960) to identify Osaka as the specific urban context.

However, in *The Sun's Burial* the castle is composed high in the frame at sunset with the city's slums in the foreground, contrasting the tourist-site icon of Osaka with criminal desperation. The red of the sunset is at once picturesque on the castle horizon, like a postcard of the exotic past, and blood-red in the streets. To a certain extent, we can see this combined figure as a multiply determined opposition: rich versus poor, tradition versus modernity, bourgeois tourists versus the unemployed prisoners of the slums, a monument of aristocracy versus the conditions of the lower class, and so on. The binary articulations of this iconic code become dialectical to the degree that they are ideologically informed. But at some point, these oppositions, in part necessary to make the film intelligible, break apart and mark instead a rupture between the two terrains: these places and what they represent have nothing in common. They are not simply in irreversible contradiction, but the gulf between them cannot be bridged. This kind of disjunctive opposition is also characteristic of Ozu's work, in the repeated framing of the tile roofs of traditional homes together with a passing train and electric wires. Does Ozu's inscription of traditional and modern mark a dialectical joining of opposites or a break between disjunctive elements, or both? A characteristic construction of Japanese culture seems to be the setting together in the same context of two irreconcilable elements, which neither resolve into a stable opposition nor break apart into fragments. Much of the dynamic tension in *The Sound of the Mountain* comes from this kind of setting together within the same narrative of the closed traditional home and the vast garden that closes the film.

Some architectural figures depend on specific cultural associations, either traditional or contemporary. The tori gate shrine in Yanagimachi's *Fire Festival* (*Himatsuri,* 1985) is a recognizably famous Shinto shrine to Japanese audiences, and the appearance of Yoyogi stadium in Oshima's *Treatise on Japanese Bawdy Songs* (*Nihon shunkako,* 1967) recalls the 1960s protest movements surrounding the Olympics for those familiar with Tokyo's postwar past. Other figures develop a symbolic dimension by intertextual contextualization and repetition. An island functions as a figure of personal and subcultural isolation in films as diverse as Shindo's *The Island* (*Hadaka no shima,* 1960), Shinoda's *Captive's Island* (*Shokei no shima,* 1966), and Kinoshita's *Twenty-four Eyes* (*Nijushi no hitomi,* 1954). An old traditional house can represent the patriarchal family system from Oshima's *Ceremonies* (*Gishiki,* 1971) to Ichikawa's *The Makioka Sisters* (*Sasameyuki,* 1983). Of particular interest here are figures of transgression represented architecturally. In Kobayashi's *Rebellion* (*Joi-uchi,* 1967), the samurai code of loyalty is marked as broken when a warrior walks across a sand garden; in Shinoda's *MacArthur's Children* (*Setouchi shonen yakyu dan,*

1984), American soldiers violate tradition by walking in their shoes on the tatami mats of a private home. At the climactic moment of rebellion against tradition in both Shinoda's *Assassination (Ansatsu,* 1964) and Yoshida's *Eros Plus Massacre (Eros purasu gyakusatsu,* 1969), all the shoji, or paper screens that mark the interior divisions of a house, are broken down. In all these cases, tradition is represented as a precise organization of space into a system of walking and looking, passage and enclosure, and transgression as the breaking of these boundaries. In *The Sound of the Mountain,* the traditional family is violated more quietly but just as strikingly by the shift from interior to exterior.

Still other architectural images accumulate multiple associations through the course of a film, so that complexity expands a single figure. The office building in Kurosawa's *The Bad Sleep Well* is one example. First appearing as the shape of a wedding cake, the office building eventually becomes the site of criminal confession in a scene set in shadows stylized according to the conventions of film noir. The building thereby comes to link the sexuality and generational heritage implicit in the wedding with the murderous corruption the film associates with the accumulation of wealth. The gate in *Rashomon* and the city park in *Ikiru* are two other examples of complex accumulative architectural figures in Kurosawa.

As architectural figures expand in significance, one of the dimensions of meaning that becomes clearer is the ideological. If the post-Bauhaus office building in *The Bad Sleep Well* is developed as a figure of ruthless individualism, then spatial enclosure is frequently used to articulate the confining tyranny of feudal tradition. In Mizoguchi's *Sansho the*

FIGURE 18. Perspectival recession in an early modern glass-covered shopping street in Asakusa, a predecessor of today's shopping malls that resembles the *passages* of Paris.

Bailiff (1954), the bailiff's walled compound becomes a principal representation of his cruelty in a Heian-period examination of the origins of feudal power. Much of the narrative turns on whether Zushio and Anju are being victimized inside or liberated outside the compound, whether the walls still stand or are burned, and whether the characters appear in the closed space of a boat, a corridor or a house, or outdoors on an open field or beach. This technique is even more relentlessly pursued in Ishida's *Fallen Blossoms* (*Hana chirinu,* 1938), in which a geisha house is represented almost entirely from the inside.[13] By restricting all camera positions to a single interior within the main body of the narrative, the visual representation of enclosure becomes almost claustrophobic and powerfully articulates the feudal restrictions on women's movement exemplified by the geisha's role. Compounding the sense of enclosure, the camera visually composes geisha both as individuals and as groups in architectural frames within the camera frame, such as within door frames, balconies, or stairwells, so motion in space is always constrained.

Only at the end of *Fallen Blossoms* does a principal character, Akira, climb to the roof and look out from a platform to see smoke on the horizon, which marks the collapse of the Tokugawa regime. The other geisha have already evacuated the house to flee from the approaching battle and fire, and Harue, the only other woman who remains, is drunk and pessimistically forecasts that nothing will change. But Akira alone separates from the group, stays behind, and looks out from the roof in a moment of erotic and political hope. The break from visual enclosure to the infinite receding space of a perspectival rooftop vista is identified with the end of feudal power, and by implication the relative relaxation of female constraints. In this context, the camera movement back to an extreme long shot of earth and sky at the end of *Sansho* may require reconsideration. The conventional interpretation of this closing shot as a Buddhist "transcendence" of worldly conditions has the unfortunate result of collapsing Buddhist detachment and the Western metaphysics of transcendence into a single figure. The figure becomes comprehensible and consistent with the rest of the film if considered as a projection of postwar humanist values into the feudal past. In this reading, traditional Buddhist compassion functions as a metaphor for 1950s antifeudal humanism, and the extreme long shot at the end joins photographic deep space with a release from suffering in much the same way that Ishida uses a rooftop vista to represent the end of feudal enclosure.

In *Sound of the Mountain,* it is not the association of perspectival space with the end of enclosed family relationships that is problematic, but its ideological significance. Kikuko is not allowed the same implied optimism as Akira in *Fallen Blossoms,* but is caught in a contradictory juncture where freedom and victimization seem inseparable. If Kikuko's independence gains her release from subordination to an irresponsible and unfeeling husband, it also costs her the system of mutual responsibility that has been her principal defense against the individual ruthlessness of men like Shuichi. Although Naruse, like Ozu, sentimentalizes the patriarchy, there is more at stake here than nostalgia. If Naruse and Kawabata too easily imagine that patriarchal authority and mutual responsibility combine in a single seamless figure, they also question whether the romantic idealism of humanist individualism should be valorized as "freedom" or criticized as isolation and powerlessness. It is in part this dilemma that *Sound of the Mountain* represents.

Kinokuniya Bookstore, as an architectural figure in Oshima's *Diary of a Shinjuku Thief* (*Shinjuku dorobo nikki,* 1969), compounds problematic ideological signification within a self-consciously multiple symbolic space. To those familiar with Tokyo, it initially identifies Shinjuku as the district in which the narrative takes place. As a notable foreign-language bookstore, it accumulates significance as a domain where Japanese and Western ideas intersect. Ironically, the open public space clearly marked as Western a decade earlier in Naruse has become for Oshima's younger generation part of a set of Japanese alternatives that now includes modernism. Known, familiar territory for young students, it becomes a space of increasingly complex interactions in opposition to the owner of the store and specific texts from the shelves. Through the older owner's role, the opposition of tradition/innovation intersects with that of owner/user, and through the texts of Jean Genet in counterpoint to Japanese authority (not unlike Derrida's counterpoint of Genet to Hegel in *Glas*) with sexuality, power, and perversity. These multiple instabilities open up within the space of the bookstore in part because of the doubling of signification across the generation gap: that which was new for the old (the relatively liberating postwar factors of public space, Western imports, and investment capital) has become old for the young (that is, linked to parental authority and feudal oppression). Part of the problem of reading architectural figures in Japanese film is recognizing the continually shifting boundaries between foreign and Japanese, and traditional versus modern, as each new generation expels from Japanese cultural tradition what had previously been integrated, or incorporates what had been innovative and invasive. In *Diary of a Shinjuku Thief,* the texts within Oshima's international market space contain contradictions and opportunities for the young as yet unread by the older generation who introduced them.

To further understand this process of multiple determination in Japanese cinema, we can concentrate on a single architectural figure as extended to nature: the garden. The traditional model for a Japanese garden derives from the Indian cosmogonic system, by way of Chinese aesthetics and cultural transmission through Korea. In this system, a symbolic mountain (Meru in India, and by transference Fujiyama in Japan) marks the center, but it does not function to centralize the garden in the same way as in the West. A mountain in traditional Japan is a taboo space, a place of gods or demons. This is precisely where one does not go or stand, and hence the mountain functions symbolically in a garden to decenter spatial arrangements. Barthes remarks on the same decentering principle of a taboo empty center in discussing the Emperor's Palace grounds in modern Tokyo:

> In accord with the very movement of Western metaphysics, for which every center is the site of truth, the center of our cities is always *full:* a marked site, it is here that the values of civilization are gathered and condensed: spirituality (churches), power (offices), money (banks), merchandise (department stores), language (agoras: cafés and promenades): to go downtown or to the center-city is to encounter the social "truth," to participate in the proud plenitude of "reality."

> The city I am talking about (Tokyo) offers this precious paradox: it does possess a center, but this center is empty. The entire city turns around a site both forbidden and indifferent,

a residence concealed beneath foliage, protected by moats, inhabited by an emperor who is never seen, which is to say, literally, by no one knows who. . . . In this manner, we are told, the system of the imaginary is spread circularly, by detours and returns the length of an empty subject.[14]

Structural decentering continues to characterize Japanese space, while its mythic and imperial origins now appear arbitrary. Mountains became recreation areas with the invention of the "Japan Alps" in the nineteenth century, and the emperor's palace had only a figurehead role from the Kamakura to the Tokugawa eras, as well as in post-Occupation Japan. Yet the empty center continues to be a significant feature in Japanese architecture, especially as part of a play of forms in exchange with the West. Frequently, this play remains unclear to Western observers or in Western writing, as evidenced by this problematic description of a contemporary Japanese reconstruction of European classical space in a 1986 issue of the *New York Times Magazine*:

> The Tsukuba building has been of particular interest to Western architects because of its obvious post-Modernism—it is a thesaurus of Western architectural history. . . . "Architecture is a machine for the production of meaning," says Isozaki, explaining that he has designed Tsukuba as a metaphor for Japan. At the center of the country, once occupied by the Emperor, there is a symbolic void. At the center of the Tsukuba square, *where one would expect a triumphant statue,* there is only a drain. [italics mine][15]

At the same time, a Japanese garden is marked by formal replication of key "natural" figures throughout Japan, such as a small stone peninsula in the pond at Katsura Villa in Kyoto to represent Amino-Hashidate, the archipelago with pine trees facing the Japan Sea celebrated in traditional poetry and painting. These representations are never full-scale or mimetic but function as miniaturized simulacra—a self-referential écriture of nature/culture as inseparable, rather than the categorical wildness imagined by an English garden. These simulacra combine with other formal compositions in a decentered space to construct an interlacing text of multiple viewpoints. Stepping stones can be turned in different directions, as at Katsura Villa, to invite the subject to various positions from which shifting visual compositions can be best observed. Many such viewpoint/composition constructs recombine the same formal/natural elements visible from other positions, so the subject and materials remain decentered and are never or rarely hierarchized by a dominant vista or overview. Specific viewpoint/compositions are also constructed to emphasize the formal play of materials and de-emphasize deep space. At Joju-in, for example, a series of bushes are spherically sculptured to flatten space: larger, round shapes appear behind smaller identical shapes, with middle sizes in no fixed depth relation to either. As a result, the eye moves forward and back without organizing space into the receding hierarchy of perspective. Hence, a Japanese garden is constructed as a decentered, multiple interlacing of simulacra and flat compositions, a space that reifies shifting positions within proximate group relationships. The écriture of a Japanese garden consistently constructs subject/object and nature/culture as fluid relations, never as categorical opposites.

In contrast, both French and English gardens work to sustain Western organizing principles. In the classical French gardens of André LeNôtre, for example (as at Versailles or the Tuileries), uniform symmetry constructs a central perspective or vista as a position of absolute visual power, a representation parallel to the reign of Louis XIV, the economic centralism of Colbert's *dirigisme,* and Descartes's cogito as a categorical and individualist subject. Interior to the linear symmetry of LeNôtre's gardens and subordinate to it, realist statuary of human figures represent nature linked with the erotic (Greek and Roman myths of seasons, rivers, and sexuality in statues that twist and turn in Baroque curves), an ideological identification of a lower agricultural class with an unconscious characterized by the categorical exclusion of the erotic from the cogito. Like the Japanese garden in a Japanese social context, the French garden both reifies Western social and psychological constructs and positions future generations within that system through a complex dialectical process that renders the construction unconscious or "natural" through redundancy. Yet as Derrida has commented in *Otobiographies* and elsewhere, it is precisely this underlying repetition of ideological constructs that most clearly emphasizes their origin as culturally arbitrary, and in need of constant symbolic reinscription to deny their constructive determination.[16]

The English garden, for all its notorious opposition to the French, seems to invert and sustain the same principles of organization. The natural or free-form landscape, advocated by Alexander Pope and Joseph Addison in opposition to French symmetry, projects outward the irregular multiple curves of the nature/erotic identification that were interiorized through sculpture in the French garden. For, example, in the work of Lancelot "Capability" Brown at Blenheim Palace and elsewhere, a hidden fence or "haha" maintains a barrier between a centralized perspectival position and the rural landscape beyond.[17] An irregular "nature" was painstakingly constructed to appear categorically opposite in its "wildness" to the individual viewing subject, still very much constructed as a cogito, and functions as a foreground to identify the rural landscape as an other to the cogito. The hierarchically centralized point of view, or vista, projecting outward to a categorical other subordinate to the individual subject—all this sustains the French system, but with the structure rendered invisible by the hiding of the fence below ground level. After its emergence in the eighteenth century, the English garden then became the world norm for landscaping, except, as Donald Greene notes in *The Age of Exuberance,* in the Far East.[18]

The Western categorical subject is embedded as a structured absence at the perspectival center of a vista facing an image of nature as a categorical other. This complex construct is not ahistorical. Its multiple determinants can be read in the development of Western painting from the Renaissance to the Enlightenment, if one reconsiders the premises of art history by way of Michel Foucault's archeology of humanism.[19] The flat iconic images of the medieval church were reinscribed during the Renaissance by means of the rectilinear architectural figures of classicism, which were used to construct the hierarchical linear symmetries of receding perspectival depth. As the viewing subject becomes centered as an individual point of view, through the structuring absence inherent in the perspectival distortion of a two-dimensional surface, architectural figuration

becomes the means by which space is reorganized to categorically separate and hierarchize self and other, private and public, interior and exterior. The later development of
landscape painting, as in the work of Nicolas Poussin and others, rendered these architectural symmetries as invisible as a hidden fence by the translation of the receding lines
of the laws of perspective into an invisible organization of nature, to extend the categorical self/other order of Renaissance humanism outward from the city to the rural
provinces beyond. This "civilization" of the countryside (etymologically, an urbanization)
is what the West ironically comes to call "nature," a romantic otherness projected outward as an image of what is excluded from the cogito of the city, as a kind of representational colonialism that parallels the English reorganization of agriculture into the great
estates of the eighteenth century. In both cases, the garden and painting, the same structure is maintained, just as in French and English variants: an absolute individualized
subject at center, with nature and the erotic subordinated as a passive other within the
hierarchical space of a perspectival vista. The further irony of the English garden is that
the rendering invisible of this complex categorical hierarchization was considered "democratic" by its advocates in contrast to the absolute monarchy implied by and associated
with the visible symmetries of French gardens. It is this ideological valorization of categorical humanism as "freedom" that *The Sound of the Mountain* problematizes by its
painfully isolating vista at the end of the film.

Gilles Deleuze and Félix Guattari in *A Thousand Plateaus: Capitalism and Schizophrenia* theorize this problem as territorialization at the psychoanalytic and ideological
bases of the Western cogito, through a disjunctive montage of historicized constructs,
from 1914 to 10,000 BC to 1440 and so on. They share with Foucault the premise that
the development of the cogito is linked to a culturally specific idea of madness as a failure to translate the collective symbolic processes of human culture into the categorical grid of individualism and nature.[20] The shadow of this idea of madness haunts the
West, according to Deleuze and Foucault, and it is perhaps this shadow that falls across
Kikuko's path in Naruse's garden. The territorializing and centralizing epistemology
of the Western cogito, which Derrida characterizes through his deconstruction of logo-
centricity "from Plato to Freud and beyond,"[21] meets an end point in the Far East. The
deterritorializing and decentering character of traditional Japanese space as articulated
through architecture appears in the emptiness of centers and of "nature" as the West
knows it, and its different emphasis on boundaries, gates, ephemera, and transitions
as the loci of signification and action. The cogito is no more present than its representational equivalents. Tooru Takahashi, in his writing on Japanese psychoanalysis and
language,[22] writes:

> In the Japanese language, the first person does not exist except in intimate combination
> with the second person . . .

This relational subject appears to be developmentally based in the extended contact of
mother and child, in contrast to the earlier separation of the child, especially the male
child, in the West, to encourage individuality:

> The binary combination appears in Japanese human relations as a repercussion of the imaginary relation of the subject with the mother . . .

Philippe Ariès theorizes that the Western concept of childhood as a separate stage of life was invented during the fifteenth and sixteenth centuries,[23] at the same historical moment as the architectural figuration of the individualist subject in perspective painting.

One could propose a Joycean multilingual wordplay to condense this cross-cultural psychoanalytic/social/representational difference into a single figure. By coincidence, the word "haha," which signifies the hidden barrier between the subject and nature in Brown's garden, is also the Japanese word for mother—specifically, one's own mother. In Japan, "haha" suggests the sustained intimate contact of mother and child at the psychoanalytic basis of a proximate relational social system. But in English, "haha" signifies the invisible barrier between self and other in a representation of nature as a categorical other. In *Sound of the Mountain,* Kikuko's motherhood is aborted as the imaginary security of the maternal role within patriarchy becomes untenable. It is not just the break of generational continuity that is represented by her isolation within the humanist vista of the garden, but the felt relational contact with the other represented by the mother's role at the psychoanalytic base of a social system knit together of mutual responsibility. Kikuko is abandoned, both by her family and by the end of the film, as an isolated individual within the perspective of deep space, with the nature of a garden recast as background, as object. In short, she is positioned as an unwilling victim in the domain of the cogito, with a future critically viewed as a position in a system of fractures between self/other, past/present, and culture/nature. The individualist alternative for women appears less as "freedom" than as a powerless silence, such as Susan Griffin articulates in her critique of pornography as the epistemological and ideological role of the feminine under the reign of humanism.[24] The poignancy of the film comes perhaps from the way that Kikuko is left suspended between an untenable traditional role and an equally untenable humanist alternative.

Sound of the Mountain is not alone among Japanese films in using architecturally figured space as a means of representing the dislocation and anxiety produced by cross-cultural conflict between East and West. Various transpositions of centered/decentered, intimate/public space appear in films frequently charged with social conflict or erotic anxiety. Interesting parallels can be found, for example, in films as otherwise dissimilar as Kuosawa's *Drunken Angel (Yoidore tenshi,* 1948) and Oshima's *Treatise on Japanese Bawdy Songs.* In *Drunken Angel,* the disintegration of a traditional Japanese community during the Occupation is represented by the centricity of a large muddy pool amidst the rubble left by bombing raids. Early in the film, the pool is identified as a source of disease by the local doctor, who alone argues on behalf of individualist and humanist values. The conflict of tradition and humanism significantly turns on the ambiguous figuration of this center. Empty as in tradition, yet presented visually in the narrative as if it were the perverse opposite of a centralized Western plaza, the pool and its disease represent conflicting values of centrality in the same space. In *Japanese Bawdy Songs,* conflicting spatial values are similarly equivalent to anxious interpersonal relationships. In a striking long take, Nakamura and Miss Tanigawa walk toward screen right in medium shot with the city scrolling by behind them as if on a flat screen. Cars passing the couple in the foreground indicate they are walking across a bridge, but the camera excludes the bridge itself from the wide-screen film frame. As a result, the erotically strained relationship between a young male student and his dead teacher's woman companion is positioned against a radically decentered public space. To represent erotic relationships dislocated in the modern educational system, Oshima's ironic critique constructs at this point a space that is neither traditional nor humanist in structure, but that radically fuses the two. What occurs in these films is not a confusion of spaces but specific compounds of conflicting values conjoined with both vitality and distress.

In Yoshida's *Eros Plus Massacre,* radical individualism and its erotic implications are directly represented in terms of the camera's construction of space. Episodes from the life of Osugi, as a historic anarchist and advocate of free love, are intercut with contemporary images of a young man and woman positioning their sexuality in relation to a camera and a projection screen. As mentioned earlier, Osugi's erotic politics triggers the destruction of all the shoji in a traditional home, so that intimate decentered spaces are replaced by one perspective vista. The extension of this radical reconstruction of architectural space to the present is presented in terms of cinema. The young man is empowered by the camera to a position of erotic dominance, while the young woman is bound to the screen. In Yoshida, the camera itself has an architecture, and an ideological imperative: the categorical separation of subject and object. *Eros Plus Massacre* is one of the most extensive elaborations in Japanese cinema of the camera's positioning of the subject in the ideological and erotic construct of humanist individualism. Yet the architecture of camera space and the ideology of perspective is also implicit in Shingo and Kikuko's discussion of the garden vista. Yoshida may rework the spatial material for emphasis and clarity, but many of his most radical assertions are perhaps surprisingly already intrinsic in Naruse.

For if there is poignancy in the garden at the end of *Sound of the Mountain,* there is also possibility. In this moment of suspension between tradition and humanism, the disjunctive break associated with the transition between the two systems is still open to be read as a means of rewriting both tradition and humanism as texts. The "haha" that signifies cartoon laughter could not inappropriately be added to the accumulating wordplay at this point, to suggest a Nietzschean inversion of disjunction into *jouissance.* The tension between two untenable positions generates a reciprocal deconstruction, undermining the truth of each system and setting all the elements of representation into play. At precisely the zero point of no possibility, where all space appears to be taken up, a rupture occurs: écriture is released from what Jameson calls the prison-house of language.[25] The possibility of inscribing a difference appears in the necessity of acting separately from all established positions. It is perhaps for this reason that *Sound of the Mountain,* and many other Japanese films that similarly sustain cross-cultural contradictions rather than imagining simpler positive resolutions or negations, remains so productive as a text. Frequently, by means of architectural figuration of incompatible spaces, they evade the false security of a transparency of meaning that represses writing, and instead approach what Foucault has called a "nonpositive affirmation."[26] Meaning is continually destabilized, and it is this destabilization that is sustained and implicitly affirmed as the necessary basis for action.

Ozu Paradoxes

Ozu's films first began to be seen in the West in the late 1950s, and were understood both as the most traditional of Japanese films and as modernist constructions. As Yoshimoto has argued, this phenomenon does not simply result from the usual range of scholarly approaches, but represents an unusually conflicted situation.[27] The paradox of Ozu's reception maps an inversion across cultural difference, whereby a traditional figure in one context can have radical potential when displaced to another.

Donald Richie, in *Japanese Cinema* (1971), argued the traditional side of this paradox when he wrote that "[Ozu] uses, for example, only one kind of shot. It is always a shot taken from the level of a person seated in traditional fashion on *tatami*. . . . It is the position from which one sees the Noh, from which one partakes of the tea ceremony. It is the aesthetic passive attitude of the haiku master who sits in silence and with painful accuracy observes cause and effect, reaching essence through an extreme simplification. Inextricable from Buddhist precepts, it puts the world at a distance and leaves the spectator uninvolved, a recorder of impressions which he may register but which do not personally involve him." Today, however, other factors have come to complicate the relationship of cinema and Zen. D. T. Suzuki's introduction of Zen to American subculture coincides with Donald Richie's analysis of Zen in Ozu's films, while Zen in Japan has since been attacked for complicity with 1930s militarism.

The difficulty in reading Ozu is in understanding how his films can be both a reactionary and oppressive tradition in Japan, as attacked by Imamura and Oshima, and simultaneously a resource for modernist innovation in the West, as theorized by Burch and Bordwell and practiced in the films of Jarmusch. Part of the confusion derives from thinking through what might be called a secular Buddhism, or the persistence of Buddhist tropes in a post-Buddhist secular society. Westerners who make pilgrimages to Ozu's tombstone to witness its inscription of *mu,* or emptiness, can be a source of amusement to people in Japan, who see the inscription as purely conventional and no more profound than "rest in peace" on a Western grave.

Ozu's metal teapot, which appears in so many of his films, is not only not simply Buddhist, but acts at two steps remove. Richie, in his 1971 discussion of Ozu in *Japanese Cinema,* significantly omits any direct mention of Zen, which is only implied at the juncture between Buddhism and the Zen aesthetics of Noh, tea, and haiku. The tea ceremony itself, invented in the sixteenth and seventeenth centuries, is a displacement of Zen into secularized aesthetics, parallel to the contemporary secularization of painting and sculpture in sixteenth- and seventeeth-century Europe. A metal teapot, such as the red one in *Equinox Flower (Higanbana,* 1958), is one step further away, displacing aesthetics into mass production and industrial design. Ozu's teapot is to Zen what European photography is to medieval iconography. Yet Buddhist figuration is not simply absent, anymore than modern portrait photography is devoid of resonance with the Holy Family.

Nishida Kitaro (1870–1945) is often cited as the first modern Japanese philosopher, and his contributions to questions of thought and cultural difference are still being actively debated. Nishida introduced the principle of emptiness into Western philosophy,[28] not as a nostalgia for a premodern past, but as a missing principle within modern discourse. Nishida's emptiness anticipates Derrida's foundational absence within a metaphysics of presence, parallel to how Heidegger's strategy of erasure returns as part of Derrida's deconstructive critique. This is not a question of influence but of parallel moves within the logic of the text.

Ozu and Nishida both construct a modern *mu,* as a secular principle of emptiness, or proto-absence. Their joint project is neither necessarily traditionalist nor modernist, but capable of either trajectory depending on the kind of reading that engages their texts. Any productive text, insofar as it introduces a break into dominant discourse, is open to such bivalent effects.

Abjection/Fissure

The figure of Zen emptiness is unstable and always at least double, oscillating between an abject complicity and a radical potential, depending on context. In Japan, Zen often represents an evacuation of individual agency complicit with imperialist or corporate domination, while in the United States, Zen can work very differently to destabilize a dominant metaphysics of presence and control.

The conflicted discourse surrounding Zen, as documented in, for example, *Rude Awakenings: Zen, the Kyoto School, and the Question of Nationalism,* often derives from tacit code or context switching within a rhetoric of universalist meaning. Zen in Japan can be legitimately critiqued as complicit with the Romanticized tradition of Japanese ultra-nationalism, while Zen in the West intersects with democratic societies to upset the ideology of universalist humanism. Karatani dismisses interest in Nishida as "Romantic,"[29] while Haver produces radical and innovative readings of Nishida[30]; both of these moves can be legitimate and important, depending on the specific institutional and discursive contexts through which they circulate.

Textual agency depends on awareness of contextual heterogeneity, and the multiple, potentially conflicted, and often unanticipated effects of any utterance. Nishida extends the secularization of "Buddhist" or post-Buddhist thought, intersecting with Western philosophy, to imagine a hybrid theorization. The principle here is that foundational figures inhabit modern secularized societies that derive from historically religious and cultural traditions that preceded secularization. These different figures remain foundational and can be read by way of literature, the arts, and cinema, although they remain repressed in the secular discourses of history, philosophy, and social sciences. Derrida's *Glas* places essays on Genet and Hegel against each other to demonstrate the reciprocity of figural and discursive texts.

Nishida can be reactionary Romanticism if read as a seamless appropriation of Japanese cultural tradition within a nostalgia for Japanese militarist imperialism. Reading then perpetuates his continued participation within the increasingly militarized institutions of 1931–45, and leads to an unresolvable debate as to whether his actions suggest sympathetic complicity or resistance within the system. Like Heidegger, who similarly became part of Nazi institutions, Nishida can also and simultaneously be read as a text that exceeds the limitations of its author. Nishida, in part, as Feenberg argues,[31] continues to challenge any Western ethnocentrism that imagines a categorical closure of philosophy against ideas from outside a Eurocentric tradition. Many of the debates surrounding Nishida have been specifically addressed in the context of the 1942 Symposium "Overcoming Modernity" and question how to work through the conflict of premodern nostalgia and postmodern potential implicit in these proceedings. Ozu too can be critiqued in terms of his wartime role, and his production of *There Was a Father* (1942) can be read as both complicit with or resistant to the war.

The hinge between reactionary and radical readings for both Heidegger and Nishida, and Ozu as well, is in part the difference between reading practices. One imagines an authoritative essence that positions authorial production as a seamless truth, and the other proposes a deconstructive textual practice that distinguishes between unsupportable assumptions and radical potential. Nishida's text, in contrast to his humanist role as an individual, proposes an emptiness at the basis of Western philosophy. By means of an antihumanist reading, his work not only anticipates Derridean absence but also Karatani's foundationless West, within the limits of available discourse during the 1930s and 1940s.

Mono no aware Revisited

When Donald Richie identifies Ozu with the aesthetic philosophy of Zen and *mono no aware,* he simultaneously notes Ozu's rejection of these arguments. In his 1974 book on *Ozu,* he writes:

> The philosophy of acceptance in the films of Ozu may be called this both because it is so deeply felt and because it has antecedents both in the Buddhist religion and in Japanese aesthetics. In basic Zen texts one accepts and transcends the world, and in traditional Japanese narrative art one celebrates and relinquishes it. The aesthetic term *mono no aware* is often used nowadays to describe this state of mind. The term has a long history (it appears fourteen times in *The Tale of Genji*), . . . Ozu did not, of course, set out self-consciously to capture this quality. To do so would have seemed to him artificial, just as the concept itself would have seemed to him old-fashioned and bookish. Nevertheless, his films are full of it, since he was. The many examples of *mono no aware* in his pictures, homely, mundane, often seemingly trivial, are none the less strong for all that.

Richie then comments in a footnote that Ozu had little faith that foreigners could appreciate his work and cites Ozu's remark, "They don't understand—that's why they say it is Zen or something like that." We should not be too quick to dismiss this contradiction as an ignorant West facing the true Japan, nor of Western insight confronting Japanese denial. Like Yoshimoto's contradiction of traditionalist and modernist readings, this conflict goes to the basis of what makes Ozu problematic and fascinating.

A major part of this dilemma has to do with how history works in visual media. A viewer may well ask whether history is not superfluous in modern film, or whether it does not simply vanish, as Fredric Jameson laments of television. Tadao Sato, however, argues that the historical contrast between medieval Europe and Japan explains the difference between American and Japanese concepts of leading men in cinema.[32] History, seemingly invisible in isolated media, often appears at points of difference like this. To read the naturalized images of film, one must notice both history and its inversion into a libidinal and political unconscious.

Ozu's films work to embody the subtle allusion of an intuitive nuance, which seems negated by any direct statement of cultural and historical context. Yet, just as Derrida argues that writing is implicated in the desire for a transparent language, so history inhabits a naturalized environment and immediate experience. Immediacy in Zen is also an ideological construction, as Bernard Faure suggests,[33] albeit it one of attention and the unrepresentable. Trained attention, by way of the unconscious, can yield the aesthetics and forcefulness of the Zen tradition, from *sumi-e,* or ink painting, to archery.

The phrase *mono no aware,* the "sensitivity of things," however, suggests more than a seamless aesthetics with Zen. When Richie first refers to *mono no aware* to describe Ozu in *Japanese Cinema* in 1971, he describes it simply as an aesthetic quality, but when he returns to the idea in his 1974 book on *Ozu,* he traces its history to *The Tale of Genji.* What he does not say, perhaps because it would seem cumbersome, is that Motoori Norinaga (1730–1801), a literary and linguistic scholar, first emphasized the term and traced it to early Japanese literature as part of an effort to define what was unique about Japanese culture. Motoori was the principal figure of the movement called *kokugaku,* usually translated as national, native, or Japanese studies. Motoori and the *kokugakushu* (nativists) sought to isolate Japanese traditions from foreign influences, such as those from China, Korea, Southeast Asia, India, or Europe. In part, *kokugaku* was consistent with the isolationist closure of Japan during the Tokugawa period, but it also represented a political resistance within the shogunate system. Harootunian argues that by proposing a "purity" of Japanese language and culture, the movement implicitly criticized the Sinocentric regime, which privileged Chinese writing and neo-Confucianism.[34] As a result, Motoori's ideas in some ways parallel those of Rousseau, in a celebration of natural language over the supplement of writing.

A century later, nativism helped legitimize the "Restoration" of the emperor in order to overthrow the shogunate, and combined with *romanha,* or Japanese Romanticism, to promote a Japanese imperialist nationalism. By the 1890s, the nativist privileging of Shinto became increasingly both a mystification of imperialist absolutism and a mode of xenophobic intolerance toward any and all cultural traditions deemed impure. Eventually, militarist and ultranationalist appropriation produced an inversion, so that nativism became a means of identification with the state rather than a resistance to it. Nationalist Shinto transformed Japanese traditions of localized *kami* into a state ideology, prefiguring both Hindu nationalism and Islamic militancy.

These were the circumstances that led to the situation that *Sansho* bitterly rejects: the attempted separation of Buddhism and Shintoism, the withdrawal of state support from

Buddhism, popular sentiment against the religion, and the iconoclastic destruction of Buddhist statues and sutras. Kofukuji, where burning Buddhist images in bonfires became routine, was the foundational site of Japanese history and culture as the first temple built for the new capital of Nara in 710.[35] Fanatic nationalism combined China, Korea, India, and the pan-Asian tradition of Buddhism, together with Europe, in a global category of the West. As Carol Gluck argues, the "foreign" was used to invent a "pure" Japan, so that Buddhism and Zen, like other groups, could only survive by subordinating their interests to the requirements of imperialist propaganda.[36]

Of course, it is not possible to extract Shinto from Buddhist ideas and practices. Almost nothing is known about Shinto before the arrival of Chinese culture, and afterward Shinto was integrated into Buddhism in practice and ideology. What Japanese culture was like before Chinese culture began to influence it is almost impossible to determine. Further, the rejection of Chinese writing, and *kanbunkan,* ironically rejects a substantial part of what is most "uniquely" Japanese. As Shunsuke Tsurumi argues, Japan's history of combining unrelated and incommensurable traditions is what makes Japan most unlike China and even Korea.[37] Asymmetry is the model for this combination of nonparallel materials, an aesthetic developed specifically in Japan and no other Asian country.

Ozu, through his own invention of cinema as a mode of writing, recovers a secularized and tacit syncretism of *mu* and *mono no aware* that was officially repressed during the war. By calling attention to these two vectors in Ozu's work, Richie tacitly suggests a contestatory project, at odds with the idea of a transparent repetition of traditional values. Accordingly, Ozu requires a differential reading, one that expects neither a total break with tradition nor a direct and transparent continuity with the past.

Unfortunately, Wim Wenders, in his voice-over narration for *Tokyo-ga,* an otherwise remarkable film on everyday life in postmodern Japan, claims to lament the present and long for Ozu as the source of "pure" images. By doing so, he positions Ozu in the place of a German idealism displaced to Japan, in a nostalgic circuit of mirrors that imagines the other as the truth of the self. In this reading, Ozu collapses into an ideology of tradition as originary presence. *Romanha,* like European Romanticism, acts as a neo-medievalism, and imagines a plenitude of Being through a direct equation of feudal narratives and modern discourse, such as the celebration of Bushido as an ethic for modern life. The transparent conflation of modern industrial mass society with "romance"— as vernacular language, as transcendent narrative, as libidinal transference—suggests a chilling nostalgia for the unchanging purity imagined by ultranationalism.

In contrast, Ozu, like Hou Hsiao-hsien, can also be read as actively translating and displacing tradition to become generative tropes within a modern context and discourse. The recurring phrase "Isn't life disappointing?" is cited by Richie as the primary example of *mono no aware.* However, this phrase is not necessarily nostalgic but potentially implies a model of radical change, a willingness to accept loss as part of a social reconfiguration. Japanese tradition associates personal loss with the passing of seasons through the trope of poignancy, and Ozu in *Tokyo Story* (*Tokyo monogatari,* 1953) locates the death of the mother in this nexus. As in nearly every Ozu film, nature in *Tokyo Story* is woven together with images of modernization, beginning with the sound of the motorized boat in the harbor and the image of a passing train that cuts through the middle of a traditional landscape. The seasons, through parallelism, can be extended to the continuing transformation of the modern world and the inevitable loss of one's own childhood world of libidinal transparency.

Given the historical context during which Ozu produces his work, it is perhaps not too much to suggest that his films can be seen to propose a politics of mourning, in counterpoint to the German "inability to mourn,"[38] and unresolved foreclosure. If this seems to conflict with other readings of Ozu's work as apolitical or reactionary, we should recall that politics always has more than one front. In 1942, Francis Ponge, Ozu's contemporary, published *Le parti pris des choses,* "the position taken by things," a book of poems suggesting that material things have political stances. Perhaps today we should reconsider *mono no aware* as a sensitivity to the position taken by things. At its most radical, Ozu's films potentially imply a disruption of declamative phrase regimes, and propose a countertext where all language is provisional and contingent, oscillating between intervention and erasure, suspended between presence and absence, irretrievably open to the other, the *arrivant,* the future.

The radicality implicit in Ozu, however, most often remains to be read.

Western *Mu*: Nomadic Tropes across East and West

A number of significant projects that emerge in the United States during the 1950s, including such classical Hollywood films as *Japanese War Bride* by King Vidor, the sculpture gardens of Isamu Noguchi, and the sound fields of John Cage, are inhabited by displaced figures from Japan. Some of the figures that tacitly circulate across national and cultural boundaries are the image of the Japanese woman, the principles of Japanese aesthetics, and the Buddhist concept of *mu* or emptiness. These figural dislocations are conventionally contained within Orientalist fantasy, but they can also combine with Western contexts to produce innovative and heterogeneous texts.

Unfortunately, the complex and conflicted repesentations that result often escape recognition in histories of film. Instead, they are overlooked or marginalized by disciplinary divisions between art and film histories, across national canons, and by debates between artistic modernism and postcolonial critique. The hybrid figures within Vidor's classical cinema, Noguchi's late modernism, and Cage's avant-garde projects can alternatively be relocated in productive relation to one another to better understand their operation and effects. Regrouping them together makes figural displacements and hybridities legible, and enables their reconsideration in a context where postmodern and postcolonial discourses intersect.

Vidor Brutalities

An elderly bespectacled Japanese man lifts a sword while clutching a monkey, and announces to his American visitor, "This is our ancient custom, which must be performed to honor the guest."

Since decolonialization, we have become most familiar with Western representations of Japan and Asia by way of Orientalism, the Romantic appropriation of Asian images for self-indulgent and self-serving fantasies of racial superiority, sexual domination, and technological control.[39] A postcolonial approach to film history can then problematize classic Orientalist film texts.[40] Many U.S. Orientalist tropes emerged in 1950s commercial narratives of Japan, from *Japanese War Bride* (1952), *Teahouse of the August Moon* (1956), and *Sayonara* (1957) to *The Barbarian and the Geisha* (1958). These tropes are subsequently extended to China, Vietnam, and Afghanistan in *Flower Drum Song* (1961), *The Green Berets* (1968), and *Rambo: First Blood Part II* (1985). John Wayne's *Green Berets* is symptomatically infamous for its concluding sunset over the ocean, a scene that could obviously be shot only in the United States, and not in Vietnam.

The exoticism of Orientalist fantasy has more recently been represented in film as multiple and reversible, as in Wong Kar-Wai's *Happy Together* (*Cheun gwong tsa sit,* 1997), in which a gay couple from Hong Kong pursues their romance in an exoticized Argentina. Ironically, Wong's film provoked a critique that it fails to represent the real Argentina, which is of course precisely the point. Exoticism may always be other than the known, but is not fixed in any one location. Jim Jarmusch's *Mystery Train* (1989) doubles this inversion, to consider Memphis as the exotic other for travelers from Japan, Italy, and England. By so doing, the film resituates the known as the other's exotic. Categories of same and other, once territorialized and seemingly predetermined, become destabilized and reversible. Once exoticism has been distinguished from an object initially imagined as fixed, other approaches become possible.

Orientalist art in part represents a discovery of the unconscious through its projection onto the exoticized other of Asia. Orientalist critique is invaluable not only insofar as it uncovers figures of domination that continue to inhabit Western discourses, but also as it enables distinctions among unconscious desire, social representations, and political effects. At its best, an Orientalist critique unpacks conflicted representations and makes possible the productive differentiation and recombination of its constitutent materials. Western representations can then also be considered insofar as they exceed Orientalist predictability and produce unexpected effects.

Japanese War Bride is a prototype not only for U.S. Orientalism in film but also for the possibilities of resistance within a closed system of classical representations. The complexity and contradiction of this film make it a case study in the representation of cultural difference. King Vidor makes a serious effort to address racial alienation and discrimination in California in the period after the release of Japanese-Americans from relocation camps, yet the film begins with a racist stereotype displaced to Japan as if it were an ethnographic discovery.

The majority of the film narrates the persecution of a young Japanese war bride in postwar California, where she has been brought by her GI husband. She struggles to survive despite local racist hostility, secretive and manipulative demonization, and systematic exclusion. The condition represented by her situation in the narrative has been perpetuated through the targeting of victims by extreme right groups in the United States from The Order to Aryan Nation. Racist hostility toward heterogeneity and intermarriage has intensified across Europe since the 1990s, in anti-immigrant rhetoric from Jean-Marie Le Pen supporters in France to Jörg Haider's in Austria. The problem extends as well to Hindu nationalist hostility toward Muslim citizens in India, Romanian discrimination against a Hungarian minority, and so on. Vidor's critique continues to engage a crucial problem in an increasingly postnational world.

There is, however, a peculiar moment near the beginning of the film that inexplicably lurches into a surrealist realm, which is ostensibly rationalized within the diegesis as grounded in traditional Japanese culture. A Japanese nurse takes her GI boyfriend home to meet her family. Her family home is recognizably a mansion of the extremely wealthy but appears within the film as if a normative Japanese house. The GI knows enough to take off his shoes before entering the house so that he will not appear to be a Western barbarian, and he is awkwardly courteous to the family. The family in turn is concentrated in the figure of the father, who insists on "honoring" the American guest through the "traditional" blood sacrifice of a monkey, prompting the daughter to protest and the GI to run out of the house in shock and disgust.

What is at stake in this peculiar sequence? In part, we are witnessing a historical version of stage irony, where we as viewers today know many things that American audiences in the 1950s presumably did not. The initial problem is that no traditional Japanese ritual anything like this ever existed. The situation is invented entirely for the film, and fiction is displaced to ethnography as if we were watching *Robinson Crusoe* or *Gulliver's Travels*. The second problem, however, is that in a socially progressive film, Vidor is not out simply to demonize the Japanese. Why, then, is this bizarre behavior attributed to the Japanese father?

Vidor's film in part attacks the traditional patriarchal family in Japan, or *ie,* celebrated in its decline by Ozu and later vehemently attacked by Oshima. The daughter here, as in Ozu, represents a radical break with traditional gender and generational norms, and the figure of woman's romantic agency appears as an emblem of a democratized Japan. The film recalls the American Occupation's odd requirement of kissing scenes in postwar Japanese films, as reconstructed in Shinoda's *MacArthur's Children* (*Setouchi shonen yakyu dan,* 1984), and the inclusion of an Equal Rights clause for women in the new Japanese constitution imposed by MacArthur.

None of this, however, explains the combined figure of brutality and monkey. John Dower's *War without Mercy,* on U.S. and Japanese propaganda images during the war, historicizes the monkey figure in the context of racist stereotypes. "Without question," Dower writes, "the most common caricature of the Japanese by Westerners, writers and cartoonists alike, was the monkey or ape." Among numerous examples, he cites Admiral Halsey's description of a naval mission as a hunt for "Monkey meat." Political cartoons from *Punch* to the U.S. Marine Corps journal *Leatherneck* depict the Japanese as monkeymen, and act as a calculated and derisive bestialization of the enemy.[41] Far from being an arbitrary or random image, the monkey figure is heavily overdetermined by a history of ideological projection.

In *Japanese War Bride,* the monkey is displaced still further to become politically surreal. The American stereotype of a bestial enemy becomes a sacrificial animal in the father's hands, his samurai sword now lifted to kill his victim. But what is being killed? Is it an innocent animal in its proximity to nature, or the Japanese militarist tradition? Is it the racist stereotype of American attitudes, or the bestial atrocities that characterized the war? Or do all these elements intersect in a knot of unresolved conflicts where atrocity and war guilt continue to inhabit Japanese and Americans alike?

In another sense, why does the monkey return as a ritual sacrifice? Sacrifice suggests a parallel figure of atrocity in Europe, especially in the context of a monkey the size of a small child. One of the emblematic figures of the Holocaust is the anti-Semitic fantasy of "blood libel," a virulent trope that charges Jews with the blood sacrifice of Christian children to make Passover matzoh. As a figure of biologized hatred and symbolic foreclosure, the medieval blood libel myth was revived by the Nazis, and has again returned among Islamic societies today to demonize Jews. All the same structural elements recur in Vidor's sequence: blood sacrifice, alien being, ritual performance. By substituting a Japanese father for the imaginary Jew, the film doubly inscribes Japan as a stereotyped object of hatred. The image thereby confuses Japan with Germany, and victims with perpetrators, in a vortex of misattribution and guilt.

Vidor's monkey sacrifice acts as a condensed figure of multiple atrocities located in the boundary space of potential intermarriage between Japanese and American families. Traces of racist bestialization and genocidal blood libel mark the gap between competing nationalist and patriarchal genealogies. These traces are then projected onto the Japanese and inverted as if initiated by the father, so that the political unconscious, to use Jameson's term, is initially represented as if belonging to the other. Such overdetermined moments figure as a boundary between discourses, as an asemic threshold where discourse collapses into foundational incommensurability. Bataille argues that a General Economy is necessarily founded in abjection, and *Japanese War Bride* suggests that the gap between incommensurable economies can become an impossible limit of reciprocal foreclosure.

The interracial couple in *Japanese War Bride* attempts to walk away from the problem by abandoning the father for marriage, but foreclosure then reappears everywhere once they arrive in the supposedly normal environment of California. Any renegotiation of memory and history, yet alone erotic desire and bonding, must first overcome the gridlock of reciprocal foreclosure at stake in figures of animals, robotic machines, and "race." Vidor's film warns that virulent exclusion will continually return despite discourses of tolerance until the determining figures of foreclosure are acknowledged and worked through.

Noguchi Displacements

In the context of the media arts, Isamu Noguchi becomes a curious hinge figure, connecting international modernism with Hollywood and the avant-garde.

Although biography has no privilege over other narratives of history, it is not unimportant either, and in the case of Noguchi is distinctive. Noguchi simultaneously produced modernist work and pioneered the habitation of a modern international space between Japan and the United States. From the mid-1960s until his death in 1988, he migrated annually between the two countries, continually crossing social and discursive boundaries. In the process, he anticipated a transnational space and mapped a Japanese/American hybridity into visual representation. The unusual circumstances of his life produce a complex narrative that circulates among multiple discourses of Japan and the United States, and of the fine arts and popular culture. Attention to his life in this context does not imply a celebration of humanist centrality neglected elsewhere, but the inclusion of the body as one organizing figure among others, which turns out to be unexpectedly suggestive in this case.

Noguchi was born in 1904 in Los Angeles to Leonie Gilmour, an American writer, and the Japanese poet Yonejiro Noguchi, who had returned to Tokyo earlier in the year. As a Nisei, or second-generation immigrant Japanese, he anticipates the progeny of Vidor's fictional couple in California.

He grew up in Japan, then after his parents separated, returned to the United States for high school and college. He studied in Paris with Brancusi, then later discovered Zen gardens and Haniwa sculpture. From this international and bicultural experience, he developed a hybrid modernism across gallery exhibition, theater design, and landscape gardens. His work is recognizable for displacing traditional Japanese figures into Western abstract sculpture, reconnecting Japanese tradition and Western modernism from an experience of both cultures. By so doing, he replies to the Western interest in Japanese tradition as a source of modernist innovation, initiated by the Impressionists, but embodies this combined figure through a hybrid ethnicity and doubling of discourses.

His work became internationally recognized, and his proposals received public support in the United States, Europe, Japan, and India. His project is ideologically international in the sense of displacing a genealogical origin from the West to Japan, opening the door to alternative national configurations of the modern. A century after the Impressionists, Noguchi's intervention quietly displaces the Western appropriation of the East by placing Asia next to Europe as a source of foundational reference. From 1953 to 1958, he designed landscape gardens for the UNESCO headquarters in Paris and by 1970 had begun a series of "void sculptures" in Japan.

Perhaps more thoroughly and persuasively than anyone else, he works through the potential radicality of Japanese tradition for modernism. He displaces Japanese aesthetics of asymmetry, raw materials, seriality, decentering, negative space, and the environmental field into the modern world. He then combines these principles with Western non-ocularcentric "abstraction," industrial production, international institutions, and the nomadic role of a deterritorialized flaneur. His work argues not just a stylistic surface but a structural connection between social representations in the Japanese past and the Western future. Both configure a decentered and nomadic subject in dynamic relation to a fluid environment, in contrast to the static hierarchies and categorical oppositions of the classical Western fine arts.

As one example, Noguchi's design of the exterior spaces (1956–58), including the Jardin Japonais, for Marcel Breuer's UNESCO building in Paris, works through a complex relation between Western modernism and Japanese traditional aesthetics. He imported rocks and stone lanterns from Japan, organized through triangulated and asymmetric compositions, for a garden of his own design. The effect is to offset Breuer's symmetrical rectilinear building in the style of international modernism with a curvilinear and asymmetrical space, so that the combination oscillates between centering and decentering the viewer, and between a hirarchical grid and a nomadic passage. By the late 1960s, Noguchi was producing a series of sky gates and void sculptures that redeployed Japanese principles of emptiness and negative space to produce modernist projects. In his *Skyviewing Sculpture* (1969) at Western Washington State College in Bellingham, Washington, for example, black painted steel constructs an open frame toward the sky. Shinto gates opening toward the environment, as at the Mt. Miwa shrine on the Kii peninsula, and minimalist Zen ink paintings are thereby refigured to position an ecological earth in relation to a cosmological setting of satellites in space.

Noguchi also crossed other discursive boundaries, and seemed able to navigate the gap between popular culture and the fine arts. In 1932, he designed a swimming pool for Josef von Sternberg, unfortunately never built, and was living in Hollywood when the Japanese military attacked Pearl Harbor. After the war, he met and married the actress Yoshiko (Shirley) Yamaguchi, who played the role of Vidor's Japanese war bride in 1952. He and Shirley were together from 1950 to 1957, until they divorced. Most of this time was spent outside the United States, since Shirley's visa was denied in 1953 due to her past associations with suspected Communists in Hollywood. This was the period when Noguchi designed and built the UNESCO garden in Paris.

The Noguchi-Vidor connection may seem curious or even uncanny, a surreal effect produced through the juncture of simultaneous but incommensurable discourses. Classical Hollywood Cinema and modernism in the visual arts have always had a complex and contradictory relationship. On the one hand, the mechanization of ocularcentric mimesis by photography and cinema allowed the handcrafts of painting and sculpture to pursue other modes of representation. MoMA (in 1935, when Alfred H. Barr Jr. hired Iris Barry) then incorporated both cinema and painting as "modern arts," and Hollywood occasionally borrowed from modernism to ornament its diegetic effects. On the other hand, as Theodor Adorno argues, mass culture institutionally repeats an aesthetically and ideologically reactionary mode of production that has no meaningful relationship with modernism and the modern.

Although Noguchi became canonized as part of high modernism, he also collaborated with the avant-garde. In 1947, he designed sets for Martha Graham, and for Merce Cunningham and John Cage's production of *The Seasons*. In the seemingly closed opposition of neoclassical Hollywood and institutionalized high modernism, the missing repressed figure is the avant-garde, which was always political and often considered pop culture an ally in its resistance to canonical fine art and dominant ideology.

His canonical status can make it easy to dismiss Noguchi today as if he were simply a representative of official corporate modernism. His simultaneous participation in the avant-garde, however, suggests other unfinished readings of his work. Noguchi can also be read against the grain as a nomadic figure who crosses categories of high modernism, corporate architecture, popular culture, avant-garde, and political art usually thought of as antagonistic.

As a Japanese-American, Noguchi's work is always haunted by the conflicted figure of race, as attested by his 1931 terra-cotta portrait head of Mexican muralist José Clemente Orozco, based on shared commitments to social reform, and his 1934 metal sculpture of *Death (Lynched Figure),* contemporary with the trials of the Scottsboro Boys and Republican filibusters against any federal antilynching bill.[42] After the Japanese attacked Pearl Harbor, he organized the Nisei Writers and Artists Mobilization for Democracy in 1942, and later attempted to improve conditions in Japanese Relocation Camps. If these efforts were failures, in the sense that rigid assignments of race, democracy and modernization remained unchanged in the Western popular imagination, they were nonetheless significant interventions and provocative failures. His hybrid idea of a Nisei Mobilization cannot be contained within an international utopianism, but instead implies a more complex field where modernization, tradition, and interracial marriage intersect in unpredictable ways.

At its most challenging, Noguchi's project returns the gaze of an Orientalizing West, and problematizes Western appropriation of Japanese tradition as a source for modernist art since the Postimpressionist citation of ukiyo-e. He reconfigures the connection between tropes of Japanese cultural tradition and strategies of Western modernism as an encounter between parallel discourses, rather than as a "primitivism," a parallelism or "next to" in Deleuze's terms rather than a privileged or subordinate origin.

One way of activating the radical potential available in Noguchi's work is to consider his failed projects as unfinished. Of these, perhaps the most conflicted and provocative is his proposal for a memorial at Hiroshima together with its refusal by local authorities. As an unfinished intervention into conflicted discourses of history after the end of the war, the proposal/refusal marks a specific impasse, and can be revisited today as a kind of conceptual art piece that rereads archival material for continuing possibilities.

Hiroshima marks an exceptional, perhaps impossible, position from which to imagine a memorial. Its challenge is to recode atrocity as a work of mourning, an irretrievable break and a "never again," evoking its potential to connect peoples across societies as common victims of an unthinkable annihilation. In response to this challenge, the conflicted discourses surrounding the Hiroshima memorial mark a pivotal crisis in the politics of representation. Noguchi's proposal was rejected, perhaps because his Nisei identity was simply conflated with the United States. The Japanese committee perhaps understandably selected a design proposed by a Japanese native, but this choice then creates other problems.

The memorial as built excludes recognition of Koreans forcibly transported to Hiroshima as slave labor in war-production factories. Only in 1970 was a small monument to Koreans killed in the nuclear devastation permitted, and then only across the river away from the central plaza, memorial, and museum, which remained "purely" Japanese. The Korean Hiroshima Memorial thereby becomes an unanticipated postmodern event, encoding not only mourning and loss but also political exclusion implied by its positioning. Its existence tacitly problematizes the official memorial's attempt to contain modernity and modernism within the figure of romantic nationalism, and ultimately race.

Today, the one monument to Korean victims that exists on the central plaza, the "Clock Commemorating the Repatriation of Those Who Chose to Return to the Democratic People's Republic of Korea," compounds the irony, since Japanese law forbids compensation to any hibakusha, or nuclear victim, who has left the country. It is as if the only Korean victims who can be acknowledged within the park are those who have excluded themselves from compensation by choice, inverting their arrival by force. In 2001, the *Japan Times* noted a memorial service at the park, where "Pak So Sung, the chief of the Hiroshima regional unit of the pro-Seoul Korean Residents Union in Japan (Mindan), spoke of those Koreans who have been unable to receive benefits under Japan's law to support hibakusha because they have left Japan, saying it is 'an issue that should be resolved while surviving hibakusha are alive.'"[43] North Korea's current claim to have nuclear weapons transforms the clock into an icon reminiscent of the Cold War, counting down minutes until disaster. The tacit exclusion of Koreans, and the Japanese government's refusal to provide compensation for non-Japanese victims, has returned in the form of a threatened repetition of the event that the official monument most sought to avoid.

Noguchi's unbuilt memorial now marks a series of unfulfilled potentials, available for rediscovery and action:

How could a postnational memorial be conceived and constructed that would include not only Japanese but Korean and Asian losses in the nuclear disaster? How could the historical memory of atrocity be fabricated to commemorate not only victimization but also the complex weave of atrocities *by* as well as *against* one's own society?

How could U.S. memorials be similarly reconceived? Another important but failed project parallel to Noguchi's was the Smithsonian's 1995 attempt to exhibit the *Enola Gay* in the context of new research questioning whether the nuclear bombings were as necessary as claimed, which was canceled after intense veteran protests. The permanent display of the *Enola Gay* at the National Air and Space Museum has since been haunted by the hegemonic foreclosure of responsibility and doubt surrounding the nuclear decision. However, the *Enola Gay* is far from the only event in U.S. history that invites recommemoration.

To invert the foreclosure of Vietnamese society in American popular culture, could a conceptualist art project extend Maya Lin's Vietnam Veterans Memorial to indicate the length necessary to include the Vietnamese dead as well as American losses? Since the wall currently consists of two 250-foot slabs to commemorate the 58,000 Americans who died, the Washington Mall is haunted by a ghost wall some five miles in length, with space for an estimated three million names written in a language that most Americans do not understand. This spectacular wall would extend past and through the Capitol dome with Thomas Crawford's bellicose 1859 "Armed Freedom" statue hovering above, or perhaps cross the Potomac in the opposite direction to refigure the Pentagon.

And then there is the monument yet to be imagined—to the 2,927 U.S. and 600,000 local dead (as of December 2006) in Iraq.

Cage Events

When he was in Kyoto in 1989, John Cage recounted, "I once asked Arragon, the historian, how history was written. He said, 'You have to invent it.'"

Zen entered the American counterculture through Black Mountain College and the Beat movement, at the moment when Bebop intersected with Existentialism to produce what Lewis MacAdams has discussed as the birth of the Cool. The pivotal juncture that connects these events was the arrival of D. T. Suzuki from Japan in 1950 to lecture at Columbia University, where his students included Cage and Kerouac.

In *Rude Awakenings,* Suzuki has since been attacked for complicity with Japanese militarism and Zen for participation in the war effort. This is ironic because, as MacAdams observes, the initial impression that most Americans had of Zen before Suzuki was its context of militarism. *Rude Awakenings* can remind us of this juncture, in place of historical amnesia, but it should not reduce reading to a logic of contamination that assumes an essentialist determining role of person and idea, rather than the effects of a text that exceed both the author and single readings. Zen has a long and complex history in Asia, deriving from the seventh- and eighth-century emergence of the movement called Ch'an in China, and its translation to modern militarism is very recent. Displaced from the problematic context of the Japanese militarist era, Zen in the United States generated a hybrid figure that both recovers a premodern historical tradition and inhabits innovative work by John Cage and the Beats with consequences for U.S. counterculture ever since.

Suzuki marks the moment when reconsideration of cultural difference allows for a more complex reading of alien culture than simply a totalized confrontation and rejection. Parallel to Kakuzo Okakura's *Book of Tea* in 1906, Suzuki's project was a self-conscious attempt to introduce tropes of Japanese cultural tradition to Western discourse. Accordingly, Suzuki's production of Zen is neither the "authentic" tradition that it appears to be to Western audiences nor the superficial and kitsch falsification of that tradition as it appears to Japanese traditionalists. Instead, Suzuki attempted a reinvention of Japanese tradition as a resource within an international and transcultural context. If this move necessarily betrays the purity and authenticity of insider traditionalists, it also opens the tradition to innovative and transformative readings that can revitalize its potential.

The radical potential of Zen in the West is in part possible because of its displacement from Japan, a displacement that produces effects regardless of Suzuki's personal contributions or limitations. Ch'an and Zen in Asia have always combined a radical openness of insight with the authoritarian closure of feudal hierarchies and the prescribed roles of master and disciple. The democratic impulses and emerging youth counterculture of the United States in the 1950s, in contrast, tended to spontaneously disregard the authoritarian aspects of Asian tradition. Suzuki acted as hinge between Japan and the West, generating this cultural dislocation and reconfiguration.

Cage never adopted Zen as a philosophy or institution but borrowed some of its tropes as operative principles in his work. His work marks the difference between antagonism and translation as discussed by Sakai,[44] between a direct resistance to the domination of both Japanese and U.S. imperialisms and the indirect agency of generative texts.

In the 1950s, parallel to Nishida and Ozu in Japan a generation earlier, a Western countercultural reading of the Zen principle of *mu,* or emptiness, displaced and inverted this traditional figure from Japanese culture to act as a proto-deconstructive absence in the United States. In the same way that Eisenstein and Pound's theory of the Chinese written character can be reread now as proto-grammatological, the figure of *mu* as displaced to the West can again be seen as anticipating Derrida's critique of the Western metaphysics of presence before this theoretical discourse was available. The figure of Zen in film and the avant-garde can then be rethought through Nishida's philosophy of emptiness, in parallel to Heideggerean erasure.

Permeable Binaries and Fluid Reconfigurations

John Cage's displacement of the *I Ching* for music coincides with the expansion of digital binarism in computing to become the dominant paradigm of the postwar era and with Norbert Wiener's citation of Chuang Tzu as a parable for cybernetics.[45]

In contrast to the Western idea of history, history in China and Japan was traditionally based on a regeneration of past representations and constructions. Western history is produced through a preservation of authentic artifacts, facilitated by an architecture of stone and founded on a metaphysics of origin. The premodern Far East instead privileged the copy to perpetuate an ephemeral precedent,[46] where buildings and statues of wood were assumed to participate in environmental processes of decay and renewal. This idea of history is based on an alternative or counter-metaphysics of cyclical time and a network of changes that continually regenerate an institutionally closed system.

A cyclical model of time is of course no longer characteristic of modern China or Japan, which have both adopted the Western calendar and metaphysics of time since the nineteenth century. However, the West continued to imagine Asia as a primitive society "behind" Western developments through at least the 1970s, when Japan grew into one of the world's most powerful economies. In contrast, modern history in Asia depends on the narrative of a radical break with past traditions. From this position, history can be reconfigured as an archive of unrealized potentials rather than a nostalgia for genealogical origins.[47] Conflicted discourses in a postcolonial context often seem to derive from a confusion of nostalgia and archive as figures of history.

When Wiener, Cage, the Beats, and others in the United States discovered a resource in premodern East Asia for an emerging electronic media society, their project implicitly engaged a reconfiguration of history not yet explicitly theorized. Although the figure of Asia in the 1950s United States continued to assume a rhetoric of origin, a sharp division emerged between nostalgic practices of neo-Orientalism and proto-archival displacements circulating as a countertext during the same moment.

In the 1950s United States, computers were monolithic mainframes, exclusively owned and operated by the centralized institutions of mass culture, from credit cards to universities. Binarism in this context, as well as during the Cold War, seemed consistent with a reduction of thought to Manichaean opposites.

Cage's reading of the *I Ching,* as a historically situated intervention, radically translates ancient Chinese tropes into a performative theorization of the emerging computer environment. The *I Ching* is a binary system with a *différance,* an operating system that is irreducibly permeable and changing, not categorical and fixed. Each element is in the process of becoming its opposite, and hence contains the germ of otherness within itself. Trigrams and hexagrams, like bytes, are a restricted set of figures constructed from a binary base. Unlike the alphanumeric system of bytes, however, hexagrams are conceived as a circulatory network of figures continually changing into one another in unpredictable ways. Categorical boundaries dissolve into thresholds, and fixed essences of Being elide into a perpetual process of Becoming.

Since the 1950s, computer binarism has radically changed and has become internalized and invisible within bits and bytes, then JPEGs and MPEGs. Binarism today is a molecular figure that inhabits all representations as a generative operator of translation, apart from the grand narratives of Manichaean opposition. Binarism has become like water, a fluidity that dissolves all images and representations into others, and a foundational indeterminacy that lies behind textual meanings and effects.

Like Brecht's 1926 essay on radio that anticipated the interactive broadcasting only realized much later by the Internet,[48] Cage's intervention transfigured the limits and possibilities of a new media context. The permeable binaries and fluid reconfigurations that Cage displaces from the *I Ching* imagine a postdigital Internet, no longer organized by alphanumeric Web pages but opening onto a dynamic full-screen videonet, at the horizon of VRML (virtual reality modeling language). That Cage's project cannot be contained within a formalist aesthetics is suggested by his call for "joy and revolution," a radical social transformation including, and not repressing, the libidinal energies of desire.

6

International Modernism

Textual Agency and the Politics of Desire

Neither Japanese nor French filmmakers initially appreciated the appellation "New Wave," which was manufactured by journalists and marketers eager to promote or attack their work. Oshima, for example, felt that the films involved were far too diverse to be reduced to a broad single category, and preferred to emphasize differences among motivations and strategies of representation. Eventually, however, the term became established, like "Cubist" or "Gothic," for a specific period and group of texts, regardless of its misleading implications. The arbitrariness of this convention, however, should not be forgotten, especially in its ethnocentric assumption that the French initiated innovation, while Japan produced only derivative imitation.

What is normally called the "New Wave" marks a shift in international context from the universal humanism of the 1950s to an international counterculture. Artistic strategies and political activism converged to become a politics of representation, to contest media transparency and dominant ideology in multiple contexts. Japan, like France, was situated between what Godard called the competing propaganda systems of the United States and the USSR and the conflict between these two dominant discourses opened a gap for new possibilities.

Oshima turned the parallel situations of France and Japan into his own strategy. When told that the title *Ai no koriida* ("love's bullfight arena," 1976) would not be understood in the West, he renamed the film *L'Empire des sens* for foreign distribution, a play on both Barthes's *L'Empire des signes* ("empire of signs") and Deleuze's *Logique du sens* ("logic of meaning" or "logic of value"). In English, the film became known as *Empire of the Senses* or *In the Realm of the Senses,* through a direct translation that unfortunately reduces both Japanese and French connotations to Orientalist sensuality.

To reconsider the films of the 1960s, I would like to historicize the phrase "New Wave" as part of a late modernism that expands beyond Western Europe and the United States. Japan, India, and other societies outside the West enter into a new kind of international modernism, no longer necessarily centered on Western developments as normative. To decenter ethnocentric assumptions and problematize historical discourse, I would like to consider Shinoda's film *Double Suicide* (*Shinju ten no Amijima,* 1969) as a kind of tutor-text, by which we can enter into some of the issues and conditions of this reconfiguration. By this gesture, I do not mean to privilege Shinoda above other filmmakers of this period, but rather to pursue shared assumptions by way of films that have received relatively less attention than they deserve.

Refolding

Shinoda's *Double Suicide* begins with what appears to be a documentary film about the Bunraku puppet theater. We see the large puppets of this specific style of Japanese theater, with their visible handlers dressed in black, and all but the main handler's face covered. In a voice-over, we hear Shinoda discussing a film production idea on the telephone, in a self-reflexive gesture that both implicates the filmmaker in the film and displaces the historical context of the puppet theater to the present.

We then enter a fiction film about doomed lovers in the eighteenth century, trapped by social conventions that bar their marriage and whose only escape is suicide together (like Romeo and Juliet). The actors of this narrative are set in an avant-garde staging with large ukiyo-e images and kanji on paper screens surrounding their performance, and accompanied by visible handlers in black as if in Bunraku.

Part of this juncture between documentary and fiction depends on a hinge between insider and outsider knowledge. Those who know something about the Bunraku theater might recognize several marks of an explicitly coded transition: the film's Japanese title, *Shinju ten no Amijima,* is announced in the stylized voice of a Bunraku narrator, and the story of this famous Bunraku play is then represented in a contemporary cinematic version. Inside a Japanese context, the transition is obvious, since the play's author, Chikamatsu Monzaemon, is as famous as Shakespeare in the West, and the play from 1720 is well known. For those international viewers who do not already know this, however, the juncture becomes a riddle, part of a hermeneutic code that can only be deciphered through extratextual knowledge. Conventionally, this kind of extratextual premise is usually explained in a subtitle or introduction added to the film for foreign distribution, to restore a potentially challenging moment to the transparency of immediately available knowledge.

Insider knowledge appears to explain much about the film. It can be helpful to know that Bunraku came into use as a term only in the nineteenth century, and named a theatrical tradition after its most famous site of production, the Bunrakuza puppet theater in Osaka. The puppet theater itself preceded its modern name, and first became widely popular in the late seventeenth century. This was the period when the dramatist Chikamatsu Monzaemon composed his librettos and presented them in Osaka in a new style devised by Takemoto Gidayu. Chikamatsu wrote narratives about the merchant class in Edo and Osaka, and the ukiyo quarter or entertainment districts in those cities, for both Bunraku and Kabuki stage performances. The film then directly cites the Tokugawa era, and the entertainment subculture within it, as the point of departure for its project.

If *Double Suicide* is read as a riddle, then the "answer" is Chikamatsu. Yet Shinoda's film participated in an era of international modernism when overseas distribution was likely. The youth movement of the 1960s, in which Shinoda's work was involved, marked a moment when young people in Japan increasingly defined themselves in modern terms and were becoming increasingly estranged from Japanese artistic traditions. In both these situations, outsider response could not only be expected but turns back on the film to recode potential readings. In this sense, understanding the transition between the two segments of the film as simply an adaptation of Chikamatsu's work to the present occludes the equally obvious emphasis of the film on an abrupt and decisive break between incompatible modes of representation.

In terms of film grammar, the combination of incommensurable styles or visual discourses cannot be safely contained in a hermeneutic interpretation; it also implies a direct equivalence of the two segments. As in Deleuze and Guattari's *Kafka, Double Suicide* can be encountered as an "experimental text" that does work. The film produces effects that exceed "interpretations" "about" a topic that leave the viewer secure in a fantasy of transcendent knowledge and a controlling subject. The film is not just an essay or metaphor "about" Chikamatsu, but its internal fissure acts as a copulative. No causal explanation or development is sufficient to justify its combination of materials, which argue on screen that this *is* that. An eighteenth-century puppet play is presented as the direct equivalent of the present, and the determining text of the Tokugawa era is represented as regulating the Japanese modern era, although its figures are repressed.

Double Suicide reinscribes history as a fold of the eighteenth century onto the 1960s, in another version of time as origami. Shinoda is not alone; Imamura produces the same fold in *Eijanaika,* suggesting a social rather than a personal reconfiguration. By again considering history as origami, I mean to imply not only Deleuze's theorization of the baroque in terms of the fold,[1] but Karatani's argument that Japan in the Showa period actively works to reinscribe Meiji events.[2] Shinoda's refolding of history problematizes the dominant historical narrative of 1950s Japanese humanism, which depends on the premise of a categorical break between a "feudal" Japanese past and a modern present that occurred in 1945.

The conceptualization of Japan as "feudal" derives from Marx, who argued that a living example of feudal society in the late nineteenth century could be found in Japan. The critique of a "feudal" Japan is then appropriated by New Deal administrators during the Occupation to legitimize the imposition of radical change, including democracy, labor unions, pacifism, and women's rights. The same idea of 1945 as an absolute break was then folded into the Cold War reversal of Occupation policies in 1948, known in Japan as the Reverse Course. Ironically, Marx's condemnation of traditional Japan as "feudal" became a determining premise of a right-wing faction in the United States that defined itself in opposition to Soviet Communism. The figure of a Japanese "feudalism" doubles and becomes unstable, so that 1945 thereafter implies conflicted readings that remain unresolved. A progressivist critique reads "feudalism" as an oppressively authoritarian land-based economy, while industrial capitalism repositions the "feudal" past as a legitimizing origin. Either way, the concept of "feudalism" identifies Tokugawa Japan with a medieval West, in an evolutionist model of history that remains centered on a European sequence as normative.

Shinoda's film proposes a different reading of the Tokugawa era, thereby problematizing the concept of "feudalism" and the evolutionary ethnocentrism the term implies. *Double Suicide* argues that a modern counterculture resists a dominant corporate society in the same way that the ukiyo entertainment subculture opposed the mercantile class during the Tokugawa. The traces of a "feudal" hierarchy in this era's samurai ruling class

FIGURE 19. Edo-era entertainment: the Minamiza theater in Kyoto.

are secondary to the growth of a mercantile economy, so that Tokugawa Japan resembles more the bourgeois centralization of seventeenth- and eighteenth-century France than a medieval economy. In contrast, Japan's entertainment counterculture seems closer to the nineteenth-century bohemian life of Montmartre, so the temporalities of Japan and the West do not directly coincide. Instead, the film argues that nothing fundamental has changed between the Edo era and the LDP, and that distortions of social relationships and desire across the two eras are consistent. No break has occurred, and illegitimate privilege organizes capital flows for the benefit of the few, founded on a simultaneous repression and incitation of desire that leads toward an eroticized death. The counterculture then and now resists the domination and brutality that regulates capital, sexuality, and language.

The counterculture of the 1960s was generated through specific historical conditions. The generation of the 1960s was raised under the Imperial Rescript on Education during the 1930s. The 1890 Imperial Rescript asked Confucian self-sacrifice to the state combined with modern knowledge and was subsequently enforced by the militarist regime.[3] In 1945, this generation was suddenly informed that everything they knew was a lie, and that democratic and socialist alternatives represented a decisive break with the past. The Reverse Course of 1948 was then experienced by this generation as a profound betrayal and a return to domination in the name of national security. After 1948, the previously disbanded industrial conglomerates, or *zaibatsu,* were restored and previously legitimized unions were suppressed. Political figures condemned for war crimes were rehabilitated, and by 1960 Kishi Nobusuke, arrested as a Class A war criminal after the war but released in 1948, became premier.[4] It was Kishi who then signed a renewed military alliance with the United States known as AMPO, which was seen by the younger generation as contravening the peace constitution and restoring militarist imperialism in Korea and Vietnam. The effect of this reversal was a generation that believed in nothing, a mass constituency with no guaranteed meanings.

Reinscription

The Imperial Rescript on Education in 1890 declared: "This is the glory of the fundamental character of Our Empire, and herein also lies the source of Our education. Ye, Our subjects, be filial to your parents, . . . should emergency arise, offer yourselves courageously to the State; and thus guard and maintain the prosperity of Our Imperial Throne coeval with heaven and earth." Any discussion of the student movement in Japan necessarily derives from this document.

Shinoda's *Double Suicide* in one sense could be said to be an essay on the possibilities of social reconfiguration in the 1960s. However, it is also a more visceral embodiment of this process and attempts to produce as well as theorize change.

Narrative action takes place surrounded by large-scale images of kanji, ukiyo-e, and Bunraku libretti on paper screens.[5] Characters are represented as inhabiting a written environment, where determining texts continually shape the possibilities and limits of social relationships and agency. Paper screens are mobile and produce a more flexible and changing space than fixed architecture, but they continue to reconstitute a familiar organization of openings and boundaries in multiple circumstances. After the beginning segment of the film, presented in the mode of a self-reflexive documentary that incorporates the voice of the filmmaker, inscribed paper screens act as a stand-in for cinema. Cinema is thereby represented as a kind of text that regulates action and reinscribes the determining figures of historically produced texts.

The visible puppet handlers, or *kuroko,* of Bunraku are combined with live actors reminiscent of Kabuki, but without Kabuki's stylized makeup; the naturalistic faces of the actors suggest both lived experience in contrast to the idealized world of the theater and cinematic representation as a new context of material conditions. The puppeteers now represent invisible forces of history in a trope that reappears recently in the anime *Ghost in the Shell,* where the criminal hacker is named the Puppet Master. Forces of economics, sexuality, language, and representation are figured as puppet handlers covered in black, as living equivalents of the "purloined letter" that appears in plain sight but remains unnoticed.

Oshima's films of the same period, *Diary of a Shinjuku Thief* (*Shinjuku dorobo nikki,* 1969) and *The Man Who Left His Will on Film* (*Tokyo senso sengo hiwa,* 1970), were both produced through Sozosha/ATG, as was *Double Suicide,* and extend and rework these ideas in the context of contemporary Tokyo and the student movement. As in Derrida, whose *De la Grammatologie* first appeared a year earlier, in 1968, text is considered as prior to speech and is expanded to include cinema and kanji as well as the roman alphabet. As in Godard, theater is positioned as prior to life and fiction prior to documentary, to suggest social practices inscribed in theatrical and cinematic texts that inform and regulate social behavior. Historically produced institutions and assumptions act as determining figures that precede the seemingly transparent reality of normative experience.

The year 1970, as Karatani notes in "The Discursive Space of Modern Japan," is known in the traditional Japanese dating system as Showa 45. It was during this period that Japanese popular discourse began using Western dating, so that the Showa 30s were succeeded by the 1970s. As a result, historical patterns of Japanese modernization can be obscured by a supposedly neutral Western system that tacitly imposes an alien teleology. Karatani makes the playful and provocative argument that the Showa period replays and reinscribes major events of the Meiji era, in a series made visible by corresponding Japanese dates. Showa 43 (1968), for example, corresponds to Meiji 43 (1910–11) as a way of suggesting that the student movement works through and reinscribes traumatic events from this earlier moment.

Japan forcibly annexed Korea in 1910, initiating a period of brutal colonization that ended only in 1945 and establishing Japan as an imperialist power. The United States had forcibly annexed the Philippines in 1898, when President William McKinley's imperialist policies set a precedent for how an expanding industrial nation could enter a world economy already divided among European imperialisms. McKinley was then assassinated at the Pan American Exposition in Buffalo, New York, in 1901 by the anarchist Leon Czolgosz. The Pan American Exposition prefigured modern theme parks as an infantilized and sanitized version of world culture, and included such exhibitions as the African Village, Alt Nürnberg, the Philippine Village, Streets of Mexico, Old Plantation, and the Beautiful Orient. This walk-in model of history has, of course, since been franchised to Japan in the form of Tokyo Disneyland.

Just as significantly, Meiji 43 was the year of the High Treason Incident in Japan, when twenty-four socialist intellectuals were arrested and executed.[6] Among them were Miyashita Takishi, who had planned to assassinate the emperor, and many, including Kotoku Shusui, who were innocent. Student activism in Showa 43 worked in contrast to oppose neo-imperialism, in the context of Japanese complicity with U.S. policy in Vietnam, and to restore radical possibility to the public sphere. Oshima's films in 1969–70 specifically address these issues and events, and derive from his earlier work on Japanese involvement with Korea in *Yunbogi's Diary* (1965) and *Death by Hanging* (1968).[7] Yoshida's *Eros Plus Massacre* (also produced in 1969) links 1960s activism with the survival of sexual and political anarchism after the High Treason Incident, through the historical figures of Osugi Sakae and Ito Noe from 1916 to 1923.[8]

Karatani's textual game is not, of course, to be taken at face value, as if history could be reduced to numerological magic. The absurdity of such a reading should clarify that his interests lie elsewhere. Instead, Karatani's dates alert us to the rhythms and repetitions of history understood not as an idealist teleology or blind succession of events but as a material process of regulating discourses and reinscribed figures.

Romanha

Rather than represent student activism directly, Shinoda instead addresses sexuality and desire by way of 1960s parallels to Tokugawa counterculture. In *Double Suicide,* sexuality is bound up with political agency parallel to Bataille's principles of a General Economy, as an outgrowth of a surrealist double revolution against both political oppression and sexual repression. Utilitarian needs are not enough for radical change; one must also address desire, and the desire of the other. In Shinoda's film, the same actress (Shima Iwashita) plays both Jihei's wife, Osan, and the geisha Koharu, with whom he becomes obsessed. This device undermines any transparent idealization of women and instead suggests that obsessive fascination is the product of a transgressive site rather than the property of an imaginary object. The lovers are caught in a potentially impossible game, seeking release from social restrictions through a funhouse of receding mirrors that only lead down an obsessional spiral to suicide.

Part of what is at stake in these images is the irony of a Left misogyny. A repeated trope during the 1960s and since has been radicality bound up with a hatred of women, an Oedipalized romance of revolution complicit with sexual violence. Hani's *Inferno of First Love* (*Hatsukoi jigoku-hen*, 1968) links modern alienation with bondage and molestation, Oshima's films (as Maureen Turim has noted) often revolve around the figure of rape, Wakamatsu's *The Embryo Hunts in Secret* (*Taiji ga mitsuryo suru toki,* 1966) notoriously sustains the premise of a woman tied up and tortured throughout most of the film, and violent manga or *hentai* today obsessively repeat a fantasy of men mutilating women. A number of films address this situation but often seem unable to do more than represent it, and thereby risk complicity with the problem being represented.

Figure 20. Oblique low-angle shots continually warp space to narrativize the Taisho sexual anarchist Osugi, in Yoshida's widescreen *Eros Plus Massacre* (*Eros purasu gyakusatsu,* 1969).

In part, these images represent an attack on the idealized woman of Japanese tradition as seen in films by Naruse and Ozu, but often in a way that the attack becomes indistinguishable from hatred of actual women. The magical thinking of unconscious fantasy directly projected into film can conflate idealized representations with living people. The goal of an egalitarian society is then ironically expressed through rage against women, as an unself-conscious vengeance for loss of infantile plenitude. Libidinal intensity operates in excess of egalitarian rationality and opens onto a politics of desire.

At their best, films like *Double Suicide* engage the libidinal and gender conditions that inhabit 1960s counterculture and work to transform them, so that a New Left can be located at the intersection of multiple discourses of radicality, from sexuality and language to economics and representation. Shinoda's film is part of a larger project during the 1960s to reconfigure the Left in an era of information. This film, like others, can act as an instruction manual to work through potentially maddening conflicts and distinguish between radical possibility and Oedipalized misogyny, between revolutionary agency and the seductive lure of suicide. The films remain to be read as a resource for working through problems of history and agency today.

The Pacific War: Reading, Contradiction, and Denial

Oshima Nagisa directed a series of documentaries produced by the Nippon Television Network from 1962 to 1978, at times when he was not actively working on feature films. His feature-length film, *The Greater East Asia War* (*Dai toa senso,* 1968), reconstructs the propaganda image of Japanese militarism through newsreels of the period. Unknown in the United States, the film remains a cautionary tale that generates new implications during a period of renewed nationalist idealism and remilitarization in the United States and Japan. Oshima's film intervenes in the context of contemporary reconsiderations of the war and its ideological representations, which in turn become understandable through an extended study of *Momotaro umi no shimpei,* a 1944 animated feature from Shochiku.

Militarizing Childhood

Momotaro umi no shimpei was one of the more striking films being shown in Tokyo during the summer of 1984. Although much more interested in promoting its new commercial features such as *Welcome Shanghai* or Yoji Yomada's latest addition to the ever-popular Tora-san series, Shochiku nonetheless included a limited re-release of *Momotaro* in Tokyo as part of their August exhibition schedule.

The production of *Momotaro umi no shimpei* was supervised by the Minister of the Navy as part of the Pacific War effort, at a moment when the euphoria and hard-line exhortation that characterized Japanese propaganda during 1942 had begun to be recast in favor of entertainment values, as Gordon Daniels describes in "Japanese Domestic Radio and Cinema Propaganda, 1937–1945: An Overview."[9] Named after the hero of a traditional story, *Momotaro* presents Disney-like anthropomorphic animals happily jumping up and down as they build airfields, load troops into planes, and seize a city similar to Singapore from the British. A series of images translates nature into culture with specific ideological determinants: the jungle setting is cleared by childlike animals with industrial construction techniques to build watchtowers, barracks, and the airfield; individual play with toys alternates with an educational group sing-along of the Japanese hiragana syllabary; the chaotically bouncing animals are organized cheerfully into the uniform ranks of a military formation; the Japanese boy who leads the animals is the sole human in the group, and so on. The story is twice interrupted and framed by flashbacks: the first is a familial memory in which a father bird recalls baby birds back home; the second is a historic retrospective of the period of European colonialization, through silhouettes of ships, maps, and bombardments. The climax of the film then becomes a sequence of grand adventure: animal troops board planes packed with parachutes and rice, take off to cheers, and sing songs in the sky; they pass through the obstacles of a dramatically visualized storm and parachute landings under fire; and the Japanese boy leader decisively confronts the British, who are surprised at cards and panic, and breaks through their evasions to claim an unconditional surrender.

Several aspects of this film seem immediately interesting. The apparent lack of racism against Europeans has been noted before in Japanese films of the militarist period. To a Western viewer familiar with the racist stereotypes of American propaganda films of the war, the Japanese representation of the British enemy seems oddly restrained. American representations of the enemy so often seem to become what they attack, from Frank Capra's *Why We Fight* series, which ironically denounces the racist policies of the Nazis by categorizing the enemy as "Huns" and their Japanese allies as "buck-toothed pals," to the lurid Oriental villain of pop culture exemplified in the Superman cartoon *The Japoteurs*. In contrast, the British in *Momotaro* are portrayed not as monsters but simply as weak, indecisive, and out of place. Indeed, there is racism in *Momotaro,* but it is the implied racial superiority of the Japanese over their Asian neighbors, as inscribed in the opposition of the Japanese boy to the animals that follow his leadership. The British are the only other human figures in the film and are seen as adults. The Japanese boy is thereby presented as decisive and vigorous youth overthrowing parental authority, but the British are also indirectly acknowledged as the only kin to the Japanese in the domain of the human, the domain of civilization and the law.

Once the figure of racism is traced out, several further layers of contradictions emerge from the filmic text, elided by its transparent and idealist style. Japanese counter-racism in the film substitutes identification with the colonizing power in place of a potential Asian solidarity against Europeans, even though the film's militarism is justified in terms

FIGURE 21. Poster for the 1984 re-release of *Momotaro umi no shimpei,* the 1944 animated propaganda film produced by the Japanese navy ministry.

of the latter. The film's second flashback represents European dominance in Asia in terms of a past superiority in technology and organization, which is used to justify Japanese military modernization in the diagetic present. Daniels writes: "As in most countries, Japanese wartime propagandists often sought to combine the romance of history with a contemporary message. In particular, films were made of historical events which could present the Pan-Asian ideal as something with deep historic roots."[10] *Momotaro* represents recent events surrounding the capture of Singapore as a response to the history of colonialization. The irony of the Japanese position is not racism against racists, as in U.S. films of the period, but the perpetuation of racism in the name of anticolonialist liberation.

What is being elided here is the profound and tragic schism between the liberal Greater East Asian Policy of the 1920s, which proposed Japanese leadership in an industrially developing Asia led by Asians, and the militarist imperialism that seized on this policy as rationalization for its brutal massacre and exploitation of non-Japanese neighbors. Since the elision of this schism served military propaganda purposes in America as well as Japan, it is only since the 1980s that comparative studies of policy documents in both wartime governments, as in Akira Iriye's *Power and Culture: The Japanese-American War, 1941–1945,* have made it possible to reconstruct the multiple contradictions that shaped the war. After the Manchurian Incident of 1931, the Japanese military was increasingly able to force policy decisions on the civilian government in Tokyo by "direct action," at times in direct conflict with government orders. This catastrophic breakdown of coordination between military and civilian administrations continued through Pearl Harbor, when simultaneous peace talks and secret first-strike plans seem authentically to have represented different conflicting factions within Japan, a conflict overcome as before only by the military forcing the issue. Yet this rupture was perceived on the outside by most Americans as treachery rather than instability. As Iriye writes,

> Americans believed that the Japanese had long schemed such an outrage even while America was trying to negotiate with them in good faith. The negotiations had been in vain, because the two countries stood for diametrically opposite principles and because the Japanese had never taken the talks seriously. . . . This was a war between "lawless forces" and the cause of "establishing a just peace," as Roosevelt said on the day after Pearl Harbor. . . . This type of fatalism helped ensure national unity in both countries. For the first time the Japanese felt united behind a national purpose; debate and bargaining among diverse groups would give way to universal sacrifice and devotion to ideal.[11]

The ideal that elides discourse also conceals atrocity, as in *Momotaro,* where the cheerful confusion of pan-Asian liberation and racist imperialism forbids any possible articulation of such militarist actions as the Nanjing massacre, in which perhaps three hundred thousand Chinese were arbitrarily slaughtered.

The Politics of Memory

Then what purpose does the re-release of *Momotaro umi no shimpei* have in the summer of 1984? During this summer, protests were mobilized against the rearmament of Japan in coordination with the American military buildup under Ronald Reagan. Such protests are generated by a lasting broad-based pacifism that originates from a popular perception of the defeat in 1945 as a discrediting of military solutions. Yet also during the summer of 1984, a controversy broke out concerning the reediting of Japanese textbooks to de-emphasize such atrocities as the Nanjing massacre, a revision of history in public educa-tion vehemently protested by the Chinese.[12]

A special issue of *Cahiers du Japon* titled "Le Japon et la guerre" was distributed in France during 1984, specifically to summarize for a Western public revisionist views on the war that had recently emerged in Japan.[13] A series of essays compare the Occupation constitution secretly dictated by MacArthur to the imposed democracy of the Weimar Republic. The essays also criticize the war-crimes trials as hypocritical since other coun-tries have also committed atrocities and argue that Japan's role in the war was to a sig-nificant degree one of self-defense. Fusao Hayashi's controversial work, *Accepting the Greater East Asia War* (*Dai toa senso kotei ron,* a series of articles published in the journal *Chuo Koron* in 1964–65), which earlier reconceptualized the Pacific War as the last stage of a hundred-year struggle between Japan and the West, is defended as having no ide-ology and no dogma. The denial of ideology inevitably conforms to a desire to erase conflict in the writing of history and reify a shift in interpretation as fixed in signifieds imagined prior to the process of description. In these terms, new information and accu-racy about the war are blended seamlessly with the rising pride of the Japanese middle class, which benefits from "the economic miracle," in order to recuperate history into a mythic origin for renewed national idealism.

Shinoda Masahiro 's film *Setouchi shonen yakyu dan* (released in New York in the sum-mer of 1985 as *MacArthur's Children*) also appeared at this time in Tokyo, and was bitterly attacked by an American reviewer as sentimentalizing war crimes by nostalgically reduc-ing the postwar period to simply a time when Japanese children heard swing music and learned to play baseball.[14] Are the 1984 releases of *Momotaro* and *Setouchi* best understood as a form of denial, as a return to an idealism that erases memories of historic criminal responsibility in a renewed military buildup? The distribution of these films seems at least partly symptomatic of a remythification of the war, parallel to what George Ball criticizes as an American attempt to fabricate a myth about Vietnam that will convert atrocity and failure into nobility and betrayal. Ball underscores the danger of these apparently innocent idealisms by a comparison to General Ludendorff's myth of a betrayed heroic Germany in 1918, which helped poison the Weimar Republic and assist Hitler's rise to power.[15]

The most powerful corrective to this wishful misrepresentation of Japan remains Oshima Nagisa's uncompromising *The Greater East Asia War,* which assembles a history of the war solely from newsreels and propaganda films of the period. By restricting the film entirely to found materials edited together within the sustained device of chrono-logical sequence, Oshima in part constructs a documentary congruent with minimalist and conceptual art practices active at that moment in the West. With all voice-over narra-tive withheld, the war appears on its own terms, without romanticism or apology, in an ironic parallel to late 1960s ethnographic films designed to respect the symbolic constructs of the filmed subject. Through this construction, the film resists categorical responses to the war in terms of idealism or denial and places the viewer in a position to decipher the hypnotic but untenable codes embedded in this cumulative social text. A narrative emerges, or is drawn out, from the propaganda necessity of univocal consistency: all new footage released had to conform to the illusion of logical policy development.

Oshima's film begins with the Japanese announcement of the attack on Pearl Harbor, dated in the sixteenth year of the Showa Emperor, and presented dramatically with both ground and air footage. Speeches from General Tojo are edited together with images of public solidarity: people in the streets, a family praying, a crowd with banners, and children donating coins. Footage follows of Japanese warships, landings on beaches, and aerial bombing runs, leading up to the surrender of the British flag by British troops at Singapore, with close-up shots of British and Japanese leaders engaged in talks. The eyelids of the British flicker abnormally fast, through a shift of camera speed that suggestively recapitulates in a newsreel context *Momotaro*'s image of the British as weak and surprised. Daniels, in his study of the original newsreels, comments on the "notable . . . depiction of General Yamashita demanding surrender from the defeated General Percival" in Singapore.[16] Iriye, in discussing the impact of these events on China, describes responses equally characteristic of Japan when he emphasizes the "symbolic significance" of Singapore: "Since Western prestige in Asia depended as much on psychological as on physical factors, their loss of face would do irreparable damage . . . when Singapore did fall. . . . Westerners seemed to be weak and irresolute, a far cry from their pretensions as masters over the Asian races."[17] Although the events are well known, Oshima's version, like *Momotaro,* restores the rhetorical figures by which a social consensus was built and manipulated in a society where consensus politics are the norm.

The univocal hysteria of wartime-controlled information accumulates in the film through parallel editing of speeches, mass meetings, and military advances. An enormous crowd before the Emperor's Palace in Tokyo raises Japanese flags in unison to the shout of "Banzai" as military bands play martial music. Japanese troops jump from planes to the sound of Wagner's "Ride of the Valkyries," march under a temple tower in Burma as local populations cheer their welcome, and advance through flamethrowers and barbed-wire beaches on Corregidor until the Americans surrender. A meeting of dignitaries from Greater East Asia, including representatives from India, is presented in the newsreels as justification for supposedly anticolonialist victories. As in *Momotaro,* the contradiction of Japanese domination and anticolonialist liberation is embedded in the text, but with the vivid addition of mass devotion to the imperial ideal undeniably present in the shots of Japanese crowds.

Unlike *Momotaro,* however, Oshima's *Greater East Asia War* becomes increasingly eerie and disturbing. University students are mobilized and sent to the front, in images that mark a shift of tone from euphoric exhortation to melancholy and sacrifice. Daniels writes: "Japanese broadcasters assumed that their audience could accept a surprising degree of seriousness. On 21 October 1943 large numbers of university students paraded in the Meiji Shrine Stadium on the eve of going to war, undeniably an occasion of great poignancy. NHK broadcast this sad occasion presumably hoping it would strengthen national resolve."[18]

Traditional Japanese arts from poetry to Kabuki emphasize melancholy events and poignancy to express the degree of heroic sacrifice its characters willingly make. Despite, and in a sense because of, this tradition, images of heroic action in the newsreels begin to be undermined by unintended suggestions of futility. Daniels concludes, "Many shorter documentaries inadvertently depicted the decline in Japan's position and the changing mood of her war effort."[19] Images of children in uniform bow to an adult soldier's speech, followed by fierce fighting on Saipan. Kamikaze pilots are intercut with MacArthur onboard ship, bombers overhead, and the Japanese population retreating to air-raid shelters to represent the totality of sacrifice. Children are seen eating en masse, sleeping on a bridge, and going to the beach to a soundtrack of cheerful music as fires and devastation spread throughout the city.

Inevitably, atomic clouds appear and a shot of the Emperor's Palace is matched to the recording of Hirohito's broadcast announcement of surrender. A crowd standing in ruins bows its head in response, Tojo is seen in a hospital bed, a Japanese official is escorted away by American MPs, and Japanese soldiers returning home by ferry are greeted by a waving crowd. The univocal voice of coordinated propaganda promoting the war gradually inverts from intensifying sacrifice to extensive disaster. The contradiction of idealized violence is pursued within the self-generating narrative of sequentially edited newsreels to its logical end of national self-destruction.

Oshima's reinscription of the war assembles the material necessary to demystify the conjunction of regressive transference and militarist ideology characteristic of sign production of the period. *The Greater East Asia War* continues to offer a warning against a nostalgic retrieval of fragmentary materials drawn from a historic moment of social hysteria, as if these offered a glimpse of a purer, more ideal time. It also recalls the moment of crisis at the end of the war for children of Oshima's and Shinoda's generation, when the reality construct of public education during the military period collapsed, suddenly revealed as a system of mutually confirming lies. Oshima has described how, having been taught that the country could never be defeated, defeat taught his generation that no teacher could be trusted.[20] The Occupation did not bring or restore truth-value to public consensus; instead it undermined all such propositions as potential fictions.

Violent Transference

In an interview, Shinoda has said of *Setouchi* that "if I had made this film twenty years ago, I might have been stabbed in the back by a right-wing assassin,"[21] because the film presents a sunny and even positive view of the defeat. Yet Shinoda seems clear, in his focus on children slightly younger than himself, to be attempting to clarify the emotional juncture where baseball and swing music carried an edge of violence. In another interview, speaking of the movie's theme song, the Glenn Miller rendition of "In the Mood," Shinoda says: "It's swinging and light, it's a wonderful tune, but a lot of Japanese war criminals were executed right behind this music. Japanese history, tradition and philosophy are very stoic, but all of a sudden it's so gay, there's all this swing music, and it seemed to me so decadent. For me the violence is built into the music."[22]

In this context, *Momotaro* becomes almost Brechtian in its now unbelievable display of primary animal signifiers to invite children's emotional transference to the war machine. With its transparency inverted by time, the film, precisely by its heavy-handedness, becomes a document of the construction of primary process into a political economy. By so doing, *Momotaro* functions to restore memory in a history of childhood as much as it threatens to erase social history in an idealized public representation of the war.

The animals in the film serve not only to subordinate non-Japanese Asians to Japanese, but to invite Japanese children to playfully identify with a subordinate position to military authority. This position is doubly inscribed through the representation of social hierarchy, which, by offering a boy leader in the absence of any Japanese adult, substitutes identification with patriarchy for patriarchy itself. By such procedures, childhood becomes as colonized as Asia.

The desire of the militarists is to close the system, to deny cultural and psychological difference by subordination to imperial power. Asia and childhood are equally categorized as if simply an other. Yet for a society to extend to childhood the kind of closure imagined by the militarists, propaganda must address childhood modes of mental process as well as establishing legitimacy among adults. On the one hand, closure has the reciprocal function of infantilizing adults as it militarizes children. On the other, rhetorical modes diversify in order to adapt the ideal of patriarchal identification to these multiple recipients. The divergent figures of rhetoric necessary to incorporate entertainment values and a child audience undermine unity at its basis of écriture even as unity of discourse is extended to its limit. Multiplicity and difference thereby reemerge within the unitary system of identification proposed.

Perhaps the fascination of films like *Momotaro, Setouchi,* and *The Greater East Asia War* derives from their ability to suggest the multiple determination of history, the interweaving of what Freud hierarchically called primary and secondary process, of childhood and public institutions at a moment when both fracture under the stress of rapid change. If we extend the deconstructive implications of *The Greater East Asia War,* films that recall or reinscribe the war become excursions into a past that begins to seem as curious as it does horrifying. In this context, nationalist idealism first dissolves into the fixed positions that embedded contradictions and drove them toward violence; then those deadly fixations themselves begin to fracture and become multiple and arbitrary.

Tomotaka Tasaka's *Airplane Drone (Bakuon),* produced at Nikkatsu in 1939, presents an interesting parallel story. The benevolent but clumsy patriarch of a farming village learns his son will fly an airplane, which their district has purchased for the air force, over their home village in a flight of gratitude. The narrative then dissolves into a series of picaresque adventures while the father/village-master rides around the village meeting and telling everyone what will happen, with the last ten minutes of the film recording the loops and dives of the aerial visit. Like *Momotaro, Airplane Drone* is filled with animals and animism. In one memorable sequence, the father apparently talks at length with a pig, as a voice on the soundtrack is matched to the movements of a pig's mouth, edited into a sequence of reaction shots with the father. Only at the last moment does the camera pan to a speaking man standing next to the pig and rationalize the dialogue.

In this film, not only the villagers but also the animals as well are mobilized into an accumulation of capital for industrial investment through the military.

Film comparisons like this can help us better understand the operation of transparency and identification as ideologically charged elements of the narrative. Most theories of transparency depend on the concept of photographic realism, or metonymic construction of the sign, as their basis, at times in conjunction with an emotional transference facilitated by such transparency and necessary to complete the effect of a seamless narrative. *Momotaro umi no shimpei,* by targeting an animated film for children, shares the Western assumption that children will read simplified drawings more easily than photography. The film then depends for its effect on identification with familiar emotional and cultural values. Yet the substitution of animated for photographic imagery tacitly acknowledges the construction of a sign designed to be self-effacing. Similarly, since the function of the film is to shift emotional values from traditional roles (the bird's familial flashback, the animals' group solidarity within patriarchy) to a pleasurable involvement with industrialization and militarism, the film implicitly admits what its surface denies: that emotional investments are arbitrary and able to shift to new positions, and are not permanently fixed by natural or divine origins.

Transparency in an ideological context might best be described not in terms of photographic realism, but as the use of a self-effacing mode of signification to facilitate a transference by its intended audience. Both *Momotaro* and *Airplane Drone* promote not so much a return to old values as a rhetoric of the old to promote unconscious emotional investment in revolutionary change. Because such films use old and familiar values to facilitate a transference, the change remains covert as well as the benefit to some at the expense of others. The violence of such radical displacement is denied in self and society (the category of the same) by the idealist assertion of direct continuity of past and future, and is projected toward the enemy within and without (the category of the other). In such a context, as *Momotaro* records, group process is relocated through mirror identifications that seamlessly join childhood to social hierarchy, and regresses from an agricultural aristocracy to an industrial nation-state with explosive violence.

Animist Industrialism

Momotaro and *Airplane Drone* can be read as myths of national power in various tellings. In both films, a group (the animals in *Momotaro,* or the village in *Airplane Drone*) is opposed to an isolated individual (the Japanese boy, or the son in an airplane), with the relationship between them marked by authoritarian hierarchy (the military, the patriarch). In both cases, the group incorporates the proximity to nature of an agriculturally based society (suggested by the animal motifs in both films), organized through the proximate group process of spoken language. The animals represent in both cases not only the economy of farm life, but the emotional investment in that form of social organization by means of childhood transference to animal signifiers. The speaking of animals suggests through fantasy the emotional investment in this environment within the circulation of spoken signs. The incorporation of animals within the dialogue also articulates an antihumanist solidarity based on a myth of full and immediate presence of nature and emotion within language. This antihumanist solidarity is emphasized in other propaganda films of the period as well. Tasaka's *Five Scouts* (*Gonin no sekkohei,* 1938), for example, is characterized by an antiheroic concern of each of the five soldiers for the others that overrides any image of heroic conquest, leadership, or glory.

In contrast to this group solidarity, *Momotaro* and *Airplane Drone* position an individual isolated from the collective circulation of language and desire and characterized by writing and machines. This individual is visually differentiated from the others (by human form, or by the airplane) in contrast to shared visual imagery by the others within spoken presence. Positioned by writing (the hiragana public education in *Momotaro* or the telegram announcing the airplane's flight in *Airplane Drone*), the individual is characterized by absence—most strikingly in *Airplane Drone,* where the son never visibly appears at all and must be inferred indirectly by the telegram, other characters' memories, a photograph, and the sight of the airplane. A similar feature in *Momotaro* is the boy leader's forceful confrontation with the British, a decisiveness achieved without waiting for group consensus and approval. This is a myth that inscribes the creation of psychology, a shift to an internalized center separate from local group presence, as a repositioning of self within the distant orders of nationalism and an industrial economy. Simultaneous with this appearance of an interiorized subject is a nostalgia for its imaginary origins in the solidarity of village life, the presence of animals, and the fullness of spoken language. In short, these films in part record the introduction of what Derrida calls a Western metaphysics of presence, which marginalizes writing in the process of acknowledging its power, as the basis of transforming a feudal society into an industrial nation-state. Although both the militarist state itself, as well as its enemies, liked to imagine not only a continuity but also a spiritual identity with a traditional Japan of the period dominated by the samurai, closer examination of these films from the period suggests that something quite different is at work here.

At the same time, the militarist adoption of an imaginary purified Shinto for subject positioning within the state specifies a difference from such parallel formations as Protestant capitalism in the West, as well as from the Buddhist aristocracy of traditional (pre-Meiji) Japan. In each case, changes in metaphysical systems historically correspond to social reorganization, to renegotiate the shifting relation between primary and secondary process in a double formation of history. Militarist Shinto might be said to propose a direct transference of animism to industrialism as the primary process foundation of a peasant-based nationalism. Because this repression of cultural development into nature or the unconscious cannot occur spontaneously but only by means of authoritarian control, animist industrialism becomes infantilized, so that the machines become toys in *Momotaro* and the villagers in *Airplane Drone* appear childishly simple and naive. The transparent idealism of these texts, then, inscribe a myth that does not simply respect peasant solidarity (as the militarists claim) but reconstructs it as a regressive psychology within state determinations of power.

To trace further these psychological configurations within state determinants requires a return to psychoanalytic considerations, and Takahashi's idea of a relational self produced in part through a use of language in which personal pronouns are often elim-inated.[23] Again, subject formation in relation to language figures so differently in Japan that one consequence is to invite deconstruction of Western metaphysical assumptions inherent in psychoanalytic theory, parallel to the critique of Freud that Derrida pursued in *The Post Card*. Yet to imagine Japan in a transcendent position outside psychoanalytic considerations would be untenable. Since the phallocentrism of patriarchal power, and, by inversion, the category of the castrated as its basis, has long figured in Japanese history, psychoanalytic categories are not irrelevant. At the same time, some specific figures, such as mirror identification and castration, seem to emerge strongly from the films. The pres-ence of psychoanalytic materials in texts combines with the rural absence or militarist repression of the cogito. This suggests that in a Japanese context psychoanalytic con-figurations can function through collective representations in the social domain while their status as internalized categories remains problematic. This shift of emphasis within psychoanalysis from the private to the social asks for a psychoanalysis of texts rather than subjects. It also asks for a critique in which ideological and psychoanalytic approaches coincide, in some ways parallel to the project of Deleuze and Guattari in *Anti-Oedipus*. Deleuze and Guattari characterize Freud's universalization of Oedipus as itself a myth, as much as the original story. In this context, the symbolic function of castration within the structure of the unconscious becomes historicized and ideological as a framework within which personal roles are constructed.

In *Momotaro* and *Airplane Drone*, the role of the peasants is positioned at a juncture of social and psychic process by a regressive reformulation of Shinto within militarist industrialism. Peasant access to power ceases to function within a local circulation of language and desire and becomes possible only by the isolation of single signs as mirror identifications with the state. Such a juncture is the site where questions concerning the mutually determining roles of ideology and psychoanalysis can be most meaningfully posed, as Deleuze and Guattari have argued. Lacan has described castration as a fanta-sized threat to the mirror identifications of phallocentrism, which must be resolved to gain access to the intersubjective situation of language. If we are willing to transpose this formulation to Japan in terms of a collective representation, then exclusion from national discourse re-creates in part the crisis that stands between self and intersubjectivity, as conceived in the West. From a pre-linguistic or pre-Oedipal position, group access to national power proceeds from mirror identifications to a reenactment of castration fan-tasy on the national stage. Given the terms of this psychosocial formation, the collective regressive fantasy of phallic same (the patriarchal family and state) and castrated other (the subhuman non-Japanese Asians, indecisive British, childhood, and so on) then seems inevitable.

To go further, one could argue that this structure was not changed by the Occupa-tion per se, but only inverted. Since the emperor was equivalent to the phallus ("chin" is a term with two meanings: it is used by the emperor as "I" and also signifies the phallus), General MacArthur was popularly named General Navel *(Heso Gensui),* as the figure above the phallus.[24] With postwar phallic power reversed to the other, the revived inter-est in the figuration of suicide and rape in postwar films could be said to function as a representation of internalized castration fantasy (violence on a personal and social scale against the category of the same). To some extent, the new Japan restores the situation of the Tokugawa, with provincial subservience shifted from the Edo shogunate to an imperially conceived Washington.

But this identification too easily erases the reconstruction of Japanese culture and psyche in relation to economic development and the West. For example, despite extensive publicity given in the West to ritual seppuku and to student suicides over exams, which match a Western Orientalist fantasy of Japanese tradition, these forms of self-destruction are relatively rare. However, approximately half of all suicides in contemporary Japan occur in response to escalating debts contracted with the *sarakin,* or loan sharks. Similarly, women in postwar Japan can sell their companionship as bar hostesses as well as being vulnerable to rape. It is capital that is now dominant, not the physical or military force frequently used metaphorically to represent that dominance. In this context, it is not Paul Schraeder's American fantasy of *Mishima* (1985) that describes the libidinal situation in Japan, but Yoichi Sai's *Mosquito on the Tenth Floor* (*Jukai no mosukiito,* 1983), a Japanese feature about a low-paid minor police official whose symbolic and self-destructive gestures of rape and violence articulate a runaway conflict between consumer ambitions and loan-shark debts. The closed system imagined by the militarists in *Momotaro* is reopened, but with the contradictions of an industrialist absolutism now buried as the foundation of contemporary capitalist development. The re-release of *Momotaro* in 1984 perhaps marks the historic juncture between attempts to deconstruct these foundations and others to reinforce them as conflicting heritages of the Pacific War.

Shifting Boundaries

Studies of propaganda date back at least to the 1930s, when John Grierson defined the subject in positive terms as an impassioned advocacy or propagation of belief, identifying the word with an etymological origin related to the defense of church doctrine.[25] More critical or negational approaches include Jacques Ellul's classic analysis of the subject during the 1960s,[26] which attempts to answer Wilhelm Reich's question of how the masses come to desire their own oppression. The purpose here is to suggest that another kind of reading is possible, which traces specific inscriptions of the interplay of psychological and social formations within the domain of representation. Such a reading provides a means of deconstructing both the idealist identifications of positive approaches and the anxiety over diminishing powers of the individual cogito so often attached to negational studies of propaganda. As a text, *Momotaro umi no shimpei* contributes to an understanding of cultural dynamics in Japan, and by extension to the Third World under the pressures of industrialization and electronic information, and to the United States at a historical moment of nostalgia for industrial and military dominance.

It is easy enough to critique *Momotaro*'s advocacy of militarism as an attempt to collapse a complex adaptive process into a single authoritarian stroke. It is more difficult to articulate the shifting boundaries within psyche and culture that occur in response to radical social and economic change, so that the mutually determining forces of subjectivity and history can be equally deconstructed and the role of desire considered in a social context.[27] *Momotaro* can be read as a text that inscribes a specific psychosocial formation in response to a specific historic juncture, and as such it can help clarify problems of social crisis and change in a contemporary world.

Pig, Insect, Carp

Pigs stampede outside the Yokosuka U.S. naval base, an insect digs through the dirt, a carp splashes in a fish tank.

Two quotations can be mobilized to frame the discussion of animals in Imamura's films. The first is by Deleuze and Guattari in *Kafka:*

> We believe only in a Kafka *politics* that is neither imaginary nor symbolic. We believe only in one or more Kafka *machines* that are neither structure nor phantasm. We believe only in a Kafka *experimentation* that is without interpretation or significance and rests only on tests of experience.

The second is by Abdelfattah Kilito in "Dog Words":

> One must bark in order to find one's way; in order to become human one must first turn into a dog.[28]

What does it mean to say a society can go mad? This question emerges in the work of Wilhelm Reich in the 1930s, when he asks why, in contradiction to Enlightenment models of the political, people choose to act against their own rational interests? This problem then haunts the twentieth century, and it returns in a different place in Frantz Fanon's interrogation of madness and colonization, then again in Lyotard's *À partir de Marx et Freud* (marking Marx and Freud as a point of departure) for further theoretical engagement with social process. Imamura in the 1960s intervenes between these moments of theorization to problematize the conditions of what Deleuze and Guattari later call schizo-capital, and his project anticipates subsequent theoretical work.

After 1960, the *Zengakuren,* or Japanese student movement, confronted specific limits as to what would be possible in the immediate future. After many years of activist resistance to the Reverse Course, or reversal of liberation-era policies introduced by U.S. Occupation forces after 1948 and institutionalized by the rise and subsequent electoral monopoly of the Liberal Democratic Party, any radical break with renewed hierarchies of power seemed indefinitely deferred. The Liberal Democratic Party, or LDP, was formed in the early 1950s with the support of the CIA as a coalition of conservative political groups, and it has dominated virtually every Japanese election since, despite endless corruption scandals. In contrast, during the brief but foundational Liberation era of 1945–48, Occupation policies had actively promoted democracy, unionization, and women's rights, while militarization and corporate monopolies, or *zaibatsu,* had been dismantled. The *zaibatsu* were and are the monolithic industrial conglomerates, like Mitsubishi, that had been central to the war effort, and their elimination had seemed to be a necessary first step toward any democratization and labor rights.

The Reverse Course instead saw the war criminal Kishi become prime minister, the *zaibatsu* regain control of the economy and then the government through the LDP, and a military alliance with the United States passed in 1950 and renewed in 1960. Kishi had been rehabilitated from his Class A war-criminal status after the collapse of the 1946–48 Tokyo War Crimes Tribunal, while AMPO, the military industrial alliance with the United States, reorganized Japan around the ideology of the Cold War. A monopoly on power by monolithic business interests protected by military force, once thought overthrown by the liberation of 1945, had not only triumphfully returned but had become entrenched. These conditions become familiar again because they appear to have incrementally returned since the 1980s, despite the relative radicality of the 1960s and 1970s that in retrospect has been ideologically recast as only a temporary disruption.

In these circumstances, Oshima produced *Cruel Tales of Youth, Sun's Burial,* and *Night and Fog in Japan* (all produced at Shochiku in 1960) narrativizing the suffocation and foreclosure of revolutionary change, with special attention to groups and institutions that had failed to support student and labor activism. Subsequently, he went on to make the radically experimental and political films for which he became best known in the West: *Death by Hanging* (1968), *Diary of a Shinjuku Thief* (1969), and *The Man Who Left His Will on Film* (1970). By this later moment, the New Left had gained worldwide recognition and revitalized activist protest in Japan and the West against a hegemonic LDP regime complicit with the U.S. escalation in Vietnam.

From 1961 to 1966, the period adrift between the AMPO renewal and the rise of the New Left, Imamura Shohei produced what are arguably his three most powerful films—*Pigs and Battleships* (*Buta to gunkan,* Nikkatsu, 1961), *Insect Woman* (*Nippon konchuki,* Nikkatsu, 1963), and *Introduction to Anthropology* (*Jinruigaku nyumon,* distributed in the United States as *The Pornographers: Introduction to Anthropology,* Imamura Prod./Nikkatsu, 1966).

FIGURE 22. A young woman surrounded by filmstrips and a photograph of infantile sexuality narrativize the student generation of the 1960s in *Eros Plus Massacre* (*Eros purasu gyakusatsu,* 1969).

In these films he addressed the same historical situation as Oshima but in different terms. Curiously, through the often arbitrary circumstances of international distribution, these films were delayed and were not seen by Western audiences until the late 1970s and after. Today, these films seem as important as Oshima's to understanding the Japanese 1960s (and parallel conditions today), although for some time they were recognized internationally by only a few scholars who had seen the films in Japanese archives.

Imamura's films take a very different route toward the problems of political impasse and desperation than Oshima's, less oriented toward principles of Brechtian distantiation and reflexive textuality that Oshima seemed to share with Godard and that made his work recognizable and appreciated by radical theorists at the time. Imamura instead produces a series of wild texts, somewhere between Kafka and Daffy Duck, and closer to Deleuze and Guattari's theorization of psychotic machines as a figure of radical break.

In Imamura's version, society breaks down under the unbearable weight of untenable hierarchies and fractures into autonomous figures and transgressions. In one sense, social conditions have become psychotogenic, but in another, mass psychosis itself constitutes a break with any past viable community. If this break is not necessarily radical, it is nonetheless irretrievable, and refigures social participation regardless of intention or will.

We may begin perhaps to notice this effect through the curious repetition of animals in Imamura's films. Pigs in *Pigs and Battleships,* the insect in *Insect Woman,* and the carp in *Introduction to Anthropology* all figure centrally in the narrative in ways that may seem at first to be idiosyncratic and inexplicable. Animals also figure prominently in Imamura's later films, from the coupling wildlife in *Ballad of Narayama* to the eel in *Unagi.* An extreme close-up of the insect in *Insect Woman,* for example, is directly intercut with human figures, yet is often critically discussed, if at all, as simply a metaphor for character motivation. The direct cut between insect and human is easily understood by way of Eisensteinian montage as a metaphor.

What if we instead pursue Deleuze and Guattari's proposal in *Kafka* for an experimental reading and set aside critical hermeneutics that translate narrative figures into easily identified signifieds in a psychologized discourse? What if we read outward from the figure as a textual machine that infects and determines the rest of these films? In each case, the significant repetition and explicit attention given to representations of animals exceeds any rational narrative explanation or character psychology. As in Kafka's "Metamorphosis," the insect in *Insect Woman* is never explained or contained within a point of view or fantasy grounded in character, but instead operates as an autonomous figure insistently edited into the film.

Imamura has described his fascination with the "lower part of the human body and the lower part of the social structure, on which the reality of daily Japanese life obstinately supports itself."[29] Despite the seeming primitivism of this rhetoric, his project is decidedly antiprimitivist. Deleuze and Guattari argue that the figure of the cockroach in "Metamorphosis" operates as a textual machine to produce deterritorialized effects, rather than as a Signifier to regulate meanings. Imamura's animals, from pig to insect and carp, work to deterritorialize nationalist narratives of history founded on primitive origins and generate counter-histories of [modern Japan] next to the official versions.

Imamura is both more cynical and more optimistic than we might expect. Cynical because his films imply that Japanese society has gone mad, rather than pursue the project of liberation that seemed clearly in reach after 1945. Yet optimistic in that madness itself already constitutes an irretrievable break with the hegemonic return to a society based on brutality and domination. The savage comedy of his 1960s films derives from the premise that a radical break with domination is no more drastic than the madness that has already occurred, and that madness ultimately leads nowhere different. If society goes mad instead of embracing radical change, then this is a remarkable preference that provokes a Nietzschean laughter, not despair. The alternative to desperation and brutality remains clear, and all that is missing is a social grasp of the difference amidst an array of proliferating misrecognitions.

Whenever participation in the social symbolic is foreclosed, whether by violence, untenable hierarchies, or propaganda infantilization, machinic effects multiply as a consequence. Imamura then figures that the most productive intervention he can make under the circumstances is a series of films that operates somewhere between a zen blow with a stick and a Nietzschean genealogy of morals, as antiviral jokes against a society infected with the morbidity of schizo-capital.

"Every revolution is a throw of the dice," as Jean-Marie Straub and Daniele Huillet paraphrased Stéphane Mallarmé, and there are never any guarantees for what will happen next.

Intersections: Anamnesis and the Libidinal Field

One of the ironies of referring to Japanese films of the 1960s as a Japanese New Wave is that the Nouvelle Vague could be said to have begun in Japan. Several of the filmic innovations later associated with the French were initiated in Japanese films like *Ikiru* (1952). The directorial voice-over that begins the film is one such device, which becomes a trademark strategy identified with Godard by the time of *Deux ou trois choses que je sais d'elle* (1966). The image of an X-ray in the place of an opening establishing shot is another, as well as the sound of traffic directly switched on when a character crosses the street to suggest shock at suddenly realizing where he is. *Ikiru* also radically reorganizes the temporality of filmic narrative by placing the central character's death in the middle of the film, then completing the story through a complex layering of flashbacks.

In 1952, these strategies appear as a direct use of filmic technique for expressive effect, displacing theatrical conventions previously normativized by classical film style in the West, from scenic unity and "realist" cinematography to invisible technique. Such strategies were characteristic of experimental films and modernist narratives in the 1920s, but were marginalized during the classical era of 1930–45 and return in the United States only with the experimental films of the 1940s and 1950s. *Ikiru* helps recall commercial narrative cinema to a modernist strategy of working through the materiality of the medium, at the same historical moment when classical technique in the United States is extended to broadcast television. Although Godard and *Cahiers du Cinéma* explicitly reject Kurosawa to celebrate Mizoguchi as "the greatest of Japanese film-makers,"[30] the ghosts of *Rashomon* and *Ikiru* haunt the Nouvelle Vague as much as any of the films that these critic/directors more directly acknowledge, not as influence or auteur but through the precedential articulation of the text. As with Yuan Muzhi's *Street Angel (Malu tianshi,* Shanghai, 1937), a film belatedly acknowledged in the West as bridging slapstick comedy and neorealism, the Japanese contribution to world cinema has often been minimized or overlooked.

Hiroshima mon amour (1959) is Alain Resnais's first feature-length film, and appears in the same year as several other first features: François Truffaut's *400 Blows* and Godard's *Breathless,* to initiate the Nouvelle Vague, and Oshima's *A Town of Love and Hope (Ai to kibo no machi),* which led to the Japanese New Wave. *Hiroshima Mon Amour* acts as a hinge between "New Waves" in France and Japan, and, although not usually considered in this way, can in one sense be said to mark an homage to Japan as one source of a new generation of filmmaking in France. As Marie-Claire Ropars-Wuilleumier remarks, Resnais's film marks a rupture with classical film practices, introducing modernist concerns with memory, ellipsis, and interweaving networks of meaning that have since become so normative that the film's initial shock effect has now become invisible.[31] The film is unusual both in the collaboration of Alain Resnais and Marguerite Duras and in its sustained address of Japan and the West in a modernist narrative. Duras knew Indochina and Asia from her own childhood experience, as described in her later novel *The Lover (L'Amant),* so her script is able to avoid the classical Orientalist stereotypes that characterize most other Western narratives of Japan during the same period.

The power relationships in the film are complex, since the narrative is centered in a Western character visiting Japan, yet that character is a woman, inverting a gendered hierarchy of unequal cultural relationships. Sato describes the *rashamen* type of film as a love story between a man from a culture implied to be superior with a woman from a supposedly inferior society. This is a type of story that not only includes most U.S. commercial narratives of Japan and Vietnam, from *Japanese War Bride* (1952), *Teahouse of the August Moon* (1956), and *Sayonara* (1957) to *Rambo: First Blood Part II* (1985), but also Japanese films made during the occupation of China, in which Japanese soldiers would be fictionally paired with native women.[32] Such narratives have a double edge, simultaneously asserting a subordination of the other while denying the violence of that hierarchy through the avowal of love as motivation. *Hiroshima mon amour* reverses the postwar *rashamen* model by presenting a European woman with a Japanese man, and by representing both characters as equals rather than as a metaphor for national domination and subjugation. Further, the inversion of *rashamen* as a trope is consistent with the film's stylistic intervention and its institutional contexts. Modernist strategies simultaneously destabilize the domination of the other implicit in the camera gaze of classical narrative, while Western domination of international production and distribution were challenged throughout the 1950s by a series of well-received Japanese films in Europe following the success of *Rashomon* at Venice.

In retrospect, *Hiroshima mon amour* acts as an intersection of several conflicting concerns that are elaborated in other texts that Resnais and Duras produced. Nevers, as the site of the French woman's war trauma, is set against Hiroshima; Duras's later novels

The War (La Guerre) and *The Lover* describe her wartime experiences in Paris and her adolescent love affair with a man of Chinese ethnicity in Vietnam. Nevers/Hiroshima articulate and displace these experiences in counterpoint, so the moral ambiguities of French collaboration with the Germans and colonialism in Indochina are foregrounded. The French defeat by the Viet Minh at Dien Bien Phu had just occurred, in 1954, and contextualizes the film's consideration of the European presence in Asia. Resnais, alternatively, came to this film after his representation of traumatic memory and Nazi death camps in *Night and Fog (Nuit et brouillard*, 1955), and inflects Hiroshima with the context of the Holocaust. His next film, *Muriel* (1963), reminds us that the Algerian War is at its greatest intensity during the production of *Hiroshima mon amour*, although it is nowhere mentioned in the film.

The film then directly engages Hiroshima as a politically polyvalent site. Hiroshima figures in the film as the setting of the narrative and home of the Japanese man, as the symbolic center of the antiwar movement that brings the French woman there as an actress in a protest film, and as the unrepresentable of mass atrocity. In the middle of the Cold War, France and Japan can both be considered as conflicted zones between the competing propaganda systems of the United States and USSR, parallel to the situation portrayed by Godard in *Masculine Feminine* (1966). The film thereby sidesteps the Manichean contest through which this parallel universe positions West and East, and pursues a radical alternative in a politics of anamnesis, atrocity, and impasse.

Hiroshima mon amour shifts the question of the Western representation of Asia from classical Orientalism to modernist limits. When questioned by an Indian woman about *India Song,* Duras, who visited India for only two hours when she was seventeen, said that she intended an "Inde métaphorique," not a documentary.[33] The film, however, also intersects with Resnais's documentary background and location shooting to create a hybrid fictional documentary, or essay, on the West and Japan. *Hiroshima mon amour* is neither the truth nor the falsification of Japan, but engages the figure of Japan as it circulates across cultural discourses. The film both recognizes and misses significant features of a Japanese context in a complex play of insight and blindness. As such, it marks the process of how knowledge is necessarily produced within discursive limits, and never as a transcendent universalism. As in Barthes's *Empire of Signs (L'Empire des signes),* the film makes no claims of total knowledge, but instead enacts what Gianni Vattimo calls "weak thought": the acknowledgment that all discursive agency is incomplete and necessarily remains open to other texts. Reading *Hiroshima mon amour* today means threading this text into and out of others, to map the possibilities of situated and limited knowledge at any given moment in history.

In *Hiroshima mon amour*, Japan remains a blank, a cipher, but a meaningful one, against which the West is challenged to recognize itself. The central characters remain nameless, in a modern space outside the social and familial hierarchies of the name. We see only a Japanese architect and a French actress in an encounter without narrative explanation of how they met. The Japanese man continually repeats, "you understand nothing," in response to the French woman's claim to see everything. The desire of the film is for a nothing as limit and exteriority of European discourse, an empty mirror in which the figure of the self is not simply confirmed by the gaze of the other but is displaced and dissolved. In this sense, the film already prefigures Barthes's reading of Japan in *Empire of Signs,* as emptiness, or absence, at the basis of cultural representation. Barthes writes his book on Japan two years after Derrida's *De la Grammatologie,* and radically rereads the emptiness of Japanese tradition as a foundational absence in contrast to the Western metaphysics of presence.

Karatani's remark that *Empire of Signs* is "nothing but the West" is most suggestive if we understand his statement as a pun, despite his disclaimer that he generally avoids wordplay. Karatani links Barthes's nothing to the introduction of the zero into European mathematics from India, where it derived from a metaphysics of the void, by way of what came to be called "arabic numbers." In medieval Europe, the zero caused consternation to theologians of presence, and only gradually took place in Western thought as a place marker. In this context, Barthes's *Writing Degree Zero* restores to Western discourse an absence that was always implicit from within, but also an emptiness that represents a site of the East within the West from the earliest moments of the modern European tradition. The East remains as a hybrid foundation available to be read from the contribution of Arabic translations to scholastic thought in Paris to the way Giotto's freestanding bell tower at the Duomo in Florence displaces minarets into Western architecture, or Moorish stripes inhabit the walls of Santa Maria Novella. *Empire of Signs* rereads the radical potential of zero as a figure through which to unhinge the sovereignty of the Western subject and open on to a free play of the text.

Hiroshima mon amour and *Empire of Signs* occupy a transitional terrain between the late modern and the postmodern. They reconfigure the Western representation of Asia from an Orientalist objectification to a modernist limit, but they do not yet enter into a postmodern hybridity that recognizes Asian voices, discourses, and texts as bound up with Europe. Insofar as Barthes translates modernist aesthetics into poststructuralist theory, *Empire of Signs* mobilizes a free play of the text; yet insofar as Asian representations remain mute within Western discourse, as a limit rather than a reconfiguration, Asia remains foreclosed from Western thought and we encounter "nothing but" the West. The position of "nothing" in the film and the book remains unstable and marks a provocative hinge between the modern and the postmodern, the West at a moment of simultaneously thinking both past and not past the structural foreclosure of the cogito.

At the same time, the approach to nothingness in the Resnais–Duras film derives from the catastrophe of the war. The East and the West, whether figured as Germany and France or as Asia and the West, arrived through total war at a point of reciprocal disaster. Hiroshima marks the end point of any possible gain to be achieved through the escalating practices of international war and its devolution into Mutually Assured Destruction, or MAD, the policy of massive retaliation and imminent apocalypse that governed the Cold War. Hiroshima and Nagasaki, as the first and only incidents of nuclear attack, are refigured after the war as emblems of a nuclear holocaust that threatens to engulf the entire world. Antinuclear protest begins in Japan, where it fuels the resistance to AMPO, but it is recognized outside Japan as part of a growing international antiwar movement. The student activists in Tokyo seen in the background of Oshima's *Cruel Tales of Youth* (*Seishun zankoku monogatari,* 1960) are part of the same social phenomenon represented in *Hiroshima mon amour* as antiwar protestors at Hiroshima. This marks the point of departure for Resnais's film, an international coalition of antinuclear activists that brings together a film crew from France and the context of Japan.

She, the textual figure, performs the subject position of French discourse as a woman in Japan, parallel to the feminine position of ideas in the French language from *la philosophie* to *la liberté. She* encounters Hiroshima through the figure of a Japanese man who remains erotically attractive and opaque at once, a self-conscious problematization of Orientalist eroticism as fascination with an unknown and unknowable other. *He,* the figure of Japan, acts as a pivotal relay into *her* unconscious through the medium of an intimate body outside the closure of conscious discourse. *He* resists Orientalist objectification by his absence from a libidinally charged scenario of romantic idealism and his dislocation of meaning into nothingness. At the limit of representation, their bodies act as erotic machines, performing obsessive libidinal forces outside the stability and placement of a shared discourse. This willed obsession derives from the Surrealist preoccupation with *l'amour fou,* an erotic madness sought out to unhinge conscious mastery and foreclosure of the other bound up with a discourse of domination. By the 1960s, the U.S. antiwar movement translated this figure into the slogan "Make love, not war."

She responds to *his* blank personification of Hiroshima by a flashback, a return to the memory of trauma, foreclosed within a discourse of international protest. *Hiroshima mon amour* not only considers Japan and the West, but addresses atrocity by way of the erotic body. Nevers, the French city on the Loire, is inscribed as a counterfigure within the film to Hiroshima, a Western city as another conflicted representation of the war. This is the city of *her* childhood, *her* youthful romance with a German soldier during the Occupation, *her* complicity with the enemy, grief at his death, and punishment after the Liberation. *She* has her head shaved like a figure from the concentration camps, and is kept hidden by her family, imprisoned in the stone basement in shame. *She* is the one who scrapes her fingers raw against the stone, bleeding against the immovable obstacle of the walls, trapped in the trauma of history. *She* is complicit with violence, in love with an enemy who kills her own people, interweaving collaboration and intimacy with fear and horror. This is how it feels to be the colonized, to be the woman in a German version of a *rashamen* film.

She lives the contradiction of *Eros* against *Thanatos,* attempting a victory of Venus over Mars, desiring that love and intermarriage could overcome death and trauma. *She* is lost instead in a trauma of complicity and irretrievable loss, sadistic punishment and suicidal guilt, madness and concentration camps, gender and genocide. Desire is empty in the face of historical trauma, an emptiness that propels the black sun of despair across the Western metaphysics of light. This is an emptiness that marks the collapse of meaning, of history and of time, not the generative emptiness of Asia. Emanuelle Riva, the actress who plays the French woman in *Hiroshima mon amour,* reappears significantly in Krzysztof Kieslowski's *Blue,* an essay on *la liberté* within his trilogy of *Blue, White,* and *Red* and the three films' calculated associations with *liberté, egalité,* and *fraternité*. In *Blue,* Riva plays a mother in an institution for the elderly, lost in a trance of television images, unable to recognize Julie, her daughter, her legacy. Julie endures the accidental death of her family to write music that commemorates the reunification of Eastern and Western Europe, pursuing her own possibilities of freedom from the East through trauma to écriture.

Nevers/Hiroshima proposes a specific exchange of representations to imagine atrocity and trauma across cultural difference. Traumatic memories haunt present time and conflict with one another, generating a complexity of narrative temporality that Deleuze discusses in *Image-Time,* and anticipating what were later called "flashbacks" as symptoms of post-traumatic stress syndrome. Much of this complexity derives from the multiple determination of unresolved conflicts, so that *Hiroshima mon amour* acts as a Western *Rashomon,* producing a break in historical discourse provoked by conflicted and unresolvable narratives of past trauma.

To return to *Hiroshima,* what about *him?*

He acts as the Other, an allegorical figure of the limit of language in the structural capacity for symbolic differentiation, a Lacanian precept identified by Homi Bhabha with the limit of incommensurability and cultural difference. Such a position is inhuman, in the sense Lyotard describes in *L'Inhumaine,* an uninhabitable position located in the unconscious, outside any stable identity or discourse through which to speak. *He* marks a shift within Western discourse from the other to the Other, as a theoretical implication of the move from Orientalist objectification to modernist limit.

The Lacanian concept of the Symbolic Other, as foundational limit of the play of self and other within the register of the Imaginary, coincides for Bhabha with Fanon's Other of categorical foreclosure, as limit of madness for the colonized subject. Fanon's colonial subject, positioned by imperialist domination as an object, occupies a site of intensely conflicted representations. The conflation of subject and object either triggers a recognition of identity as Symbolic masquerade and site of reinvention, or the misrecognition of identity as truth collapses into contradiction and madness.

Bhabha's linking of these two concepts depends on the recognition of foreclosure as a structural foundation of Western discourse, a premise Lacan has argued as a categorical foreclosure of otherness preliminary to the formation of the cogito, which is necessary in order to create the illusion of a self-contained individual apart from the differential process through which identity is produced. Such foreclosure, according to Lacan, is structurally indistinguishable from psychosis and represents the position of madness implicit within the cogito. Bhabha's reading of Fanon implies the export of madness by an imperialist cogito to the position of colonized object. As Teresa Brennan argues in *History after Lacan,* madness and Western history are bound up together, and their connection becomes recognizable from the position of the colonized. At this point, the Other of foreclosure coincides in both Lacan and Fanon.

If the impossible position of the Other does not yet allow *him* to speak, it nonetheless marks a crucial move from the closures of the Imaginary and the Symbolic to open onto the indeterminacy of the Real. If *his* voice is not yet intelligible, the absence of known meaning has been located as the site from which transcultural representation necessarily begins.

He: nothing. *She:* everything. Against a metaphysics of knowledge as visual mastery and verbal presence, the figure of Japan introduces an unstable absence. The "nothing" of *Hiroshima mon amour* figures in the text in several ways simultaneously. On one hand, nothing recalls the Asian principle of a generative emptiness, the void of Buddhist tradition. On the other, it argues a "nothing but" of postcolonial critique, the structural blindness of Western discourse to the reading and comprehension of an incommensurable discourse of Asia. In yet another sense, or absence, nothing represents the zero of Western discourse, figured as the negation and abjection of difference, visited in apocalyptic form on Japan at Hiroshima. Nothing can then invert to suggest denial and foreclosure as figural determinants of discourse. And then again, nothing implies the unrepresentable of atrocity, the failure of narrative discourse to address what escapes representation. Nothing becomes the asemia or absence at the foundation of the text, the annihilation of totality and truth as claims of power, and the irretrievable break between discursive worlds.

But to what other world does this asemic border lead?

He is an architect. But an architect of what? Of the Palace of Industry, built during the Meiji era as a monument to modernization and the only building still standing at the epicenter after the bomb fell? This ruin is one of the first prominent Japanese buildings we see in *Hiroshima mon amour,* intercut with the opening dialogue of the two lovers to document the scene of Hiroshima. Or of the Peace Museum at Hiroshima, the modernist building seen next in the same sequence? Or of war industries, like a Japanese Albert Speer, unseen in the film but the reason cited by the United States for selecting Hiroshima as a legitimate target? Or of Architecture as metaphor for Western thought, a retrospective possibility introduced by Karatani's book of that name?

Exilic Japanese Women

Is it possible to imagine and theorize a reply to *Hiroshima mon amour*'s modernist representation of Japan? If Resnais and Duras's modernist text radically inscribes Japan as a significant absence within Western discourse, is there a parallel representation of the West within a Japanese discourse that opens up similar questions of gender, representation, and cultural difference?

Hiroshima mon amour may seem to be unique in its modernist problematization of Japan as a figure within a Western-inflected international discourse. Although Imamura's *Pigs and Battleships* engages the United States as a figure within a Japanese modernist text, representations of the West are rare in Japanese film, and neither location shooting in the West nor significant production involvement by women seem possible in the Japan of the 1960s. By the 1980s, Japanese women begin producing feature films outside Japan and avant-garde video inside Japan, but these possibilities are prefigured by avant-garde film and video in the United States in the 1960s. If we are to imagine and theorize these components of a reply to Western representations of Japan, it becomes necessary to include transnational avant-garde media as part of Japanese film history.

Enter Kusama. Yayoi Kusama inverts the terms of *Hiroshima Mon Amour* in productive ways and allows us to imagine an intertextual dialogue between Resnais and Kusuma that problematizes the *he* and the *she* within the film. Or perhaps better, a polylogue between Resnais and Duras on one side of the ocean and Kusuma and Warhol on the other.

How are we to understand Kusama in relation to Japan and the cultural production of sexual difference? International modernism provides the context for Kusama's entrance into the New York art scene, but this is a discourse founded on a universalist aesthetics that transcends historical tradition and national origin. Kusama's Japanese heritage would seem to be merely a local inflection of a shared modernity, exotic rather than substantial. In this sense, any consideration of Japan as a foundationally different context might seem to detract from Kusama's recognition as a serious and important international artist.

The problem, however, is different from the assumptions of universalist humanism that inhabit much of the rhetoric that surrounds 1960s avant-garde work. Kusama's ethnic ancestry is neither an essentialist race, character, or discourse that guarantees specific artistic behavior, nor does it vanish in the imaginary light of international transparency. Kusama's link to Japan positions her work in relation to Japanese cultural tradition as one register among others available to generate connotations and resonance. She may or may not have intentionally or unconsciously woven such representational strategies into her work; this is a different question. The point is rather that Kusama, like Yoko Ono and Shigeko Kubota, combines an embodied Japanese context with transcultural hybridity and gendered agency at a time when such issues were not yet part of a theoretical discourse. As a result, shifting cultural registers and destabilized sexualities inhabit their work but remain occluded within dominant art criticism. What would later be understood as proto-theoretical projects appear instead as intuitive practices particular to the "artist" as center of her or his work.

Yayoi Kusama

Yayoi Kusama has been recently rediscovered in the West, after she was chosen to represent Japan at the 1993 Venice Bienalle. Her earlier career in the United States has since been commemorated by a traveling exhibition, "Love Forever: Yayoi Kusama, 1958–68,"[34] that recalls her participation in the New York art scene. Although she, like many artists, rejects inclusion in movements or categories, art historians and critics have noted how her work anticipated many other developments, from minimalism to the later work of Louise Bourgeois. Since her return to Japan in 1973, where she was institutionalized for mental illness, her work had largely been forgotten, despite a popularity that at the time had rivaled Andy Warhol's. Ironically, she has said in interviews that she had originally left Japan because her work had not been accepted because of her mental illness.

Her work in Japan has a different character than the work she produced in the United States, a difference Akira Tatehata describes as "more literary."[35] During her education, she was trained in *Nihonga,* or "Japanese-style painting," which she later abandoned for abstract work and international modernism. She describes herself as an outsider, but has said that she never felt "Japanese."[36] In New York she gained many friends and supporters, including Donald Judd and Joseph Cornell. She produced paintings, sculptures, installations, and performance art based on what she called her hallucinations, in works called *Infinity Nets, Accumulations, Aggregations,* and *Accretions.* She came to use polka dots as a device, often covering walls, dancers, images, and objects with dots. She also designed a room to produce infinite mirror recession, before Lucas Samaras's *Mirrored Room 2* (1966), which she exhibited in several contexts.

Her images and performances became increasingly erotic, to reject what she saw as the conservative and narrow-minded attitudes of American audiences. Her use of direct sexual images at the time paralleled sexual representation in Warhol, Jack Smith, and Carolee Schneeman, among many others. In her *Accumulations* she covered furniture and objects with stuffed fabric to resemble proliferating phalluses, and she staged happenings with nude dancers at the New York Stock Exchange, Central Park, and the sculpture garden of the Museum of Modern Art. In one of her manifestos, she wrote:

> Become one with eternity, Obliterate your personality.
> Become part of your environment. Forget yourself.
> Self-destruction is the only way out! On your trip, take along one of our live bodies. . . .
> My performances are a kind of symbolic philosophy with polka dots. . . .
> Two and three and more polka dots become movement. Our earth is only one polka dot
>   among the million stars in the cosmos.
> Polka dots are a way to infinity.
> When we obliterate nature and our bodies with polka dots, we become part of the unity of
>   our environment, I become part of the eternal, and we obliterate ourselves in love.[37]

"Obliteration" became the word she used to describe the goal of her work.

Her project is documented in a film, *Kusama's Self-Obliteration,* produced in collaboration with Jud Yalkut in 1967. Kusama's role in the production is ambiguous, since Yalkut made the film and Kusama either cooperated or directed, depending on the report one consults. In either case, the piece represents one of the earliest film projects by a Japanese woman, apparently only possible in exile. Yoko Ono and Shigeko Kubota also produced avant-garde films and videos in New York during this period, and by the 1980s women were making independent video in Japan. Japanese women after 1945 increasingly participated in the arts, as evidenced in literature from Fumiko Enchi's *Masks* (*Onna-men,* or "woman-face,"1958) to Banana Yoshimoto's *Kitchen* (1988). Mizoguchi's *My Love Has Been Burning* (*Waga koi wa moenu,* 1949) retrospectively traces the role of women activists to the "freedom and people's rights movement" of the 1880s. However, Kusama represents a possible entry point for considering Japanese women not only as representations in film but also as beginning to produce their own work in this medium.

Kusama's career in the United States is a case study of Japanese women in exile, traveling abroad to produce work that would have been impossible to produce in Japan. Many of the tropes that surround her work, from mental illness and foreign reception to different works in different contexts, are similar to conditions faced by other artists in exilic circumstances. Principal among these tropes are the reciprocal effects of international appeal and cultural amnesia, where a claim of transnational universality is situated uneasily next to initial rejection at home and a subsequent forgetting of her contributions abroad.

Not Zen

"My paintings," Kusama declared in 1964, "had nothing to do with Impressionism or with Zen Buddhism."

The interest in pop culture by avant-garde artists during the 1960s is often misconstrued today as simply a moment when pop consumerism was legitimized as extending or replacing the traditional fine arts. However, artists from Warhol to Kusama, Nam June Paik and Yoko Ono, were committed to a hybridity of avant-garde practices with a new public media sphere, building on the Dada and Surrealist tradition of the avant-garde as partner with an energized pop culture in transforming public space. In this utopian project, the arts functioned as a figure of nonalienated labor to transform social life, recoding the repressive trance of robotic control and ideological conformity into a free play of productive desire. The sexual body foregrounded in avant-garde performances of the 1960s acted as a signifier of *jouissance* within a larger project of social transformation. Only later did direct sexual representation devolve into a pornographic product in the service of a renewed consumer isolation. To recover the radical potential of this era, it is necessary to recognize a free play of productive desire exploding the narrow institutionalized maze of fetishized products.

In one interview, Kusama explained that she represented phalluses because she was afraid of them, and her representations presumably allowed her to negotiate that anxiety. In retrospect, it is now possible to see her work as decentering the phallus through serial repetition, and domesticating transcendent claims of power through resituating disembodied male organs as part of the furniture and clothing of everyday life. Although she was uneasy about the category of feminism, her images nonetheless provide a parodic critique of phallocentrism long before the idea became part of a theoretical apparatus in the United States. Her images also displace sexual attitudes from Japan, where the body was never conceived as a taboo in itself but was only transgressive if desire conflicted with other obligations. In another sense, however, Kusama's images subvert Japanese conventions that since the Tokugawa era restricted sexual entertainment as a privilege for men, by recoding sexuality as equally available to women. Through tacit displacement and hybridity, her work transforms sexual hierarchies in both Japanese and Western contexts into nodal and rhizomatic desire.

Another way that Kusama's work transfigured sexuality was through what might be called the absence of Zen. Kusama had several reasons to feel alienated from Japan.

She considered her mental illness to have derived from an abusive mother, leaving her
no sentimental attachment to her immediate family or ancestry. She also felt that Japan
had rejected her as an artist because of her mental illness, leaving her no place in a
national public sphere. When she arrived in New York, she embraced not only international modernism as a context to escape the prison of national identity, but the radical
individualism of an artist generating work solely from her own experience. She accordingly rejected any categorization of her work within any groups or traditions, from
Impressionism and Surrealism to Japanese or Zen.[38] Then what are we to make of her
concept of self-obliteration and its resonance with a Zen environment, immediacy, and
emptiness?

Kusama's obliteration acts as a critique of the cogito and its foreclosure of otherness,
multiply configured as sexuality, the environment, and race. As an intervention during
the growing escalation of the Vietnam War, obliteration recodes militarized foreclosure
of the other into a symbolic violence redirected against a narcissistic and ethnocentric
identification of self. Huey P. Newton of the Black Panthers argued this same principle
as "revolutionary suicide," and both ideas appropriate the Nietzschean idea of self-
fashioning as a fundamental part of social change. When Kusama takes her nude dancers
to the Museum of Modern Art during the Vietnam War, she is already proposing a radical alternative to the suicide bombers who destroyed the World Trade Center. The violence of modernization and cultural dislocation can only be negotiated, she implicitly
tells us, by shifting domains to a politics of desire. What Georges Bataille would call the
"restricted economy" of utilitarian needs is not enough to eliminate mass destruction.
One must also acknowledge and address the desire of the other, an act that consequently
dissolves the paranoid enclosures of an individualized self as sole determining figure of
national identity.

Kusama's obliteration without Zen extends the secularization of Zen that had already
characterized the Tokugawa era in Japan. Since the sixteenth century, and parallel to
Renaissance secularization in the West, Zen principles had been increasingly transformed
into an aesthetics, from tea rituals and landscape gardens to ink painting. These principles then became part of a Japanese cultural context, without religious institutions or
doctrines for their continuation. This is part of the joke at stake when Japanese observers
make fun of Western tourists who imagine that the character for *mu* on Ozu's tombstone
represents some great insight. In Japan, the figure is commonplace, and represents the
continuation of tropes derived from a religious past into a secular present. What continues is not the religion or even the aesthetics as such, but the determining figures. Kusama's
Not-Zen, then, is paradoxically like John Cage's Zen in its deterritorialization of determining tropes, so that figural elements are dislocated from Japanese institutions and discourses and circulate within a Western context.

Even when Kusama is being most a part of the international avant-garde scene in New
York, her discourse remains inhabited by tropes from a Japanese context. In a sense, it
is precisely her rejection of a Japanese identity that makes it possible to recognize figural
assumptions in her work that remain disjunctive in the context of the West and contribute to the radical effects her work produced.

Sliding Registers

In a postmodern context, it becomes possible to theorize both cultural reconfigurations and mass media stereotypes, and to trace the conflict between these figural modes as a product of history. Daily life is situated at the intersection of multiple registers of information, from semiotic codes and institutional contexts to genetic recombination. Essentialist stereotypes work through the trope of conflation, so that the myth of "race," for example, depends on a conflation of culture and ethnicity. The "Yellow Peril" of U.S. anti-immigrant paranoia and the 1924 prohibition of Oriental immigration, on the one hand, and anti-Western representations of weak, doddering Europeans during the Japanese militarist era, on the other, operate through the same principle of misrecognition and misrepresentation. Between these dangerous conflations of "race" and a deconstructive reading of multiple registers lies one project of history, the work of a social recoding from one figural mode to another. The 1960s marks a period when racism in the United States had been fundamentally discredited in the aftermath of the Holocaust and the civil rights movement, but a theoretical model of symbolic registers had not yet emerged. How does ethnicity and culture figure in this transitional moment?

The relation between Warhol and Kusama traces one such situation, where ethnicity and cultural difference are at stake but have not yet been worked through. Kusama's work in the New York art scene from 1958 to 1968 participates in a double register of ethnicity, both as "Japanese" in the United States and as a woman in exile from Japan, but would have been recognizable as such to very few. Her work appears as an autonomous production in New York, but its distinctive character evokes a tacit cultural difference that was difficult to put into words. One could say in retrospect, perhaps, that her work can be read in relation to Japanese cultural traditions while it simultaneously disavows any direct or essentialist connection. In this ambiguous space, atmospheric words like "style," "character," or "personality" tend to appear to describe intuitively the tension between a discredited determinism and an as yet untheorized textuality.

On the surface, Kusama's work is like Warhol's. Strategies of serial representation and performative sexuality intersect, while collapsing distinctions of public and private space, and of fine art and popular culture. Kusama's *Infinity Nets* and *Accumulations,* for example, are as serial in construction as Warhol's soup cans, yet with a difference. While Warhol translates mass production into a strategy of serial repetition, Kusama's use of the same device can be read in relation to such Japanese traditional representations as the thousand Buddhas at Sanjusangendo temple in Kyoto. The question is what precise relation these two contexts have at the moment when Kusama is producing her work. It is unlikely that U.S. audiences in the 1960s would have been able consciously to connect seriality to Sanjusangendo, but the motivation of her work would nonetheless seem different than the impersonal mass production of Warhol's premise.

Seriality threatens the ideology of humanist individualism in a Western context, so that Warhol's work provoked uneasy responses from boredom to robotic alienation. Kusama's work, in contrast, seems playful, unencumbered by alienation or a humanist anxiety about machines. This tacit but evocative difference traces an unhinging of determinist necessity behind "Japanese" representation and marks a shift toward a figural production of images. The generative figures that inhabit Kusama's work are neither religious nor genetic, but the consequence of her childhood in Japan, her accession to the Symbolic from within the context of Japanese institutions and discourses. Displaced to an exilic context, they generate an artistic discourse with a difference, one that eludes direct naming.

Similarly, Warhol's performative sexualities derive from the New York counterculture, the gay sexual underground, and strategies of transgression. Kusama's parallel play with nudity and phallic proliferation has a different effect in its casual disjunction between the sexual body and an expressive self. However peculiar this effect may seem within Anglo-American Puritan traditions of polarized repression and incitation, it is consistent with Japanese constructions of the body. From the Tokugawa era through contemporary Love Hotels, sexuality has been figured in Japan not as taboo in itself but only transgressive if personal desire comes in conflict with social responsibility. Men traditionally have benefited from sexual privileges at the expense of women, but women were part of the same system. Again, the effect does not depend on direct reference to Japanese tradition but is produced as an embodied discourse deriving from a Japanese childhood, or what in the West would be called the unconscious.

Kusama's film *Kusama's Self-Obliteration* implies the conjunction of a Western unconscious and Japanese embodiment. Filled with "psychedelic" light patterns and kinetic effects, it documents her painting, sculpture, and performance art within the context of American counterculture. Co-produced by Jud Yalkut, the film suggests an inversion between a Japanese embodiment and the Western figure of a "mind-expanding" opening to the unconscious. Kusama's return to a mental institution in Japan in 1973 was no doubt determined by her personal condition and not a social or political context, but nonetheless it suggests an allegorical madness at the conjunction of such incommensurable embodiments. It is perhaps not too much to suggest that its title, *Self-Obliteration,* implies a hinge between suicidal destruction and a deconstructive absence of meaning at the basis of representation.

7
Postmodern Networks

Stress Fractures

In Japan, a new generation of narrative filmmakers began producing work in the 1980s that seemed to reject the stylistic innovations and self-reflexivity of the so-called Japanese New Wave of the 1960s, and instead returned to a style of character centricity and classical continuity typical of the 1950s period of "humanist" films. This apparent reversal raises questions about the economic and social situation from which this younger generation in Japan produced films, about the periodization of Japanese filmmaking by generational sequence, and about the theoretical context through which we can approach their films. I would like to examine what might be called a "neohumanist" style in terms of the internal stress, contradictions, and fractures it produces, both within the films in a postmodern context and in the concept of postmodernism if it is to embrace cross-cultural work. Throughout the discussion, the word "humanist" is intended to evoke not only the specific period of the 1950s in Japan, but the ideological and structural premises of such a style in the sense Foucault has articulated.[1]

It is surprising that a younger generation of significant narrative-feature practitioners emerged at all. As Tony Rayns has pointed out, the major studio system in Japan was in crisis just as it was in the West,[2] the old apprenticeship system was in decline, and the studios seemed unwilling to invest the venture capital necessary for new directors to develop. As a result, the budgets and distribution necessary to support commercial production went to increasingly superficial films, both inside the studios and among such new big-budget independent producers as the publisher Haruki Kadokawa.[3] At the same time, no national grants or private foundations existed to fund individual artists, and alternative institutions that promoted new work, such as Image Forum, the Pia information magazine and film festival, and the Imamura school for new directors, lacked the financial resources to support feature production.

Despite this, Oguri Kohei, Morita Yoshimitsu, Yanagimachi Mitsuo, Sai Yoichi, and Ishii Sogo, and others produced distinctively new narrative work and gained commercial distribution against the economic odds. Their means of producing a first feature film were diverse, but depended almost entirely on their own initiative.[4] Sato Tadao has noted that "most of these new directors have, on their own, found backers for their debut films."[5] Oguri studied at the Imamura school and worked as assistant director for Shinoda before gaining the unconventional support of the industrialist Kimura Motoyasu to make his first film, *Muddy River* (*Doro no kawa,* 1981). Morita moved directly from 8mm experimental films to a self-financed 35mm feature production, then was commissioned to direct three soft-core erotic films (or "pink eiga") before making *The Family Game* (*Kazuko geemu,* 1983). Yanagimachi began working in documentary and educational films, and made his first feature as a 16mm documentary on motorcycle gangs, *God Speed You: Black Emperor!* (original title in English, 1976); *Himatsuri* (also known as *Fire Festival,* 1985) was produced by the Seibu department store chain as his fourth feature. Sai was first assistant on Oshima's *In the Realm of the Senses* (*Ai no korida,* 1976) and directed for television in 1981 before making *Mosquito on the Tenth Floor* (*Jukai no mosukiito,* 1983) as his first theatrical feature. Ishii formed his own production company at the age of nineteen on the basis of a prize-winning 8mm film, turning out features on bike gangs and rock music before making *The Crazy Family* (*Gyakufunsha kazoku,* 1984).

Regarding the decentralization of funding sources for new directors, Oguri remarked, "The owner of a small factory gave me support, and I was quite lucky. It is true that there has been a sort of mythology saying that film could only be produced in the studios of the major film companies, and I think I could destroy this myth. And it is possible that one day the owner of a dry-cleaning shop might support financially the production of a film in the future. Why not?"[6]

Initial low-budget independent productions have then opened some doors at the major studios, which also own theater chains for commercial distribution, but new independent production always remains precarious. Oguri's next film, *For Kayako* (*Kayako,* 1984) was sponsored by the Himawari Theater Group. Kyoko Hirano has discussed the new independent production groups currently supporting new work, such as the New Century Company, which produced *The Family Game,* and the Directors' Company, which enabled Ishii to produce *The Crazy Family.*[7] Both groups were founded in the early 1980s, and sometimes cooperate with the older Art Theater Guild, as with *Mosquito on the Tenth Floor,* produced by New Century for ATG.

Inventive financing has been a characteristic of innovative filmmaking since long before Luis Buñuel produced *Las Hurdes* with twenty thousand pesetas won by a worker in a lottery, and it has always had as its purpose the breaking of new ground outside the established conventions of an industry bent on standardizing production to maximize short-term mass-market profits. Yet this new work is striking in its apparent rejection of the stylistic innovations that characterized the generation of the so-called Japanese New Wave of Oshima, Shinoda, Imamura, Yoshida, Hani, and others. Self-reflexivity and distanciation as techniques to interrogate cinematic representation seem replaced by an unproblematic centricity of character and proairetic codes within classical continuity editing and the narrative unity of Aristotelian exposition, development, and catharsis. Rayns also argues of the new generation that "their films have no formal characteristics that would not be equally viable in a western film."[8] In short, many of the values of the classic Hollywood film that Bordwell, Thompson, and Staiger have attempted to delineate have returned to the foreground in Japan as a normative narrative system for a younger generation marking a departure from their immediate past.[9]

To some extent, conservative market forces could be said to have effected a change in style from the 1960s to the 1980s. Contemporary films by "New Wave" filmmakers such as Oshima's *Merry Christmas, Mr. Lawrence* (*Senjo no Merry Christmas,* 1983), Imamura's *Vengeance Is Mine* (*Fukushu suru wa ware ni ari,* 1979), and Yoshida's *The Promise* (*Ningen no yakusoku,* 1986) were also produced in a style more consistent with classical conventions than the same filmmakers' work a decade or two earlier. Yet Oguri argued against the work of the previous generation on theoretical grounds, not for marketing convenience:

> The previous generation, for example, Mr. Oshima, had a very clear opinion. He liked to express his opinion, his personal image. The generation previous to mine made films created by their rapid camera work. When the director has a more and more precise, clear opinion, the cameras will work more and more frequently. And therefore, the face of the director himself appears in the film. That is exactly what I do not like the films to be. . . . Avoiding the showing of one's own face is not to be considered as weakness. And that does not mean I have no opinion to express.

In one sense, Oguri recapitulates a critique of montage as a formalist subjectivism withdrawn from social context, not unlike André Bazin's argument against Eisenstein on behalf of Jean Renoir and the neorealists.[10]

Muddy River makes a parallel argument visually through its choice of a black-and-white neorealist-like style to represent the small boy Nobuo's perception of working-class life in the Osaka of 1956. Stylistically, the film is also set in the late 1940s or 1950s, representationally parallel to the work of early Roberto Rossellini or Vittorio de Sica in postwar Italy, or to the Occupation-era and 1950s work of Kurosawa, Chiba, Kobayashi, or Kinoshita in Japan. This is the era of cinematic humanists, who in Japan drew on Western styles of representation to emphasize antifeudalistic individualism in film. Close-ups of emotional responses centered on screen, which were normative in the West, became advocacy for individualist subjectivity in Japanese consensus society. Such techniques contrasted sharply with the tendency toward decentered long shots and impassive facial expressions in work by the older generation of Ozu, Mizoguchi, and Naruse. These alternative strategies perhaps correspond more closely to the cultural specificity of traditional Japan as Noël Burch and others have argued, but must have seemed to the humanists to have been linked with feudal values promoted by the militarists.

Unlike the simpler use of black-and-white to create a cinematic atmosphere of nostalgia, as in Woody Allen's *Manhattan* (1979), Oguri constructs a new film completely consistent with the stylistic principles of a different era, so much so that audiences not knowing its date of production might easily mistake it for a rediscovered older film. Yet Oguri's choice of neorealist technique is not the same as its use in an immediate postwar context. Inevitably an intertextual reflexivity creeps in, which could not have character-ized films of the earlier period. Oguri was born in 1945, and for him a representation of this period recaptures his own era of childhood. Ironically, the past remembered in *Muddy River* reinscribes realist technique as a self-reflexive sign of the past, producing the par-adoxical phenomenon of a nontransparent photographic realism.

The work of these new directors also recalls another 1950s, the decade of the first youth films. The raw energy, sexuality, and emotional violence that pervades the work of Ishii, Sai, Yanagimachi, and others of their generation recall Nakahira Ko's *Crazed Fruit* (*Kurutta kajitsu,* 1956), generally acknowledged as the first Japanese youth film, and the precursor of such important early work of the "New Wave" as Oshima's *Cruel Tales of Youth* (*Seishun zankoku monogatari,* 1960) and *Sun's Burial* (*Taiyo no hakaba,* 1960), Ima-mura's *Pigs and Battleships* (*Buta to gunkan,* 1961), and Hani's *Bad Boys* (*Furyo shonen,* 1961). In an interview, Sato Tadao has given this new generation of directors a socio-logical context:

> So what remains of the cinema public? Young people or university students; and as these categories of the population have a rather dark vision of the world, the films reflect their conceptions and contain many scenes of violence and pornography. . . . And this provokes a kind of schizophrenic crisis: if one goes to the cinema, one has an image of a violent, erotic Japan, it's an inferno; and if one looks at television, it's heaven, paradise, all human relations are harmonious and everything works well.[11]

Yet more is at stake here than a sociology of self-indulgent adolescence, as Sato is the first to admit. In another context, he writes,

> These directors have the ability to depict a subtle uneasiness that underlies Japan's super-ficial stability.[12]

Even in the understated work of Oguri, a series of images suggests an overwhelming loss. *Muddy River* sustains a vision of a childhood irretrievably past, and *For Kayako* pre-sents Koreans in Japan with their country and culture permanently left behind. When questioned about this, Oguri responded by citing history:

> Since 1868, what we have accomplished and what we have experienced is tremendous. As you know, Japan has been first-rate in its economy and has been successful in the innova-tion or invention of highly technological products, but I am not at ease with them, and I don't think this is my personal problem. I think this is a problem with all the people.

A pervasive anxiety circulates through these films, at times understated and melancholy, and at times exaggerated and hysterical, but always linked to the conflict between tra-dition and modernization. Although this conflict operates throughout the history of Jap-anese film, and is one of its distinguishing features of cultural specificity, these films can help clarify how this conflict has been reconfigured in a postmodern context.

Several concerns introduced earlier now make a return in the postmodern context. To begin, Rayns argues that the lives of the younger generation in Japan are fundamentally like those in the West. This critique can serve as an important corrective to the kind of nostalgia that characterizes, for example, Wim Wenders's "search for pure images" in his quest for Ozu in *Tokyo-ga*. Yet the denial of cultural difference is no more adequate than exoticism as a means to understand current work. In a more cautious passage, Rayns acknowledges the problem:

> To say that Japanese cinema has been through the same financial, structural and aesthetic upheavals as American, British and French cinema is not, of course, to deny the cultural specifics that make a Japanese film Japanese. But identifying cultural specificity is not as easy nowadays as it was in the days when Mizoguchi, for instance, unfolded elaborate sequence-shots with the detached precision of a painter of *emakimono* picture-scrolls.[13]

Leaving aside for the moment the question of whether Mizoguchi's difference is as easy to understand as it might appear, it is useful to begin any discussion of modernism and tradition in Japan and the West by recalling the pattern of inversions that characterizes the use of these terms in different contexts. Many of the characteristics that the West associates with modernism (such as decentering, repetition, minimalism, relativism) are associated in Japan with tradition, while many of the features of a Western democratic cultural tradition (centrality, uniqueness, expressivity, individualism) define the modern for Japan. This is more than a superficial difference related to the study of Japanese prints by Postimpressionists in the West. Nor can it be simply subordinated to a cultural evolutionism that sees traditional Japan as parallel to an earlier feudal stage of development in the West, which Japan will leave behind through even more Westernization. The problem is closer to that of a structural inversion within alternative organizations of an industrial society.

Accordingly, postmodernism undergoes a curious shift when transferred to Japan. For the purposes of this discussion, postmodernism can be described as a shift within cultural production away from the progressivist teleology of high modernism toward an interplay of multiple modes of representation, a shift not unrelated to the redistribution of power in the movement of society from an industrial economy to an information economy.[14] In the West, a renewed interest in Dada during the 1970s served to reestablish a play of forms rigidly proscribed by such critical advocates of high modernism as Clement Greenberg. The shift that occurs in applying this description to Japan is that high modernism comes to mean the high point of Taisho humanism, while the "New Wave" begins to seem like an extension of modernist individualism to directorial stylization and international distribution. It is noteworthy in this context that Kurosawa and Oshima both received international funding late in their careers for new work, despite their apparently irreconcilable differences of style and purpose. In contrast, the new narrative paradoxically appears as a tactic to dislocate the progressivist teleology that hierarchized late modernist modes of representation over alternative models.

The misleading term "New Wave" inevitably prioritizes Japanese work in a way that emphasizes aesthetic strategies that seem to mirror those of the West, specifically those self-reflexive and distancing elements critics celebrated in Godard, while ignoring equally important work in a Japanese context that has no clear Western parallel. As a result, by the 1980s such films as Oshima's *Diary of a Shinjuku Thief* and *I Left My Will on Film* had long been distributed and appreciated in Europe and the United States, but *Sun's Burial* and *Night and Fog in Japan* were "discovered" by Western audiences only in retrospect, and *Dear Summer Sister* and his television documentaries remain unappreciated or unknown. Equally severe problems have occurred with the Western reception of the work of Shinoda, Imamura, Yoshida, Hani, and others of the era. If these filmmakers are to be grouped as a "New Wave" and the new generation as a "Next New Wave,"[15] then it is important neither to exaggerate nor ignore cultural specificity in the production of meaning. Considering the full range of innovative production during this period, it seems clear that for Oshima and the others, distanciation and self-reflexivity formed one aesthetic strategy among many and was never prioritized as a dominant technique as it seemed to become for critics in the West. Japan never developed a single teleologically determined style during this period, while the ideological dominance of distanciation and reflexivity in the works of Godard and Jean-Marie Straub and Daniele Huillet that characterized critical writing of that period in the West conforms to the pattern of high modernism. In maintaining this nonhierarchized play of forms, Japan, as is sometimes remarked, has been postmodernist for some time. One could in retrospect also question whether these aesthetic strategies are indeed as central to the Nouvelle Vague, and even to Godard and Straub–Huillet, as they once seemed.

Given this context, the "neohumanist" direction of the new generation functions to dislodge the role of artist as hero, or center of a body of work, and reemphasize the film as text. Also, as we have seen, reflexive elements continue in the new work, perhaps unavoidably, so there is more continuation of pattern and purpose than might at first appear.

Yanagimachi's *Himatsuri,* for example, to consider a 1985 work that received reasonably wide distribution and critical attention in the West, is a film constructed on principles of conflict and paradox congruent with the characteristic features of postmodernism, yet this aspect of the film tends not to be fully appreciated in the West. Arthur Nolletti, in his otherwise excellent analysis of the film, acknowledges that "Yanagimachi's cinema is nothing if not paradoxical." Yet he still argues that the film fails psychologically to justify Tatsuo's murder of his family and suicide that ends the film, and that aspects of the film's structure remain inaccessible.[16]

Nolletti provides a unitary reading of *Himatsuri* in which Tatsuo figures as a primitive animist in the contemporary world, resisting to the death the commercial development of his native island. To support his thesis, he quotes from his interview with the director:

> I wanted to go back to the Jomon Period [a pre-agricultural, prehistoric time, c. 7000 BC–300 BC] and incorporate that period of mythology into contemporary life in a very concrete way. Back then human beings and animals were not separated, but were harmonic and fused. It was modernization that separated animals and human beings.[17]

This interpretation has several problems, despite Yanagimachi's apparent affirmation. Since Buddhism arrived in Japan together with the importation of Chinese characters for writing, Shinto and Buddhism have been intertwined since the beginning of recorded history. Any attempt to separate Shinto from Buddhism creates an almost purely imaginary scene, since even with extensive archeological research very little can be known of that society. Shinoda's *Himiko* makes precisely this point, by enacting a speculative story of prehistoric intrigue and female shamanism in deliberately stagelike settings to indicate the limitations of our knowledge. *Himiko* ends with a call to explore the tumuli of prehistoric Japan in order to increase public knowledge of the period.

As Shinoda's film makes clear, such research was opposed by the militarists, who wanted Japan's origins to remain mythic. It was the militarists who first insisted on the imaginary scene of a "pure" Shinto, uncorrupted by such foreign ideas as democracy and Buddhism, and they enforced this fantasy through terror. In *Himatsuri,* Tatsuo's aggressively masculine Shintoism can be understood only in the context of contemporary neonationalist political movements in Japan. Far from being a character left over from the Jomon, Tatsuo paradoxically promotes a contemporary individualism based on the imaginary Shinto purity of the militarists. *Himatsuri* is in a way a rural version of Yanagimachi's first feature, *God Save You: Black Emperor!*, which documents the fascination with authoritarian relationships among motorcycle gangs disenfranchised from the mainstream of Japanese society. This dimension of meaning is far from trivial in light of right-wing death threats against critics of the emperor at the time of Hirohito's funeral, and the lure of authority became even more troubling after the 1989 military suppression of pro-democracy demonstrators in Tiananmen Square.

In *Himatsuri,* however, Tatsuo is also identified with ecological resistance to overdevelopment. The figure Tatsuo is not so much a psychological character as a cultural allegory of the odd coincidence of aims among neoconservatives and radical ecologists. As such, his actions are less understandable as individually motivated than as a representation of conflict and paradox among social and psychological forces in contemporary Japan. Yet if the ambiguous character of Tatsuo's romanticized brutality cannot be read as an unequivocal advocacy of his position, neither can the film be reduced to an alternative unitary reading grounded in sociological contradictions. Yanagimachi uses poetic relations among images to sidestep unitary determinations and consider the complex interaction of desire and ideology with presence and history. Tatsuo makes love to the prostitute Kimiko on board a fishing boat at night, witnessed by Ryota, in a scene intercut with images of the first train to arrive in the village long ago. Rather than being grounded as one character's memory, the images of the younger Tatsuo and Kimiko greeting the first train's arrival function as counterpoint to the entire situation of sexuality among the three characters on or near the boat. Similarly, the film ends without ever identifying a single character as responsible for dumping the oil that kills the fish. Although Tatsuo's guilt is strongly implied, the last oil slick appears after his death. In both these sequences, questions of unitary character-centered determination are left unresolved. Consequently, industrial development, intimacy with nature, and the flow and breaking of desire are left to be mutually and multiply determining, rather than being fixed within a psychology or a sociology.

The potential for misinterpretation of current work derives at least in part from a confusion of history as it figures in the work of the humanist era and that of the New Wave. In Kurosawa's *Throne of Blood,* for example, the past figures as a seamless tradition, so that elements from Kabuki and Noh are mixed interchangeably. This figuration of tradition as a categorical sameness is consistent with the evolutionist ideology of the humanist period, which imagined a direct progression from the feudal past to a humanist present. In contrast, Shinoda's *Double Suicide* conceives of Japanese tradition as disjunctive, so that anti-expressive elements from Bunraku and Noh work in conflict with the emotional expression of Kabuki. In this context, disjunctive elements in the past function as symbolic resources to articulate representational issues in cinema. Because of its "neo-humanist" surface, it is easy to imagine that *Himatsuri* intends to be centered consistently on character within narrative unity, but the film instead assumes the disjunctive and multiply determined sense of history that emerged during the New Wave.

Like Oguri's *Muddy River* and other contemporary work, *Himatsuri* is interesting because it asks us to break apart assumptions of how history, signification, and aesthetic strategies are configured by combining in the present elements from apparently contradictory periods in the past. By so doing, the films enable us to better understand the work of past generations as well as constructing rhetorical tools for addressing issues in the present. What is at stake in these observations seems to be a strategy of double coding, like that of Charles Jencks,[18] within the process of what Lyotard calls a language game.[19] Two incompatible systems of meaning (humanist, antihumanist) are embedded in the same text. This sustained disjunction makes it possible for each system to deconstruct the other, so as to avoid the centrality of either as metanarrative, and to construct a signifying process based instead on continuing dislocation.

Tokyo Intertext

In an early print of *Tokyo Story* distributed in the United States, an English subtitle succinctly translated the father's response on first seeing the city: "Tokyo is a big."

Tokyo, like Paris, Berlin, Rio de Janeiro, and New York, developed into a metropolis at the same historical moment that cinema emerged as a means of articulating social and cultural formations. Cinema and the city of Tokyo have been interactive in translating premodern Japan into industrial and information economies in modern and postmodern situations. Tokyo has been completely rebuilt twice in this century, after the Kanto earthquake of 1923 and after the American firebombing of 1945, while cinema has continually reinscribed how the city functions as a signifying process. As a result, Tokyo acts an intertextual terrain, where "landscape," which Karatani theorizes as a specifically Western construction, is precariously interwoven with a non-Western context.

Predictably, the first appearance of Tokyo to the West is in terms of absences, what characteristics of Western cities it lacks. Kenneth Frampton, like other Western scholars of urban design, has noted the "total absence of relatively static public places, of agoras and squares" in the Japanese organization of the city.[20] Similarly, Roland Barthes in *Empire of Signs* conceives of the Emperor's Palace as an empty center at the heart of Tokyo, which to Western experience seems to be a paradox: a central space where no one goes.[21]

Next, according to the modernist trope of seeking contemporary patterns in traditional societies, Tokyo is seen as linking advanced industrial development with an idealized tradition and with nature. Frampton argues that "the processal nature of motopia was already present, to some extent, in the traditional Japanese city." For Barthes, the decentering absence at the heart of Tokyo forces traffic "to make a perpetual detour," and enter into continual circulation. These tropes link the city mobilized by industrial transport to Japanese traditional respect for dynamic processes in the environment.

If we wish, we can then imagine the Japanese positioning of industrialization within tradition and nature as mirroring developments in the West. Barthes implies that Tokyo's urban decentering parallels the "quadrangular, reticulated cities (Los Angeles, for instance)" in the West that lack a clear center. Reyner Banham, in his analysis of Los Angeles, considers the automobile as one of the city's key ecological components, and by using an ecological model for thruways locates late industrial dynamics in the context of environmental processes.[22]

If we are to unravel Tokyo from this rhetorical system of lacks, origins, and mirrors, we need to set aside the framing orientation of Western cities without thereby lapsing into an idealist fantasy of pure difference. The characteristics of Tokyo assembled by

FIGURE 23. Tokyo is haunted by traces of Edo-era sites familiar through ukiyo-e images, although most have been rebuilt in concrete. Nihonbashi is now hidden under an expressway. One that survives is Shinabazu Pond in Ueno Park.

Frampton's and Barthes's separate approaches are of a decentered and dynamic circulation linked both to late industrialization and to traditional Japanese models of environmental processes, without either the centrality or the quadrilateral grid of Western cities.
Yet Frampton also notes that the grid is part of Japanese tradition, not a pattern apart
from it. One of the inversions encountered by comparing Japanese and Western cities is
that the grid, borrowed from T'ang China, was the model for the earliest Japanese urban
development at Kyoto. In contrast, Western cities developed unifying macroscopic patterns as a relatively late historical development: as concentric circles (say, Paris or Washington, D.C.) or as a grid (the Quartier Mazarin in Aix-en-Provence, or Manhattan).
Edo, and later Tokyo, departed from this model rather than moving toward it. Yet other
theoretical models exist for decentered nongrid patterns.

In *A Thousand Plateaus*, Gilles Deleuze and Félix Guattari theorize a model of social
formations on the basis of the rhizome, conceived as a decentered, heterogeneous, and
interconnected lattice of living components. Unlike Western cities, Tokyo seems organized on this basis, dispersed among multiple district centers, no one of which predominates. This rhizomelike structure is indirectly represented in Japanese film insofar as
the representation of a specific district often characterizes a narrative. The distinction
between Asakusa and Shinjuku, for example, can be significant. Chiba's *Downtown* (1957)
depends on recognition of Asakusa, Tokyo's oldest district, still in ruins in a story set just
after the war. In contrast, Oshima's *Diary of a Shinjuku Thief* records the Shinjuku of the
1960s, before the skyscrapers were built that now dominate its skyline.

At the same time, Tokyo functions as a palimpsest, a layered surface recalling the
Edo period through contemporary signs. In Morita's *The Family Game,* for example, shots
of the Sumida River at night from the family's high-rise apartment could recall Edo's
summer fireworks over the Sumida represented in ukiyo-e prints. History has become
spatialized and marked by its absence, as Fredric Jameson has argued of postmodernist
capitalism. In considering Jameson's description of this process, Tokyo could more easily
be compared to American than European cities. As in the United States, Tokyo's past
has been radically erased and is recalled almost entirely through place names and historical reconstructions, such as the Asakusa Kannon Temple. This erasure is a trace of the
firebombing of the city on the night of March 9–10, 1945, an event everywhere inscribed
but nowhere discussed. As a result, the site of the eighteenth century's largest city is now
virtually a new metropolis, founded on the repression of history.

In Japanese film, Tokyo approaches the status of an infinite intertext. Like Paris or New
York, the city is continually reinscribed through film as a representation of cultural deterritorialization and reterritorialization. The city becomes a figured space from which
transtextual operations proceed. Gérard Genette's work on intertextuality, *Palimpsests:
Literature in the Second Degree,* needs to be conceived in terms of Deleuze and Guattari's
theories of territorialization in *A Thousand Plateaus* and elsewhere. The discursive practices that constitute a culture are positioned by the production of multiple texts, which
both regulate and are embedded in urban development.

FIGURE 24. The Meiji era introduced the idea of vast public space, as in the Tokyo National Museum in Ueno Park.

The concept of territorialization here intersects with Kojin Karatani's use of the term "landscape" to reconsider the pioneering Japanese modernist writer Natsume Soseki (1867–1916). Brett de Bary argues that Karatani's *Origins of Modern Japanese Literature* articulates the major concerns of the Japanese postmodern movement by its critique of "literary history" and its radical attempt to redefine modernity. Karatani describes modernity as a discursive space that emerged through a rupture or "overturning of a semiotic constellation" that preceded it. As a result of a series of inversions *(tento)*, modernity makes it possible for both "landscape" as a Western formation of exterior space and the "interiority" of the psychological novels for which Soseki is most well known to emerge. According to de Bary, Karatani plays on the ambiguity of the modern Japanese word for landscape, *fukei*, to confuse the distinction between object and representation. By so doing, *fukei-ga,* as the Meiji word for Western landscape painting, functions to expose its own conventions of representation:

> Once a landscape has been established, its origin is repressed from memory. It takes on the appearance of an "object" which has been there, outside us, from the start. An "object," however, can only be constituted within a landscape. The same may be said of the "subject" or self. The philosophical standpoint which distinguishes between subject and object came into existence within what I refer to as "landscape." Rather than existing prior to landscape, they are products of it. (Karatani, trans. de Bary)[23]

To make the point, de Bary cites a story told by Janine Beichmann, in her book on modern "realist" techniques in the poetry of Masaoka Shiki (1867–1902), about the teaching of Western landscape in Japan. Instructed by the Italian painter Antonio Fontanesi to go out into Tokyo and sketch landscapes, Japanese students returned empty-handed, reporting that they could find nothing suitable to sketch, that is, that there was no "landscape" there. Only after the painter clarified the assignment to emphasize an observational practice separate from specific subject matter did the students begin to paint.[24] Cinema can be said to mechanize these conventions of Western representation as it records the industrializing modern city as object, thereby performing simultaneously the reconstitution of subject, object, and representation that Karatani suggests by "landscape." This is the sense in which cinema's function in representing the city should be considered.

Figuring Out the City

In the cinematic representation of Tokyo, some specific tropes recur that can be addressed as figures of absence, of margins, and of interweavings. At times, Tokyo figures as the absence of some other city such as Onomichi or Kamakura. As such, it often figures as a trope of the loss of tradition, as in Ozu's *Tokyo Story* or Naruse's *Sound of the Mountain*. Similarly and just as frequently, Tokyo appears as a trope of the new, as in the industrial oil-storage tanks of Ozu's *Tokyo Chorus* (1931) or the high-rise office buildings in Kurasawa's *The Bad Sleep Well* (1960). Shun-Ichi J. Watanabe argues in his analysis of Tokyo as metropolis that since the Meiji period Tokyo has represented modernity to the Japanese, whether as a symbol of progress or of sybaritic behavior.[25] This modernity has been created through a series of rebuildings, each time after a major disaster.

A related urban trope includes the repeating representations of Tokyo as a devastated wasteland, as in Kurosawa's *Drunken Angel,* where the city surrounds a disease-infested muddy pit, or as social paralysis, as in the bureaucracy of Kurosawa's *Ikiru.* Both tropes continue in current films: *Crazy Family* imagines the Americanized suburbs transformed into a wasteland by an outburst of nihilistic self-destruction, and *The Family Game* represents the city as a domain of suffocating social pressures. Tropes of devastation and paralysis confront history as rupture, as impasse, and as break.

Given the scale of disaster that has affected Tokyo in the twentieth century, it is surprising only that images of devastation do not appear more often than they do. As a result of the Kanto earthquake on September 1, 1923, perhaps 100,000 people died and 1.4 million were left homeless. Fires burned for five days, leaving most of the city in ruins. Twenty-two years later, during the American firebombing of the city in March 1945, an *akakaze* or red wind swept across the Tokyo plain. The U.S. Strategic Bombing Survey, which later evaluated the effects, concluded that "probably more persons lost their lives by fire at Tokyo in a 6-hour period than at any time in the history of man." The estimated 100,000 dead during this one night far surpassed the death toll at Dresden (35,000) and approximated the initial losses at Hiroshima (118,000).[26] Yet film representations of these disasters are virtually nonexistent. What few images of fires we have are indirect, as in the fire that destroys Sansho's compound in Mizoguchi's *Sansho the Bailiff,* or the fire that destroys the Golden Pavilion in *Conflagration* (1958), Ichikawa's version of Mishima's *Kinkakuji.* In Edo, before the Meiji regime banned flammable building materials, devastating fires were an annual event and quick rebuilding became the norm of the Tokugawa period. But the capacity for a quick recovery does not entirely explain the absence of representation.

The trouble the Japanese have with history is often represented in 1980s Japanese films in terms of an unwanted older generation. In Itami's *The Funeral* (1984), the one older man who remembers the war comically dies, but other films suggest that the past does not fade away so easily. In Yoshida's *The Promise,* the older generation is represented as a despicable grandmother who wants to die, and is finally murdered with all other members of the family implicated. In many other films, from *Tampopo* to *Family Game,* the older generation is simply absent. Japan's militarist past is an inconvenient intrusion on such 1980s concerns as the international expansion of Japanese business interests, as Japanese filmmakers can remind us. At times, historical temporality is encoded in terms of the city's spatial dimensions. In Ishii's *The Crazy Family,* a father in desperation begins digging beneath the living room of a new house to build a separate room for the family's grandfather. As a result, the film inscribes the city as layered archeologically, with the older generation buried alive below, the middle generation on a crumbling main floor, and the younger generation isolated upstairs as if lost in outer space. Jameson's spatialization of history is here linked to the trope of devastation through the destruction of the house, which concludes the film. The energy of *Crazy Family* comes in part from its rediscovery of the discontinuity at the basis of history, which contemporary Japan so often struggles to repress.

Barthes's conception of the Emperor's Palace as an empty center is politicized in Hara Kazuo's gonzo documentary *The Emperor's Naked Army Marches On (Yuki yukite shingun,* 1987). Obsessed with his memories of the war, Okuzaki Kenzo is barred from entering the Emperor's Palace to make his accusations that Hirohito was guilty of war crimes, and thereby is forced into circulating around Japan to interrogate reluctant witnesses of Japanese atrocities. Here the city of the empty center and processal circulation is reinscribed as founded on repression and driven by guilt.

As another trope, the selection of a specific district can represent the shifting margins of postwar Japanese society. *Downtown* represents the scrapping of tradition through the ruins of Asakusa, the old district. Tradition is marginalized by the industrial and economic recovery in progress under the American Occupation. This process is visually articulated by the roaring trucks at the end of the film that force the central woman character into the ditch. Later, *Diary of a Shinjuku Thief* represents Shinjuku as student territory during the 1960s, when the radical *Zengakuren* student organization actively formed the margins of Japanese society. Harajuku in turn is marked as belonging to the 1980s younger generation in Yoichi Sai's *Mosquito on the Tenth Floor.* Sai's margins are represented as alienated pastiche in terms of the teen dancers who ritually perform in coordinated group costumes of bikers' leather, 1950s party dresses, or disco satin.

FIGURE 25. Classical columns and modernist minimalism combine in a prewar cinema theater in Tokyo.

Tropical Weave

Mosquito on the Tenth Floor is a provocative conjuncture of multiple tropes. Sai's film, written by rock singer Uchida Yuya, who also stars in the film, is of the type that claims to be based on an actual incident. The incident in question concerns a Kyoto police patrolman named Hirota, who was convicted in 1978 for attempting to rob a bank and for taking bank employees hostage. In the film, the central character, a low-paid policeman, acts out of frustration with his dead-end job, his divorce, and his inability to afford consumer goods. He threatens loan-company employees with a gun in a climax reminiscent of Al Pacino's character in *Dog Day Afternoon,* but he is captured without gunfire or killings and is led away by police.

In this film, the city is figured in terms of shifting margins (the police character's daughter at Harajuku) and as paralyzing social pressures. The policeman is consumed by escalating debts to the *sarakin* or loan sharks, which were originally contracted to finance consumer purchases. When meeting his ex-wife at a bar for an angry confrontation, the city appears outside at night as an infernal industrial landscape, ironically presented as a scenic tableside view. At home, in a tenth-floor walk-up apartment, the central character is isolated in an empty room with a computer video game. In this satirical representation of the postmodernist moment, Tokyo is reconfigured as mass cellular isolation amidst an industrial wasteland, where desire is repressed and explodes as rape or rage or is marginalized as cool Harajuku pastiches.

The police civil servant in the film is from a social class that has always been marginalized in Tokyo, the underpaid service-industry worker who was once typed as "the well-dressed poor" *(Yofuku saimin)*.[27] In the film, the figure of a policeman who breaks the law is ironic, and functions less to suggest official corruption than to argue that Japan consumes those who labor near the bottom of the pay scale.

Allegories of Cultural Dislocation

Imamura Yohei's film *The Ballad of Narayama (Narayama bushiko,* Toei, 1983) ostensibly retells the story of a primitive Japanese cultural practice in which anyone over the age of seventy must be taken into the mountains and abandoned to die. In the film, this tradition is introduced in the form of a ballad, which is then implied to be the basis of the historical reconstruction of the film's narrative. Much of the film details the harsh conditions and survival strategies of a rural community represented as close to nature, through frequent intercutting of animal behavior that parallels human activities. Snakes are seen coiling when humans have sex, and animals devour one another when humans die in the competition for food.

What is the significance of this narrative, this film, and Imamura's interest in producing it, in the historical context of 1983? Why this fascination with cruelty and harsh conditions, at precisely the moment when Japan's economy reaches its peak and competes for world prominence? Why is this narrative set so strongly in nature, when Japan has become a postindustrial landscape where natural environments are restricted to parks?

The Narayama narrative acts as a naturalized symbolic landscape, constructed from a series of embedded figural elements, often marked by complexity and inversion. As such, the film becomes a model for understanding how history operates as a landscape before it can develop a temporality or dialectic, parallel to Karatani's discussion of "landscape" and Jacques Derrida's revisiting the concept of *chora* in Plato's *Timaeus,* initially addressed by Julia Kristeva as a space for semiotic intervention preceding discourse. I understand Kristeva's use of the term "semiotic" here to be closely linked to Lyotard's concept of the figural, as inhabiting discourse and being linked to the unconscious, and prefiguring the organization, character, and limits of discourse constructed through it.

My interest in Imamura's film comes from its capacity to demonstrate the way that history works through a series of embedded figures, always indeterminate at their limit but never simply open to intentional change. In particular, the film makes the operation of embedded figures visible through a series of cross-cultural displacements and symbolic inversions, generated by the complex and interwoven conflicts of tradition and modernization, as well as Asian and Western modes of thought and representation, that constitute life in contemporary Japan.

The combined effects of these displacements and inversions, both generative and destructive, can be organized through the concept of cultural dislocation. Severe cultural dislocation often accompanies the process of economic and social modernization in non-Western countries, and Japanese film has represented this experience from the longest tradition of modernization and filmmaking outside Europe and the United

States. As a result, Japanese film can function to articulate *aporias* and crises that tend to recur outside the West. In these terms, then, I will argue that *The Ballad of Narayama* is constructed through figures of cultural dislocation, and that the multiple allegories implicit in these figures articulate the conflicted political and historical positioning of the "postmodern" Japanese subject.

Abandoned Parents

The central figure of Imamura's film might at first appear to be the abandonment of parents. In *Narayama,* the old woman, Orin, insists that her son carry her to the top of the mountain to die, even though she is neither sick nor disabled, because she has reached the age of seventy and the village rule demands it. She waits only long enough to arrange wives for her sons before she leaves, and her son weeps at the necessity of leaving her. In contrast, Mata, an old man, has become mad and seems to pose a more serious threat to his family's survival. When he is carried to the mountain by his own son, Mata resists abandonment before being thrown over a cliff. Whether or not justified in the narrative by survival, the film emphasizes the gratuitous cruelty of abandonment to death by freezing.

The figure of abandoned parents is part of the recurring trope of an unwanted older generation that appears in several films produced at about the same time. Juzo Itami's

FIGURE 26. Kinokuniya Bookstore in the Shinjuku district of Tokyo, the site of Oshima's *Diary of a Shinjuku Thief.*

The Funeral and Sogo Ishii's *The Crazy Family* were both released in 1984, and Yoshige Yoshida's *The Promise* in 1986. All of these films represent an antagonistic and even violent rejection of an older generation as legitimate and justifiable, in either comic or dramatic terms.

In *The Funeral*, Itami satirizes both the traditional family system and Ozu's filmic respect for it, through the deliberate casting of Chishu Ryu, the actor identified with the role of an idealized father through his reappearance in many of Ozu's films. In Itami's film, Chishu Ryu plays a Buddhist priest who conducts a farcical funeral for an obnoxious old man whose death seems only to inconvenience the consumer lifestyle of his descendants.

In Yoshida's *Promise,* the grandmother of the Morimoto family dies unnaturally, and police discover that everyone in her family had reason to hate her and wish her dead. Here the grandmother is represented as monstrous and the grandfather as senile, and the official investigation of their roles in the family uncovers a web of mutual betrayal and disgust. The eventual failure of the police to resolve the crime only serves to implicate everyone in a process explicitly addressed in the film as euthanasia.

In Ishii's *Crazy Family,* Katsuhiko has no place in his new home for his elderly father, Yasukini, and he hits on the idea of digging under the living room to create a basement for him. Yasukini's military uniform appears dramatically out of place in this consumer family, and building a basement apartment for him quickly becomes an image of trying

FIGURE 27. By the 1980s, electronic imaging had become an integral part of the environment, as depicted by this giant outdoor television screen in Shinjuku.

to bury the past and one's parents with it. Burial is an image in *Narayama* as well, in a more explicitly cruel form. The Ameya family is accused of stealing food by others in the village, and as punishment the entire family is buried alive.

The repeating figure here is a deliberate rejection, burial, or killing of a family's oldest generation, seen as an inconvenience, tyranny, or threat to survival by their children and grandchildren. The repetition of this symbolic murder of ancestors across several films suggests its overdetermination as a figure to negotiate the chasm between an aging generation educated in the militarist and imperialist values before the war and the Americanized consumer generations that have followed.

The violence of this figure is produced in part by its absolute inversion of the traditional Confucian respect for one's ancestors. The subordination of self to family elders was a basic premise of the educational system before 1945, and it was central to the construction of a patriarchal society hierarchically identified with the emperor. What is being killed is not just the parents, but the system of respect for the parents, which was fundamental to a cultural identity now hopelessly obsolete.

Yet the violence of this rejection cannot help but recall the eugenics movement of the 1930s, as discredited by Nazi genocidal policies and their link to prewar Japan. Brutality against a class of people seen as unnecessary is in this sense an imported idea from the West, yet from the prewar period that remains difficult to address openly in contemporary Japanese discourse. The newness of this genocidal idea strikes so deeply that it seems, or can be imagined to be, primitive. But the primitive resonance of mass death is an invention of the industrial era, and the displacement of euthanasia into a primitive Japanese past is an invention of *Narayama*.

Anthropology

To return to Imamura's film, *The Ballad of Narayama* is conspicuously a remake—in this case, of Kinoshita Keisuke's film of the same name produced at Shochiku in 1958. Kinoshita's version of the film is highly theatrical, and sets the narrative within the apparatus of the Kabuki stage. Joseph Anderson and Donald Richie's description of the film in *The Japanese Film: Art and Industry* is succinct:

> It opened like a Kabuki—the curtain drawn to disclose the first scene—and throughout used *nagauta,* the voice and samisen accompaniment that describes and comments on the action. . . . Division between scenes often consisted of sudden light changes at which whole sections of the scenery slid away; intimate conversations were accented by careful spotlighting; the entire background would drop to reveal the next scene.[28]

In other words, far from setting the narrative in nature, as Imamura does, Kinoshita adopts an antirealist style prefiguring the Brechtian use of Kabuki by Shinoda Masahiro in *Double Suicide* (*Shinju ten no Amijima,* 1969). While Imamura shoots on location in rural Japan, Kinoshita emphasizes the mythic unreality of the narrative involved. Interestingly, the distance and artificiality of Kinoshita's version historically precedes the immediacy and brutality of Imamura's. The landscape of this narrative must be visibly constructed before it can be lived as raw experience.

Kinoshita's film, in turn, was based on the celebrated first novel by Shichiro Fukazawa of the same name, which was published in the magazine *Chuo Koron* in 1956 and awarded its New Man prize.[29] Fukazawa grew up outside literary circles, and his writing departed considerably from established conventions. It was precisely this departure that led to his recognition in the immediate post-Occupation era as characterizing a new kind of identity and experience.

Fukazawa's title, *Narayama bushiko,* could more accurately be translated as *A Study of the Songs of Narayama,* suggesting an anthropological or folkloric analysis of primitive culture. The anthropology involved here, however, is deliberately fake. Fukazawa's story, though seeming to retell a genuine Japanese tradition, was entirely fabricated on the basis of several ancient legends. In other words, anthropology is deployed as a narrative figure, to reinvent the possibilities of culture and identity.

As in Shinoda's *Himiko* (1974) and Kumai Kei's *Sandakan 8 (Sandakan hachiban shokan bokyo,* 1974), anthropological discourse functions first to disrupt the prewar notion of a sacred origin for Japanese society that precludes analysis. *Himiko* is the story of a prehistorical Japanese shamaness, stages this role in Brechtian fashion, and ends by demanding the opening of ancient tumuli for archeological research. *Sandakan 8* was originally written as an anthropological investigation of wartime-forced prostitution, an issue recently brought into public view by the Japanese government's belated apology to the

FIGURE 28. A group of teenagers in Harajuku park in Tokyo adopts a U.S. rebel image from the 1950s. By the 1980s, the historic preservation of American pop culture had become performative.

mostly Korean women forced into servitude as "comfort girls" during World War II, before being made into a film with a journalist in the role of the anthropologist. In both these cases, the discourse of Western social science functions to challenge the cult of the emperor, with its insistent mystification of prehistory and its denial of wartime guilt.

In this context, it is noteworthy that Fukazawa's publication of *An Elegant Fantasy (Furyu mutan)* in 1960, between the productions of Kinoshita's and Imamura's films, was widely read as a direct attack on the Emperor system. The story provoked a violent response from right-wing fanatics, who threatened Fukazawa's life, and forced him into hiding and a later renunciation to survive. The scandal surrounding these events has resulted ever since in an unspoken but de facto prohibition of any direct representation of the emperor in the arts.[30]

The parallel of this case to the condemnation of Salman Rushdie by the Islamic hierarchy in Iran, and Rushdie's subsequent hiding in the West, should not be ignored. In both cases, narrative interventions were greeted with attempts at suppression by terror, to enforce the exclusion of specific determining figures from permissible discourse. In a perverse twist on the Hebrew tradition of the unnameability of God, the absence of these figures is determined not by the grammatological limits of language, but by the simple condition that anyone who speaks them will be killed. The absence of the emperor or of Allah from artistic representation is a conspicuous sign of the institutional violence of their figuration.

Biology

Unlike *Himiko* and *Sandakan 8, Narayama*'s anthropology does not argue for an accurate analysis of historical conditions but instead remains entirely imaginary. The figure of anthropology here reduces the resonant and overdetermined imperialist mystification of prehistory to an alien landscape of mute and brutal forces. The "new man" of 1950s Japanese humanism emerges as a split subject in opposition to a newly "objective" nature, now reinvented as distant and harsh materiality. In this sense, Fukazawa's *Narayama* shares a symbolic landscape with the youth films of the 1950s, from *Crazed Fruit* to Oshima's *Cruel Tales of Youth,* in their linking of raw sexuality and violence to the isolation of the individual growing up in the ruthlessly commercial environment of postwar Japan. Imamura's earliest films were part of this period, and they emphasize this connection through the images of sexuality and cruelty that punctuate his film.

If the figure of anthropology reduces history to a flat materiality, then biologism reanimates that materiality with the newly impersonal forces of sexuality and death. Fukazawa described himself by saying, "Writing for me is a biological act."[31] Biology, as part of a Western landscape, reduces social relationships to a direct equation with animal behavior, as articulated in Imamura's repeated cross-cutting. In Imamura's *Narayama,* sex is repeatedly linked to snakes: when Matsu and Kesa make love, two snakes are seen coiling together; when they later make love when Matsu is pregnant, a snake sheds its skin; when Tatsuhei accuses Risuke of having sex with a dog, rats are seen chewing on a snake, and so on. At the same time, death is linked to images of eating: when the Ameya family is buried alive for threatening the fragile food supply that barely prevents star-vation, an owl is seen devouring a mouse. Far from being "natural," this reduction is part of the violence that constructs the naturalized conditions of contemporary Japan.

This representation of history also comes closer to Georges Bataille's idea of a General Economy, in which the erotic forces of expenditure and excess participate in the fields of production and consumption, than to Hegel or Marx. In one sense, *Narayama* seems like a Japanese *Man of Aran,* insofar as a brutal struggle for survival is presented as bio-logically natural, while the capitalist forces that construct such an image (in Flaherty's *Man of Aran,* the estates of English absentee landlords just across the channel from the Aran Islands; in *Narayama,* the images of multinational corporations) are rigorously kept offscreen. But Imamura's enduring interest in inventing the primitive as a foil for exam-ining contemporary conditions has never been limited to the naturalization of what Bataille would call a restricted economy. Imamura's idea of the primitive is always charged with erotic forces that swallow up and transform human intentions, making individual characters into fools, pests, and survivors.

Mountains

If the conflicted figures of abandoned parents, an anthropologized prehistory, and a biologized nature are all at work in *Narayama*'s landscape, then many of the conflicts of these representations are condensed in the central figure of the mountain named in the title of the story and the films (*yama* is Japanese for mountain). In traditional Japan, mountains were places of terror, the abode of the spirits, outside human community. In contrast, Western influence in the nineteenth century reconceived of mountains as places of beauty and recreation, so that the central mountain range of Japan has come to be known as the Japan Alps, in honor of the European model through which they could be seen as significant. Today, Japanese mountains are filled with busloads of middle-class vacationers and skiers. As yet another inflection, the mountain image is translated through Mount Fuji into a site of nationalist identification, and secondarily into the historical logo of the Shochiku Film Studio, which produced the first version of *Narayama*. Part of the irony of Imamura's *Narayama* comes from the mobilization of all these conflict-ing meanings simultaneously, so that the terror of Orin's self-willed expulsion from the village coincides with an idealized beauty of nature, and both are enfolded within a com-mentary on Japanese cultural identity.

The mobilization of beauty and terror, identity and death, at the same site, parallels the Western concept of the sublime, which Lyotard discusses as approaching the post-structuralist concept of limit or *aporia* within the rhetoric of Romantic literature. Like Mont Blanc in Shelley's poem of that name, *Narayama* becomes so conflicted a figure in the narrative that it cannot be thought. Simultaneously central as a primary signifier of hierarchical organization, and the mark of an *aporia* or impossibility of any such system, *Narayama* can be seen as emblematic of conditions in a postmodern but non-Western culture. Monumental asemia is then represented through a visual rhetoric that plays against *romanha,* or Japanese Romanticism. Everyday life sets up familiar objects in the

FIGURE 29. A group of girls in Harajuku Park in Tokyo is dressed in the American bobby-sox style from the 1950s.

environment as both the signs of a specific cultural identity and the simultaneous marks of its destabilization and impossibility, suspended between the enforcement of cultural authority and its dissolution in a transcultural information economy. The intensely conflicted figures that construct this history as landscape hover like cruel ghosts or electronic transmissions in their insistence and instability.

Diasporic Japan

A street banner in *Gaijin* reads: "Bem-vindo ao Bairro Oriental."

In 1991, when I attended the French Film Festival in Sarasota, the best film was not as precisely French as one might imagine. The film was titled *Urga,* and it was indeed produced primarily with French financing, but it was shot in Mongolia by a Russian director. The story concerned the importation of Japanese television sets to a remote village for programs alternating between George Bush and Chinese music.[32] I remember thinking, as much as I love this film and as much as I love France, is it really necessary to call this film French?

To be more precise, is it possible to rethink the relationship between filmic representation and cultural identity without categorizing films by national traditions? How can one address films that cut across boundaries rather than fitting securely within them? Increasingly we live in a diasporic world of international co-productions and multiple identities, yet we continue to write film histories organized by national tradition and authorship. This habit of thinking marginalizes some of the most interesting films now being produced and obscures the complex cross-cultural experiences that now constitute everyday life for almost everyone on the planet.

One way to address the problem of the nation is to consider its erasure as a governing trope of cultural analysis. The trope of the nation, as a specific form of cultural production interiorized within a language, a population, and/or a territory, has been much discussed by postcolonial criticism, but the trope often creates as many problems as it solves in approaching the issues of ethnicity and subjectivity in a transnational information economy. However, if transnational formations are discussed, the rhetoric of a depoliticized transcendental idealism often surfaces instead, and the appropriation of signifiers like "democracy," "humanism," and "opportunity" into an imaginary global universalism can quickly drain the discussion of any historical specificity or complexity. Alternatives that refuse the false binarism of nationalist enclosure versus an imaginary transcendence might be explored through a tropic analysis of culturally specific texts.

First, one could constitute a set of materials by looking for films that seem to fall between cultures, rather than resting securely inside one. This procedure might produce an odd collection of films, a little like the Borgesian encyclopedia Foucault mentions at the beginning of *Les mots et les choses*. This set might include Tizuka Yamasaki's *Gaijin* (1980), a film made in Brazil by a woman of Japanese ancestry; but also King Vidor's film *Japanese War Bride* (1952), packed with stereotypes yet also oddly sensitive at points

FIGURE 30. Mountains, once conceived as outside civilization, are now areas for recreation in Japan. The Japan Alps were renamed after the Swiss during the Meiji era (1868–1912).

to cultural dislocation; and Ozu's *I Failed, But . . .* (1930), a pastiche of a Buster Keaton–like figure in a Japanese university with American college football pennants on his dorm walls. Further, one could include a series of reciprocal relationships between curious pairs of films: the two films titled *Black Rain* made in 1989, one an American action film set in Japan, the other an adaptation by Shohei Imamura from the famous novel on the bombing of Hiroshima (the Japanese seem to prefer the first, although American critics accuse it of being racist); or the two sensations juxtaposed by coincidence at the 1991 Cannes Film Festival, Madonna's *Truth or Dare* and Akira Kurosawa's *Rhapsody in August,* his meditative reminiscences of the bombing at Nagasaki, in which children wearing T-shirts marked USC and MIT investigate traces of the disaster.[33]

What do these films and reciprocal relationships have in common? Marginalized by any consideration of cinema based on the dominant characteristics of a national style, these films and the relationships among them are nonetheless fascinating examples of the way that visual and rhetorical figures cut across cultural boundaries to generate new possibilities of meaning. They seem irretrievably "postmodern," not in the Jamesonian sense of erasing history,[34] but in the opportunity they offer for reinscribing history as the productive intersections of incompatible systems of meaning. They become linked as history to the postmodern by actively articulating a kind of double coding, although not the double of classic and modern that Charles Jencks notes in postmodern architecture, but a double of tradition and modernization that complicates our understanding of the "modern."

One could expand the list to China: *The Sound of Music* (U.S., 1965) as the one American film popular in China during the Cultural Revolution; and *Street Angel* (China, 1937), the sole extant example of a genre that might be called slapstick neorealist musical, cast with a central character modeled after Charlie Chaplin and set in the streets of Shanghai with a singing woman refugee from the Japanese invasion of Manchuria (Godard's *Une femme est une femme* is the only film that remotely parallels this stylistic mix, but Godard's film uncharacteristically omits the politics). One could also locate similar defining examples from Korea, Vietnam, India, and countries throughout the so-called Third World: the five remakes of *Rambo* produced in India, for example,[35] or films by Vietnamese filmmakers on the Vietnam war, produced both inside a postwar Vietnam and in exile, that represent the conflict through the memory and expressive subjectivity of a central female character.[36] In restricting the present discussion to the boundary between Japanese film and the West, I am not seeking to privilege this one set of possibilities but only to clarify issues by addressing texts within a specific set of cross-cultural parameters. By shifting attention from Japan as cultural enclosure to Japan and the West as a set of permeable boundaries, I hope to open Japanese film to productive relationships with Asian, African, and Latin American texts, and not seal it off further as a unique or idealized other.[37]

At their most interesting, films that cut across boundaries can foreground the rupture between systems of meaning as a site for generating new tropes. These new tropes can in turn become determining figures for a repositioning of knowledge and social action: in short, marks of an epistemic break. Generated through radical incongruity, these tropes are normally marginalized as derivative or unsuccessful; yet they constitute a type of production that circulates throughout film history and deserves greater recognition on its own terms. One area of parallel knowledge recently rewritten in this way has been the history of Japanese modern art in the early twentieth century, long dismissed as derivative of the West but recently reconsidered in its own terms as a mode of radical production.[38]

The writing of cultural history, in film, the arts, and elsewhere, has become a terrain filled with ironic artifacts embedded in its own texts. Why, for example, did it take a surrealist artist in the 1930s to collect a kachina doll of Mickey Mouse from Native Americans in the Southwest, while anthropologists excluded it from consideration in a discipline regulated by the master trope of cultural purity?[39] This exclusion has by now become ironic, since the notion of cultural purity that once seemed to respect the autonomy of another culture functioned instead to isolate cultural difference within the stereotype of the primitive.[40] The trope of a kachina Mickey undermines the positioning of Native American culture as a pure object of study by modern anthropology, and is instead richly informative for studying the reciprocal reading of modernization and mass culture by Native Americans. Yet this complex artifact was excluded by an anthropology that insisted on reading in one direction only, imagining that information could be legitimate only if it flowed exclusively from the native to the modern outsider and was constructed solely in terms of the Western cogito.

Similarly, why does film history continue to be written in terms of national cinemas, despite a poststructuralist methodology that now rejects essentialist assumptions as illusory? One thinks, for example, of Thomas Elsaesser's excellent book on New German Cinema, which was awarded the Jay Leyda prize for its contribution to film scholarship; yet at the same historical moment, Germany's boundaries were dissolving both internally with the collapse of the Berlin Wall and externally with the approach of the Maastricht EU Treaty in 1992, inscribing a shift from cultural enclosure to interactive formations. Is this phenomenon like the explosion of auteurist books in film literature after the "death of the author," a convenient figure for delineating a body of texts liberated by the elimination of any ontological pretensions, much as we continue to admire the "sunrise" long after we understand it does not take place? Or has national categorization become an ironic artifact of contemporary Western discourse, not yet able theoretically to work through the implications of its own changed assumptions? Does the premise of nation function now as cultural purity did before—to isolate cultural difference within stereotypes and exclude reciprocal processes of reading that defy easy categorization?

How might one begin to set loose the concept of circulating tropes that move across cultural boundaries without lapsing into superficial or reductive methods? Homi K. Bhabha's *Nation and Narration* (1990) and Bill Ashcroft, Gareth Griffiths, and Helen Tiffin's *The Empire Writes Back: Theory and Practice in Post-Colonial Literatures* (1989) both contributed to this discussion by examining the constituting tropes in nationalist and postcolonialist discourses. Here, though, I would like to shift the emphasis away from the writing or rewriting of nationalist and imperialist ideologies that might be called the problem of the trace: the conflict of different meanings inherent in cross-cultural reinscription that generates multiplicity and dislocates meaning in both cultures involved.

I am not unaware of the rhetorical landmines embedded in this discursive terrain: namely, the powerful critique that the term "cross-cultural" itself can work to neutralize a political analysis of drastic inequities of power among the cultures in question by reducing conflict to an idealized play of the signifier. However, by addressing conflict through the problem of the trace, I do not wish in any sense to de-emphasize the role of power in the construction of texts, but rather to caution against any assumption that power can be easily understood as a single operation of resistance to dominant ideology.

Japan is instructive in this regard because it violates postcolonialist models in several respects: never a colony, it nonetheless suffered from Western domination; its resistance to domination translated directly into cultural isolationism, myths of ethnic superiority and neo-imperialist militarism; it survived nuclear attack and was transformed by the American Occupation paradox of forced democracy; and, as a non-Western culture, it is now a powerful participant in the "First World" economy. Despite this atypical situation, it is important not to set aside Japan as unique and unrelated to other developing countries, a move that replicates precisely the right-wing ideology of Japanese neonationalists. Once a unitary nationalist model is discarded, several features of Japanese modernization have significant parallels elsewhere. For example, in the Middle East, military isolationism and myths of cultural superiority seem widespread, in relation to a culturally specific process of modernization not yet fully understood. The U.S. attempt to replicate the Japanese example of forced democracy in Afghanistan and Iraq is under way, with great violence and unpredictable results. In the former Yugoslavia, the resistance to past Soviet domination all too easily translated into ethnic conflict and cultural isolationism, which reduced the potential for economic and political development to catastrophe.

A tropic analysis of Japanese films can help to cross the limitations of national boundaries and read parallel formations elsewhere. Some of these issues can be addressed through a reading of Tizuka Yamasaki's *Gaijin: A Brazilian Odyssey* (*Gaijin: Caminhos da Liberdade,* Brazil, 1980), a film that seems central to these problems in part because it is so marginal to other discourses. At first glance, it is an anomaly: since Japanese women in Brazil have not previously seized international attention, in the United States the film may seem to compete for obscurity through its representation of the other's other. Part of the problem here is that Japan is rarely discussed in terms of a diaspora, despite Alberto Fujimori's election as president of Peru. The Japanese outside Japan, if mentioned at all, tend to be subordinated to specific national frameworks, as in the discussion of Asian-American films in the United States, or as in Yamasaki's role in Brazil. Yet it is specifically the screening of *Gaijin* in the United States that interests me, as a further displacement of an already dislocated cross-cultural narrative.

The story of *Gaijin* negotiates epic concerns: a woman's voice-over situated in the São Paulo of 1980 recalls her arrival in Brazil with eight hundred Japanese in 1908, her backbreaking work on a coffee plantation and eventual flight to a textile factory in the city at the onset of World War I. Along the way, a series of images and transactions maps the circuitous route by which she ceases to think of herself as a Japanese temporarily away from her homeland and begins to act as a person permanently committed to making a life in a new land. The film's title, *Gaijin,* is Japanese for "foreigner" or "outside person," and initially implies the Brazilians as seen by the Japanese, but later reverses to designate the central character's status in Brazil. As the first film by a Brazilian woman of Japanese descent, the narrative appears as a quest for origins by a contemporary filmmaker: not just any immigrant's story, but one autobiographically linked to the filmmaker's own life. At the same time, the cross-cultural and political resonance of the narrative is suggested by the co-authorship of Yamasaki's script by Jorge Duráu, an exiled Chilean, who had lived in Brazil since the Pinochet coup.

Much of the layered contextual framing of the narrative develops in the credit sequence during the first five and a half minutes of the film, although the significance of much that occurs can be understood only retrospectively in relationship to all that follows. The film begins with a siren, a siren that is not diagetically grounded until nearly the end of the film as the signal for the central character's workday to begin at the textile factory, and the title "São Paulo 1980." Shots of the skyline and traffic are followed by a banner stretched across a crowded street that reads "Irashai" ("welcome" in Japanese, but written in the roman alphabet) and below that "Bem-vindo ao Bairro Oriental" ("welcome to the Oriental district" in Portuguese). Other signs juxtapose "Korea House" (in English) and "ar condicionado," and Chinese characters with part of a word in roman letters.

This inextricable urban weaving of languages and writing systems then abruptly cuts to a more tranquil scene: a group of Japanese children crouch together in traditional costume chanting a game as a woman paces behind them and a Japanese flute plays, all marking the scene as Japan before the title acknowledges "Japão 1908." A rickshaw arrives, and an old woman stares out of a crowd as a man's voice reads a posted sign: "They want people to go to Brazil." The story locates the Japanese woman's role from motherhood to old age in relation to both childhood and group process, all of which occurs before we see the central character.

The voice-over then initiates a dialogue between an unseen woman identified retrospectively with the São Paulo of 1980 and the diagetically present image of Japan in 1908, claiming that image as memory: "It was year 41 of the Meiji era," a period characterized by the rapid importation of Western goods and ideas. This voice continues as the shot changes to a young woman in kimono standing in a field, "I was only 16 years old," locating the subject of this discourse in an image for the first time. Her name, however, is significantly withheld until much later in the narrative. Instead, the woman's identity is established in relation to a network of relatives, the *uchi* of intimate family relationships: "My brother wanted to go to Brazil. He had to have a family to be eligible. I decided to go too. I had to marry. Our family was made up of my brother Yassuji Kobayashi, my cousin Mitsuo Ueno, and the man chosen to be my husband, a friend of my brother's, Ryuji Yamada, whom I didn't know." In this concatenation of specific names, the absence of the speaker's name is conspicuous, but it can be inferred at the outset as suspended unstably between two others: Kobayashi, her family name now left behind, and Yamada, her name as married to a man yet unknown. Both names define her status not as a Western interiority but within the group identity of the patriarchal *uchi,* an identity distributed among relational kinship positions and regulated hierarchically by the name and power of the father.

If the narrative of the film could be said to be oriented around a single axis, then its development would chart the change in this woman's subjectivity from a subordinate position within a group process to an interiority constructed through memory and loss. In this development, the film maps a trajectory not unlike that of Watanabe in Kurosawa's *Ikiru* (1952), a character who struggles to learn a Western sense of individual initiative that violates traditional Japanese values of obligations and consensus. As in *Ikiru,* there is no simple, direct route by which such a transformation can be apprehended; a sign amidst the traffic in São Paulo at the beginning of *Gaijin* displays the universal traffic icon for "no through route." Instead, the character proceeds through a series of stages, each marked by a reconfiguration of subject/object relations and driven by irreversible loss. In *Ikiru,* the loss of traditional Japan after the Occupation is represented by Watanabe's terminal cancer; in *Gaijin,* the same loss of tradition much earlier in history is marked by emigration.

In *Gaijin,* the name of the central character is withheld until relatively late in the action. She is asleep, and seen on screen enveloped by darkness when her husband calls her name for the first time: "Titoe!" At this moment in the narrative, she is exhausted by her first day's labor at the coffee plantation, yet in panic she awakens and apologizes, "gomen nasai," then immediately offers to fix the evening meal, which she has forgotten. Itami's film *Tampopo* has satirized this self-sacrificing image of the ideal Japanese wife through an episode in which a terminally ill woman is roused from her deathbed to prepare one final meal for her family before expiring. In *Gaijin,* Titoe's husband is not represented as being this absurd; he simply tells her to go to bed. The anxiety over meal preparation represents a traditional role that is being dismantled, and her naming recognizes her as a subject in the process of a relatively autonomous reformation.

The darkness out of which Titoe is named combines a double significance: the death of the traditional role bound by multiple obligations, and the emergence of an interiorized subject. Three deaths mark stages of this loss during the narrative, only slightly displaced from Titoe. A Japanese baby dies on the train that is transporting the immigrants from their ship to the plantation. Later, a mother goes mad from the extreme conditions they are forced to endure and hangs herself, elegantly dressed in full kimono. Finally, Titoe's husband, Yamada, dies during an epidemic. These three deaths destroy the three points of the traditional family role: child, mother, and father.

Concurrent with the progression of these deaths is a series of images marking the developing interiority of Titoe's emerging Brazilian self. When the Japanese first see the inadequate housing that has been assigned to them at the plantation, the camera follows Titoe as she enters a crumbling house, in a shot that sustains an image of her alone moving through its interior rooms. Later, she marks her possession of that interior by cleaning and setting up a mirror, yet the mirror does not reflect her own image. Instead, the mirror still later reflects her husband Yamada's face, at the moment when he forces her to first have sex with him. The trope of Titoe's constructed interiority is accordingly marked first by the space of an interiority and the possibility of reflection, then by the reflected gaze of a dominant other. Only near the end of the film is the mirrored husband replaced by a photograph of him after his death, which repositions his role as an absence at the moment Titoe first takes decisive action of her own by moving away from the plantation to work at a factory in São Paulo.

During the credit sequence at the beginning of the film, this trope of a constructed interiority is both foreshadowed and completed. Titoe's departure from her home village is represented by her turning away from the community that formed her and following a cart with the three men she joins en route to Brazil. Visually she recedes into the perspectival depth of the screen, into a visual interiority that becomes significant in retrospect. Then, after she disembarks at the harbor in Santos, the camera pauses to frame her on the left as the director's credit appears on the right of the screen: the ancestral character is marked by the director's signature long before she receives a character name within the diagesis. The directorial signature claims this character as a myth of origin, as the genealogy of an interiority that was not always preexistent, but which constructed, at a certain moment in history, the possibility of a subject who could speak in an individual voice. That voice is recognized as the condition that renders possible the making of this film by a direct descendant.

The origin of the signature is thereby traced to the absence of any preexisting individualized subject, and instead marks the subject of the film's making as deriving from the disjunctive constructions of Japanese and Brazilian formations of self. This is perhaps the trope of cross-cultural dislocation most forcefully inscribed in the film, but it is not the only trope that can be linked outward to other cross-cultural situations.

To return to the credit sequence once again, one could note the positioning of music in relation to the image claimed by the narrator's voice-over as a memory of Japan. Although the image of "Japão 1908" is initially synchronized with the music of a Japanese flute, the flute is replaced by Western choral music from the tradition of Gregorian chant and Christian oratorio. The moment of this replacement occurs immediately after the words, "I had to marry," which mark Titoe's decisive break with her birth family and her native culture. In other words, this moment of originary memory is inscribed in the film with what *The Empire Writes Back* describes as an "irretrievable hybridity." No Japanese cultural purity can be found at the origin of Titoe's transformation, but instead the earliest moment is already marked by the presence of the West. The use of Christian religious music specifies further the character of that hybridity: as the quest for origin that is inscribed within the Christian and humanist metaphysics of the subject, and that is absent from the traditional Japanese construction of self.

In considering *Gaijin,* I have addressed three specific tropes that seem to recur and circulate in many texts constructed at the boundaries, the tropes of constructed interiority, the signature, and irretrievable hybridity. Constructed interiority is a trope of humanist subjectivity as self-consciously represented in a posthumanist or postmodern context. Irretrievable hybridity is a different kind of trope that intersects with the constructed interiority in *Gaijin* as both its precondition and its limit. Hybridity marks the boundary between *uchi* and humanist subject formations that both initiates Titoe's transformation and constitutes the filmmaker's signature as a trace of multiple subjectivities.

These three tropes constitute only part of this film's complex textual weave. However, it is not my purpose here to work through a comprehensive reading of the film, but rather to consider a cross-cultural analysis pursued by a study of tropes that cut across national boundaries. History is always at least double: the intersection of a transformational subjectivity with social and economic change constitutes a dynamic process of reinscription that can be difficult to describe. At the same time, subjectivity now shifts and multiplies in a cross-cultural context that might simultaneously be called postcolonial and postmodern. A sustained tropological analysis may offer the best means of addressing the multiple variables at work here, while sidestepping the misleading enclosures of national identity and authorship. When effectively developed, this approach can help articulate the conflicting distributions of power and desire unavoidably at stake in the process of cultural dislocation and change.

Paper Screen

American responses to Japanese video seem to fall into predictable patterns. First comes the claim that it looks just like New York video, or, in other words, that it is derivative. Second, that there is no longer a unique Japanese style, but rather a world culture of film and video. Despite these alternative expectations of a unitary discourse, whether centered or decentered, a recurrent suspicion seems to remain that there is somehow nonetheless a unique Japanese way of making images. Barbara London writes of Japanese videotapes that are "Eastern in sensibility,"[41] and Nakaya Fujiko, writing about Ina Shinsuke's work, suggests that there is a difference between Japanese and Western perceptions of the same material, even within the same global context.[42]

Articulating the precise interplay of same and difference in Japanese and American video can be elusive. What appears to be different can in a more careful reading turn out to be quite similar, and what seems the same can be most alien. This problem is also, it seems to me, at the heart of what makes Japanese video so intriguing and is perhaps an inexhaustible subject. Nonetheless, one can attempt a few preliminaries to understanding the interplay of same and difference in the Japanese electronic arts by specifically focusing on two videotapes: Ina Shinsuke's *Flow (2)* (1983) and Idemitsu Mako's *Great Mother, Yumiko* (1984).

First, some historic observations may help create a context for this discussion. The history of Japanese video is succinct and interconnected, and can be historically introduced through two bursts of activity: one organized in the period 1971–74, when equipment first became available and artistic exchange first occurred with America and Europe, and a second in the early 1980s, when equipment became more available to independent artists and at the same time more sophisticated. A history of the first moment is available in English in the catalog for the Museum of Modern Art exhibit *Video from Tokyo to Fukui and Kyoto,* edited by Barbara London in 1979. The second moment is documented by Nakaya Fujiko's program notes for *Japanese Television and Video: An Historical Survey,* a 1984 exhibition presented by the American Film Institute (AFI). What interests me here is not to repeat that information but to observe certain interconnections between these two periods of work, between video art in Japan and the West, and between video art and experimental film in Japan.

Video art began in Tokyo at approximately the same time that it did in New York, with video art works and events produced and exhibited in 1968–70. The first intensive activity occurred slightly later, however, with the conjunction of three different kinds of work. During this period, three different groups were organized in Tokyo by Japanese video artists: *Video Earth* was founded by Nakajima Kou in October 1971, followed by *Video Hiroba,* an inter-artists' collective, and the Video Information Center, a cultural archive of videotaped theater, performance, and lecture events, in 1972. Related to these developments were visits to Japan by video artists active in America, bringing with them examples of American video art. These included Michael Goldberg of Vancouver, who began a four-month stay in Japan in November 1971; John Reilly and Rudi Stern, whose "American Video Show" at the American Center in Tokyo was held in August 1973; and Shigeko Kubota's "Tokyo–New York Video Express," an exhibition of American and Japanese video art in Tokyo in January 1974. At almost the same time, Japanese video art began to be exhibited in the West. In Vancouver in 1973; at "Open Circuits," a Museum of Modern Art conference in New York City in 1974; and at Anthology Film Archives in New York, the Institute of Contemporary Art in Philadelphia, and the "Thirteenth Biennale of São Paulo" in Brazil in 1975. The interdependency of these activities can be suggested in several ways. Michael Goldberg, for example, during his visit to Japan, organized the first Tokyo video show with Japanese artists, at the SONY building in February 1972. Participants in this exhibition were the founders of *Video Hiroba* (a group whose name means "Public Square Video"), and several artists who helped form this group were later represented in the 1984 AFI exhibition in the United States, including Kawanaka Nobuhiro, Matsumoto Toshio, and Hagiwara Sakumi. Nakaya Fujiko, another co-founder of this group, presented tapes by *Video Hiroba* members at Vancouver in 1973, the first Japanese video show in the West, and wrote introductions to the later Japanese video exhibitions, *Video from Tokyo to Fukui and Kyoto* in 1979 and the AFI's *Japanese Television and Video: An Historical Survey* in 1984, the latter of which Nakaya also curated.

Another connection that can be observed in the history of Japanese video is with the development of Japanese experimental film. In the United States, artists have tended to make a choice between the two media, to move decisively from one to the other (like Ed Emshwiller or Woody Vasulka), or to use one for characteristic effects in the other (such as Scott Bartlett or Bob Brodsky and Tony Treadway). In Japan, however, a much greater tendency seems to exist for artists to be active in both media simultaneously. Of artists screened in the 1984 AFI video exhibition, for example, Matsumoto Toshio, Hagiwara Sakumi, and Idemitsu Mako also had film work included in the Japanese Experimental Film program of 1980, curated by Donald Richie and organized through the Japan Society and the American Federation of Arts. Matsumoto Toshio, Hagiwara Sakumi, and Kawanaka Nobuhiro also had film work included in the Japanese Experimental Film Show in Chicago in 1983, organized by Chicago Filmmakers and the Art Institute of Chicago. Not surprisingly then, the history of Japanese experimental film as it has been exhibited in the West is intertwined with that of video during the 1970s. Matsumoto's film work, for example, was included in the program of *New Japanese Avant-Garde Cinema* at Millennium and Film Forum in New York City in 1974, the same year his video work first appeared in "Open Circuits" at MoMA; these programs were followed by a "Computer and Video Films" program including Japanese work at Film Forum in 1976, a "Japan Film and Video" program at the Center for Media Study in Buffalo in 1977, and a "Japanese Avant-Garde Film" program at MoMA in 1978.

A second burst of activity both in Japanese work itself and in the visibility of that work in the United States can be located in the period after 1980. In the United States, past Japanese work in video and experimental film received major summative exhibitions in "Video from Tokyo to Fukui and Kyoto," which circulated from New York to Long Beach and Vancouver in 1979, and Donald Richie's "Japanese Experimental Film 1960–80," which first circulated in 1981–82. By this time, however, newer work was beginning to appear in Japan. The Scanimate Synthesizer, used in Matsumoto's *Mona Lisa,* marks an entry point for Japanese artists not only to more sophisticated equipment but to relatively unexplored processed imagery. Image Forum was founded by Tomiyama Katsue in Tokyo in 1976 as a center for experimental film and video, and began to publish *Gekkan Image Forum* as a magazine of critical writing concerning these media forms. Also in Tokyo, the PIA Film Festival, founded in 1977, began to include noncommercial young filmmakers; and Video Gallery Scan was founded by Nakaya Fujiko in 1980, followed by its Video Art Network as an outreach of video art to small towns. Many new artists active in film and video have since become visible in the West, both at the "Japanese Experimental Film Show" in Chicago and the AFI video exhibition.

This interrelated history of video art in Japan and the United States has initiated a process of recognition, exchange, and misperception founded on a systematic interplay of similarities and differences between the two cultures. In one sense, it is possible to maintain that there is no Japanese film or video any longer, but only a world culture in which film and video is produced from multiple decentered sources. This is a tempting assertion, with sushi, Hondas, and futons in Manhattan and a lavish display of Japanese goods at Bloomingdale's, matched by Kentucky Fried Chicken, baseball, and Miki Masu in Tokyo, a city where all the rock performers sometimes seem to sing in English regardless of national origin. World trade and electronic communication have established an extensive system of exchange between these two cultures, which has erased the strikingly different appearances that previously marked the distance between West and East. As a result, contemporary Japanese feature films such as Morita's *The Family Game* and Sai's *Mosquito on the Tenth Floor* all show families in Western-style apartments, driving cars, watching television, and wearing Western clothes, while the shoji, kimono, teapots, and arranged marriages of Ozu and Naruse have almost vanished, except in period films. Japanese video art could also be argued to be reminiscent of U.S. styles. *Video Hiroba* could be said to emerge from a philosophy of community and documentary use of video parallel to that of Global Village and Downtown Community Television in New York. Nakajima Kou's video diary *My Life* (1974–78) could be said to parallel autobiographical tendencies articulated by Rosalind Krauss in her essay on video and narcissism in *October.* Films such as Matsumoto's *White Hole* (1979) could be said to document feedback, waveform-constructed geometries, saturated color, and soundtrack glissandos parallel to early electronic synthesis by Skip Sweeney, Stephen Beck, Dan Sandin, and others in the United States, differing primarily by the far more limited access to video synthesis in Japan. Giant video manufacturers such as SONY and Mitsubishi notwithstanding, Japanese video artists have always had greater difficulty gaining access to equipment, lacking facilitative resources in Japan parallel to the arts councils and private foundations in the West. Because access to sophisticated video equipment by independent artists in Japan has been delayed, it can become tempting for American viewers to see Japanese video art as somehow "following" U.S. developments, in the same way that Japanese film is sometimes thought to "follow" the history of film in the West.

However, the opposite argument can also be made: that Japanese/U.S. (East/West) difference has always been a matter of conflicting systems of relationships among elements, not in visual appearances or materials per se. The elements themselves have been in a process of exchange for much longer than is usually recognized. For example, tempura is a style of cooking the Japanese first learned from the Portuguese, and Hokusai's ukiyo-e (woodblock prints) make use of Western perspective in a Japanese context before the arrival of Commodore Perry. Ironically, through an unconscious process of self-recognition, it was the postperspective prints of Hokusai and Hiroshige that were first discovered by nineteenth-century Europe and proclaimed as the climax of a "pure" Japanese tradition, not unlike the way tempura is now represented as stereotypically Japanese. Along these lines, it should also be recalled that the names "Japan" and "China" themselves come from exportable merchandise to serve Orientalist fashions in the West, and would not be recognized as names of countries by most Asians. In other words, there never was a "pure" Japanese culture apart from outside influences, except as an idealized object imagined through a denial of the circulation that makes such perceptions possible.

One way of distinguishing systematic from apparent differences is to consider the relation of traditional and modernist visual styles in Japan and the West. In many cases, as in the past, what is considered stylistically most modern in the West is a feature of what is most deeply traditional in Japan. This relationship is of course not accidental, since modernist visual styles are to a large extent based on a rediscovery of archaic and non-Western cultures and techniques. However, even familiar elements of Japanese tradition are not often reconsidered systematically in this context. Minimalism, for example, if conceived as a radical reduction to basic materials, can be traced back at least to the influence of Zen in the Kamakura period, as articulated in the aesthetics of Yoshida Kenko and the concept of *wabi* (usually defined as simplicity or understatement), and in artistic work from *sumi-e* (ink painting) and Noh theater to the influence of the tea ceremony on architecture after the Momoyama period. Carl Andre's sculpture is not that far from the rock garden at Ryoanji. Serial imagery, like that of Warhol's Marilyn Monroe series, goes back in Japan at least to Sanjusangendo, the Heian period hall in Kyoto with a thousand identical statues of the Buddhist bodhisattva figure. Process art in the West has its parallel in the Japanese valuing of the ephemeral, articulated by Kenko's statement that "the most precious thing in life is uncertainty," or the concept of *sabi* (aging in harmony with nature). It was a deliberate cultural choice that the Japanese constructed their most valuable cultural objects, such as statues and temples, from wood, so that they remain perpetually vulnerable to imminent destruction by fire. This principle is perhaps most clearly inscribed in the Shinto temple of Ise, which is deliberately destroyed and reconstructed on a periodic basis, and has been continually since the introduction of Buddhism to Japan. Yet this same ephemeralization is inherent in the video image, which exists nowhere in physical space—neither on magnetic tape nor on the flickering phosphors of the screen—but attains its apparent stability only through the retina's persistence of vision as assembled by the cerebral cortex. The flow of Ina Shinsuke's tape *Flow (2)* is as deeply rooted in Japanese tradition as it is contemporary, in the same way that the traditional Japanese practice of miniaturization (as in the invention of the folding fan) finds a contemporary practice in the production of electronic circuitry after the transistor.

To continue this point a little further: it has been frequently noted that environmental art finds its Japanese parallel in the still-present neolithic heritage of Shinto involvement with nature, as with the placement of the Itsukushima Shrine at the edge of the sea on mountainous Miyajima Island. Less noticed is that the antihumanist shift of postmodernism, from a phenomenological emphasis on the individual human subject to the psychoanalytic repositioning of subjectivity as fundamentally bound to an other, parallels the Japanese concept of hara—"self" conceived not as subjective interiority but as a relational position.[43] In addition, textuality and imagery, which mix freely on the video raster

FIGURE 31. Electronic layering of water, rock, and vegetation in Ina Shinsuke's *Flow (2)* (1983).

(programmable equally by computer and camera), have always done so in Japanese cal-
ligraphic painting, in which kanji (Chinese characters) and landscape continually exchange positions and techniques of inscription. In short, Hokusai, who appears to be the
essence of tradition to Western eyes, is in fact quite modern, while aspects of postmodern
styles in the West can appear quite traditional in Japan. What does appear modern to
the Japanese, in the sense of being relatively new and antitraditional, are such aspects of
video as camera perspective and mechanical reproduction, as well as such principles as
a splitting between nature conceived as object and the individual as isolated subject.
Such "modern" principles and techniques of course were first introduced to Japan during
the Meiji period, and have therefore become in a sense a tradition of their own. So the
postmodernist participation in a world culture from Japan involves an interplay of traditional and modernist practices quite different from that of the West. The question for
a Western observer of Japanese video, then, concerns not only a system of cultural differences but a pattern of breaks and reinscriptions unfamiliar even to postmodernist
artists and critics in the West, who both do and do not share a common world culture
with contemporary Japan.

To consider this issue more carefully, it becomes important to consider not only historic relationships and systematic differences, but the construction of meaning in specific
tapes. Ina Shinsuke's *Flow (2)* and Idemitsu Mako's *Great Mother, Yumiko* seem helpful
in this respect. *Flow (2)* presents camera and colorized imagery of rocks and flowing
water within a shifting irregular grid, and appears at first to be quite similar to the Western combination of environmental and abstract material in such films and videotapes as
Paul Sharits's *Stream: Sections: Sectioned: Sectioned* (1968–71) and William Gwin's *Irving
Bridge* (1972). *Great Mother, Yumiko* shows a young couple struggling with their mother
through television, and may also appear like the interweaving of melodrama and media
in 1980s U.S. narrative uses of video, such as Cecelia Condit's *Possibly in Michigan* (1983)
and media/theater pieces by Mabou Mines. Yet the Japanese tapes differ radically in their
construction of meaning, and the apparent visual similarity of these several pieces can
help confuse the issue. Because of the Western priority of the "new" object (an ideological value related to individualism and marketability), visual similarity can be easily dismissed as derivative imitation. Yet in Japan, precise repetition of the old or the respected
is a deeply traditional value, with meaning generated indirectly through articulation
within an appropriate context. For example, the quotation of memorized poetry became
itself a creative act when the selection of verse precisely fitted a contemporary occasion.
In the same way, in the films of Ozu, cliches become powerful means of expression as
understated voicings of complex situations. Stylistic analysis may again be only partially
helpful here.

In a Japanese context, *Flow (2)* inevitably constructs meaning through a series of intertextual relationships not present in the West. The flow of the title and of the water on
the screen not only connects with video's flow of electrons, the flow of energy in a post-
Einsteinian universe, and the flow of information through the nervous system, but
constructs its aesthetics parallel to those of Kenko, who inverted the Buddhist sense of
loss inherent in the transitory nature of life into a figure of desire. In Japan, the world

has always been conceived as an active process, except for the brief period of imported nineteenth-century science. Newtonian mechanics and inertia passed through Japan like a cloud over Kyoto, vanishing before it could be fixed into a habit of meaning. Ina's nature is framed like an Eastern not a Western landscape, that is, not at the distance of perspective space like an untouchable other, but as material surfaces composed within reach, much like the gardens and walkways composed within a frame by gates and paper screens in traditional architecture that act as passages and not barriers. The organization of imagery within a grid parallels the construction of shoji (paper screens), not the Cartesian organization of space recalled by Eadweard Muybridge and Sol LeWitt. The asymmetry of the grid in *Flow (2)* is as Japanese as the irregular street plan of Tokyo in contrast to the Chinese regularity imported for Kyoto. The restrained use of materials (water and rock) is as minimal as a stone garden, yet the luminous flatness of video color recalls Momoyama-era gold-screen painting. With this much traditional grounding of meaning, what is contemporary about the piece is not the aesthetics and values directly but their displacement into an electronic context, in which Shinto respect for nature becomes a post-Minamata advocacy of the environment in an urban industrial society.

Perhaps more important in our understanding of the piece is the construction of nature itself as a sign. In the West, even in postmodernist works, nature tends to be configured either as subject or as object, even as those values begin to be undermined. In William Gwin's *Irving Bridge,* nature is presented as meditative subject, a mirror of the observing subject centered within camera perspective. In Paul Sharits's *Stream: Sections: Sectioned: Sectioned,* however, flowing water is filmed and then intercut with itself according to a formal system, to present nature as an impersonal object or material parallel to the flow of the film material through the projector. Both Gwin and Sharits use a movement toward abstraction to undermine these initial positionings of nature as subject or object. Gwin's understated use of a colorizer produces a fluid imagery not unlike the tradition of abstract expressionism, while Sharits's accumulation of scratched lines into the emulsion comes more from the constructivist concern with line and surface. In both cases, flickering abstraction serves to undermine the categorical construction of meaning into subject or object through a more active interplay with retinal response. Significantly, the result is nonverbal and nonrepresentational, so that the price of freedom from Western categorical logic is a schism with language parallel to the perceptual unconscious described by Anton Ehrenzweig in *The Psychoanalysis of Artistic Vision and Hearing.*

In contrast, as Nakaya Fujiko writes about Ina's work, "The Japanese relationship to nature is often a communal give and take, rather than an attitude of reverence or sublimation." Nature in Japan exists as a dialogue, a process of exchange that is empty until marked as a sign. In the construction of a garden, the material does not become "nature" until it is composed. As a sign, the arranged material marks a relation of subject and object, a site of exchange that creates meaning. Nature is neither "object" (outside signification, it remains empty in the Japanese system of meaning, not a privileged "reality" as in the West) nor "subject" (not interiorized or transcendent). At the same time, language and image are not separate. The interdependent relationship between language and representation is too complex to discuss here, but it should be noted that Japanese art, like the Chinese, never found it necessary to eliminate representation in order to achieve the free play of formal materials that the West discovers in "pure" abstraction (consider Sesshu Toyo or Chu Ta). As a result, Japanese visual representation both eludes categorical signification and coincides with language and writing as a mode of inscription. This mode of representation produces a play of relational positions, not the division of objects, subjects, and abstraction familiar to the West. Nature in *Flow (2)* is a system of signs not unlike the pieces in the Japanese game of Go. In the game, smooth white shell is opposed to rough black stone; in the tape, a system of exchange involves black and white/color, water/rock, and periodic waves/static texture.

Great Mother, Yumiko provides an opportunity to discuss other problems that occur in Western criticism of contemporary Japanese work. In this tape, a woman videomaker (Idemitsu Mako) inscribes the relationship between a young contemporary couple and the continuing influence on their lives of the maternal parent. The mother's advice and control is represented by a giant speaking face on a television screen within the video image in which the young couple appears, and the couple's alternating romance and abuse plays against this other. Rather than embark on an extended reading of this narrative, I will comment here on a single issue raised by this tape: the contradictions within Japanese tradition, against which contemporary media work constructs its own complexity. Too often Japanese film and video is written about in the West as if it were a single,

FIGURE 32. A modern daughter and mother share a meal in relation to traditional roles, figured by way of a video screen next to a contemporary television broadcast. Idemitsu Mako, *Great Mother, Harumi* (1984), from the Great Mother series.

coherent project based simply and directly (if at all) on a uniform tradition. Connection with the cultural context, if observed, tends to be described in terms of progress from traditional to modern techniques ("realism," for example), or alternatively as a resistance to that "progress" as foreign or class domination. Yet both traditional visual and performance arts and modern practice in Japan have their own breaks and contradictions, and the play of one against the other is the source of much meaning generated in contemporary work.

For example, to consider only the relation of theater to film and video, commercial cinema can be traced back to Kabuki as one among several sources for narrative models (and Kabuki in turn to Bunraku, the puppet theater), as reworked through the stylistic innovations of Shimpa (the Meiji-era sentimental drama) and Shingeki (or realist "modern drama"). This kind of history stresses the development of visual realism, and can be misleading insofar as it implies that such films as Ichikawa's *An Actor's Revenge* pose radical alternatives to dominant narrative practice simply because of an antirealist surface drawn parallel to Kabuki. Kabuki itself is a late development in Japanese theater. It emerges from the same urban merchant class that came to power after the Meiji restoration and practices the same principles of emotional expressivism and viewer identification that underlie commercial narrative cinema. Within Japanese tradition, the apparently antirealist makeup design of Kabuki serves as the equivalent of a cinematic close-up to emphasize strong emotion, in contrast to the relative fixity of iconic representation in the masked theatrical forms (Noh, Bugaku) that preceded Kabuki.

Postmodernist media work in Japan has tended to take an alternative approach, which is visible in Idemitsu's *Great Mother* series, and depends on a kind of double articulation that inverts Western expectations about camera imagery, "realist" aesthetics, and presentation of self in everyday life. First, Noh theater functions in Japanese tradition as a more effective antirealist countertradition than Kabuki to the ideology of Meiji-era liberal humanism naturalized through the aesthetics of realism. Noh, as an alternate source for a postmodernist project, constructs meaning indirectly through allegory and distance, rather than expression and identification, so its influence is not barred from the unmasked photographic realism of cinema. Rather, photographic realism itself becomes reconceived as a kind of mask, a purely visual falsification of the multisensory texture of life, which, because false, can function as a kind of mask. Films from the Japanese New Wave by Oshima, Yoshida, Imamura, Shinoda, and others first explored this possibility. This tendency continues in Japanese new narrative video, intensified by the low-resolution antirealist iconic surface of the raster. In *Great Mother, Yumiko,* the close-up face of the mother, inserted into the diagesis by means of a screen within a screen, calls our attention to the use of camera-image as mask. At the same time, the relatively realistic image of the couple works a little differently—Western costume can itself function as a kind of mask in a society where traditional dress is increasingly associated with the traditional roles of formal occasions. A change of costume is not simply a matter of fashion, but constructs a change of role and position in society, much as a mask constructs an alternate role on stage. Costume here functions as a means of signification, not as an expression of personal feeling, as perhaps could most clearly be seen during the 1980s in the juxtapositions of grouped costumes presented for public exhibition by teenagers dancing to rock music in Harajuku each Sunday.

The *Great Mother* series, however, is not restricted to masks as a postmodernist use of Noh. Idemitsu not only draws on Noh as a representational model, but uses it as a means of confronting sexual role ideology in Japanese society. Noh theater, with its precise ritual repetition of the roles of Waki and Shite, consistently assigns fixed positions for sexual roles. The Waki, though nominally secondary, is always unmasked and male, that is, a positioning of the male role as central observing self. It is only the Shite, nominally the central character, that varies—god, ghost, madness, woman, demon—in short, the other from a position of male centrality. That all roles in Noh (as in all other Japanese traditional theater) are played by men should only underscore this point. Idemitsu begins to question these positions: like Kristeva, she is concerned with the role of the mother, not the father, and as producer of images she no longer takes for granted that the sole viewing position should be conceived as male. By so doing, she not only ironically inverts camera realism into a kind of mask, but proposes to unmask the ideological determination of the male self behind the aesthetics of realism.

None of this is to say that contemporary Japanese work can or should be conceived as a remote other in relation to postmodernist work in the West. But the means by which Japanese video art constructs meaning to achieve what at times are parallel goals with the West can be quite different. As a result, much of what is most interesting and challenging about these works inherently is lost in a rush to fit them into categorical universals or opposites. Japanese texts instead can be far more productive when engaged in a process that respects and works through their specificity. They invite a more careful reading in both local and global contexts that would recognize their breaks, shifts, and contradictions. In such a moment, video texts become events that bristle with nuance and possibility.

Epilogue: Next

Japan, film, and history are no longer the indisputable means of organizing media representations that they once were. It has become possible to imagine an "end" of Japanese film history, parallel to other "ends" or transitions around the world. Film ceases to be the dominant medium in society as computers, the Internet, and interactive games emerge as significant media practices. "Japan" begins to be so much a part of the world economy that its cultural productions begin to define entire media niches. A younger generation has now emerged in the United States and Asia that assumes new types of alternative media narratives, from *Pokémon* and Nintendo to manga and anime, are normative. At the same time, "history," in the sense of isolated national traditions, begins to dissolve into a world economy of representations, produced and negotiated from different singular positions. These changes appear as a horizon within the hegemonic closure of globalization, where nation, cinema, and history continue to be predominant institutions, but now with foreseeable limits.

The array of CD-ROMs produced in Japan in the early to mid-1990s traces some of the effects of these changes. As Tim Murray has noted, early practices of such new media as CD-ROMs often experiment with the possibilities and effects of new contexts. Later developments, in order to gain a foothold in the mass market, are far more likely to adapt to hegemonic norms. As a result, Shono Haruhiko's *Gadget: Invention, Travel & Adventure* (Synergy, 1994) marks a moment when CD-ROMs, given the technological capacity for increased memory and faster computers, moved toward the narrative hierarchies and seamless continuity of Classical Hollywood Cinema. In contrast, Shono Haruhiko's alternative *Alice: An Interactive Museum* (Synergy, 1994) and especially Kusakabe Minoru's earlier *Refixion II: Museum or Hospital* (Synergy, 1992), though technically more "primitive," are conceptually more ambitious and suggest a more challenging set of future possibilities.

Manga Space: The Graphic Inflection of Digital Imaging

The Japanese word "manga" has the inclusive meaning of cartooning, comic page or book, or animated film. Manga, in its sense of cartooning, has been important at least since the eighteenth century, when sketches by Hokusai and other Japanese artists contributed to the counterculture of the Tokugawa era. Manga could be traced back even further, to the Choju Giga, a twelfth-century Japanese handscroll with a representation of Buddha as a frog.[1] By the eighteenth century, artists in Western Europe were using the medium of the cartoon as a preparation for oil painting, yet Japanese sketches are a far more distinct art form linked to wood-block prints, or ukiyo-e, as one of the first mass-produced art forms around the world.

By the 1960s, the manga of comic books had become an important part of a new counterculture, as commemorated in Oshima's film *Band of Ninja* in 1967. This kind of manga has always reached both adult and child audiences in Japan, anticipating the later Western development of an adult audience for underground comics and the graphic novel. By the 1990s, anime, which is an abbreviation of the Japanese word *animeshon,* had become the primary introduction to Japanese film for a new generation, marketed in combination with pocket electronic games.

At the same time, manga, in its broader sense, can be understood as the graphic inflection of the visual image in contrast to the production of cinema with a camera. As artists in the early 1990s began to engage with the new media of CD-ROMs and the Internet, the camera became one more form of computer input, intersecting with graphic arts as a double mode of visual inscription increasingly found together. I would like to discuss the implications of this development, as represented by such Japanese projects as the CD-ROMs *Alice* and *Museum or Hospital,* and the Internet sites of Masahiko Sato and *The Nanjing Massacre Museum.*

Since the 1990s, anime has become one of Japan's biggest cultural exports, important enough for Dave Kehr to call it Japanese film's "Second Golden Age."[2] Anime is both written about too much in one sense and not enough in another. On the one hand, an enthusiastic fan base accumulates massive collections of production circumstances and narrative detail. Like the accumulation of trivia by film buffs, this is a potential archive of valuable material, as well as being entertaining for its own sake. On the other hand, anime also invites historical and theoretical engagement. Historical consideration might note, for example, the limited distribution and curious reception given in the United States to Miyazaki Hayao's *Princess Mononoke* (*Mononoke hime,* 1997). At the time, *Mononoke* was the only Miyazaki production to open commercially in the United States, and the film earned only two percent of the Japanese box-office revenues of $154 million.[3] Miyazaki's subsequent film, *Spirited Away* (*Sen to Chihiro no kamikakushi,* "The Voyage of Chihiro Spirited Away," 2001), became the most popular film in Japanese history, earning $234 million in box-office returns to date, exceeding *Titanic* at $208 million. Yet initially there were no plans whatsoever for U.S. distribution, after the disappointing U.S. response to *Mononoke.* When the film was eventually released through Disney, critics observed that it still failed to receive the kind of promotion that it deserved, comparable to other Disney films. Why is there this enormous disparity of response?

Like Rintaro's *Metropolis* (2001), *Spirited Away* is a hybrid text, freely mixing cultural traditions from the West and Japan to produce multiply resonant narratives. Both anime generate their stories through a complex visual pastiche of multiple styles and densely constructed images, far from the standardized sketches and minimal movement of conventional mass-produced animation. *Metropolis* historicizes and updates the concept of the metropolitan center by fusing Berlin and New York City in an era of information monopoly. *Spirited Away* begins with theme park reconstructions of Meiji-era buildings in a pseudo-Western style, then combines the *Odyssey* and Japanese folk tales as resources for a female coming-of-age story. Both of these narratives suggest that the simulations of new media, despite their initial appearance as superficial and fake, can by the slightest of inversions open onto history as a complex and transformative archive. U.S. mass audiences, however, often seem to treat the Western elements of these narratives as transparent while responding to Japanese elements as alien. Children, on the other hand, encountering Japanese cultural representations first through anime, seem struck by the absence of polarized good and evil, in narratives that continually recognize some degree of goodness even in evil characters and evil impulses in the good.

Ueno Toshiya, who contributed his essay "Japanimation and Techno-Orientalism: Japan as the Sub-Empire of Signs" to the Yamagata International Documentary Film Festival, engages anime theoretically, and I am indebted to his work.[4] Rather than pursue the question of cultural difference, however, I would like to take a different tack. What specific contribution does manga or anime make to digital imaging in a world context? Is there a specific inflection of cyberspace that we could call mangaspace?

There are a number of practical reasons for the resurgence of the graphic image in a video and Internet context. The rate of information for video is so high, with an uncompressed video signal requiring 65 MB/sec by one estimate, that processing video on a computer has been very difficult. This is why it took ten years for Internet video to move from postage-stamp size to a little bigger, and even with a broadband connection is unable to duplicate broadcast television. Compression software has been crucial to make computer video possible, which unavoidably restricts its capacity for complex visual dynamics. However, even a full television image has only 525 lines of information, compared to 10,000 lines per inch for a 35mm photographic print. The abbreviation of the image inherent in television is compounded by moving to the Internet, which moves in the opposite direction from HDTV's attempt to replicate 35mm quality electronically.

Slowed down to ten frames per second in the earliest stages, computer video reconstituted frame-by-frame animation as a necessary entry into cyberspace. The reduction of the video image in time and resolution also characterizes the beginnings of virtual reality, where visualization is dynamically reconstructed from a database, and animation is again the interface that makes it possible. Early VR simulations of walking through the interior of an airplane fuselage, for example, looked like a 3D schematic diagram, to minimize the information per second being processed to continually rescan the screen. In the same way, CD-ROMs in the early to mid-1990s privileged graphic animated imagery in order to save disc space, then limited to 650 MB. Since then DVDs, faster chip speeds, broadband, and HDTV have dramatically increased information capacities, enabling a return to camera realism and the illusion of continuous motion as normative modes of production. We should not forget, however, that long before camera realism became normative in digital media, manga-like sketches and animation-like stepped motion were the foundational processes through which spatiality and representation were reconceived. Graphic inflection shaped the formation of cyberspace in its earliest stages, and that heritage remains with us.

In a precise historical parallel, Émile Reynaud's 1889 Praxinoscope animations also preceded twentieth-century cinema. Animated drawing preceded cinema for many of the same reasons that it played a formative role again in digital video: because these strategies are technically simpler at a specific developmental moment and thereby are more easily accomplished. The graphic inflection of digital media may, however, be more than a passing stage of development. Digital video collapses what had long been thought to be a fundamental and categorical distinction between camera imagery and graphic art. Images can now be transferred back and forth between nonlinear editing software, inevitably modeled after cinema, and image processing and compositional software, modeled after photography and painting. Once camera imagery and painting occupy the same place, representation opens onto a horizon of pixel-by-pixel reorganization interacting with camera movement. The return of manga in a digital age marks this intersection of graphic representation and video footage, in anticipation of a kind of visual production not yet known. Classic Hollywood Cinema and broadcast television offer no models for these new conditions, since computer animation tends to be restricted to the insertion of animated characters into a camera space, or vice versa, and digital processing is reduced to transitions in sports coverage or so-called special effects within narrative realism.

Alice, in contrast, is an early CD-ROM transformation of *Alice in Wonderland* into an archive of Western popular culture. After entering the virtual space of the narrative through a door with a light and a thumping noise from inside, the viewer-protagonist discovers an empty room with water dripping on the floor. From this puddle springs a bookcase, which contains volumes that transport the viewer to a residential apartment crammed with artifacts and paraphernalia, each of which in turn opens onto other possibilities and events. Although Alice's rabbit appears prominently, so do record albums from 1950s Broadway musicals, glass cabinets of knick-knacks, books of photographs, and so on. Although the format of a room as a CD-ROM interface to organize a range of thematically unified materials and objects later became commonplace, *Alice* is distinguished by its seeming incoherence, its almost Dadaist juxtaposition of incommensurable objects. Like Mark Dion's gallery installations modeled after archeological digs and natural history exhibits, *Alice* becomes an ethnographic archive asking us to uncover what this array of materials has in common to mark it as a specific set of cultural productions.

Museum or Hospital is an early CD-ROM that opens with the rounded exterior of a postmodern building. Inside, the viewer-protagonist is positioned as a fly's-eye view, in a variation on Kafka's cockroach, buzzing around a museum space. The walls exhibit paintings that are oddly embodied and leap out at the viewer when looked at too intently, with dynamic and amorphous shapes that suggest Bataille's nonocularcentric sexualities. One door of this gallery leads irreversibly through a locking metal gate into the concrete block corridors of a prison asylum. Through peepholes in heavy iron doors, one sees large machines in operation and bestial robotic creatures that slowly turn to return the gaze and approach the viewer. This is a text that suggests Foucault's work on prisons and asylums, and his histories of madness and sexuality, as interrogations of those kind of images called "art." In *Museum or Hospital,* institutions are founded on the forced enclosure of animals and machines, reminiscent of Deleuze and Guatarri's critique of schizo-capital.

By the end of the 1990s, Sato Masahiko created a Web page called "Mutsumi-so's apartment," including a low-resolution camera that hourly changed its minimal image, comparable to a manga sketch. Her page is addressed to "the people of the world," and includes photos from Kentucky and Texas as well as her home in Fuchu City of Tokyo. She attempted to write her homepage in English as well as Japanese, although she was only able to produce a single page in translation when she began. If much has been written about the limits of English-language education in Japan, her ambition and sense of herself is, nonetheless, that of a hybrid personality in a global context. If Sato's project seems unremarkable in the United States, where every teenager seems to have their own Web page and take global communication for granted, we should remember to contextualize these conditions. In Japan, women have been far more excluded from media production even than in the United States, and Idemitsu Mako's 1980s video work remains one of the first examples of women's media production inside Japan. For a young woman in Japan today to begin her life with access to electronic media production as a starting point is worth noting. From Japan, it is also obvious that American media hegemony is not bilateral. The ability to initiate messages from Japan to the world, rather than only respond to messages initiated from the United States, marks a radical and perhaps still utopian change. This is, however, the context from which Miyoshi and Harootunian edited *Japan in the World* in 1993. The Internet shifts the foundational assumptions of international communication, so that decentralized voices previously excluded or marginalized begin to participate in public discourse. If these voices have not yet received the reply they deserve, it is not now for lack of the capacity to speak.

Guo Peiyu also has an instructive Web page. Guo came to Japan from China in 1989 to study Japanese contemporary art, but after living in Japan, he became discouraged by how little most people seemed to know about the Japanese invasion of China and the atrocities committed from 1937 to 1945. As a result, he initiated a series of artistic projects to investigate the issue of historical memory, only to be canceled or banned by several exhibition sites because of discomfort or right-wing pressure. Eventually, he began "The Museum of Nanjing Massacre" in his Tokyo apartment to commemorate the three hundred thousand people murdered by Japanese soldiers in 1937–38. He explains, "To me the Japanese are only aware of their status as 'victims' not as 'instigators.'" His museum displays three thousand clay faces, like a manga parody of the traditional trope of a thousand Buddhas, leaving the other 277,000 faces to the "Japanese conscience." Guo then publicized his project with photos and text on the Internet. Parallel to the changing role of women in Japan and the world, Guo's intervention suggests the changing role of different voices within Asia, speaking across national boundaries to address what has been foreclosed from national discourse.

Since these different projects are not seeking a historical synthesis, no new normative model emerges. At the same time, the singularity of each productive intervention does not depend on any monological discourse for circulation and effect. Instead, these texts continually regenerate and reconfigure possibilities from the heterogeneous conditions and multiple discourses of history conceived as a laboratory and archive.

None of this means that manga is the future of digital media, anymore than animated productions in the nineteenth century were to be the future of cinema in the twentieth century. What mangaspace suggests instead, to paraphrase Godard's *Le gai savoir,* is that any future media will need to address some of the issues and ideas worked through in early digital formats, and continue to be engaged in manga as a proto-digital entry point.

History and Heterology

What is [culture]? Is there such a thing as Japanese culture? Or American culture? Or comparative culture? Or has cultural difference become irrelevant in a globalized modern society? Perhaps we need a new word, one that reconfigures the meanings of culture, history, and the symbolic field.

[Culture], for lack of a better word, is a palimpsest: the inscription of current social institutions, practices, and discourses takes place over a series of past social contexts now occluded but only partially erased. Traces of past social texts continue to inhabit current practices, often as unconscious assumptions or determining figures.

[Culture] operates as a network of discourses, institutions, and practices that intersect and indirectly affect one another within a social context. Discourses are sites of knowledge, power, and agency that transform material conditions into specific social practices and effects. They are woven into the immediate environment rather than standing apart from or above it. Discourses are constructed or inscribed in texts to record and transmit knowledge and agency across generations and are regulated through determining figures. Figures inhabit, embody, and situate discourses in relation to the materialities of writing, sexuality, labor, and the sensorium. [Culture] is thereby configured as a heterogeneous array of intersecting figures and discourses within an intertextual network or *aufschreibesysteme*.

Borrowing from Michel de Certeau, the study of such a dynamic array could be called heterology. In his foreword to de Certeau's book, Wlad Godzich explains, "*Heterology* is a term that has come to designate a philosophical countertradition that, in shorthand, could be described as being deeply suspicious of the Parmenidean principle of the identity of thought and being."[5] The concept invites the study of otherness in its multiplicity, through the dislocation and inversion of foundational tropes across intersecting discourses and cultural horizons, without a single universal framework to contain the play and contestation of *différance* within an idealist system.

Closure is established within discourses and cultures alike by abjection, or foundational foreclosure of incommensurable difference, to stabilize the boundaries of an imagined community. Figures nonetheless circulate across discursive and cultural boundaries, generating a variety of intensities and effects. Each discourse contains its own temporality, or history, in syncopation with others, and the break between discourses is marked by a series of what Karatani calls inversions. Heterology works to trace complexity and contradiction across discourse networks as a means toward a micropolitics of localized interventions.

No conclusions or endings are possible, yet a number of things can be said.

History has reached several ends, or endings, in the twentieth century. History reached one of its end points in the Holocaust and the consequent collapse of the Western idea of history as inevitable progress. With the dropping of the bomb at Hiroshima and the subsequent Cold War policy of Mutually Assured Destruction, the premise of total war led toward the possibility of a nuclear holocaust that would end all history. Increasing scientific knowledge and technology could no longer be seen as a guarantee of improving conditions, with the effect that any sense of teleological goal for modernization and development was undermined. This effect is irreversible, despite triumphalist claims such as Francis Fukuyama's that liberal capitalism has achieved the best of all possible worlds. Such claims attempt to restore a utopian idealist version of dominant history, founded on a repression of the Holocaust and its effects.

Another end was documented by Victor Burgin's *The End of Art Theory,* when the institutionalized isolation of art from the supposed contamination of social and political contexts could no longer be sustained. The Marxist idea of a totality of effects across a social field undermined how "art for art's sake," a movement that initially broke with the regulation of thought by religion, had itself become canonized as a neo-idealism. At the same time, multiple totalities began to intersect, so that a totality of effects could also be recognized in psychoanalysis, textuality, and representation, ethnicity, gender, postcoloniality, and postnationalism, among others. Privileging any single totality over others began to seem complicit with totalitarian thinking, and the postmodern critique of grand narratives broke with unitary and totalized models of history.

Yet another end came with Young's *White Mythology,* departing from Derrida's critique to problematize Hegelian models of history at the core of Western ethnocentric evolutionism and a neocolonialist ethos. Multiple historical trajectories are possible en route to modernization, and no single model can be considered correct or best. At the same time, accelerating communications brought these multiple histories into increasing contact, with intersections, contestations, and hybridities as a result, and the heterological complexity of a networked society.

This being said, the consequent heterologies do not compose a system. Insofar as terms like "heterology," "hybridity," "postmodern," and the like have become fetishized and repetitious, then they have become as misleading and useless as any other idealist terms. The problem, however, is not in these terms as opposed to others, but in the limits of language and representation as such. Texts always remain to be read and can never be exhausted, repressed, or monopolized by established readings, yet terms are also easily subsumed in the regime of the sign and mistaken for concretized objects rather than dynamic events. Figural agency always exceeds any discourse, and surprises us with inventions where all is assumed as already known.

Hence, the availability of what is conventionally called Japanese film history as an archive says nothing about what can or will happen next. The most effective new work will draw on and transform past precedents, but not in any way yet known. What we can do is consider the issues at stake and the strategies in play in new media texts, while recognizing that all current practices are transitional. The next move cannot be recognized in the midst of a foundational shift, but any productive project must continue to work through the issues and strategies engaged here.

Appendix

Japanese Networked History: A Metachronology of
Culturally Significant Events in Relation to Film

Films are primarily listed in the sequence of their diagetic setting, citation, or connotation, and only occasionally according to when they were produced or viewed, as indicators of how history is continually reconstructed. Entries in italics mark additional points where one era significantly intersects with another. Other entries are compiled from several general history sources.

All entries are selective and not comprehensive, to call attention to intertextual links that might otherwise be overlooked. Entries are exemplary and not authoritative and are sometimes selected from a set of contested possibilities. The goal is to displace the idea of history as singular, definitive, and absolute, and instead suggest an approach to history as interactive, transformative, and heterological.

Contemporary cultures continually interact with the past by altering the archive of available artifactual evidence, gaining unexpected insights through new methodologies and generating new models for the future from materials previously discarded. Derived from limited information, and with major areas uncertain or unknown, history is volatile, unstable, and unpredictable, even while providing a dynamic model of cultural complexity and change.

PALEOLITHIC

200,000 BCE   No definitive evidence for paleolithic culture in Japan, but peoples presumably came from different areas of Asia and South Pacific; predominant strain is Mongoloid, with considerable mixture of Malayan; Japanese language appears related to both Polynesian and Altaic

Ancestors of Ainus among earliest peoples (16,000 remain in Hokkaido today), but early history and relation to neolithic cultures unknown

NEOLITHIC

Jomon

3500–250 BCE   Neolithic hunters and gatherers live in pit dwellings, develop corded
                decoration on pots into high relief (*joomon* = cord-marking)

Yayoi

250 BCE–250 CE   Invaders from Korea bring advanced agricultural techniques and
                 bronze casting; stimulate incised pottery and *dotaku* (bronze bells)

                 Yayoi pots (named after the place first found) are wheel-made and
                 less elaborately decorated than Jomon, but they are fired at higher
                 temperature and technically superior

2nd century BCE   Bronze and iron tools enter Japan from Asia

100 BCE   Rice culture (originating from South China or Southeast Asia)
                 begins to appear and revolutionize culture, establishing basis for the
                 economy until the industrial era

1884   *Pots discovered at Yayoi, define pre-Yamato period*

Yamato Period (300–710)
Formation of the ruling class

Protohistoric period: Kofun

0–400 CE   Immigrants from the Asian continent (China, Manchuria, and Korea,
                 with possibly an oceanic or Malay strain) displace the Ainu race
                 (source of many place names, e.g., Mount Fuji, and probably many
                 Shinto beliefs) as primary occupants of Japan

0 CE   Probable historic date of Jimmu Tenno's rule in Yamato as first
                 emperor of Japan and founder of the imperial line, unbroken
                 through today

712–720   Kojiki *(712) and* Nihon Shiki *(720) chronicles written to record myths
                 and consolidate imperial house—claims divine origin of Jimmu Tenno's
                 founding of empire, mythically dated 660 BCE*

2nd century CE   Himiko, shamaness queen, unifies country after period of civil strife

                 Relation to Yamato clan unknown

3rd–5th   *Pimiku (Himiko) recorded in Chinese histories:* History of the
century CE   Kingdom of Wei, *c. 297 CE, and* History of the Latter Han Dynasty,
                 compiled c. 445 CE

3rd–6th century CE	Rise of imperial Yamato clan— Haniwa ("circle of clay") sculpture and *kofun* (monumental burial mounds, e.g., earthworks tomb of Emperor Nintoku near Osaka)
	Shinoda's *Himiko* (1974)— calls for opening the imperial tombs for archeological research
	Teshigahara's *Face of Another* (1966)— Haniwa sculpture on shelves in protagonist's apartment
mid-4th century	Empress Jingo establishes Korean colony (abandoned 7th century)
	Shinto shrines at Izumo and Ise, periodically rebuilt, probably initiated in this period

Early Historic: Asuka (552–645)

beginning 5th century	Chinese script officially adopted for court scribes
	Three kingdoms of Korea (Paekche, Silla, and Koguryo) serve as route for sporadic contacts with China
6th century	Buddhism introduced from China, succeeds through efforts of Prince Shotoku (572–621); native polytheistic religion named Shinto in contrast
	Clan rivalry develops—dominant Soga clan promotes Buddhism
7th century	Soga overthrown by Fujiwara clan—administrative reforms introduced that are modeled on Chinese T'ang empire
680–693	Horyuji temple built near Nara on site of Shotoku's palace and temple, now oldest wooden building in the world; murals completed by 711, Yumedono (Dream Hall) by 739; parallels Six Dynasties architecture in China
1884	*Yumedono Kwannon (80-inch wooden statue, Asuka period) discovered inside Yumedono tabernacle at Horyuji by Ernest Fenollosa, curator of Oriental Art at the Museum of Fine Arts in Boston*
1949	*Horyuji frescoes destroyed by fire, temple reconstructed*

Nara/Heian
Period of Court aristocracy

Nara

694–710	Fujiwarakyo built as capital city, imitating China's T'ang capital Chang-an
710–84	Heijokyo (Nara) built as capital city, imitating China's Chang-an

Kojiki (712) and *Nihon Shiki* (720) chronicles written to record myths and consolidate imperial house—claims divine origin of Jimmu Tenno's founding of empire, mythically dated 660 BC

Military forces maintained in northeast against Ainu—helps develop military clans

784–794   Capital moves to Nagaoka

Heian

794   Capital moves to Heian-kyo (Kyoto)

mid-9th   T'ang in disorder, Chinese influence ends
century

10th–11th   Feudalism emerges—taxes paid to provincial landowners
centuries
               Murasaki Shikibu, a court lady, writes *Genji monogatari (A Tale of Genji);* male writers preoccupied with Chinese literary imitations

               Mizoguchi's *Sansho the Bailiff* (1954)—
               attacks rise of manorial system in late Heian

12th century   Rivalry of military clans leads to decline of Fujiwara

               Taira Kiyomori (fl. 1150s–1181) and his clan take power; first political executions in 300 years

               Mizoguchi's *New Tales of the Taira Clan* (1955)—
               conflict between decadent court and rising warrior class

1185   Taira clan defeated by the Heike (Minamoto) at pivotal sea battle in the Shimonoseki straits

Kamakura/Muromachi
Period of military clans

Kamakura

1185   Minamoto Yoritomo given the title shogun (sei-i tai-shogun, or "barbarian-subduing great general") by the emperor, and establishes administrative center (Bakufu, "camp office") at Kamakura, far from Kyoto

               Debut of samurai and of hara-kiri

               Jodo-Shinsu, Nichiren, and Zen Buddhist sects arise—Zen becomes associated with the samurai ideal

               Yoritomo fears his powerful brother, Yoshitsune, and tries to have him killed. Yoshitsune flees to Hiraizumi to take asylum with his old friends the Fujiwaras, where he is betrayed and killed at Takadachi Castle in

1189. The diminutive Yoshitsune and his equally famous companion Benkei become the heroes of numerous legends and Kabuki dramas

Kurosawa's *Those Who Tread on the Tiger's Tail* (1945)— Pacific War propaganda version of Yoshitsune, undercut by Chaplin-like Benkei

13th century	Zen-inspired landscape painting; monumental statue of Amida Buddha erected at Kamakura
	Labyrinthine politics: Emperor at Kyoto is the puppet of the Fujiwara clan, who in turn are controlled by the Minamoto shogun at Kamakura, himself a puppet of the Hojo clan
1274 and 1281	Attempted invasions by the Mongol Emperor of China, Kublai Khan—fleet for the second larger invasion (150,000 men) destroyed by typhoon ("kamikaze"—"the divine wind")
	Kamakura administration impoverished by invasions, in disrepute
Beg. 14th century	Money replaces rice as principal medium of exchange
1331	Hojo deposes and exiles the emperor, Go-Daigo, who had been plotting to overthrow the Bakufu
1333	Go-Daigo reemerges, with warrior support and defections from Hojo; one of his commanders attacks and overruns Kamakura
	Last Hojo regent, family and 800 retainers commit mass hara-kiri
	Ashikaga Takauji of the house of Minamoto sets up another member of the imperial line as emperor, creating rival court and civil war
Muromachi	
1339	Ashikaga Takauji has himself appointed shogun, establishes government in Muromachi district of Kyoto
14th–15th centuries	Trade and commerce increase: Japanese seafarers establish closer contacts with China, while Japanese pirates harass the China coast from Shantung to the Pearl River
	Important harbor communities develop as a result, including Sakai, port of Osaka, ruled by local merchants
	Ashikaga shoguns live in luxury and aestheticism in Kyoto, in contrast to poverty and disorder of provinces; emperor reduced to dire financial straits
	Era of almost continuous violence, amounting to full-scale civil war over many years

1358–1408	Yoshimitsu as shogun, patron of the arts; landscape gardening, classical drama, tea ceremony, and flower arranging flourish and establish standards of excellence
1445–90	Yoshimasa as shogun, also patron of the arts
15th century	New art forms become established: Noh theater (Zeami), Renga (linked verse), *sumi-e* (ink painting; Sesshu)
1542 or 1543	Portuguese, driven off course on way to Macao, land at island off Kyushu
1549	Francis Xavier, Spanish Jesuit, visits Kagoshima in Kyushu
	Portuguese merchants and sea captains from Macao introduce Western trade and smooth-bore muskets
16th century	The "age of the overthrow of the higher by the lower": conditions chaotic, law and order breaks down, great houses overthrown by bandit chiefs
	Kurosawa's *Rashomon* (1950)— set in Kyoto during 16th-century civil wars
	Kurosawa's samurai epics also set during 16th-century civil wars— e.g., *Seven Samurai* (1954) and *Hidden Fortress* (1958)

Azuchi-Momoyama

1578	Oda Nobunaga (1534–82), a *daimyo* of central Japan, first to use muskets as part of strategic military force; subjugates neighbors and becomes leading figure in Japan
	Unable to become shogun, as Taira, because the title is traditionally reserved for a member of Minamoto clan; emperor and Ashikaga shogun alike become nominal powers, subservient to Nobunaga
	Nobunaga builds superior wood castle on stone base at Azuchi by Lake Biwa; attacks Buddhist strongholds on Heizan near Kyoto and slaughters the women and children who survive
	Favors Jesuit missionaries with land grant for seminary near Azuchi, though he himself is without religion
1582	Nobunaga killed in a surprise attack
1582–90	Toyotomi Hideyoshi (1536–98), son of peasant foot soldier and noted for small stature and ugliness, completes unification of Japan: defeats rival *daimyo* and Nobunaga's surviving sons, achieves stand-off and then alliance with Ieyasu

Defeats Shingon Buddhists (crucifies leaders), suppresses resistance in Kyushu with 250,000 soldiers, then captures last resisting fortress at Odawara (southwest of modern Tokyo)

Hideyoshi establishes efficient system of central administration, rearranges feudal allotment of fiefs so potential rivals are checked by loyal supporters

Obtains title of Kampaku from emperor (could not be shogun except through adoption), enforces division between samurai and peasantry (no samurai allowed to become townsmen, weapons confiscated from peasants)

Builds castle at Osaka far stronger than Nobunaga's at Azuchi, and palaces near Kyoto (Juraku mansion and Momoyama palace at Fushima); trade with Macao (Chinese silk) and Manila highly valued

Hideyoshi's extravagant entertainments promote a craze for the ostentatious; prosperity enjoyed by the few, while conditions of the peasantry are severe

Era of Sen Rikyu, greatest of tea masters

Christian converts grow to 300,000 (of 15–20 million total population), including several *daimyo;* anti-Christian edicts of 1587 not enforced

Nagasaki virtually governed by Jesuits (Portuguese in loyalty), who act as translators and accept percentage of commercial profits while confining evangelism to samurai class

Rivalries develop with Spanish Franciscan and Dominican friars from Manila, who address the poor, sick, and outcast

1592 and 1597	Hideyoshi sends invading army of 200,000 to Korea, as intended preliminary to conquest of China (megalomanic folly, but outlet for thousands of restless warriors)

Osima's *Sun's Burial* (1960)—
image of Osaka castle repeatedly framed by slums

Teshigahara's *Rikyu* (1989)—
Sen Rikyu's tea ritual, in era of Hideyoshi's Korean invasion

1597	Hideyoshi martyrs 26 Franciscan friars and converts by crucifixion at Nagasaki, having come to take seriously the threat that missionaries could precede foreign invasion
1598	Hideyoshi dies, leaving his heir Hideyori under guardianship led by Ieyasu

1600	Ieyasu meets Will Adams, the English pilot of a Dutch vessel that reaches Japan with 24 survivors out of a crew of 100

Tokugawa
Period of merchant urbanization

1600	Tokugawa Ieyasu (1542–1616) defeats rivals at battle of Sekigahara
1603	Ieyasu appointed shogun (eligible as member of Minamoto clan)
	Fiefs redistributed according to the alliances at Sekigahara, as basis of new system of centralized administration
1605	Ieyasu abdicates in favor of son Hidetada; nominally retires while Hidetada heads shogunal administration at Edo
1609	Dutch begin trade with Japan
1613	English begin trade with Japan
	Will Adams teaches Ieyasu about Europe, math, and navigation and is appointed diplomatic agent with Dutch and English traders; forbidden to return to England, Adams is granted an estate, marries a Japanese woman, and dies in Japan
1612–14	Ieyasu issues edicts prohibiting Christianity, having learned that northern Europe would trade without religion; orders expulsion of priests, demolition of churches, and renunciation by converts
1616	Ieyasu overcomes last supporters of Hideyori after long siege of Osaka castle (Christians, including Jesuits and friars, are among castle defenders); Hideyori and his mother and principal retainers commit suicide
1616	Hidetada suceeds Ieyasu
	Intensifies measures against Christians, torture used to root out alien faith seen as subversive
1623	English close trading post in Japan, due to low profits
1637–38	Shimabara rebellion assumes Christian character; insurgents in castle at Hara are massacred
	Christianity now seems eliminated (but secret practices rediscovered among local families in Kyushu in 1865)
1637–39	National Isolation declared and enforced by beheadings and ship burning; Japanese forbidden to leave or return, Spanish and Portuguese banned

1640	Ship from Macao brings gifts to Iemitsu as new shogun; all but 13 are beheaded at Nagasaki and the vessel is burned—the rest are sent back to Macao as messengers
	Japan now effectively closed to outside contact and trade, except for Dutch and a few Chinese at Nagasaki
	Iemitsu, third Tokugawa shogun, builds Toshogu Shrine, Nikko, in honor of his father, Ieyasu
17th–18th centuries	Edo era characterized by growth of urban culture, and interior colonization of provinces
	Building of Himeji castle (1609), Kiyomizudera temple in Kyoto (1633)
17th–19th centuries	New artistic forms emerge: popular literature (Saikaku), Kabuki and Bunraku in theater (Chikamatsu), ukiyo-e in art (Utamaro, Hokusai, Hiroshige), haiku in poetry (Basho)
20th century postwar	*Nikko, Himeji, and Kiyomizudera become primary tourist sites*
	Mizoguchi's *Life of Oharu* (1952)— story from Saikaku based in late 17th century
	Shinoda's *Double Suicide* (1969)— countercultural rediscovery of Bunraku puppet plays
1853	Commodore Matthew Perry arrives with Black Ships off Uraga, forces opening with West
1854	Trade agreement with United States, allows use of port at Yokohama

Meiji
Imperial restoration and modernization

1867	Imperial Restoration replaces shogunate; feudalism abolished
	Reforms: clans replaced by prefectures, Christianity legalized, solar calendar adopted
	Railroads, postal system, education
1875	Monumental torii gate built at Itsukushima Shrine, Miyajima (shrine since 6c)
20th century postwar	*Miyajima torii gate becomes emblem of Japan for tourism*
1877	Satsuma rebellion

1879	Former President Ulysses S. Grant unexpectedly approves of the Noh theater, especially resurrected for his official visit, thereby saving it from extinction
1884	*Yumedono Kwannon (80-inch wooden statue, Asuka period) discovered inside Yumedono tabernacle at Horyuji by Ernest Fenollosa, later curator of Oriental Art at the Museum of Fine Arts in Boston*
1884	*Pots discovered at Yayoi, define pre-Yamato period*
1885	Cabinet system established
1889	Meiji Constitution promulgated
1890s	Young men from China come to study in Japan, and return converted to Western political ideas
1894–95	Sino-Japanese War: Japan's modernized forces overwhelm the Chinese and annex Taiwan
	Oshima's *Empire of Passion* (1978)— **ghost story set in 1895, during era of Meiji militarization**
1904	Russo-Japanese War
1906	Kakuzo Okakura, a former student of Fenollosa, writes *The Book of Tea* in English to promote foreign appreciation of Japanese traditions
1910	Japan annexes Korea
1910–11	High Treason Incident: 24 socialist intellectuals arrested and executed
1911	Kobayashi Ichizo founds Takarazuka all-girl revue in Kobe-Osaka at terminus of his railway line to attract travelers
Taisho	
1912	Taisho begins
1914–15	Japan seizes German-leased territory and sphere of influence in Shantung at outbreak of World War I, negotiates treaty with Chinese dictator Yuan Shih-k'ai recognizing Japanese dominance in Shantung, Manchuria, and Inner Mongolia—provokes massive upsurge of nationalist feeling in China
1915–16	Socialists and anarchists including Osugi Sakae attempt to organize labor; Ito Noe becomes editor of Seito ("Bluestocking"); Osugi advocates free love as rejection of traditional obligations, becomes lovers with Kamichika Ichiko and Ito Noe, in addition to wife, Hori Yasuko; Kamichika stabs Osugi, but he survives

Yoshida's *Eros Plus Massacre* (1969)—
juxtaposes Osugi's sexual anarchism with 1960s student activism

1923   Kanto earthquake and fire destroys Tokyo–Yokohama area, killing
            100,000; in the aftermath, vigilante crowds massacre 6,000 Koreans,
            and police arrest anarchists, communists, and leftists, some of whom
            are murdered in prison, including Osugi Sakae and Ito Noe

Early Showa

1926   Hirohito, known for his Western interests in biology and golf,
            becomes emperor

1920s   New generation of Western-influenced youth, *mobos* and *mogas*
            (Marx, or modern, boys and girls)

            Japan appears to be moving toward liberal democracy as an outcome
            of modernization

            Matsuda's *Bantsuma: The Life of Tsumasaburo Bando* (1980)—archive
            releases Futagawa's *Orochi* (1925) and excerpts from *Backward Current*
            (1924) and *A Shadowy Character* (1925)

            Kurosawa's *No Regrets for Our Youth* (1946)—
            links postwar Japan to 1920s liberal era

            Kurosawa's *Rashomon* (1950)—
            based on Akutagawa stories written in 1920s

1929   Depression begins

1931–33   Manchurian Incident: Japan occupies Manchuria (1931), establishes
            puppet state of Manchukuo under the last Manchu emperor (1933);
            militarists begin to leverage success in Manchuria into increasing
            control of Japanese government

            Japanese rapidly builds basis of modern economy in Manchuria, with
            a dense railway network, and heavy and light industries, on a scale
            unmatched elsewhere in China; intensifies after outbreak of war
            (1937)

            Kobayashi's *The Human Condition, Part I* (1959)—
            a pacifist drafted and sent to administer Manchurian slave labor

1935–36   Japanese occupy neighboring Jehol and try, but fail, to control all of
            northern China

            Chiang forced to form united front against Japanese invaders, despite
            preference to crush Communists and provincial rivals

Mizoguchi's *Sisters of the Gion* (1936)—
harshly criticizes both modern and traditional roles for women

Oshima's *In the Realm of the Senses* (1976)—
story of Sado's sexuality set in 1936, with militarist background

1937–38   Japan responds to united front by invading in force, occupying most
of north and central China, together with coastal ports and all centers
of modern industry; Nationalists retreat into impregnable mountains
of Szechwan and the southwest

December   Nanjing massacre: after Nanjing falls, the Japanese Imperial Army
1937–   launches a massacre for six weeks
January 1938
According to the records of several welfare organizations that bury
the dead bodies after the Massacre, around 300,000 people, mostly
civilians and POWs, are brutally slaughtered (more than in the later
bombings of Hiroshima and Nagasaki combined)

Kumai's *Sandakan No. 8* (1974)—
investigates enslavement of wartime "comfort women"

1941–42   Japanese advances in Pacific War: bombing of Pearl Harbor, Singapore captured from British, United States expelled from Philippines

1944   Japanese offensives add more territory in China

1944–45   Firebombing of Tokyo and atomic bombs on Hiroshima and
Nagasaki; Japan accepts unconditional surrender

Postwar

1945–52   U.S. Occupation under General Douglas MacArthur

1946   New Constitution dictated by MacArthur, ostensibly by Japanese:
includes equal rights for women, and Article IX prohibiting war;
emperor retained as constitutional monarch, but divinity denied

1948   General Tojo and others executed as war criminals; Cold War causes
United States to reverse initial plans to break up the *zaibatsu* and
demilitarize Japan

Shinoda's *MacArthur's Children* (1984)—
reconstructs immediate postwar period of baseball and war crimes

Kurosawa's *Rashomon* (1950)—
wins first prize at Venice and international attention for Japanese film

1951	U.S.–Japanese Mutual Security Pact signed; television broadcasting begins
1952	End of Occupation

Kurosawa's *Ikiru* (1952)—
humanist individualism requires transformation of self

Ozu, *Tokyo Story* (1953)—
parents visit ungracious children preoccupied with business

1955	Liberal Democratic Party (LDP) forms conservative alliance with business, begins unbroken control of the Diet, which continues for 38 years
1956	Prostitution made illegal
1958	Kinkakuji destroyed by fire
1960	Security Pact renewed despite massive protests by the *Zengakuren* and others

Oshima's *Cruel Story of Youth* (1960)—
youth cynicism after futility of *Zengakuren* protests

1960s	"Age of uncertainty"

"Economic miracle" begins: income doubles during the decade and Japanese families acquire the "three treasures" (television, refrigerator, and washing machine) and the "three C's" (color television, camera, and car)

1964	Shinkansen bullet train route opens between Tokyo and Kyoto

Imamura's *Insect Woman* (1963)—
determined survival of excluded despite abuse

Teshigahara's *Face of Another* (1966)—
Kobo Abe story of visceral dislocation in modern conditions

1970–1980s	Era of external shocks *(shoku):* yen shocks (massive currency revaluations of 1971 and 1985) and oil shocks (massive price increases of 1973 and 1979–80); Japan responds with resilience, and competitiveness increases rather than weakens

Western books arguing that Japan has caught up with the West, such as Kahn's *The Emerging Japanese Superstate* (1970) and Vogel's *Japan as Number One* (1979), are popular in Japan and contribute to growing national self-confidence

1974   Prime Minister Tanaka convicted of taking Lockheed bribe, resigns
            but remains power behind the scenes

1980   Japan produces more automobiles than the United States

1981   Japan produces 70 percent of the world's computer chips

1982   Ministry of Education proposes revision of textbooks to downplay
            Japanese war atrocities, but withdraws proposal after intense Chinese
            and Korean protest

1980s   Second postwar generation (born in the sixties) comes of age, called
            "new human beings" *(shinjinrui);* by the late 1980s, 65 percent of the
            population was born after the end of the Pacific War

            Morita, *The Family Game* (1983)—
            satirizes upward mobility and exam pressure

            Idemitsu, *Great Mother, Yumiko* (1984)—
            refigures family system in relation to television

1985   Japan becomes the world's major financial power: largest creditor
            and net investor, with largest banks and stock markets in the world

1980s   "Japan bashing" in United States; boom in Japanese books explaining
            U.S. hostility as part of a worldwide Jewish conspiracy

1986   Scandal over Prime Minister Nakasone's remarks that Japan's success
            is due to a homogeneous population, while the mental level in the US
            is lower because "there are blacks, Puerto Ricans and Hispanics"

            Itami's *A Taxing Woman* (1987)—
            satirizes corruption in business and government

            Hara's *The Emperor's Naked Army Marches On* (1988)—
            invasive protest of emperor's complicity in wartime atrocities

            Kore-Eda's *Nobody Knows* (2004)—
            based on a 1988 incident of abandoned children in Nishi-Sugamo

1988–89   Recruit Cosmos financial scandal affects almost the entire LDP
            hierarchy; Kaifu selected as unlikely prime minister because he alone
            was untouched

1989   Hirohito dies, Showa reign ends; new Emperor Akihito begins
            Heisei ("achieving peace") reign—controversy over Shinto elements
            of funeral and enthronement ceremonies that suggest the emperor is
            still divine

Kurosawa's *Dreams* (1990)—
postmodern series of episodes on representation and history

Álvarez and Kolker's *The Japanese Version* (1991)—
notes the Japanese appropriation of Western popular culture

1993	After endless scandals, the LDP finally loses an election, and Hosokawa becomes prime minister as head of a new government coalition pledged to reform and an improved standard of living for average salarymen
	New Premier Hosokawa Morihiro, grandson of Prince Konoe Fumimaro, who was charged as a Class A war criminal, publicly states as one of his first official acts that Japan's military actions in the 1930s and 1940s were "an aggressive war and a wrong war"
	Government organizes compensation packages for some former "comfort women"; confronting wartime misdeeds remains a difficult process for Japan, although polls consistently show that more than half the population believes the country owes Asia an apology for Japanese atrocities
	Kim Young Sam, first democratically elected civilian president of South Korea, when asked about "comfort women" compensation, said, "It is not your money we want. It is the truth we want you to make clear. Only then will the problem be solved."
1994–2005	LDP returns to power, but only as part of unstable coalitions
1995	Major earthquake hits Kobe, the worst in Japan since 1923
	Aum Supreme Truth cult releases sarin nerve gas in rush-hour subways in Tokyo, leaving 11 dead and 3,796 injured

Guo Peiyu opens the *Nanjing Massacre Museum* (1995)—
apartment museum and Internet site in Tokyo
http://arts.cuhk.edu.hk/NanjingMassacre/NMGP.html

1996	Prime Minister Murayama Tomiichi apologizes for "mistaken national policy" of "colonialism and aggression"; the right wing insists that Japan's "guilt" is a fiction created by Japan's conquerors, but many believe Murayama does not go far enough, must begin with admission that Hirohito himself largely conducted the war, and offer compensation to those who suffered
1998–2005	Worst economic slowdown in more than half a century

Hello Kitty (1999)—
Japanese pop culture grows increasingly popular across Asia

Channel 2 founded in Japan (1999)—
Internet chat site rapidly becomes major cultural phenomenon
http://www.2ch.net

2001   Koizumi Junichiro leads LDP to victory by promising reform,
           becomes most popular prime minister in postwar period

2005   Renewed protests in China against Japanese textbook revisions and
           refusal to acknowledge war atrocities

2005   Koizumi leads LDP to one of the largest parliamentary majorities in
           modern Japanese history, then is succeeded by Shinzo Abe as prime
           minister in 2006

Notes

Preface

1. By 1928, Japan was producing more films per year than any other nation in the world, yet it was a rare occasion when a single film, Naruse Mikio's *Wife, Be Like a Rose* (*Tsuma yo bara no yoni,* 1935, distributed abroad as *Kimiko*), was commercially distributed in the United States. See Richie, *A Hundred Years of Japanese Film,* 44 and 60–61.

2. Translations of contemporary Japanese theory into English have increased dramatically since the late 1980s, beginning with the two anthologies by Masao Miyoshi and H. D. Harootunian, *Postmodernism and Japan* (1989) and *Japan in the World* (1993); two books by Kojin Karatani, Brett de Bary's edited translation of *Origins of Modern Japanese Literature* (1993) and Sabu Kohso's translation of *Architecture as Metaphor: Language, Number, Money* (1995); and Naoki Sakai's ambitious *Traces: A Multilingual Journal of Culture Theory and Translation,* which began publication in 2001.

3. Notably, Noël Burch argued for a reconsideration of 1930s Japanese cinema after the New Wave and Kinugasa's *Crazy Page* received renewed attention after the cinematic innovations of the 1960s. Before then, these films had been neglected both in postwar Japan and outside Japan.

4. Taisho and Occupation-era cinemas were reconsidered by Joanne Barnardi (2001) and Kyoko Hirano (1992), respectively, after the 1980s.

5. Oshima Nagisa, *100 Years of Japanese Cinema* (*Nihon eiga hyaku-nen,* 1995), a documentary film commissioned by the BFI as part of a global retrospective on the 100th anniversary of film. For a discussion of the film and Oshima's corresponding book, *Fifty Years after the War: One Hundred Years of Film* (*Sengo 50 nen, eiga 100 nen,* 1995), see Cazdyn, *The Flash of Capital,* 79–81.

6. Spivak, *Death of a Discipline.*

Introduction

1. Karatani, "The Discursive Space of Modern Japan," in Miyoshi and Harootunian, eds., *Japan in the World,* 288–315.

1. Thresholds

1. See also Agamben, *Infancy and History: Essays on the Destruction of Experience.*
2. Karatani, "The Discursive Space of Modern Japan."
3. See the remarkable chapter, "Historiography: Nation, Narrative, Capital," in Cazdyn, *The*

Flash of Capital, 52–87, which includes a discussion of Tanaka's and Richie and Anderson's projects, 66–72.

    4. Ibid., 56–62.

    5. Eisenstein, "The Cinematographic Principle and the Ideogram," 28–44.

    6. See, for example, Minamoto, "The Symposium on 'Overcoming Modernity,'" in Hesig and Maraldo, eds., *Rude Awakenings*.

    7. Foucault, preface, in Deleuze and Guattari, *Anti-Oedipus*.

2. Dislocations

    1. Jencks, *What Is Post-Modernism?* 14.

    2. Jameson, "Postmodernism, or The Cultural Logic of Late Capitalism," 53–92; Lyotard, *The Postmodern Condition: A Report on Knowledge*.

    3. Mitsuhiro Yoshimoto discusses two of my earlier essays that have since been revised as part of this chapter. See Yoshimoto, "The Difficulty of Being Radical: The Discipline of Film Studies and the Postcolonial World Order," in Miyoshi and Harootunian, eds., *Japan in the World*, 342–44; and Yoshimoto, *Kurosawa: Film Studies and Japanese Cinema*, 24–28. Yoshimoto critiques the Other, in its sense of abjection and foreclosure, and the cross-cultural effects of cultural hegemony. What he does not discuss is the Other in its post-Lacanian sense of language and textuality, or destabilization and heterogeneity across cultural contexts that exceed and resist domination. He argues for a resistance to Western domination, while the purpose of my essay and chapter is to resist the domination of Eurocentric narratives of history by way of Karatani's model of inversion.

    4. For a contemporary Japanese theoretical reconsideration of modernism from a postmodernist position, see de Bary, "Karatani Kojin's *Origins of Modern Japanese Literature*," in Miyoshi and Harootunian, eds., *Japan in the World*, 235–57.

    5. Ives, *The Great Wave: The Influence of Japanese Woodcuts on French Prints*, 11–12.

    6. Yoshimoto is concerned that considering the unanticipated effects of humanism implies that Western imperialism somehow empowered Japan, but the argument here is very different. In contrast to the Eurocentric narrative of Japanese dependency and the counter-imperialist claim of a Japanese purity uncontaminated by the West is that Japan constructed a social agency from modern conditions independent of Western intentions. See Yoshimoto, "The Difficulty of Being Radical," 344. See also the discussions of Choshu and Chakrabarty elsewhere in the text.

    7. Rimer, "Tokyo in Paris/Paris in Tokyo," in Takashina and Rimer, *Paris in Japan*, 68. See also Kawakita, *Modern Currents in Japanese Art*; Smith, *The Japanese Print Since 1900*; and Terada, *Japanese Art in World Perspective*.

    8. Yamanouchi, *The Search for Authenticity in Modern Japanese Literature*, 36.

    9. Ibid., 4.

    10. For example, Yoshimoto dismisses Doi's idea of *amae* (see Yoshimoto, *Kurosawa*, 403 n. 24) because of his later association with the *nihonjinron*. Although *nihonjinron* ideas of "uniqueness" are dangerous nonsense, they are not the only way of reading Doi. Sasaki credits Doi historically with introducing psychoanalytic research in Japan, before the founding of the Groupe Franco-Japonais du Champ Freudien.

    11. For a history of psychoanalysis in Japan, see Takahashi, "La psychanalyse au Japon," in Jacquard, ed., *Histoire de la psychanalyse*, 417–38.

    12. Kiev, *Transcultural Psychiatry*.

    13. Burch, *To the Distant Observer*.

14. See, for example, Peterson, "A War of Utter Rebellion: Kinugasa's *Page of Madness*," *Cinema Journal* 29 (Autumn 1989): 36–53.

15. Burch, *To the Distant Observer*, 16–17 and 154–85.

16. Bordwell and Thompson, *Film Art*.

17. Desser, *Eros Plus Massacre*, 109–10.

18. This and the preceding quote are from Rimer, *Paris in Japan*, 50, 78.

19. Rimer, *Paris in Japan*, 66.

20. Ibid., 68.

21. Burch, *To the Distant Observer*, 126 n. 4.

22. Ibid., 269.

23. See Komatsu's entries on Japanese film in *The Oxford History of World Cinema;* Hirano, *Mr. Smith Goes to Tokyo;* and MacDonald, *Mizoguchi*.

24. Tony Rayns's critique of Barthes.

25. Burgin, "Re-Reading *Camera Lucida*," in *The End of Art Theory*, 71–92.

26. Worth and Adair, *Through Navaho Eyes*.

27. Burch, *To the Distant Observer*, 269.

28. Ibid., 9.

29. Ibid., 100–107.

30. Yoshimoto disputes this description of *giri* as being insufficiently nuanced. While a nuanced reading would be welcome, many films of the 1950s and 1960s are engaged in a radical critique of traditional values and thus represent *giri* as bound up with emperor worship and obligations to corporate bosses. See Yoshimoto, *Kurosawa*, 385 n. 43.

31. Seward, *Japanese in Action*, 72.

32. Morley, *Pictures from the Water Trade;* and Mellen, *Natural Tendencies*.

33. Whymant, "Adapting to Life in Japan Has Costs for Westerners," *International Herald Tribune*, May 26, 1986, 5.

34. Aumont, *Montage Eisenstein*, 1–5.

35. Lyotard, *The Postmodern Condition*.

3. Incisions

1. Wellbery, foreword to Friedrich A. Kittler, *Discourse Networks: 1800/1900*, x.

2. Hugh Tomlinson and Barbara Habberjam, translators of Deleuze's books on *Cinema*, describe his process as "concept creation 'alongside' the cinema." See their Translators' Introduction," in Deleuze, *Cinema 1: The Movement-Image*, xi.

3. DeFrancis, *The Chinese Language*, 83–85, 92–93.

4. Karatani, *Origins of Modern Japanese Literature*, 44, 55.

5. Eisenstein, "The Cinematographic Principle and the Ideogram," 28–44; Pound, *ABC of Reading* and *Guide to Kulchur*.

6. Eisenstein, "The Cinematographic Principle and the Ideogram." This and the two following quotes are from pp. 28–30.

7. Fenollosa, *The Chinese Written Character as a Medium for Poetry*. This and the following quote are from pp. 8–10.

8. Whorf, *Language, Thought, and Reality*, 55.

9. Ibid., 134–59. See also Sapir, *Language*.

10. Peirce, *Collected Papers*. A brief introduction to Peirce's tripartite distinction can be found in Hawkes, *Structuralism and Semiotics*, 128–30.

11. Pound, *ABC of Reading*, 26, and *Guide to Kulchur*, 16.

12. See, for example, Derrida, *Of Grammatology,* and "Scribble (pouvoir/écrire)," introduction to William Warburton, *Essai sur les hiéroglyphes des Egyptiens.*

13. Foucault, *Discipline and Punish;* and Lacan, *The Four Fundamental Concepts of Psycho-Analysis.*

14. Ulmer, *Applied Grammatology,* 6.

15. Derrida, *Of Grammatology,* quoted in ibid., 6.

16. Ibid., 6–7.

17. Eisenstein, "The Cinematographic Principle and the Ideogram," 28.

18. Burch, *To the Distant Observer,* 126 n. 4.

19. Musée national d'art moderne, Centre Georges Pompidou, *Japon des Avant-Gardes: 1910–1970;* Japan Society, *Paris in Japan.*

20. Doi, *The Anatomy of the Self.* See also Doi, *The Anatomy of Dependence.*

21. Lacan, *Le séminaire, livre I: Les écrits techniques de Freud,* 7. In this and the following quotation, the translation is mine. The two passages in French are "Le maître interrompt le silence par n'importe quoi, un sarcasme, un coup de pied. C'est ainsi que procède dans la recherche du sens un maître bouddhiste, selon la technique *zen.* . . . La pensée de Freud est la plus perpétuellement ouverte à la révision"; and "D'ou se prouve que le mot d'esprit est au Japon la même du discours le plus commun, et c'est pourquoi personne qui habite cette langue n'a besoin d'être psychanalysé, sinon pour régulariser ses relations avec les machines-a-sous—voire avec des clients plus simplement mechaniques."

22. Nancy and Lacoue-Labarthe, *The Title of the Letter,* 23.

23. Ellie Ragland-Sullivan, *Jacques Lacan and the Philosophy of Psychoanalysis,* 20.

24. Nancy and Lacoue-Labarthe, *The Title of the Letter,* 24 n. 5.

25. Richie, *Japanese Cinema,* 191.

26. See Brooks, *The Melodramatic Imagination.*

27. Richie, *Japanese Cinema,* 190–91.

28. Anderson and Richie, *The Japanese Film,* 86–87.

29. Regarding the scarcity of surviving materials from this era, see Burch, *To the Distant Observer,* 111.

30. Anderson and Richie, *The Japanese Film,* 39.

31. See Peterson, "A War of Utter Rebellion"; and Burch, *To the Distant Observer,* 123–39. Peterson argues that Kinugasa was a modernist, while Burch sees him as a traditionalist.

32. See also Burch, *To the Distant Observer,* 110–16. In his discussion of Ito, Burch provides a formalist critique of *The Red Bat,* the only film from this school that he had been able to see. He does not, however, discuss the influence of socialism on *chambara*, and instead sees the form as an expression of a dominant class. I am indebted to Larry Greenberg of Matsuda Films and Kyoko Hirano of the Japan Society for their assistance in my seeing *Orochi* and *Jirokichi,* and to Akira Shimizu of the Japan Film Library Council and the Film Center of the National Museum of Modern Art in Tokyo for enabling me to see *The Red Bat.*

33. Sato, *Currents in Japanese Cinema,* 20; Richie, 7–8; Bowers, *Japanese Theatre,* 208–12; Burch, *To the Distant Observer,* 59–60.

34. Bowers, *Japanese Theatre,* 201–8.

35. Ibid., 208–11.

36. Ibid., 210. See also Burch, *To the Distant Observer,* 59–60.

37. Shattuck, *The Banquet Years.*

38. See de Bary, "Karatani Kojin's *Origins of Modern Japanese Literature,*" and Karatani, "One Spirit, Two Nineteenth Centuries," in Miyoshi and Harootunian, eds., *Japan in the World,* 235–57; and Karatani, *Origins of Modern Japanese Literature,* 27, 87, 186, 192–93.

39. Bowers, *Japanese Theatre,* 212.

40. Anderson and Richie, *The Japanese Film,* 27–28.

41. Ibid., 31.

42. Anderson and Richie, *The Japanese Film,* 403; Sato, *Currents in Japanese Cinema,* 19.

43. Lacan, "Aggressivity in Psychoanalysis," 8–29.

44. See Pefanis, *Heterology and the Postmodern,* 11–14.

45. Lacan, *Écrits,* 146–78.

46. Sasaki, "La psychanalyse au Japon," 13.

47. Ibid., 15–16.

48. Takahashi, "La psychanalyse au Japon," 417–38.

49. Karatani, "The Discovery of Landscape," 11–44.

50. Derrida, *The Post Card;* Miller and Richardson, *The Purloined Poe;* Smith and Kerrigan, eds., *Taking Chances.*

4. Kyoto/Venezia

1. Deleuze and Guattari, *Kafka.*

2. Deleuze, *Cinema 1: The Movement-Image.*

3. The term belongs to the translators, in their phrase "Deleuze is engaged in the work of concept creation 'alongside' the cinema," to summarize Deleuze's project throughout both books of arguing a parallelism between cinema and philosophy. Tomlinson and Habberjam, Translators' Introduction, in Deleuze, *Cinema 1: The Movement-Image,* xi.

4. See Bass, "L Before K," introduction to Derrida, *The Post Card,* vii.

5. Haver, "A Preface to Translation," cited by Brett de Bary in her introduction to Karatani's *Origins of Modern Japanese Literature,* 7.

6. Richie, *The Films of Akira Kurosawa,* 36.

7. Storry, *A History of Modern Japan,* 182.

5. Reconsidering Humanism

1. Cazdyn, *The Flash of Capital,* 52–87.

2. Dower, *Embracing Defeat: Japan in the Wake of World War II.*

3. Vattimo, *The Transparent Society.*

4. See Chakrabarty, *Provincializing Europe.*

5. Benedict, *The Chrysanthemum and the Sword.*

6. See Desser, *Eros Plus Massacre,* 32–33; and Turim, *The Films of Oshima Nagisa,* 9.

7. See Tsurumi's invaluable work in *An Intellectual History of Wartime Japan, 1931–1945* and *A Cultural History of Postwar Japan, 1945–1980.*

8. Masuda, *Living Architecture,* 5.

9. Grilli, ed., *Japan in Film.*

10. Yamaguchi, "Theatrical Space in Japan: A Semiotic Approach," 1.

11. Bowers, *Japanese Theatre,* 39–43.

12. Burch, *To the Distant Observer,* 161. See also Polan, "La Politique formaliste: Noël Burch."

13. See also Burch's discussion of this film in *To the Distant Observer,* 202–14.

14. Barthes, *Empire of Signs,* 30.

15. Giovannini, "Arata Isozaki," 26–65.

16. Derrida, *The Ear of the Other.*

17. Greene, *The Age of Exuberance,* 151–52.

18. Ibid., 152.

19. See, for example, Francastel, *Histoire de la peinture Française I;* and Foucault, *The Order of Things.*

20. Foucault, *Madness and Civilization.*

21. Derrida, *The Post Card.*

22. Takahashi, "La psychanalyse au Japon," in Jaccard, ed., *Histoire de la psychanalyse,* 417–38. The two quotes cited appear on p. 437; the translations are mine. The French reads: "Dans la langue japonaise, la première personne n'existe que dans une combinaison intime avec la deuxième personne . . ." and "la combinaison binaire se trouve dans la relation humaine des Japonais comme un retentissement de la relation imaginaire du sujet avec la mère."

23. Ariès, *Centuries of Childhood.*

24. Griffin, *Pornography and Silence.*

25. Jameson, *The Prison-House of Language.*

26. Foucault, "A Preface to Transgression" (first published in *Critique,* nos. 195–96 [1963]: 751–70), in *Language, Counter-Memory, Practice,* 36.

27. Yoshimoto, "The Difficulty of Being Radical," 339–40.

28. Nishida, *Intelligibility and the Philosophy of Nothingness.*

29. Karatani, in conversation at the University of Florida (2001).

30. Haver, *The Body of This Death.*

31. Feenberg, "The Problem of Modernity in the Philosophy of Nishida," in *Rude Awakenings,* 151–73.

32. Sato, *Currents in Japanese Cinema,* 15–30.

33. Faure, *The Rhetoric of Immediacy.*

34. Harootunian, *Toward Restoration,* 24–32.

35. Ooka, *Temples of Nara and Their Art,* 23–24.

36. Gluck, *Japan's Modern Myths,* 134–35.

37. Tsurumi, *An Intellectual History of Wartime Japan,* 122–23.

38. Mitscherlich and Mitscherlich, *The Inability to Mourn.*

39. See, for example, Schueller, *U.S. Orientalisms.*

40. See Marchetti, *Romance and the "Yellow Peril."*

41. Dower, *War without Mercy,* 77–93 and 182–85.

42. "Filibuster Ended as Senate Shelves Anti-Lynch Bill," *New York Times,* February 22, 1938.

43. *Japan Times,* August 6, 2001.

44. Sakai, *Translation and Subjectivity,* 1–17.

45. Wiener, *Cybernetics.*

46. Stille, *The Future of the Past.*

47. See, for example, Okada, *Figures of Resistance.*

48. Brecht, "The Radio as an Apparatus of Communication," 41–45.

6. International Modernism

1. Deleuze, *The Fold.*

2. Karatani, "The Discursive Space of Modern Japan."

3. Reprinted in Yoshida and Kaigo, *Japanese Education,* 2–3.

4. Buruma, *The Wages of Guilt,* 61.

5. See Bock, *Japanese Film Directors,* 361–63.

6. See Gluck, *Japan's Modern Myths;* and Minichello, ed., *Japan's Competing Modernisms,* 128, 184.

7. See Turim, *The Films of Oshima Nagisa.*

8. See Desser, *Eros Plus Massacre,* 200–212.

9. Daniels, "Japanese Domestic Radio and Cinema Propaganda, 1937–1945," 120.

10. Ibid., 126.

11. Iriye, *Power and Culture,* 36–37.

12. Chinese protests against Japanese textbooks continue today; see, for example, Onishi, "Mollified by China's Move to End Protests, Japan Urges Talks," *New York Times,* April 21, 2005, A4.

13. "Le Japon et la guerre," *Cahiers du Japon,* special number 1984.

14. Bornoff, *"Setouchi Shonen Yakyudan," Japan Times,* July 7, 1984.

15. Ball, "Block That Vietnam Myth," *New York Times,* May 19, 1985, E21.

16. Daniels, "Japanese Domestic Radio and Cinema Propaganda," 126.

17. Iriye, *Power and Culture,* 50–51.

18. Daniels, "Japanese Domestic Radio and Cinema Propaganda," 120.

19. Ibid., 128.

20. Interview with Nagisa Oshima by Maureen Turim and Scott Nygren, at Oshima Productions, Tokyo, July 7, 1984.

21. Bock, trans., "Dialogue on Film: Masahiro Shinoda," 10–13.

22. Bennetts, "Director Views Violence of Peace," *New York Times,* May 28, 1985.

23. Takahashi, "La psychanalyse au Japon."

24. Seward, *Japanese in Action,* 6.

25. Grierson, *Grierson on Documentary,* 280.

26. Ellul, *Propaganda.*

27. See also Lyotard, *Économie libidinale.*

28. Abdelfattah Kilito, "Dog Words," in Angelika Bammer, ed., *Displacements: Cultural Identities in Question,* xxii.

29. Bock, "Dialogue on Film," 293.

30. Milne, *Godard on Godard,* 70.

31. Ropars-Wuilleumier, "How History Begets Meaning."

32. Sato, *Currents in Japanese Cinema,* 200–203.

33. Michalczyk, *The French Literary Filmmakers,* 124.

34. Lynn Zelevansky et al., *Love Forever: Yayoi Kusama, 1958–68.*

35. "Interview: Akira Tatehata in conversation with Yayoi Kusama," in Hoptman et al., *Yayoi Kusama.*

36. Ibid., 9.

37. Kusama, "Manhattan Suicide Addict (extract) 1978," in Hoptman et al., *Yayoi Kusama,* 124.

38. "Interview with Gordon Brown (extract) 1964," in Hoptman et al., *Yayoi Kusama*, 103.

7. Postmodern Networks

1. See, for example, Foucault, *The Order of Things.*

2. Rayns, "Nails That Stick Out," 98–104.

3. See also Hirano, "Japanese Cinema: Recent Independent Films."

4. See also Tessier, ed., *Le cinéma Japonais au présent, 1959–1984.*

5. Sato, "Rising Sons," 58–62, 78.

6. From my interview with Kohei Oguri at the Cinémathèque Française, Paris, December 3, 1985. I wish to express my appreciation to Tomoyuki Sakurai, director of the Paris liaison office of the Japan Foundation, for acting as translator. All references to quotations from Oguri, both direct and indirect, throughout the article are taken from this interview.

7. Hirano, "Japanese Cinema: Recent Independent Films."

8. Rayns, "Nails That Stick Out," 99.

9. Bordwell, Thompson, and Staiger, *The Classical Hollywood Cinema*.

10. See, for example, Bazin, "The Evolution of the Language of Cinema," in *What Is Cinema?*, 23–40.

11. Daney, "Notes Nippones," 26–34.
"Alors qu'est-ce qui reste comme public de cinéma? Des jeunes gens ou des universitaires; et comme ces catégories de la population ont une vision du monde assez noire, les films reflètent leurs conceptions et contiennent beaucoup de scènes de violence et de pornographie. . . . Et ça provoque une espèce de crise schizophrénique: si on va au cinéma, on a une image du Japon violent, érotique, c'est l'enfer; et si on regarde la télévision, c'est le ciel, le paradis, toutes les relations humaines sont harmonieuses tout marche bien" (translation mine).

12. Sato, "Rising Sons," 78.

13. Rayns, "Nails That Stick Out."

14. See Lyotard, *The Postmodern Condition;* Jameson, foreword to Lyotard, *The Post-Modern Condition;* Foster, ed., *The Anti-Aesthetic;* Jencks, *What Is Post-Modernism?;* Clucas and Sovronsky, eds., "Peter Wollen on Post-Modernism."

15. This phrase appeared in a Japan Society program publicizing these films for an initial American audience.

16. Nolletti, "Mitsuo Yanagimachi's *Himatsuri,*"49–59. Nolletti is not alone in his assessment of the film's supposed failures. *Variety,* for example, as Nolletti notes, claimed: "It's certainly not easy, from the information included in the film, to understand his motives" (*Variety,* May 22, 1985, 115).

17. Nolletti, interview with Yanagimachi, quoted in Nolletti, "Mitsuo Yanagimachi's *Himatsuri,*" 153.

18. Jencks, *What Is Post-Modernism?*

19. Lyotard, *The Postmodern Condition*.

20. Kenneth Frampton, "Regional Identity and Urban Form."

21. Barthes, *Empire of Signs,* 30–32.

22. Banham, *Los Angeles: The Architecture of Four Ecologies*.

23. Karatani, *Origins of Modern Japanese Literature,* 34.

24. Ibid., 6.

25. Watanabe, "Metropolitanism as a Way of Life, 403–29.

26. Selden, "The Atomic Bomb," 6–8, 17–18.

27. Watanabe, "Metropolitanism as a Way of Life," 415.

28. Anderson and Richie, *The Japanese Film,* 276–77.

29. Tessier, *Cinéma et littérature au Japon,* 52.

30. See Treat, "Beheaded Emperors and the Absent Figure in Contemporary Japanese Literature," 100–115.

31. Tessier, *Cinéma et littérature au Japon,* 52.

32. Nikita Mikhalkov, *Urga* (1991), produced by Michel Seydoux, in Mongolian, Russian, and some Chinese with English subtitles.

33. Canby, "Madonna and the Master at Cannes," *New York Times,* May 19, 1991, H13–17.

34. Jameson, "Postmodernism, or The Cultural Logic of Late Capitalism," 53–92.

35. See Iyer, *Video Night in Katmandu,* 3.

36. Dang Nhai Minh, *Quand Viendra le Dizième Mois (Bao gio cho den thang muoi)* (Vietnam, 1984); Lâm Lê, *Poussière D'Empire* (France-Vietnam, 1983).

37. See also Gómez-Peña, "Border Culture: The Multicultural Paradigm," 93–103, for a related discussion within the context of Latino arts and culture in the United States.

38. See Rimer, *Paris in Japan;* and Smith, *The Japanese Print Since 1900.*

39. Carpenter, *Oh, What a Blow That Phantom Gave Me!,* frontispiece and p. 69. According to Carpenter, the kachina Mickey is a Zuni artifact, c. 1950, collected by William Copley.

40. For a discussion of the anthropological and avant-garde politics of primitivism, see Clifford and Marcus, *Writing Culture;* and Leighton, "The White Peril and *L'Art Negre,"* 609–30.

41. London, ed., *Video from Tokyo to Fukui and Kyoto.*

42. Nakaya, *Japanese Television and Video.*

43. I am familiar with this concept through a manuscript by Merry I. White and Lois K. Taniuchi, "The Anatomy of the Hara: Japanese Self in Society."

Epilogue

1. See Lee, *A History of Far Eastern Art,* 311.

2. Kehr, "Anime, Japanese Cinema's Second Golden Age," *New York Times,* January 20, 2002.

3. Brook, "A Wizard of Animation Has Japan Under His Spell," *New York Times,* January 3, 2002; and *Spirited Away*'s online press kit.

4. Toshiya, "Japanimation and Techno-Orientalism: Japan as the Sub-Empire of Signs," Yamagata International Documentary Film Festival, 1999. (http://www.city.yamagata.yamagata.jp/yidff/ff/box/box9/en/b9enf2-1.html.

5. Godzic, "The Further Possibility of Knowledge," in Michel de Certeau, *Heterologies,* vii.

Bibliography

In cases of translation or republication, I have included, when possible, the dates of initial publication in order to draw attention to the shifting contexts through which texts are produced and read.

Agamben, Giorgio. *Infancy and History: Essays on the Destruction of Experience*. Translated by Liz Heron. New York: Verso, 1993. Originally published as *Infanzia e storia* (Turin: Einaudi Editore, 1978).

Anderson, Joseph L., and Donald Richie. *The Japanese Film: Art and Industry*. Rutland, Vt.: Charles E. Tuttle, 1959; expanded edition, Princeton: Princeton University Press, 1982.

Ariès, Philippe. *Centuries of Childhood: A Social History of Family Life*. Translated by Robert Baldick. New York: Vintage, 1962. Originally published as *L'Enfant et la vie sous l'ancien régime* (Paris: Librairie Plon, 1960).

Ashcroft, Bill, Gareth Griffiths, and Helen Tiffin. *The Empire Writes Back: Theory and Practice in Post-colonial Literatures*. New York: Routledge, 1989.

Aumont, Jacques. *Montage Eisenstein*. Translated by Lee Hildreth, Constance Penley, and Andrew Ross. Bloomington: Indiana University Press, 1987. Originally published as *Montage Eisenstein* (Paris: Albatros, 1979).

Bammer, Angelika, ed. *Displacements: Cultural Identities in Question*. Bloomington: Indiana University Press, 1994.

Banham, Reyner. *Los Angeles: The Architecture of Four Ecologies*. Harmondsworth, U.K.: Penguin Books, 1973.

Barthes, Roland. *Camera Lucida: Reflections on Photography*. Translated by Richard Howard. New York: Hill and Wang, 1980. Originally published as *La chamber claire* (Paris: Éditions de Seuil, 1980).

———. *Empire of Signs*. Translated by Richard Howard. New York: Hill and Wang, 1982. Originally published as *L'Empire des signes* (Geneva: Albert Skira, 1970).

———. *Roland Barthes*. Translated by Richard Howard. New York: Hill and Wang, 1977. Originally published as *Roland Barthes par Roland Barthes* (Paris: Éditions de Seuil, 1975).

Bazin, André. *What Is Cinema?* Translated by Hugh Gray. Berkeley and Los Angeles: University of California Press, 1967. Selected from *Qu'est-ce que le cinéma?* (Paris: Éditions du Cerf, published in four volumes, 1958–65).

Behr, Edward. *Hirohito: Behind the Myth*. New York, Vintage, 1990.

Benedict, Ruth. *The Chrysanthemum and the Sword: Patterns of Japanese Culture*. Boston: Houghton Mifflin, 1946.

Bernal, Martin. *Black Athena: The Afroasiatic Roots of Classical Civilization*. New Brunswick, N.J.: Rutgers University Press, 1987.

Bernardi, Joanne. *Writing in Light: The Silent Scenario and the Japanese Pure Film Movement*. Detroit: Wayne State University Press, 2001.

Bhabha, Homi K. *The Location of Culture*. London: Routledge, 1994.

———, ed. *Nation and Narration*. New York: Routledge, 1990.

Blouin, Claude R. *Le chemin détourné: Essai sur Kobayashi et le cinéma japonais*. Quebec: Hurtubise, 1982.

———. *Dire l'éphémère: Entretiens avec N*. Quebec: Hurtubise, 1983.

Bock, Audie. *Japanese Film Directors*. New York: Kodansha, 1978.

Bordwell, David. *Ozu and the Poetics of Cinema*. Princeton: Princeton University Press, 1988.

Bordwell, David, and Kristin Thompson. *Film Art: An Introduction,* 2nd ed. New York: Alfred A. Knopf, 1986.

Bordwell, David, Kristin Thompson, and Janet Staiger. *The Classical Hollywood Cinema: Film Style and Mode of Production to 1960*. New York: Columbia University Press, 1985.

Bowers, Faubion. *Japanese Theatre,* 4th ed. Rutland, Vt.: Charles E. Tuttle, 1982.

Brecht, Bertolt. "The Radio as an Apparatus of Communication." In *Brecht on Film and Radio*. Translated and edited by Marc Silberman. London: Methuen, 2000.

Brennan, Teresa. *History after Lacan*. New York: Routledge, 1993.

Brooks, Peter. *The Melodramatic Imagination: Balzac, Henry James, Melodrama, and the Mode of Excess*. New Haven: Yale University Press, 1976.

Budick, Sanford, and Wolfgang Iser, eds. *The Translatability of Cultures*. Stanford: Stanford University Press, 1996.

Burch, Noël. *To the Distant Observer: Form and Meaning in the Japanese Cinema*. Berkeley and Los Angeles: University of California Press, 1979.

Burgin, Victor. *The End of Art Theory: Criticism and Post-Modernity*. Atlantic Highlands, N.J.: Humanities Press International, 1986.

Buruma, Ian. *Behind the Mask: On Sexual Demons, Sacred Mothers, Transvestites, Gangsters, and Other Japanese Cultural Heroes*. New York: Pantheon, 1984.

———. *The Wages of Guilt: Memories of War in Germany and Japan*. New York: Farrar, Straus and Giroux, 1994.

Campbell, Jan. *Arguing with the Phallus: Feminist, Queer, and Postcolonial Theory—A Psychoanalytic Contribution*. New York: Zed Books, 2000.

Cazdyn, Eric. *The Flash of Capital: Film and Geopolitics in Japan*. Durham: Duke University Press, 2002.

Chakrabarty, Dipesh. *Provincializing Europe: Postcolonial Thought and Historical Difference*. Princeton: Princeton University Press, 2000.

Cheng, François. *Chinese Poetic Writing*. Translated by Donald A. Riggs and Jerome P. Seaton. Bloomington: Indiana University Press, 1982. Originally published as *Écriture poétique chinoise* (Paris: Éditions du Seuil, 1977).

Clifford, James, and George E. Marcus. *Writing Culture: The Poetics and Politics of Ethnography*. Berkeley and Los Angeles: University of California Press. 1986.

La Cinémathèque Française, La Fondation du Japon et Hiroko Govaers. *Le cinéma Japonais: De ses origines à nos jours*. Catalog in two parts. Paris: Cinémathèque Française, 1984–85.

Coward, Harold, and Toby Foshay, eds. *Derrida and Negative Theology*. Albany: State University of New York Press, 1992.

Dale, Peter N. *The Myth of Japanese Uniqueness*. New York: St. Martin's Press, 1986.

Daney, Serge. "Notes Nippones." *Cahiers du cinéma,* no. 343 (January 1983): 26–34.

Daniels, Gordon. "Japanese Domestic Radio and Cinema Propaganda, 1937–1945: An Overview." *Historical Journal of Film, Radio, and Television* 2, no. 2 (1982): 120.

Davis, Darrell William. *Picturing Japaneseness: Monumental Style, National Identity, Japanese Film.* New York: Columbia University Press, 1996.

de Certeau, Michel. *Heterologies: Discourse on the Other*. Translated by Brian Massumi. Minneapolis: University of Minnesota Press, 1986.

————. *The Writing of History*. Translated by Tom Conley. New York: Columbia University Press, 1988. Originally published as *L'Écriture de l'histoire* (Paris: Éditions Gallimard, 1975).

DeFrancis, John. *The Chinese Language: Fact and Fantasy*. Honolulu: University of Hawaii Press, 1984.

Deleuze, Gilles. *Cinema 1: The Movement-Image* and *Cinema 2: The Time-Image*. Translated by Hugh Tomlinson and Barbara Habberjam. Minneapolis: University of Minnesota Press, 1986. Originally published as *Cinéma 1: L'Image-mouvement* and *Cinema 2: L'Image-temps* (Paris: Éditions de Minuit, 1983, 1985).

————. *The Fold: Leibniz and the Baroque*. Translated by Tom Conley. Minneapolis: University of Minnesota Press, 1993. Originally published as *Le pli: Leibniz et le baroque* (Paris: Éditions de Minuit, 1988).

————, and Félix Guattari. *Anti-Oedipus: Capitalism and Schizophrenia*. Translated by Robert Hurley, Mark Seem, and Helen R. Lane. New York: Viking, 1977. Originally published as *L'Anti-Oedipe* (Paris: Éditions de Minuit, 1972).

————. *Kafka: Toward a Minor Literature*. Translated by Dana Polan. Minneapolis: University of Minnesota Press, 1986. Originally published as *Kafka: Pour une littérature mineure* (Paris: Éditions de Minuit, 1975).

————. *A Thousand Plateaus: Capitalism and Schizophrenia*. Translated by Brian Massumi. Minneapolis: University of Minnesota Press, 1987. Originally published as *Mille Plateaux,* vol. 2 of *Capitalisme et Schizophrénie* (Paris: Éditions de Minuit, 1980).

————. *What Is Philosophy?* Translated by Hugh Tomlinson and Graham Burchell. New York: Columbia University Press, 1994. Originally published as *Qu'est-ce que la philosophie?* (Paris: Éditions de Minuit, 1991).

Derrida, Jacques. *Dissemination*. Translated by Barbara Johnson. Chicago: University of Chicago Press, 1981. Originally published as *La dissémination* (Paris: Éditions de Seuil, 1972).

————. *The Ear of the Other: Otobiography, Transference, Translation*. Translated by Peggy Kamuf and Avital Ronell. Lincoln: University of Nebraska Press, 1985. Originally published as *Otobiographies: L'Enseignement de Nietzsche et la politique du nom propre* (Paris: Éditions Galilée, 1984).

————. *Of Grammatology*. Translated by Gayatri Chakravorty Spivak. Baltimore: Johns Hopkins University Press, 1976. Originally published as *De la grammatologie* (Paris: Éditions de Minuit, 1967).

————. *Points . . . : Interviews, 1974–1994*. Edited by Elisabeth Weber. Translated by Peggy Kamuf et al. Stanford: Stanford University Press, 1995. Originally published as *Points de suspension: Entretiens* (Paris: Éditions Galilée, 1992).

————. *The Post Card: From Socrates to Freud and Beyond*. Translated by Alan Bass. Chicago: University of Chicago Press, 1987. Originally published as *La carte postale: De Socrate à Freud et au-delà* (Paris: Flammarion, 1980).

————. "Scribble (pouvoir/écrire)." Introduction to William Warburton, *Essai sur les hiéroglyphes des Egyptiens*. Paris: Aubier-Flammerion, 1977.

Desser, David. *Eros Plus Massacre: An Introduction to the Japanese New Wave Cinema*. Bloomington: Indiana University Press, 1988.

Doi, Takeo. *The Anatomy of Dependence*. Translated by John Bester. New York: Kodansha, 1973. Originally published as *Amae no kozo* (Tokyo: Kobundo, 1971).

———. *The Anatomy of Self*. Translated by Mark A. Harbison. New York: Kodansha, 1986. Originally published as *Omote to ura* (Tokyo: Kobundo, 1985).

Dower, John W. *Embracing Defeat: Japan in the Wake of World War II*. New York: W. W. Norton, 1999.

———. *War without Mercy: Race and Power in the Pacific War*. New York: Pantheon, 1986.

Eco, Umberto. *Travels in HyperReality: Essays*. Translated by William Weaver. San Diego: Harcourt Brace Jovanovich, 1986.

Ehrenzweig, Anton. *The Psychoanalysis of Artistic Vision and Hearing: An Introduction to a Theory of Unconscious Perception*. London: Sheldon Press, 1975.

Ehrlich, Linda, and David Desser, eds. *Cinematic Landscapes: Observations on the Visual Arts and Cinema of China and Japan*. Austin: University of Texas Press, 1994.

Eisenstein, Sergei. *Film Form*. Edited and translated by Jay Leyda. New York: Harcourt, Brace and World, 1949.

Ellul, Jacques. *Propaganda: The Formation of Men's Attitudes*. Translated by Konrad Kellen and Jean Lerner of *Propagandes* (Paris: Librairie Armand Colin, 1962). New York: Alfred A. Knopf, 1965.

Faure, Bernard. *The Rhetoric of Immediacy: A Cultural Critique of Chan/Zen Buddhism*. Princeton: Princeton University Press, 1991.

Feenberg, Andrew. "The Problem of Modernity in the Philosophy of Nishida." In *Rude Awakenings*, ed. James W. Heisig and John C. Maraldo, 151–73.

Fenollosa, Ernest. *The Chinese Written Character as a Medium for Poetry*. Ed. Ezra Pound. San Francisco: City Lights, 1936.

Foster, Hal, ed. *The Anti-Aesthetic: Essays on Postmodern Culture*. Port Townsend, Wash.: Bay Press, 1983.

Foucault, Michel. *Discipline and Punish: The Birth of the Prison*. Translated by Alan Sheridan. New York: Vintage, 1979. Originally published as *Surveiller et Punir: Naissance de la prison* (Paris: Éditions Gallimard, 1975).

———. *Language, Counter-Memory, Practice: Selected Essays and Interviews*. Ithaca: Cornell University Press, 1981.

———. *Madness and Civilization: A History of Insanity in the Age of Reason*. Translated by Richard Howard. New York: Mentor, 1967. Originally published as *Folie et déraison: Histoire de la folie à l'âge classique* (Paris: Librairie Plon, 1961).

———. *The Order of Things: An Archeology of the Human Sciences*. Translated by Alan Sheridan. New York: Vintage, 1973. Originally published as *Les mots et les choses* (Paris: Éditions Gallimard, 1966).

Frampton, Kenneth. "Regional Identity and Urban Form." Included in papers from "Metropolis: Locus of Contemporary Myths," U.S.–Japan Symposium on Urban Life and Culture, sponsored by the Japan Society and the National Institute for Research Advancement, Tarrytown and New York, October 1–4, 1982.

Francastel, Pierre. *Histoire de la peinture Française I: Du Moyen-Âge à Fragonard*. Paris: Éditions Gonthier, 1955.

Fukuyama, Francis. *The End of History and the Last Man*. New York: Free Press, 1992.

Gallop, Jane. *The Daughter's Seduction: Feminism and Psychoanalysis*. Ithaca: Cornell University Press, 1982.

Genette, Gérard. *Palimpsests: Literature in the Second Degree.* Lincoln: University of Nebraska Press, 1997. Originally published as *Palimpsestes: La littérature au second degré* (Paris: Éditions du Seuil, 1982).

Giovannini, Joseph. "Arata Isozaki: From Japan, A New Wave of International Architects." *New York Times Magazine,* August 17, 1986, 26–65.

Gluck, Carol. *Japan's Modern Myths: Ideology in the Late Meiji Period.* Princeton: Princeton University Press, 1985.

Gluck, Carol, and Stephen R. Graubard, eds. *Showa: The Japan of Hirohito.* New York: W. W. Norton, 1992.

Godzic, Wlad. "The Further Possibility of Knowledge." In Michel de Certeau, *Heterologies: Discourse on the Other.* Translated by Brian Massumi. Minneapolis: University of Minnesota Press, 1989.

Goody, Jack. *The East in the West.* New York: Cambridge University Press, 1996.

Greene, Donald. *The Age of Exuberance: Backgrounds to Eighteenth-Century English Literature.* New York: Random House, 1970.

Grierson, John. *Grierson on Documentary.* Boston: Faber and Faber, 1979.

Griffin, Susan. *Pornography and Silence: Culture's Revenge Against Nature.* New York: Harper Colophon, 1981.

Grilli, Peter, ed. *Japan in Film.* New York: Japan Society, 1984.

Groupe Franco-Japonais du Champ Freudien. *Lacan et la chose Japonaise.* Paris: Navarin Éditeur, 1988.

Hane, Mikiso. *Japan: A Historical Survey.* New York: Scribner, 1972.

———. *Peasants, Rebels, and Outcastes: The Underside of Modern Japan.* New York: Pantheon, 1982.

Harootunian, H. D. *Things Seen and Unseen: Discourse and Idealogy in Tokugawa Nativism.* Chicago: University of Chicago Press, 1988.

———. *Toward Restoration: The Growth of Political Consciousness in Tokugawa Japan.* Berkeley and Los Angeles: University of California Press, 1970.

Haver, William. *The Body of This Death: Historicity and Sociality in the Time of AIDS.* Stanford: Stanford University Press, 1996.

Hawkes, Terence. *Structuralism and Semiotics.* Berkeley and Los Angeles: University of California Press, 1977.

Hayward, Susan, and Ginette Vincendeau, eds. *French Film: Texts and Contexts.* New York: Routledge, 1990.

Heisig, James W., and John C. Maraldo, ed. *Rude Awakenings: Zen, the Kyoto School, and the Question of Nationalism.* Honolulu: University of Hawaii Press, 1994.

Hirano, Kyoko. "Japanese Cinema: Recent Independent Films." *CineVue* 1 (November 1986): 4–5.

———. *Mr. Smith Goes to Tokyo: Japanese Cinema under the American Occupation, 1945–1952.* Washington, D.C.: Smithsonian Institution Press, 1992.

Hoptman, Laura, Akira Tatehata, and Udo Kultermann. *Yayoi Kusama.* London: Phaidon, 2000.

Iriye, Akira. *Power and Culture: The Japanese-American War, 1941–1945.* Cambridge, Mass.: Harvard University Press, 1981.

Ives, Colta Feller. *The Great Wave: The Influence of Japanese Woodcuts on French Prints.* New York: Metropolitan Museum of Art, 1974.

Iyer, Pico. *Video Night in Katmandu, and Other Reports from the Not-So-Far East.* New York: Vintage, 1989.

Jaccard, Roland, ed. *Histoire de la psychanalyse,* vol. 2. Paris: Hachette, 1982.

Jameson, Fredric. "Postmodernism, or The Cultural Logic of Late Capitalism." *New Left Review,* no. 146 (July–August 1984): 53–92.

———. *The Prison-House of Language: A Critical Account of Structuralism and Formalism*. Princeton: Princeton University Press, 1972.

Japan Society. *Paris in Japan: The Japanese Encounter with European Painting*. New York: Japan Society, 1987.

Jencks, Charles. *What Is Post-Modernism?* New York: St. Martin's Press, 1986.

Karatani, Kojin. *Architecture as Metaphor: Language, Number, Money*. Edited by Michael Speaks. Translated by Sabu Kohso. Cambridge, Mass.: MIT Press, 1995. Originally published as *In'yu to shite no kenchiku* (Tokyo: Kodansha, 1983).

———. "The Discovery of Landscape." In *Origins of Modern Japanese Literature*. Durham: Duke University Press. Translated and edited by Brett de Bary. Originally published as *Nihon kindai bungaku no kigen* (1980).

———. "One Spirit, Two Nineteenth Centuries." In *South Atlantic Quarterly* 87 (Summer 1988): 615–28.

———. *Origins of Modern Japanese Literature*. Translated and edited by Brett de Bary. Durham: Duke University Press, 1993. Originally published as *Nihon kindai bungaku no kigen* (Tokyo: Kodansha, 1980).

Kato, Shuichi. *A History of Japanese Literature,* vols. 1–3. Translated by David Chibbett. New York: Kodansha International, 1979. Originally published as *Nihon bungaku shi josetsu* (Tokyo: Chikuma Shobo, 1975–80).

Kawakita, Michiaki. *Modern Currents in Japanese Art*. Translated by Charles S. Terry. New York: Weatherhill/Heibonsha, 1974. Originally published as *Kindai bijutsu no nagare,* vol. 24 of the Heibonsha Survey of Japanese Art (Tokyo: Heibonsha, 1964).

Kilito, Abdelfattah. "Dog Words." In *Displacements: Cultural Identities in Question,* ed. Angelika Bammer, xxii.

Kittler, Friedrich A. *Discourse Networks: 1800/1900*. Translated by Michael Metteer with Chris Cullens; foreword by David E. Wellbery. Stanford: Stanford University Press, 1990. Originally published as *Aufschreibesysteme 1800/1900* (Munich: Wilhelm Fink Verlag, 1985).

Kristeva, Julia. *Revolution in Poetic Language*. Translated by Margaret Waller. New York: Columbia University Press, 1984. Originally published as *La révolution du langage poétique* (Paris: Éditions de Seuil, 1974).

———. *Strangers to Ourselves*. Translated by Leon Roudiez. New York: Columbia University Press, 1991. Originally published as *Étrangers à nous-mêmes* (Paris: Fayard, 1989).

Kurosawa, Akira. *Something Like an Autobiography*. Translated by Audie E. Bock from *Gama no abura*. New York: Vintage, 1983.

Kusama, Yayoi. "Manhattan Suicide Addict (extract) 1978." In Hoptman et al., *Yayoi Kusama,* 124.

Lacan, Jacques. *Écrits*. Translated by Alan Sheridan, New York: W. W. Norton, 1977. Selected from *Écrits* (Paris: Éditions du Seuil, 1966).

———. *The Four Fundamental Concepts of Psycho-Analysis*. Edited by Jacques-Alain Miller. Translated by Alan Sheridan. New York: W. W. Norton, 1981. Originally published as *Le séminaire de Jacques Lacan, Livre XI, Les quatre concepts fondamentaux de la psychanalyse* (Paris: Éditions du Seuil, 1973).

———. *Le séminaire, livre I: Les écrits techniques de Freud*. Paris: Éditions du Seuil, 1975.

Lacoue-Labarthe, Philippe. *Typography: Mimesis, Philosophy, Politics*. Cambridge, Mass.: Harvard University Press, 1989.

Lagny, Michèle, Marie-Claire Ropars, and Pierre Sorlin with Geniève Nesterenko. *Générique des années 30*. Vincennes: Presses Universitaires de Vincennes, 1986.

Laplanche, Jean. *Essays on Otherness*. New York: Routledge, 1999.

Lee, Sherman. *A History of Far Eastern Art*. New York: Harry N. Abrams, 1964.

Leighton, Patricia. "The White Peril and *L'Art Negre:* Picasso, Primitivism, and Anticolonialism." *Art Bulletin* 72 (December 1990): 609–30.

London, Barbara J., ed. *Video from Tokyo to Fukui and Kyoto.* New York: Museum of Modern Art, 1979.

Lyotard, Jean-François. *Dérive à partir de Marx et Freud.* Paris: Union Général d'Éditions, 1973.

———. *The Differend: Phrases in Dispute.* Translated by George Van Den Abbeele. Minneapolis: University of Minnesota Press, 1988. Originally published as *Le différend* (Paris: Éditions de Minuit, 1983).

———. *Discours, figure.* Paris: Klincksieck, 1971.

———. *Lessons on the Analytic of the Sublime: Kant's Critique of Judgment, [sections] 23–29.* Translated by Elizabeth Rottenberg. Stanford: Stanford University Press, 1994. Originally published as *Leçons sur l'analytique du sublime* (Paris: Éditions Galilée, 1991).

———. *Libidinal Economy.* Translated by Iain Hamilton Grant. Bloomington: Indiana University Press, 1993. Originally published as *Économie libidinale* (Paris: Éditions de Minuit, 1974).

———. *The Postmodern Condition: A Report on Knowledge.* Translated by Geoff Bennington and Brian Massumi. Minneapolis: University of Minnesota Press, 1984. Originally published as *La condition postmoderne: Rapport sur le savoir* (Paris: Éditions de Minuit, 1979).

———. *Sur la constitution du temps par la couleur dans les oeuvres recentes d'Albert Ayme.* Paris: Édition Traversiere, 1980.

Lyotard, Jean-François, and Jean-Loup Thébaud. *Just Gaming.* Translated by Wlad Godzich. Minneapolis: University of Minnesota Press, 1985. Originally published as *Au juste* (Paris: Christian Bourgeois, 1979).

MacAdams, Lewis. *Birth of the Cool: Beat, Bebop, and the American Avant-Garde.* New York: Free Press, 2001.

MacCabe, Colin. *Godard: Images, Sounds, Politics.* Bloomington: Indiana University Press, 1980.

McDonald, Keiko. *Mizoguchi.* Boston: Twayne, 1984.

MacKenzie, John M. *Orientalism: History, Theory, and the Arts.* Manchester: Manchester University Press, 1995.

Marchetti, Gina. *Romance and the "Yellow Peril": Race, Sex, and Discursive Strategies in Hollywood Fiction.* Berkeley and Los Angeles: University of California Press, 1993.

Marks, Laura U. *The Skin of the Film: Intercultural Cinema, Embodiment, and the Senses.* Durham: Duke University Press, 2000.

Masuda, Tomoya. *Living Architecture: Japanese.* New York: Grosset and Dunlap, 1970.

Mellen, Joan. *Natural Tendencies.* New York: Dial Press, 1981.

———. *Voices from the Japanese Cinema.* New York: Liveright, 1975.

———. *The Waves at Genji's Door: Japan Through Its Cinema.* New York: Pantheon, 1976.

Metz, Christian. *Language and Cinema.* Translated by Donna Jean Umiker-Sebeok. The Hague: Mouton, 1974.

Michalczyk, John J. *The French Literary Filmmakers.* Toronto: Associated University Presses, 1980.

Miller, John P., and William J. Richardson. *The Purloined Poe: Lacan, Derrida, and Psychoanalytic Reading.* Baltimore: Johns Hopkins University Press, 1988.

Milne, Tom, trans. and ed. *Godard on Godard.* New York: Viking, 1972.

Minamoto Ryoen. "The Symposium on 'Overcoming Modernity.'" In *Rude Awakenings: Zen, the Kyoto School, and the Question of Nationalism,* ed. James W. Heisig and John C. Maraldo, 197–229.

Minichello, Sharon A., ed. *Japan's Competing Modernities: Issues in Culture and Democracy, 1900–1930.* Honolulu: University of Hawaii Press, 1998.

Mitscherlich, Alexander, and Margarete Mitscherlich. *The Inability to Mourn: Principles of Collective Behavior.* Translated by Beverley R. Placzek. New York: Grove Press, distributed by

Random House, 1975. Originally published as *Die Unfähigkeit zu trauern* (Munich: Piper, 1967).

Miyoshi, Masao, and H. D. Harootunian, ed. *Japan in the World*. Durham: Duke University Press, 1993.

———, ed. *Postmodernism and Japan*. Durham: Duke University Press, 1989.

Morley, John Christopher. *Pictures from the Water Trade: Adventures of a Westerner in Japan*. New York: Harper and Row, 1985.

Musée national d'art moderne, Centre Georges Pompidou. *Japon des Avant-Gardes: 1910–1970*. Paris: Éditions du Centre Pompidou, 1986.

Nakaya, Fujiko. *Japanese Television and Video: An Historical Survey*. Los Angeles: American Film Institute, 1984.

Nancy, Jean-Luc, and Philippe Lacoue-Labarthe. *The Title of the Letter: A Reading of Lacan*. Translated by François Raffoul and David Pettigrew. Albany: State University of New York Press, 1992. Originally published as *Le titre de la lettre* (Paris: Éditions Galilée, 1973).

Nishida, Kitaro. *Intelligibility and the Philosophy of Nothingness*. Honolulu: East-West Center Press, 1958.

Nolletti, Arthur. "Mitsuo Yanagimachi's *Himatsuri:* An Analysis." *Film Criticism* 10 (Spring 1983): 49–59.

Nolletti, Arthur, Jr., and David Desser, eds. *Reframing Japanese Cinema: Authorship, Genre, History*. Bloomington: Indiana University Press, 1992.

Nowell-Smith, Geoffrey, ed. *The Oxford History of World Cinema*. New York: Oxford University Press, 1996.

Okada, H. Richard. *Figures of Resistance: Language, Poetry, and Narrating in "The Tale of Genji" and Other Mid-Heian Texts*. Durham: Duke University Press, 1991.

Ooka, Minoru. *Temples of Nara and Their Art*. Translated by Dennis Liska. New York: Weatherhill/Heibonsha, 1973, 23–24.

Oshima, Nagisa. *Cinema, Censorship, and the State: The Writings of Nagisa Oshima, 1956–1978*. Edited by Annette Michaelson. Translated by Dawn Lawson. Cambridge, Mass.: MIT Press, 1992.

Pefanis, Julian. *Heterology and the Postmodern: Bataille, Baudrillard, and Lyotard*. Durham: Duke University Press, 1991.

Peirce, Charles Sanders. *Collected Papers,* 8 vols. Edited by Charles Hartshorne, Paul Weiss, and Arthur W. Burks. Cambridge, Mass.: Harvard University Press, 1931–58.

Polan, Dana B. "La politique formaliste: Noël Burch." In Joël Magny, ed., *Theories du cinéma, CinémAction,* no. 20. Paris: L'Harmattan, n.d.

Pound, Ezra. *ABC of Reading*. Norfolk, Conn.: New Directions, 1960.

———. *Guide to Kulchur*. Norfolk, Conn.: New Directions, 1952.

Quandt, James, ed. *Shohei Imamura*. Toronto: Toronto International Film Festival Group, 1997.

Ragland-Sullivan, Ellie. *Jacques Lacan and the Philosophy of Psychoanalysis*. Urbana: University of Illinois Press, 1986.

Rayns, Tony. "Nails That Stick Out: A New Independent Cinema in Japan." *Sight and Sound* 55 (Spring 1986): 98–104.

Richie, Donald. *The Films of Akira Kurosawa*. Berkeley and Los Angeles: University of California Press, 1970.

———. *A Hundred Years of Japanese Film*. Tokyo: Kodansha, 2001.

———. *Japanese Cinema*. Garden City, N.Y.: Doubleday, 1971.

———. *Japanese Cinema: An Introduction*. New York: Oxford University Press, 1990.

Ropars-Wuilleumier, Marie-Claire. "How History Begets Meaning: Alain Resnais' 'Hiroshima

Mon Amour' (1959)." In *French Film: Texts and Contexts,* ed. Susan Hayward and Ginette Vincendeau (New York: Routledge, 1990), 173.

―――. *Le texte divisé: Essai sur l'écriture filmique.* Paris: Presses Universitaires de France, 1981.

Said, Edward W. *Orientalism.* New York: Vintage, 1979.

Sakai, Naoki. *Translation and Subjectivity: On "Japan" and Cultural Nationalism.* Minneapolis: University of Minnesota Press, 1997.

―――. *Voices of the Past: The Status of Language in Eighteenth-Century Japanese Discourse.* Ithaca: Cornell University Press, 1992.

Sapir, Edward. *Language.* New York: Harcourt, Brace, 1921.

Sato, Tadao. *Currents in Japanese Cinema.* Translated by Gregory Barrett. Tokyo: Kodansha, 1982.

―――. "Rising Sons." *American Film* 11 (December 1985): 58–62, 78.

Schrader, Paul. *Transcendental Style in Film: Ozu, Bresson, Dreyer.* Berkeley and Los Angeles: University of California Press, 1972.

Schueller, Malanie. *U.S. Orientalisms: Race, Gender, and Nation in Literature, 1790–1890.* Ann Arbor: University of Michigan Press, 1998.

Seidensticker, Edward. *Low City, High City: Tokyo from Edo to the Earthquake.* New York: Alfred A. Knopf, 1990.

―――. *Tokyo Rising: The City Since the Earthquake.* Cambridge, Mass.: Harvard University Press, 1983.

Serceau, Daniel. *Mizoguchi: De la révolte aux songes.* Paris: Éditions du Cerf, 1983.

Seward, Jack. *Japanese in Action.* New York: Weatherhill, 1983.

Shattuck, Roger. *The Banquet Years: The Arts in France, 1885–1918.* New York: Harcourt, Brace, 1958.

Shawcross, Nancy M. *Roland Barthes on Photography: The Critical Tradition in Perspective.* Gainesville: University Press of Florida, 1997.

Singer, Kurt. *Mirror, Sword, and Jewel: A Study of Japanese Characteristics.* New York: George Braziller, 1973.

Smith, Joseph H., and William Kerrigan, eds. *Taking Chances: Derrida, Psychoanalysis, and Literature.* Baltimore: Johns Hopkins University Press, 1984.

Smith, Lawrence. *The Japanese Print Since 1900: Old Dreams and New Visions.* New York: Harper and Row, 1983.

Spivak, Gayatri Chakravorty. *Death of a Discipline.* New York: Columbia University Press, 2003.

Stille, Alexander. *The Future of the Past.* New York: Farrar, Straus and Giroux, 2002.

Storry, Richard. *A History of Modern Japan.* Baltimore: Penguin Books, 1972.

Sutcliffe, Anthony, ed. *Metropolis 1890–1940.* London: Mansell Publishing, 1984.

Takashina, Shuji, and J. Thomas Rimer, with Gerald D. Bolas. *Paris in Japan: The Japanese Encounter with European Painting.* New York: Japan Society, 1987.

Tanazaki, Junichiro. *In Praise of Shadows.* Translated by Thomas J. Harper and Edward G. Seidensticker. New Haven: Leete's Island Books, 1977. Originally published as *Inei raisan,* 1933 (reprinted, Tokyo: Sogensha, 1975).

Terada, Toru. *Japanese Art in World Perspective.* Translated by Thomas Guerin. New York: Weatherhill/Heibonsha, 1976. Originally published as *Sekai no naka no Nihon bijutsu,* vol. 25 of the Heibonsha Survey of Japanese Art (Tokyo: Heibonsha, 1966).

Tessier, Max, ed. *Cinéma et littérature au Japon, de l'ère Meiji à nos jours.* Paris: Éditions du Centre Pompidou, 1986.

―――. *Le cinéma japonais au présent, 1959–1984.* Paris: L'Herminier, 1984.

Treat, John Whittier. "Beheaded Emperors and the Absent Figure in Contemporary Japanese Literature." *PMLA* 109 (January 1994): 100–115.

Tsurumi, Shunsuke. *A Cultural History of Postwar Japan, 1945–1980*. New York: Routledge and Kegan Paul, 1987.

————. *An Intellectual History of Wartime Japan, 1931–1945*. New York: Routledge and Kegan Paul, 1986.

Turim, Maureen. *The Films of Oshima Nagisa: Images of a Japanese Iconoclast*. Berkeley and Los Angeles: University of California Press, 1998.

Ueda, Akinari. *Ugetsu Monogaari: Tales of Moonlight and Rain*. Translated by Leon Zolbrod. Tokyo: Tuttle, 1984.

Ueno, Toshiya. "Japanimation and Techno-Orientalism: Japan as the Sub-Empire of Signs," Yamagata International Documentary Film Festival, 1999. (http://www.city.yamagata.yamagata.jp/yidff/ff/box/box9/en/b9enf2-1.html).

Ulmer, Gregory L. *Applied Grammatology: Post(e)-Pedagogy from Jacques Derrida to Joseph Beuys*. Baltimore: Johns Hopkins University Press, 1985.

Vattimo, Gianni. *The Transparent Society*. Translated by David Webb. Baltimore: Johns Hopkins University Press, 1992. Originally published as *La società transparente* (Milan: Garzanti, 1989).

Watanabe, Shun-Ichi J. "Metropolitanism as a Way of Life: The Case of Tokyo, 1868–1930." In *Metropolis 1890–1940*, ed. Anthony Sutcliffe.

Whiting, Robert. *You Gotta Have Wa*. New York: Vintage, 1990.

Wiener, Norbert. *Cybernetics; or, Control and Communication in the Animal and the Machine*. New York: John Wiley, 1948.

Whorf, Benjamin Lee. *Language, Thought, and Reality*. Ed. John B. Carroll. Cambridge, Mass.: MIT Press, 1971.

Worth, Sol, and John Adair. *Through Navaho Eyes: An Exploration in Film Communication and Anthropology*. Bloomington: Indiana University Press, 1975.

Yamaguchi, Masao. "Theatrical Space in Japan: A Semiotic Approach." *Japan and America: A Journal of Cultural Studies* 1 (Spring 1984, Space Issue): 1.

Yamanouchi, Hisaki. *The Search for Authenticity in Modern Japanese Literature*. New York: Cambridge University Press, 1980.

Yoshida, K., and T. Kaigo. *Japanese Education*. Board of Tourist Industries, Japanese Government Railways, 1937.

Yoshimoto, Mitsuhiro. *Kurosawa: Film Studies and Japanese Cinema*. Durham: Duke University Press, 2000.

Zelevansky, Lynn, Laura Hoptman, Akira Tatehata, and Alexandra Munroe. *Love Forever: Yayoi Kusama, 1958–68*. Los Angeles: Los Angeles County Museum of Art, 1998.

Filmography

Unless otherwise noted, films were produced in Japan. They are listed chronologically, and distribution resources are given at the end of the entries.

Shibata Tsunekichi, *Maple Viewing* (*Momiji-gari,* 1898).

Tanaka Eizo, *The Living Corpse* (*Ikeru shikabane,* 1917).

Robert Weine, *The Cabinet of Dr. Caligari* (Germany, 1919).

Osanai and Murata, *Souls on the Road* (*Rojo no reikon,* 1921).

F. W. Murnau, *Nosferatu* (Germany, 1922).

Futagawa Buntaro, *The Outlaw* (*Orochi,* 1925).

Kinugasa Teinosuke, *A Page of Madness* (*Kurutta ippeiji,* 1926; also translated as *A Crazy Page*). Video, Facets.

Kinugasa Teinosuke, *Crossways* (*Jujiro,* 1928).

Ozu Yasujiro, *I Failed, But . . .* (*Rakudai wa shita keredo,* 1930).

James Whale, *Frankenstein* (U.S., 1931).

Ito Daisuke, *Jirokichi the Ratkid* (*Oatsurae jirokichi goshi,* 1931).

Tanaka Tsuruhiko, *The Red Bat* (*Beni komori,* 1931).

Ozu Yasujiro, *Tokyo Chorus* (*Tokyo no gassho,* 1931).

Luis Buñuel, *Las Hurdes* (Spain, 1932).

Robert Flaherty, *Man of Aran* (UK, 1934).

Ozu Yasujiro, *An Inn in Tokyo* (*Tokyo no yado,* 1935). DVD, Facets.

Mizoguchi Kenji, *Poppies* (*Gubijinso,* 1935).

Kinugasa Teinosuke, *The Revenge of Yukinojo* (*Yukinojo henge,* 1935).

Mizoguchi Kenji, *Osaka Elegy* (*Naniwa eregy,* 1936). Video, Facets.

Mizoguchi Kenji, *Sisters of the Gion* (*Gion no shimai,* 1936). Video, Home Vision.

Yuan Muzhi, *Street Angel* (*Malu tianshi,* China, 1937).

Ishida Tamizo, *Fallen Blossoms* (*Hana chirinu,* 1938).

Tasaka Tomotaka, *Five Scouts* (*Gonin no sekkohei,* 1938).

Tasaka Tomotaka, *Airplane Drone* (*Bakuon,* 1939).

Shinko Film Corporation, *Japanese Film History* (*Nihon eiga-shi,* 1941).

Ozu Yasujiro, *There Was a Father* (*Chichi Ariki,* 1942).

Navy Ministry, *Momotaro umi no shimpei* (1944).

Kurosawa Akira, *No Regrets for Our Youth* (*Waga seishun ni kui nashi,* 1946). Video, Home Vision.

Kurosawa Akira, *Drunken Angel* (*Yoidore tenshi,* 1948). DVD, British Film Institute.

Mizoguchi Kenji, *My Love Has Been Burning* (*Waga koi wa moenu,* 1949).

Kurosawa Akira, *Rashomon* (1950). DVD, Criterion.

Ozu Yasujiro, *Early Summer* (*Bakushu,* 1951). DVD, Criterion.

Kurosawa Akira, *Ikiru* (1952). DVD, Criterion.

King Vidor, *Japanese War Bride* (U.S., 1952).

Mizoguchi Kenji, *Life of Oharu* (*Saikaku ichidai onna,* 1952). DVD, Facets.

Kinugasa Teinosuke, *Gate of Hell* (*Jigokumon,* 1953).

Ozu Yasujiro, *Tokyo Story* (*Tokyo monogatari,* 1953). DVD, Criterion.

Mizoguchi Kenji, *Ugetsu* (*Ugetsu monogatari,* 1953). DVD, Criterion; Film, EmGee.

Mizoguchi Kenji, *Sansho the Bailiff* (*Sansho Dayu,* 1954). Video, British Film Institute.

Kurosawa Akira, *Seven Samurai* (*Shichinin no samurai,* 1954). DVD, Criterion.

Naruse Mikio, *Sound of the Mountain* (*Yama no oto,* 1954).

Kinoshita Keisuke, *Twenty-four Eyes* (*Nijushi no hitomi,* 1954). DVD, Facets.

Satyajit Ray, *Pather Panchali* (India, 1955).

Nakahira Ko, *Crazed Fruit* (*Kurutta kajitsu,* 1956). DVD, Criterion.

Alain Resnais, *Night and Fog* (*Nuit et brouillard,* France, 1956).

John Ford, *The Searchers* (U.S., 1956).

Mizoguchi Kenji, *Street of Shame* (*Akasen chitai,* 1956). Video, Facets.

Daniel Mann, *Teahouse of the August Moon* (U.S., 1956).

Chiba Yasuki, *Downtown* (*Shitamachi,* 1957).

Joshua Logan, *Sayonara* (U.S., 1957).

Kurosawa Akira, *Throne of Blood* (*Kumonosujo,* 1957). DVD, Criterion.

Stan Brakhage, *Anticipation of the Night* (U.S., 1958).

Kinoshita Keisuke, *Ballad of Narayama* (*Narayama bushiko,* 1958). Film, Kino International.

John Huston, *Barbarian and the Geisha* (U.S., 1958).

Ichikawa Kon, *Conflagration* (*Enjo,* 1958). Video, Facets.

Ozu Yasujiro, *Equinox Flower* (*Higanbana,* 1958). Video, New Yorker.

Jean-Luc Godard, *Breathless* (*À bout de souffle,* France, 1959).

François Truffaut, *400 Blows* (*Les quatre cents coups,* France, 1959).

Alain Resnais and Marguerite Duras, *Hiroshima mon amour* (France, 1959). DVD, Criterion.

Ichikawa Kon, *Odd Obsession* (*Kagi,* 1959). Video, Nelson.

Oshima Nagisa, *A Town of Love and Hope* (*Ai to kibo no machi,* 1959). DVD, Facets.

Kurosawa Akira, *The Bad Sleep Well* (*Warui yatsu hodo yoko nemuru,* 1960). DVD, Criterion.

Ichikawa Kon, *Bonchi* (*Bonchi,* 1960).

Oshima Nagisa, *Cruel Tales of Youth* (*Seishun zankoku monogatari,* 1960). Video, New Yorker.

Shindo Kaneto, *The Island* (*Hadaka no shima,* 1960). Video, Movies Unlimited; Film, EmGee.

Oshima Nagisa, *Night and Fog in Japan* (*Nihon no yoru to kiri,* 1960). DVD, Facets

Oshima Nagisa, *The Sun's Burial* (*Taiyo no hakaba,* 1960). Video, New Yorker.

Hani Susumu, *Bad Boys* (*Furyo Shonen,* 1961). Video, Movies Unlimited.

Henry Koster, *Flower Drum Song* (U.S., 1961).

Imamura Shohei, *Pigs and Battleships* (*Buta to gunkan,* Nikkatsu, 1961).

Jean-Luc Godard, *A Woman Is a Woman* (*Une femme est une femme,* France, 1961).

Ichikawa Kon, *The Outcast* (*Hakai,* 1962).

Ichikawa Kon, *An Actor's Revenge* (*Yukinojo henge,* 1963). Video, New Yorker; DVD, British Film Institute.

Imamura Shohei, *Insect Woman* (*Nippon konchuki,* Nikkatsu, 1963).

Andy Warhol, *Kiss* and *Sleep* (U.S., both 1963).

Alain Resnais, *Muriel* (France, 1963).

Shinoda Kaneto, *Assassination* (*Ansatsu,* 1964).

Teshigahara Hiroshi, *Woman in the Dunes* (*Suna no onna,* 1964). DVD, Image Entertainment.

Robert Wise, *The Sound of Music* (U.S., 1965).

Oshima Nagisa, *Yunbogi's Diary* (*Yunbogi no nikki,* 1965).

Shinoda Masahiro, *Captive's Island* (*Shokei no shima,* 1966). DVD, CD Japan.

Wakamatsu Koji. *The Embryo Hunts in Secret* (*Taiji ga mitsuryo suru toki,* 1966).

Imamura Shohei, *Introduction to Anthropology* (*Jinruigaku nyumon,* aka for U.S. distribution *The Pornographers: Introduction to Anthropology,* 1966). DVD, Home Vision.

Jean-Luc Godard, *Masculine Feminine* (*Masculin féminin,* France, 1966).

Jean-Luc Godard, *Two or Three Things I Know about Her* (*Deux ou trois choses que je sais d'elle,* France, 1966).

Oshima Nagisa, *Band of Ninja* (*Ninja bugeicho,* 1967).

François Truffaut, *Fahrenheit 451* (France, 1967).

Yayoi Kusama, *Kusama's Self-Obliteration* (U.S., 1967).

Kobayashi Masaki, *Rebellion* (*Joi-uchi,* 1967). DVD, Criterion.

Oshima Nagisa, *Treatise on Japanese Bawdy Songs* (*Nihon shunkako,* 1967).

Oshima Nagisa, *Death by Hanging* (1968). Film, New Yorker.

Oshima Nagisa, *The Greater East Asia War* (*Dai toa senso,* 1968).

John Wayne, *The Green Berets* (U.S., 1968).

Hani Susumu, *Inferno of First Love* (*Hatsukoi jigoku-hen,* 1968).

Oshima Nagisa, *Diary of a Shinjuku Thief* (*Shinjuku dorobo nikki,* 1969). Film, New Yorker.

Shinoda Masahiro, *Double Suicide* (*Shinju ten no Amijima,* 1969). DVD, Criterion.

Yoshida Yoshishige (Kiju), *Eros Plus Massacre* (*Eros purasu gyakusatsu,* 1969).

Oshima Nagisa, *The Man Who Left His Will on Film* (*Tokyo senso sengo hiwa,* 1970). Film, New Yorker.

Oshima Nagisa, *Ceremonies* (*Gishiki,* 1971).

Paul Sharits, *Stream: Sections: Sectioned: Sectioned* (1968–71).

Sol Worth and Ted Adair, cameras to the Navaho (U.S., 1966–72).

Oshima Nagisa, *Dear Summer Sister* (*Natsu no imoto,* 1972).

William Gwin, *Irving Bridge* (1972).

Shinoda Masahiro, *Himiko* (1974).

Godard and Miéville, *Içi et ailleurs* (France, 1974).

Kumai Kei, *Sandakan 8* (*Sandakan hachiban shokan bokyo,* 1974).

Godard and Miéville, *Numéro deux* (France, 1975).

Yanagimachi Mitsuo, *God Speed You: Black Emperor!* (*Baraku empororu,* 1976).

Oshima Nagisa, *In the Realm of the Senses* (*Ai no korida,* 1976). DVD, Fox Lorber.

Oshima Nagisa, *Empire of Passion* (*Ai no borei,* 1978). DVD, Facets.

Nakajima Kou, *My Life* (1974–78).

Woody Allen, *Manhattan* (U.S., 1979).

Imamura Shohei, *Vengeance Is Mine* (*Fukushu suru wa ware ni ari,* 1979). DVD, Home Vision; Film, Kino International.

Matsumoto Toshio, *White Hole* (1979).

Tizuka Yamasaki's *Gaijin: A Brazilian Odyssey* (*Gaijin: Caminhos da Liberdade,* Brazil, 1980).

Oguri Kohei, *Muddy River* (*Doro no kawa,* 1981).

Imamura Shohei, *Why Not?* (*Eijanaika,* 1981). DVD, Facets; Film, Kino International.

Imamura Shohei, *Ballad of Narayama* (*Narayama bushiko,* 1983). Video, Home Vision.

Morita Yoshimitsu, *The Family Game* (*Kazuko geemu,* 1983).

Ina Shinsuke, *Flow (2)* (1983).

Ichikawa Kon, *The Makioka Sisters* (*Sasameyuki,* 1983). DVD, Facets.

Oshima Nagisa, *Merry Christmas, Mr. Lawrence* (*Senjou no Merii Kurisumasu,* 1983). Video, Live/
     Artisan; DVD, C Logic.

Sai Yoichi, *Mosquito on the Tenth Floor* (*Jukai no mosukiito,* 1983).

Cecelia Condit, *Possibly in Michigan* (1983).

Ishii Sogo, *Crazy Family* (*Gyakufunsha kazoku,* 1984).

Oguri Kohei, *For Kayako* (*Kayako,* 1984).

Itami Juzo, *The Funeral* (*Ososhiki,* 1984). Video, Fox Lorber.

Idemitsu Mako, *Great Mother, Yumiko* (1984).

Shinoda Masahiro, *MacArthur's Children* (*Setouchi shonen yakyu dan,* 1984). Video, Universal Studios.

Yanagimachi Mitsuo, *Fire Festival* (*Himatsuri,* 1985). DVD, Kino Video; Film, Kino International.

Paul Schraeder, *Mishima* (U.S., 1985). DVD, Warner.

George P. Cosmatos, *Rambo: First Blood Part II* (U.S., 1985).

Wim Wenders, *Tokyo-ga* (Germany, 1985).

Yoshida Yoshishige (Kiju), *The Promise* (*Ningen no yakusoku,* 1986).

Itami Juzo, *Tampopo* (1986). DVD, Fox Lorber.

Hara Kazuo, *The Emperor's Naked Army Marches On* (*Yuki yukite shingun,* 1987). Film, Kino
     International.

Imamura Shohei, *Black Rain* (*Kuroi ame,* 1989). DVD, Image Entertainment.

Ridley Scott, *Black Rain* (U.S., 1989).

Jim Jarmusch, *Mystery Train* (U.S., 1989).

Kurosawa Akira, *Dreams* (*Yume,* 1990). DVD, Warner; Film, Swank.

Zhang Yimou, *Raise the Red Lantern* (*Da hong deng long gao gao gua,* 1991). DVD, Razor.

Kurosawa Akira, *Rhapsody in August* (*Hachi-gatsu no kyôshikyoku,* 1991). DVD, MGM.

Louis Álvarez and Andrew Kolker, *The Japanese Version* (U.S., 1991). Video, Center for New
     American Media.

Alek Kishishian, *Madonna: Truth or Dare* (U.S., 1991).

Nikita Mikhalkov, *Urga* (aka *Close to Eden,* Russia/Mongolia, 1991). Video, Paramount.

Reflexion II, *Museum or Hospital* (Synergy, 1992).

Krzysztof Kieslowski, *Blue* (France, 1993).

Imamura Shohei, *The Eel* (*Unagi,* 1997). DVD, New Yorker; Film, New Yorker.

Wong Kar-Wai, *Happy Together* (*Cheun gwong tsa sit,* Hong Kong, 1997). DVD, Kino Video.

Miyazaki Hayao, *Princess Mononoke* (*Mononoke hime,* 1997). DVD, Miramax.

Wachowski Brothers, *The Matrix* (U.S., 1999).

Oshima Nagisa, *Taboo* (*Gohatto,* 2000). DVD, New Yorker; Film, New Yorker.

Rintaro, *Metropolis* (*Metoroporisu,* 2001). DVD, SONY Pictures.

Miyazaki Hayao, *Spirited Away* (*Sen to Chihiro no kamikakushi,* 2001). DVD, Walt Disney.

Kore-Eda Hirokazu, *Nobody Knows* (*Dare mo shiranai,* 2004). DVD, MGM.

Distribution Information

Many historical Japanese films can be seen only at museums, embassies, film festivals, or through specialized film archives. The Filmography includes distribution information at the end of entries when Asian films are available, usually with English subtitles.

Availability has shifted in recent decades. When Japanese film was first internationally distributed, high-quality 16mm reduction prints were widely available. Since then, VHS and DVD versions have made many films accessible for study, while 16mm prints of historical Japanese films have become uncommon and may be in poor condition. Video means a loss of visual quality compared to film, but some video transfers, especially by Criterion, can be excellent, often providing a restored and more complete version than has been available previously.

Film and video sources distribute their materials differently. Some distributors list an address, telephone number, and fax number, but several distribute exclusively through a Web site. Other sources, including New Yorker Video, do not distribute directly or have stopped distributing videos or DVDs that can be obtained elsewhere. These videos can be found only through third-party dealers such as Amazon. The listings below incorporate these variations.

VHS/DVD Sources

Amazon
http://www.amazon.com/

British Film Institute
21 Stephen Street
London W1T 1LN
Telephone: +44 (0)20-7255-1444
Telephone: Video and DVD Publishing (0)20-7957-8957
http://www.bfi.org.uk/

CD Japan
1-10-12-2F Nihonbashi Horidome
Chuo, Tokyo 103-0012, Japan
Fax: 81-3-3665-4942
http://www.cdjapan.co.jp/

C Logic
Available through Amazon

Center for New American Media
http://www.cnam.com/

Criterion
http://www.criterionco.com/
Available through Amazon

Facets Multimedia
1517 W. Fullerton Avenue
Chicago, IL 60614
Telephone: 773-281-9075
Fax: 773-929-5437
http://www.facets.org/

Fox Lorber
Available through Amazon

Home Vision Entertainment
20525 Nordhoff Street, Suite 200
Chatsworth, CA 91311
http://www.homevision.com/

Image Entertainment
20525 Nordhoff Street, Suite 200
Chatsworth, CA 91311
http://www.image-entertainment.com

Kino Video
333 W. 39th Street, Suite 503
New York, NY 10018
Telephone: 212-629-6880
Telephone: 800-562-3330
Fax. 212-714-0871
http://www.kino.com/video/

Live/Artisan
Available through Amazon

MGM DVD
http://www.mgm.com/video.do

Miramax
Available through Amazon

Movies Unlimited
http://www.moviesunlimited.com/

Nelson Entertainment
Available through Amazon

New Yorker Video
http://www.newyorkerfilms.com/
Available through Amazon

Paramount Home Entertainment
5555 Melrose Avenue
Hollywood, CA 90038
Telephone: 323-956-5000
http://www.paramount.com/
homeentertainment/

Razor Digital Entertainment
12031 Ventura Blvd., Suite 3
Studio City, CA 91604
Telephone: 818-766-8400
Fax: 818-766-8401
info@razordigitalent.com
http://www.razordigitalent.com/

SONY Pictures
http://www.sonypictures.com/homevideo/

Universal Studios Home Entertainment
http://homevideo.universalstudios.com/
Available through Amazon

Walt Disney Video
500 S. Buena Vista Street
Burbank, CA 91521
http://disneyvideos.disney.go.com/

Warner Home Video
P.O. Box 30620
Tampa, FL 33630-0620
Telephone: 800-364-6928
whvcustserv@emsi.echomail.com
http://whv.warnerbros.com/

Film Distributors

EmGee
6924 Canby Avenue, Suite 103
Reseda, CA 91335
Telephone: 818-881-8110
Fax: 818-981-5506
http://emgee.freeyellow.com/

Kino International
333 W. 39th Street, Suite 503
New York, NY 10018
Telephone: 212-629-6880
Telephone: 800-562-3330
Fax: 212-714-0871
http://www.kino.com/

New Yorker Films
Telephone: 212-645-4600
Fax: 212-645-3030
http://www.newyorkerfilms.com/

Swank Motion Pictures
201 S. Jefferson Avenue
Saint Louis, MO 63103-2579
Telephone: 1-800-876-5577
http://www.swank.com/

Index

NOTE: All names are alphabetized by family name followed by personal name, although only Western usage separates the two with a comma.

Scott Nygren is associate professor of film and media studies in the Department of English at the University of Florida.